Home
Is the Hunter

The Nature | History | Society series is devoted to the publication of high-quality scholarship in environmental history and allied fields. Its broad compass is signalled by its title: nature because it takes the natural world seriously; history because it aims to foster work that has temporal depth; and society because its essential concern is with the interface between nature and society, broadly conceived. The series is avowedly interdisciplinary and is open to the work of anthropologists, ecologists, historians, geographers, literary scholars, political scientists, sociologists, and others whose interests resonate with its mandate. It offers a timely outlet for lively, innovative, and well-written work on the interaction of people and nature through time in North America.

General Editor: Graeme Wynn, University of British Columbia

Claire Elizabeth Campbell, *Shaped by the West Wind: Nature and History in Georgian Bay*

Tina Loo, *States of Nature: Conserving Canada's Wildlife in the Twentieth Century*

Jamie Benidickson, *The Culture of Flushing: A Social and Legal History of Sewage*

William J. Turkel, *The Archive of Place: Unearthing the Pasts of the Chilcotin Plateau*

John Sandlos, *Hunters at the Margin: Native People and Wildlife Conservation in the Northwest Territories*

James Murton, *Creating a Modern Countryside: Liberalism and Land Resettlement in British Columbia*

Greg Gillespie, *Hunting for Empire: Narratives of Sport in Rupert's Land, 1840-70*

Stephen J. Pyne, *Awful Splendour: A Fire History of Canada*

Liza Piper, *The Industrial Transformation of Subarctic Canada*

NATURE | HISTORY | SOCIETY

Home Is the Hunter

The James Bay Cree and Their Land

HANS M. CARLSON

FOREWORD BY GRAEME WYNN

UBC Press • Vancouver • Toronto

20 19 18 17 16 15 14 13 12 11 10 09 08   5 4 3 2 1

Printed in Canada on ancient-forest-free paper (100% post-consumer recycled) that is processed chlorine- and acid-free, with vegetable-based inks.

Library and Archives Canada Cataloguing in Publication

Carlson, Hans M.
     Home is the hunter: the James Bay Cree and their land / Hans M. Carlson.

(Nature, history, society, ISSN 1713-6687)
Includes bibliographical references and index.
ISBN 978-0-7748-1494-2 (bound); ISBN 978-0-7748-1495-9 (pbk.)

     1. Cree Indians – James Bay Region – History. 2. Cree Indians – Québec (Province) – Nord-du-Québec – History. 3. Cree Indians – Hunting – James Bay Region. 4. Cree Indians – Hunting – Québec (Province) – Nord-du-Québec. 5. Cultural landscapes – James Bay Region. 6. Cultural landscapes – Québec (Province) – Nord-du-Québec. 7. James Bay Region – Environmental conditions. 8. Nord-du-Québec (Québec) – Environmental conditions. I. Title. II. Series.

E99.C88C39 2008   971.4'11500497323   C2008-903453-8

Canadä

This book has been published with the help of a grant from the Canadian Federation for the Humanities and Social Sciences, through the Aid to Scholarly Publications Programme, using funds provided by the Social Sciences and Humanities Research Council of Canada.

UBC Press gratefully acknowledges the International Council for Canadian Studies for financial support through its Publishing Fund.

Part of Chapter 6 appeared previously in Hans M. Carlson, "A Watershed of Words: Litigating and Negotiating Nature in Eastern James Bay, 1971-75," *Canadian Historical Review* 85, 1 (2004): 63-84. Reprinted by permission of University of Toronto Press (www.utpjournals.com).

UBC Press
The University of British Columbia
2029 West Mall
Vancouver, BC V6T 1Z2
604-822-5959 / Fax: 604-822-6083
www.ubcpress.ca

For my mother and father

Contents

Maps, Figures, and Tables

Dignity and Power

by Graeme Wynn

I n the second half of the twentieth century, enormous technological might and great engineering skill were devoted to the construction of massive new hydroelectricity generating facilities to power an expanding Canadian economy and satisfy growing consumer demand for electrical appliances. From the St. Lawrence Seaway (which was as much a power scheme as it was a navigation system) to Kitimat in remote northern British Columbia, megaprojects dominated the news as they re-configured drainage systems, re-ordered landscapes, and re-placed people. Celebrated as modern marvels, widely publicized in the contemporary media, and quickly incorporated into school textbooks around the world as examples of human ingenuity, these projects betokened a new era of confidence in peoples' capacity to order the world to their purposes. They reflected a powerful conviction that shaped Canadian economic development in the quarter-century after the Second World War. Characterized, in general, by political scientist James C. Scott as "high modernism," this ideology is best summarized, in his words, as "a strong, one might even say muscle-bound version of the self-confidence about scientific and technical progress, the expansion of production, the growing satisfaction of human needs, the mastery of nature (including human nature) and, above all, the rational design of social order commensurate with the scientific understanding of natural laws."[1]

Early in the 1950s, the largest privately funded construction project to that point undertaken in Canada reversed the flow of one of the major northern tributaries of the Fraser River in British Columbia. Behind the

Kenney Dam, in the Nechako River canyon southwest of Prince George, an enormous, sinuous reservoir rose and extended a couple of hundred kilometres upstream. From its western limit the water plunged nearly 800 vertical metres – "nearly 16 times the height of Niagara Falls," the literature informs readers – through a 16-kilometre-long tunnel "as wide as a two-lane highway, drilled and blasted through the coastal mountains," into the penstocks of "a cathedral-shaped powerhouse ... drilled and blasted 427 metres inside the granite base of Mount DuBose" near Kemano. There, eight generators – each producing over 100 megawatts – sent power along an 82-kilometre transmission line "across some of the most rugged mountain territory" in the province, to drive an aluminum smelter (that processed alumina concentrated from bauxite drawn from British Guiana and Jamaica) near the newly built town of Kitimat.[2] But even this "marvel of the time" was overshadowed when the turbines of the Barnhart and Beauharnois powerhouses on the St. Lawrence began to spin later in the decade. They were the second- and third-largest hydroelectric plants in the world (behind "Stalin's concrete pyramid," the Kuibyshev Dam on the Volga River), capable of producing 3,600 megawatts of power between them.[3]

In the 1960s these projects had their counterparts in Manitoba and Newfoundland-Labrador. Faced with the challenge of harnessing low-gradient, north-flowing rivers subject to freeze-up and low flow when demand for electricity is greatest (during the winter), engineers dammed the Churchill River, flooded about 1,500 square kilometres of land, and redirected much of the river's flow through a 180-kilometre-long network of lakes, channels, and rivers into the Nelson River. At the same time, the outlet of Lake Winnipeg was dammed to allow better regulation of water levels feeding the four electricity generating stations on the Nelson drainage. A few years later the government of Canada's easternmost province capitalized on the kinetic energy of another Churchill River, in Labrador (which descends 300 metres in approximately 30 kilometres) by blasting an enormous underground powerhouse, 300 metres long and fifteen storeys high, out of the rock of the Canadian Shield at Churchill Falls. Some four hundred huge transmission towers marching across the northern muskeg carried five million or so kilowatts of electricity from this remote location into the Quebec electricity grid, 200 kilometres to the south.[4]

Promotional literature and propaganda films touted the benefits of these developments and boasted that they would have no negative environmental consequences. In retrospect, however, it became clear that their human and ecological effects were profound. As Peter Kulchyski, a leading scholar of indigenous affairs born and raised in Manitoba noted, the Nelson River, "once a pristine source of life, became silty and dangerous" and Native peoples found "logs blocking access to shores; undrinkable water; water levels that fluctuated according to no locally known logic, making travel unsafe; interred bodies exposed; islands slowly washed away," in their traditional territories.[5]

Along the St. Lawrence, some 11,000 hectares of land were inundated behind the Long Sault Dam; in all, over 9,000 residents were displaced by the Seaway project and new settlements were built to replace towns and villages flooded by rising waters.[6] According to the Canadian government's *Report of the Royal Commission on Aboriginal Peoples,* the Kitimat-Kemano power project proceeded in ways that shocked commissioners hearing the details in the 1990s. By their soberly worded account, the local Cheslatta T'en people were treated as an afterthought, with completely inadequate regard for their rights. The government initiated the surrender negotiations just as the dam was completed and flooding was about to begin. The flooding began before the surrender. The families were told to start moving without assistance the day after the surrender was signed. Because of the spring thaw, they had to leave most of their belongings behind. The homes and many belongings of the Cheslatta were destroyed before most families could move their effects to the new location. There was no housing or land provided for families or livestock at Grassy Plains (50 kilometres north, where they were relocated) for the entire summer. When land was finally purchased for the Cheslatta, moneys were taken from individual compensation allotments to pay for it – contrary to the Cheslatta understanding of the surrender agreement. The new lands were not established as reserve lands, and the rights the Cheslatta had enjoyed as a result of living on reserves were lost for many years. Graveyards above the planned flood level were washed away.[7]

Yet there was little contemporary concern about the collateral costs of these extraordinary efforts at ecological re-engineering. Omelettes could not be made without breaking eggs. Such changes were "a matter of modern progress and international prosperity."[8]

Like the projects that preceded it, the James Bay hydroelectric initiative began with optimism and happy confidence that great works were under way. Described by Quebec premier Robert Bourassa as "the project of the century," when he announced it in 1971, the James Bay scheme was to unleash the potential of the underdeveloped north as it confirmed Quebec's mastery of the brute-force technologies that had enabled so much economic development during the 1960s. It would, said Bourassa, provide "the key to the economic and social progress ... the political stability ... and ... the future" of his province (see p. 207, this volume).[9] According to the Bechtel Corporation, the giant engineering firm responsible for the project, it was "appropriately named La Grande," because it was "one of the largest undertakings ever mounted." It involved the diversion of several rivers in an area to the east of James Bay that was "larger than the state of New York." It would generate "a whopping 10,300 megawatts" of power. Millions of cubic yards of fill, hundreds of thousands of tons of steel and concrete, 70,000 tons of explosives, vast engineering skill, and "an enormous amount of determination" were necessary to realize the technocratic, political, and ideological dream of completing the modernization of Quebec.[10] Altering nineteen waterways, creating twenty-seven reservoirs, and spending tens of billions of dollars were, it seemed, all in a proverbial day's work. The territory, which a Hydro-Quebec brochure later described as "now being molded to man's needs," seemed too remote and too vast to warrant much concern.[11] Without the necessity of environmental impact assessments, construction of the James Bay access road began soon after Premier Bourassa announced the project. Neither the indigenous Cree nor the Inuit to the north were advised of the province's plans.

Yet the road to northern development was not simply paved by Bourassa's good intentions. To the surprise of the Quebec government, indigenous and popular opposition to the James Bay scheme was strong, effective, and almost immediate. In the radical, democratic environment of the late 1960s, marked by the rise of the counterculture movement, student empowerment, the stirrings of popular environmentalism (symbolized in Canada by the establishment of Greenpeace in Vancouver), and a broad-based reaction against the might of what American President Dwight Eisenhower had termed, in 1961, the military-industrial complex, there was growing suspicion of corporate and government megaprojects.[12] Atop all of this, in 1969, the Canadian government raised the political ire of indigenous peoples across the country by proposing plans to further the assimilation of Native Canadians, including the abolition of treaty rights and native reserves. Although these ideas were later set aside, they too contributed to the changed climate of public sentiment into which Premier Bourassa's James Bay dream was launched.

Within weeks of the Quebec government's establishment of the James Bay Energy and Development corporations, financial assistance from the Arctic Institute of North America allowed Cree leaders to meet in Mistassini. For some, this marked the beginning of a "process by which the Cree of Quebec ... [came] to see themselves as belonging not just to family and village but to a regional ethnic and political unit, to a nation."[13] Before the year was out, rising public unease had led to the establishment of a Federal-Provincial Task Force on James Bay Ecology, and the beginning of work on the social impacts of northern development by researchers in McGill University's Programme in the Anthropology of Development. Within a year, Helene Lajambe, a student at McGill University, and others had founded the James Bay Committee, a grassroots coalition of hunting and fishing groups, indigenous organizations, and several environmental and conservation interests.[14] Buoyed by the support, in May 1972, lawyers for the Indians of Quebec Association (IQA) filed for a permanent injunction against development that would damage Cree land and opened a new segment of what Hans Carlson (p. 21, this volume) describes, felicitously, as "the spider's web of words and meaning that clings so delicately to the forests of the North." Granted after months of hearings (well treated in the pages that follow), in November 1973, the injunction was overturned on appeal a week later. Responding to an offer to negotiate from Premier Bourassa, the IQA and the Cree entered a warren of discussion that led successively to the formation of the Grand Council of the Crees (separate from the IQA) in August 1974, an agreement in principle between Quebec and the Cree people shortly thereafter and, in November 1975, approval of the James Bay and Northern Quebec Agreement, a modern-day treaty that awarded resource and governance rights, as well as monetary compensation to Native peoples.[15]

Many factors and innumerable individuals shaped this outcome, but the work of journalist and (later) filmmaker Boyce Richardson warrants brief attention here because it was instrumental in reshaping public awareness of (and sympathy for) the plight of the James Bay Cree. Originally from New Zealand, where his career as a journalist began, Richardson arrived in Canada in 1954, after working in various capacities in Australia, India, and England. By 1957 he was with the *Montreal Star*. Between 1960 and 1968 he was the London correspondent of that newspaper and then, after a short stint as drama and film critic, became one of its associate editors. Between 1969 and 1971 he produced a number of important essays on the rising threat of pollution, on Canadian urban problems, and on "the emerging Indian."[16] Then he resigned to pursue a freelance career. Having spoken out against the James Bay scheme, he was invited, shortly thereafter, by the IQA, to make a film about the development proposal. By his own account, Richardson knew very little, at the time, of Native peoples in Canada, of the circumstances of the James Bay Cree, or of the challenges of filmmaking. He accepted the invitation because he held an inherent sympathy for "the little guys." Whatever Bourassa's rhetorical claims for the massive project, Richardson recognized that it would impose unprecedented southern demands and massive change on the Cree people of northern Quebec.

Disappointed by his first impressions of Mistassini, Richardson quickly realized that he was misreading northern circumstances. Common and widely propagated views of the Cree as unsophisticated, dependent people did not fit the more complicated, compelling conditions that he encountered.[17] Possessing the journalist's concern for the here and now, and a sharp appreciation of the value of human experience as a vehicle for effective communication, Richardson utilized visual images and the spoken word to convey, with attention-grabbing power, both the vulnerability of Cree life ways and "the beauty, harmony, and strength that the Crees found in their most natural habitat, the bush." His first film, released in 1973 as *Job's Garden,* found its centre in the gentle wisdom of Cree hunter Job Bearskin and his wife Mary, to illuminate their "profound understanding of the Human role on this Earth." Technically unsophisticated, it delivered a very clear message. For Bearskin (who stood implicitly for all of his people in this), the land was a garden, both practically and mythologically: it provided resources for daily living and served, in an Edenic sense, as a place of cultural origin.[18]

Job's Garden was soon followed by *Cree Hunters of Mistassini,* which Richardson co-directed with Tony Ianzelo for Canada's National Film Board. This superbly filmed account of a winter season at Sam Blacksmith's hunting camp north of Chibougamau echoed Job Bearskin's point that people, plants, and animals grew and flourished together in the "wilderness." Charismatic and immensely competent in the bush, Sam Blacksmith (who died, aged at least 95, as this foreword was being written) evinced a simple but profound wisdom and, because the film won international acclaim and a large audience, he "became known and respected in many parts of the world as a quintessential spokesman for the central values of Cree life." As Richardson reflected years later on hearing of Sam Blacksmith's death, he and his friends Ronnie Jolly and Abraham Voyageur, who shared his camp in the year that the film was made, "provided a powerful demonstration to the outside world of the viability of Cree hunting life, and its importance in the scheme of things, natural, human and animal." Indeed, Colin Low, one of Canada's leading documentary filmmakers in the latter half of the twentieth century, reportedly argued that *Cree Hunters* "created such an impact as to have brought about a profound change in government policy towards the so-called Indians under their charge."[19]

In the 1970s, Richardson focused on the immediate dangers that hydro development schemes posed to patterns of subsistence in the north. Almost two decades later, as debate over the development of more dams on the Grand-Baleine River intensified, he returned to portray in a third film, *Flooding Job's Garden,* the sweeping, detrimental effects of hydro development upon the environment and upon Cree communities now struggling to find a balance between assimilation and the preservation of their traditional values and way of life.[20] Each of these three films document, in ways that are entirely compelling, patterns of contemporary existence among the Crees. They are not beyond critical comment, however. Three shortcomings require consideration. First, Richardson's earliest films construct Cree hunting as a traditional practice. This gives them a very strong retrospective dimension, despite their of-the-moment currency. Yet, by treating customary behaviour as age-old, they render tradition static, flatten the past by denying the possibilities of change and adaptation, and (ironically and surely inadvertently) rob the Cree of agency. Second, as Richardson has explained elsewhere, the filmmakers shaped the picture they portrayed in *Cree Hunters* (by transporting hunters to kill moose and returning the meat to camp by plane, and by flying in nails that allowed construction of a larger-than-usual hunting lodge).[21] Finally, the fragments of existence offered by these films fascinate and inform, but as Bill Nichols has observed in a general commentary on documentary filmmaking, "the information never vanquishes the fascination." It is the very "otherness" of indigenous lives that holds the camera and thwarts "the documentarist's urge to move away from the concrete and local in order to provide perspective."[22]

Anthropologist Clifford Geertz has reflected upon the inherent tension between a focus on local detail and the search for larger horizons by drawing a distinction between "inscription" and "specification" – "between setting down the meaning particular social actions have for the actors whose actions they are, and stating, as explicitly as we can manage, what the knowledge thus attained demonstrates about the society in which it is found, and beyond that about social life as such" – and it is here, in the space opened by this tension, that Hans Carlson's *Home Is the Hunter* makes its luminous contribution to improving our understanding of the complex relationships between people and places.[23] Indeed, part of Carlson's purpose in the pages that follow is to think again about the connections that link individuals, cultures, and places. In his view every hunter is "embedded both in hunting culture and in physical nature" and, unable to separate "cultural self from physical self," each lives "within a single spatial phenomenon that influences, but does not wholly determine," his/her actions. This is important because it recognizes the dynamic qualities of cultural life. As Carlson has it: "while various aspects of culture (even traditional culture) and environment may reinforce one another, at times there is a tension between them that pulls the individual in different directions" (p. 20).

In the end, Richardson's and Carlson's extended efforts to better understand James Bay and its people point in markedly different – but nonetheless complementary – directions. Richardson, the journalist, offers an historical tableau as he illuminates a particular moment of harrowing change. Carlson, the thoughtful scholar, focuses on the past, but like all historians, he writes out of a particular time and place and his historical inquiries are inflected by current concerns. "Only by taking the long view," he insists, "do the changes occurring in the present seem understandable as something more than blind, unstoppable decline for both land and people. Only by connecting the history of the land with what is happening to the land today can we find a meaning that will help lead to the future" (p. 25). *Home Is the Hunter* reverberates with a sense of time and change and hope, as it displays the knowledge, insight, and wise judgment that its author has developed through a quarter of a century of thinking about "what lies beyond the spruce trees and the running rivers" of the north (p. XXIII). More than this, Carlson's book echoes one of the classics of modern social history, E.P. Thompson's *The Making of the English Working Class,* in its insistence on rescuing the Cree from the "condescension of posterity" (and the flattening message of the celluloid medium) by recognizing both their human dignity and their competence in maintaining a rich and distinctive (but always supple and evolving) connection with the land through centuries of potentially disruptive contact with fur traders, missionaries, bureaucrats, engineers, and other newcomers to their territory.[24]

In Carlson's telling, the story of James Bay and its people "is a prime example of the integration and exploitation of remote environments within an increasingly global economy and, consequently, within the expanding global scope of environmental social justice concerns." But it is much more than this. Concerned to move beyond the story of "wires and words" (important though it is) that "integrated this distant region into the technical geography of an international electrical grid" as the La Grande project moved to completion, Carlson anchors his account in the

Cree's own complex stories about (and understanding of) their "immemorial phenomenal world," Eeyou Istchee. These two words, he avers, "don't seem to describe a physical territory so much as a complex relationship between land and people, where neither one has control of the other, and where "land" means not just ground but all the various beings with whom the Cree interact. This is the land in all its totality ... and it involves an understanding of all the life that surrounds and includes the Cree." Complicated associations and interactions – "physical and metaphysical, human and other-than-human" – mould place and people together. In this cultural narrative, the land is a web of relationships, Eeyou Istchee, not the resource cornucopia or piece of real estate that newcomers saw in the territory east of James Bay (pp. 4, 6, 11, 204).

These two perceptions – one enshrined in the metaphysical understanding of indigenous hunting peoples and the other in the outsiders' marketplace narrative of ownership, control, and sovereignty – are the poles about which Carlson's powerful account circles. For centuries, since Henry Hudson met Chakaapash on the shores of James Bay, they have been central to the long narrative negotiation in which Natives and newcomers have been engaged, not only over land, but also over animals, home, identity, meaning, and history in this remote territory. By recognizing this and by taking the long view, by seeing the changes precipitated by the La Grande project as the most recent in a series of adjustments produced by Cree-white contact through the decades, Carlson renders the arc of Cree history intelligible to outsiders and makes it relevant to the people living east of James Bay today. His is an original, and much-needed, synthesis, a story anchored in the records of newcomers, fur traders, missionaries, scientific explorers, and the work of twentieth-century scholars, that offers new insight into and understanding of the region and its people.

In sum, the message of these pages is that the Cree are a strong and adaptable people who have had impressive success in maintaining their intimate web of relationships to place – their particular metaphysical narrative – against the stories (and the consequences associated with them) that others have told about their land. In the early years of contact, the remoteness of this place from centres of European activity and the meagre numbers of fur traders and missionaries who ventured among the Cree muted the effects of "marketplace" views in Cree territory. Carlson's perspective here is clear and distinct. Rather than pondering the "impact" of the fur trade on indigenous society, he tries to tease out the negotiated meaning of the trade, to understand how it was understood and talked about by people at the time, and how that changed their worlds.[25] In this view, the trade cannot be understood in unequivocal terms. It neither simply shackled the Cree to the mercantile economy (otherwise known as the Hudson's Bay Company) nor enrolled them unambiguously in a partnership with European traders. It was, rather and also, a relationship with the land and with other people on the land that was interpreted from within a Cree understanding of the world. So, too, in religion. The handful of Christian missionaries who worked in the James Bay area never simply imposed their beliefs upon the Cree. Nor, by and large, were their teachings rejected out of hand. Here as elsewhere, interaction produced syncretism. "Christianity changed the Cree, [but] the Cree actively worked to change Christianity to fit with the environment and their understanding of it." European faith gained new meaning "where material need met conceptual need" among the people of James Bay (p. 129).

Late in the nineteenth century, outside pressures on Cree ways of life intensified. More people, trappers, bureaucrats, scientists, tourists, "extractors" all, came into the area from the south to take something (be it furs, knowledge, or pleasure) from the region. Sometimes they brought devastating diseases among its people. Their cumulative effects were enormous; environmental degradation, sickness, and immiseration undermined Cree lifeways and heightened their dependence upon others. More transient, and less dependent upon the resources and inhabitants of the region than Hudson's Bay Company traders and missionaries had been, the growing tide of newcomers also interpreted the area as outsiders, creating a lens through which the region could be understood from afar. Rooted in an epistemology of nature and culture very different from that of the Cree, this outside narrative understanding of the region and its inhabitants relegated Native peoples to the margins of the larger society's perceptions. This marginalization was reversed to some degree in the second quarter of the twentieth century, when the Hudson's Bay Company, the government, and the Cree worked together to establish beaver reserves (that revitalized both the population of *Castor canadensis* and the – somewhat redefined – hunt). As "conservation and Native cultures became a part of popular, intellectual understanding, Cree hunting became more central to the narratives of conservation, government action, and academic study" (p. 170). But indigenous practices were also flattened, remarkably quickly and effectively, by this process "into the story of a museum piece." Although the hunt of 1950 was conducted on leased land, governed by official regulation, and depended upon maps, monitoring, and counting – and differed in all these ways from the hunt of a century before – it was widely regarded as an "ancient tradition reborn." For several of those most closely involved in the beaver reserve program, "Indian practice" was reduced to "something essential and ahistorical" (pp. 179, 191). By ignoring historical change, or at least foreshortening and simplifying it into a story about the dramatic disruption of age-old practice by white trappers late in the nineteenth century, this view erases precisely what Carlson so deftly and convincingly insists upon in these pages: "the historical power of Cree hunting and Cree hunters in negotiating with Europeans, and all the changes that this negotiation brought – both good and bad" (p. 191).

This is important. Through centuries of perturbation produced by the incursion of newcomers, new ideas, and new technologies into their homeland and the construction of new narratives that challenged their own conception of Eeyou Istchee, the Cree of James Bay have adjusted – and changed – to sustain the core of their ancient narrative. In recognizing this, Carlson acknowledges the resilience of the James Bay Cree but he also marks the roots of their strength, the nucleus of the dignity they exhibited when the legal proceedings of the 1970s "took the material facts of Cree life and placed them into the very different narrative framework of science and progress" (p. 205). Despite all that had gone before, these events revealed, in stark and arresting ways, the enormous inherent differences in the two sides' understandings of their worlds and themselves. When the judge conducting the hearings against the La Grande development asked Job Bearskin (the central character in Boyce Richardson's first film) for his address, he was met with incomprehension. Pressed by the court, Bearskin eventually responded, "I have come from what I have survived on," and then, still perhaps somewhat bemused by the question, that he was "from this land."[26] For those whose home-place it would flood, the hydro project was not simply a matter of dams and reservoirs, but (as the sometime Grand Chief of the Crees, Mathew Coon Come, noted) "a terrible and vast reduction of [their] entire world."[27] Reflecting on the events of the 1970s and the developments that followed, Chief Violet Pachanos, the elected leader of the Cree Nation of Chisasibi, observed that "the price we paid for being modern is high, a lot higher than anyone ever imagined."[28] To read Carlson's elegant and moving book is to come a little closer to understanding what that price, measured not in dollars and cents but in terms of human worth, might be, to appreciate the importance of understanding the stories by which individuals and societies order experience and act in the world, and to ask whether the histories we construct for ourselves help us to remember – or forget?[29]

Acknowledgments

First, thanks and love to my parents, Laura and Thor, for always encouraging me to do what interested me and made me happy – also for allowing me space when I wasn't really sure what that was. Thanks particularly to Abigail, Brooks, and Kate – there are so many other friends that should be named – all of you inspired and encouraged me throughout this whole process. Thanks to Mike Hermann, not only for the beautiful maps within but also for being a great companion in northern travels: there's more to come, I hope. Particular thanks to my Cree friends – Charlot Gunner, Smalley Gunner, Morley Gunner, Daniel Blacksmith, Ray Blackned, Anna and Dave Bosum, and Margaret and William Cromarty – for sharing a little of what lies beyond the spruce trees and the running rivers. What I got right in this work is largely due to them; what I got wrong is due purely to my own inability to see. Special thanks also to Abbot Fenn and the Keewaydin Foundation who gave me my first opportunity to travel in the North; Abbot and many others at Keewaydin have remained involved and interested in this work from the beginning, and I hope they find something of interest within. I would also like to thank Scott See for introducing me to Canada as a topic of study and for all the help he has given along the way as academic advisor and good friend. Thanks also to Dick Judd and Stephen Hornsby for their ideas, advice, and support. Thanks finally to Chris Rasmussen for introducing me to an aspect of the historical discipline that could hold my love of the North and my love of history so that one complemented the other.

Many institutions have supported this work over the years. Thanks to the history department and the Canadian-American Center at the University of Maine. Thanks also to the Fulbright Foundation; the Canadian Embassy in Washington, DC; the Institute of Canadian Studies at the University of Ottawa; and the Center for the Study of Canada at SUNY Plattsburgh. And thanks to the Canadian Federation for the Humanities and Social Sciences and its Aid to Scholarly Publications Program and to the International Council for Canadian Studies Publishing Fund. The funding and institutional support I have received has made this work possible.

Thanks to everyone at UBC Press: Holly Keller for managing the production, Joanne Richardson for a vigorous and valuable edit, and particularly Randy Schmidt, who took an interest in this work when it was only an idea and who has remained an enthusiastic supporter to the end. Finally, thanks to Graeme Wynn for including this work in the Nature, History, and Society Series and for writing the Foreword.

Home
Is the Hunter

I

Introduction: Why James Bay?

*In some truly unimproved natural setting – one well
removed from the reach, the sights, and maybe especially
sounds of our wonted culture – surrounded by the
immemorial phenomenal world, whether trees, ocean,
or the waves of prairie grasses, a change may overtake us,
precisely to the extent that we are willing to remain where
we are and resist what will be a gathering temptation to
return to more certain comforts. It will not quite be fear,
but it will be next to this: a kind of existential humility
born of a sense of all the life that surrounds and includes
us and that will go on without us. And this is the ground
of myth – fear or humility and submission to the still
unfathomed mystery of Life.*

– *Frederick Turner,*
Beyond Geography[1]

It was while sitting in a canoe in the middle of Coldwater Lake in July
of 1982 – my usually talkative bowman strangely silent that day, the
rest of the group far ahead – that I experienced for the first time something that until then I thought of as simply a figure of speech: deafening
silence. Part of it was being in the middle of a large northern lake where
we were alone – alone in a way that is hardly possible most places – and
part of it, too, was the weather. There wasn't a breath of wind to riffle the
water, and the air pressure was falling, dulling the crispness of the world.
Low pressure, which usually brings sounds from far off – a dog barking
in the distance, birds high up in the forest trees, a decrease in the psychic
size of the world that marks the impending rain – that day brought only
an absence of sound. The world was all of a sudden unimaginably immense. I had the sense that sounds should be coming to me from across

the water, but all that came was a quiet that made me want to clear my throat, whistle, hum a tune – just for the ludicrous reassurance that I could still hear some noise. It was both disturbing and exhilarating, and we sat, both of us, I think, experiencing the same feelings. I don't know what it was that made us break the moment – not fear, I don't think, though something equally human – there were no words that I can remember, just a seemingly simultaneous decision to pick up our paddles and be on the move. Maybe we both lost our nerve at the same time, but the splash of the blades in the water and the thump of the paddle shafts against the gunwales was comforting. The movement was comforting too.

What we experienced that day, I think, was the bush – the land in some of its totality. That's the only way to describe it, for the bush is a presence in James Bay, it is manifest and obvious in its size and reality. There's no avoiding it, even if you travel, as we did, with a good supply of food and a radio for communication and safety. I don't want to portray the bush as a harsh place, though it certainly can be at times. I've spent many summers there but only a little time in the winter, and I have to rely on the stories of those who know, and on my own imagination, to understand the work needed to traverse that country in the snow and cold: hard work, involving a flow of energy from the land, focused through human activity and put back into the land in the act of living; hard work, too, involving a flow of imagination, focused through human culture, and fitted to the world in stories of people and place that explain the immensity that I glimpsed. It's the land that I want to investigate in this book – not simply the environment, but that larger presence manifest in that silence on Coldwater Lake.

The Cree name this land "Eeyou Istchee," which is translated most often as "The People's Land" but refers to more than simply the physical or political occupation of this northern region – important though these are to the Cree today. Sometimes it seems as though "Eeyou Istchee" would be better translated as "The Land's People" as this pushes against the inherent notions of ownership and control present in the usual translation. The words don't seem to describe a physical territory so much as a complex relationship between land and people, where neither one has control of the other and where "land" means not just ground but all the various beings with whom the Cree interact. This is the land in all its totality, I think, and it involves an understanding of all the life that surrounds and includes the Cree.

And so while I want to look at Frederick Turner's "immemorial phenomenal world," I don't believe that it's the fear that he references that is the grounding of the story of the land that I want to tell (at least, I want to believe that it isn't). His notion of humility provides a better way of seeing the land as it offers an acknowledgment of the futility – maybe the irrationality – of human hubris, and this resonates with what I know about the worldview of the Cree people who live on the land in James Bay. The fear, I think, comes from another place, a non-Native place, and, oddly, perhaps it comes from our cultural perception of the humility, the hope in the land, that is so central to the Native hunter's perspective. The hunter's humility seems quaint to us. The sense of hope that the hunter cultivates scares us, too; it scares us because we don't dare to believe in it, knowing as much as we think we do about the material world that surrounds us. And we do know so much about this world and its makeup. The sheer weight of that "rational" knowledge demands a faith of its own, which, in many ways, drives away hope in anything else. These are the seeds of fear and hubris in our modern world that so disturb the Cree and other Native peoples. I have been affected by that hope in the land, even as it challenged me that day twenty-five years ago and still confuses me today. James Bay has taught me that hope makes some sense, that we ought to pay it some attention, and that maybe there is another "rational" way of understanding this northern land. If there is a larger, philosophical reason for telling this story, then this is it.

This is a story about Cree hunters and their relationship with the land of James Bay, but it's also the story of how James Bay has become integrated into the rational vision and economy of North America and how local energy and imagination have been challenged – not lost – in the process. Both the energy flow and the imagination are important here. A very real part of James Bay's integration has involved the disruption of local energy flows through the environment; this has been the primary economic link with the South. For thirty-five years, Quebec has been developing hydro power in the bay, and now megawatts of power are generated where falls of water once shook the earth around them. Energy once spent in sound and natural motion has been transformed into the hum and crackle of electricity, siphoned off to the South, and the power in these places that once moved the human imagination has now been lost. Their ability to thunder in the heart is gone, and for every unit of energy that is gained in this process something less tangible is certainly lost. The power and the noise are now in our control, are being controlled for our needs, and here is the major social/environmental reason for telling this story.

James Bay is a prime example of the integration and exploitation of remote environments within an increasingly global economy and, consequently, within the expanding global scope of environmental social justice concerns. Like so many places around the world, James Bay is a place where our desire for resources has disrupted environments and the local cultures that depend on them. The reshaping of the landscape in order to extract energy from this remote region is, in part, an environmental issue, but it has a significant cultural component as well. In reality, there are few environmental concerns that do not involve concerns about people too, and, as I look at culture and environment in these pages, it is with this in mind. We can learn meaningful lessons from events in northern Quebec, but we will have to think carefully about how culture and environment, past and present, are linked in both our words and our actions. Much land has been flooded, but more has been changed by the introduction of multiple and massive high-tension lines across the landscape and by the network of roads that transport logs to the South just as the wires transport electricity. These things have changed the way people can think about their land as well as how they can use it. The Cree hunter, who does not know what loggers have done to his land, arrives on his trapline with a sense of foreboding that was unknown in the past. The Cree mother who is told that methyl mercury from decaying plants beneath the new waters has poisoned the fish receives a warning that may save her body but that jeopardizes her faith in a traditional food supply that, for millennia, has fed her people both physically and spiritually. All of this calls into question our use of James Bay for our own needs – our alteration of culture and nature – and makes clear the importance of investigating the long history of this land.[2]

In addition to what we extract, what we bring into the region is also transformative. This is maybe best seen in the introduction into the James Bay region of fossil-fuel technologies. Like most places on the earth now, James Bay is full of engines and furnaces that ease people's lives but that also change their relationships with the land around them. There is no doubt that technology changes our perceptions of the environment and that travelling at 100 kilometres per hour in a truck or on a snowmobile potentially allows a sense of power and separation, a sense of hubris, that is not possible in a canoe or on a sled. Engines have a sound that breaks the quiet of the bush, they speak out and comfort humans by assuring them that they can still hear something familiar. In their own way, they are telling a story about all of us; or maybe it's better to say that they are pushing people towards changing the story they tell about the land. Theirs can be a harsh guttural sound, a Greek chorus behind a new narrative – adding emphasis, maybe heightening emotions – feeding technological hubris to narratives of people's place in the environment.

Technology has the potential to do all this, although, for a long time, the James Bay Cree have maintained themselves through many narrative and technological encounters. Some of our stories, like our technology, are old news now, so simple formulations of the ways that technology brings environmental and cultural change are of little value. Some of those changes were forged into the knife blades and metal pots that Henry Hudson traded near Waskaganish, in 1608; others were embedded in the Cree-language bibles and prayer books produced by John Horden and his fellow missionaries in the nineteenth century. There are analogies here for the present, but these phenomena were in large part domesticated, even indigenized, by the Cree and were added to traditional culture even as that culture changed. So care is needed in defining the nature of change.

That said, the new stories that are recited to the metre of modern technology may be different from the old stories – harder to domesticate – because these stories and technologies function so closely together. These are the stories that, as Marx pointed out, redefine the world as commodity, not simply as raw material for production, and that allow technology a free reign. They abstract nature into manipulable pieces that can be ordered, harnessed to human need with the aid of modern technology, and sold. These two aspects of our culture also work together with the stories of sovereignty, an advancing Canadian jurisdiction over the Canadian Shield and the Arctic that began in the late nineteenth century and came to maturity after the Second World War. The North is resource-rich and is the economic foundation for a nation – two nations really, for the sovereignty inherent in "Maître chez nous" is also important to understanding James Bay history. In the 1960s, the flowering of Quebec nationalism and the assertion of Québécois control over their economic and cultural lives changed the world both inside and outside the St. Lawrence Valley. And the Québécois, more than any others, have carried both new technologies and new stories onto the lands of the Cree. More than any others, they have also tied this region to the global marketplace, and all this marks today as a new period in James Bay, albeit one connected to other historical processes occurring on this continent.

And here is a final reason for telling this story. Much of North America was transformed by the combined power of the Christian, yeoman narrative, with the economics and technology of proto-capitalist and capitalist agriculture, but this cultural package came up hard against the rocks and muskeg of the Canadian Shield. On Cree land, hunting and its narrative remained dominant, interacting with the world outside but remaining internally defined for centuries, until this new package of stories and technology arrived. Rapid and dramatic change came to James Bay not with the mere arrival of white fur traders, or even later with Anglicans and Roman Catholics and their application of certain aspects of Western narrative culture, but only with the combined power of modern technology and narratives about people's place on the land. The Cree, like other Natives in the past and many other people around the world today, are dealing with these combined forces. So James Bay is an important part of our modern environmental awareness, but it can also teach us something important about the meaning of our cultural expansion on this continent both in the past and in the present.

These are the larger issues that I want to cover as they relate to James Bay, but before I do that I want to engage briefly with my own personal history with the land as it has a great deal to do with my interpretation of larger events. In canoeing through this country my companions and I were lucky enough to be guided by hunters who had been born in the bush and who had been raised there before the massive intrusion of outsiders and their technology. On my first trip our guide was Daniel Blacksmith, on future trips it was Charlot Gunner. It is to these men that I owe a great part of the inspiration to write in the first place, and part of what I perceived that day on Coldwater Lake has to do with them. I make no claims to writing this from the Cree perspective (I genuinely hope to see that story written someday); rather, I am writing this as a white American who caught a glimpse of something out of the corner of his eye while travelling up there and who has attempted to understand the great quiet that he sensed on the land and also the quiet sense of place that struck him in watching the grace with which Daniel and Charlot move through the bush. I don't use the term "grace" lightly as I see the tinge of romanticism there, but the word works for me, freighted as it is. There was a sense of connectedness, of selflessness in relation to their surroundings that made the bush that Daniel and Charlot moved through a different place from the "wilderness" that I traversed. It would probably be better to say that they were moving through a different story – one that was intimately connected with that great quiet.

I went north at first to find a wilderness and to live out some very romantic images that I had in my head from reading fur trade stories. The fur trade, for all the revisions that have been made of it, is still one of the great epics of North American history, and my imagination was captured by the sweep of that story – the grand adventure, as I saw it. I suppose I found some of what I was looking for, but it became clear to me very early on that for those Cree trappers this was not a wilderness, not an adventurous re-enactment, not a scenic getaway from the world to the south. This was a present-day world that was whole, self-contained, and internally defined if you were in tune enough to understand it. I was not that bright. All I can say is that I caught a glimpse of something and that I have spent quite a while trying to figure it out, trying to see it as a part of the modern world.

In 1982, my first impression of Mistissini Post – one of the then eight Cree communities in the region – was not positive: it seemed like a squalid little town on the edge of the forest, and I was anxious to get out of it. I didn't understand then that all of the Cree villages were in the process of rapid transformation due to the massive hydroelectric project that had been started on the La Grande River. I was disappointed in the Hudson's Bay Company trading post, which looked like any hardware store back home; I was disappointed with all of the motorized canoes I saw on the beach (the Cree boy waterskiing behind one of them was almost more than I could take); I was just disappointed. I had a story in my head – one that I am more than a little ashamed of now – and this place was not living up to my expectations. My expectations, of course, had come from stories about the past, from the belief that the Cree had been unaltered by the passage of time; and this was not so different from my perception that the region's environment, "the wilderness," had not changed either. Both of these were serious errors.

When we left the village and began to travel along the eastern shore of Lake Mistassini, things were more like what I had expected. The bush, hardly unchanged from time immemorial, at least gave that impression. It was the cultural juxtaposition of that which I expected and that which I didn't expect that continued to confuse me. Daniel had a proficiency in the woods that I admired greatly. He used the traditional crooked knife (*mogedagen*) to carve everything from axe handles to ladles; he also carried a radio (today it would be a satellite phone) to talk to his wife when he could get reception. The cognitive space here was as vast and as confusing as was the silence on Coldwater Lake, and it was even harder to put into words, particularly since I was expecting to find some kind of mythic Indian in the forest primeval. I continue to have these experiences up North, sitting in a traditional tent listening to someone speaking Cree on a cellphone and hearing the occasional reference to some professional hockey team or Hollywood movie. I have learned to laugh at the irony that my mind insists on creating out of those moments. It really is all in my head.

Over the course of seven summers I had the opportunity to travel more
in the region – far to the north along the Arctic Ocean, too – and to continue to ponder the world up there and its relationship both to the world
I had expected to find and to my own world back here at home. This book
is largely my attempt to figure out that relationship, though it is more than
that too. I came very quickly to care about the Cree and their land. I have
been compelled to try to speak to them through this story, though I am
sure that Charlot and Daniel will never read it. I find myself enmeshed
in a conversation with this place that makes me want to tell about it, and
this seems all the more pressing to me since Quebec has, this last January
2007, announced the beginning of the next phase of hydro development
in James Bay. This time it will be the Rupert River that will be dammed
and its energy harnessed to the power grid. This will bring another wave
of environmental and cultural change to the region, and I am involved in
it not only because of my relationship to the region but also because of
my relationship to the northeastern electrical grid. Hydro-Québec wants
to generate more power to grow the Quebec economy; it also wants to sell
some of it to me for my computer, lights, and woodshop. The electrical
ligaments that tie the regions together are important and so, too, are the
intellectual sinews that will continue to bind cultures even more closely
together. We need to think about the meaning of all of this not only
from a material, environmental point of view but also from a cultural,
even metaphysical, point of view. If the resources of James Bay are going
to be a part of our world, then so are the people who live there and their
worldviews. We need to engage all of this as best we can.

So for me, discussing current issues also means coming to grips with
our past cultural interactions and the fact that we have still not fully
integrated Aboriginal peoples and their land into our own history. My
hope in meditating on James Bay is not only to identify some of the many
environmental issues but also to raise some of the related cultural issues
that linger in our relationship to Aboriginal peoples everywhere. I even go
as far as to hope that I can offer something that will help to identify some
solutions to these issues. There is something in the Cree story, as I have
been able to put it together, that goes right back to that day on Coldwater
Lake, to the humbling sense brought on by the immensity of the bush,
and the hope that lies out there still.

I'm aware that I am taking on a responsibility in speaking about the
Cree and their land. This has the potential to be useful, although there
is no assurance of that. I've talked a lot about the lessons that James Bay

can teach us and what we need to consider, but, if we are not careful, this use of their land and their history has the potential to be just as exploitatively extractive as has our resource use. The words of Kiowa writer and philosopher N. Scott Momaday seem appropriate here to emphasize this potential danger: the storyteller, he writes,

> is he who takes it upon himself to speak formally. He assumes responsibility for his words, for what is created at the level of his human voice. He runs the risk of language, and language is full of risk – it might miscarry, it might be abused in one or more of a thousand ways. His function is essentially creative, inasmuch as language is essentially creative. He creates himself, and his listeners, through the power of his perception, his imagination, his expression. He realizes the power and beauty of language; he believes in the efficacy of words.[3]

I am creating something in language here, in my own language, and Momaday's words remind me to keep in mind that other story of the land, the one that is not in my language – the story I believe our guides were moving through and that I believe is still very much alive in James Bay. His words push me to try to find a way to incorporate that story's presence into my own, even if I don't understand it in all its complexity. They also continue to remind me that this is not the only story that can be told, it's simply the one that I am capable of telling.[4]

As I touched on above, when the Cree speak of their land they mean more than just the ground on which they stand, the land that can be mapped two-dimensionally and scattered with cadastral lines to show property, jurisdiction, even sovereignty. What they mean by land is the entire multidimensional web of beings that occupies eastern James Bay: people, animals, plants, earth. So their story is one of place but also one of the complicated relationships – physical and metaphysical, human and other-than-human – that have shaped land and people together. The land is full of their names, their stories, their personal memories about these relationships, and all of these inhabit the remembered earth. These narratives, even if they remain something of a mystery, a linguistic and symbolic world that we are as unprepared for as we are to make our living by hunting on the land of the bay, become a responsibility for anyone who wishes to speak about the Cree and their land. The responsibility is to remember that these stories are not curiosities but, rather, have past and present meaning on the land.[5]

In 1492, this continent was not only demographically robust but also imaginatively and narratively robust, and the latter is relevant to the way that the past led into the present. In James Bay it was Cree words and stories that formed part of the geography that was the local environment, a place where hunting defined the Cree world, where humans and other-than-humans lived together in the reciprocal gift exchange of the hunt. And, most important, those stories continued to shape historical events even when, in the seventeenth century, the region became connected with the economy and discourse of European peoples.[6] I say "connected with," not "overshadowed by," because European stories did not flourish on the land there any more than did English wheat. All that the English brought became part of James Bay's geography and needs consideration, but not as the dominant force that shaped the history and environment of James Bay as it exists today. In the specific events and chronology of its history, James Bay is different from many places where Europeans came and stayed; however, in that James Bay today demands more than an understanding of what was brought there from the outside, it is just like other places.[7]

Momaday again points the way in his own telling of Kiowa history. With his inclusion of personal as well as documented ecological and even mythological events, he pushes the reader to feel the weight of multiple ideas, even if they cannot be completely understood or assimilated within the framework of our expectations of what history should be. All the words created around a people are meaningful for him, all of them function to shape the historical events that involved Natives and non-Natives. Significantly, too, he demands a consideration not only of people and their words about each other but also of nature and our various cultural and personal relationships to it. The individual, he tells us in an often-quoted line, "ought to concentrate his mind on the remembered earth. He ought to give himself up to a particular landscape in his experience, to look at it from as many angles as he can, to wonder about it, to dwell upon it. He ought to imagine that he touches it with his hands at every season and listens to the sounds that are made upon it. He ought to recollect the glare of noon and all the colors of the dawn and dusk." For him, the land is sacred, invested with human meanings and actions that supersede any economic or political definitions of it.[8] Momaday's words are quoted so often because they resonate. They echo within my own desire to consider more carefully the role of environment and human culture in James Bay; they also echo in modern Native demands for the inclusion of their perspectives in our dealings with them over land and resources.[9]

This centrality of both land and language, I believe, means conceiving of the Cree and James Bay before contact as a self-contained environment of work and words into which Europeans entered in order to trade, proselytize, and inquire. As Europeans worked to survive, they worked to change this environment, though they never reshaped James Bay exclusively in their own image: for centuries, they did not have the numbers or power to even try. As in so many other places, in James Bay European modes of subsistence were not immediately successful, and newcomers were thrown back on Native subsistence. Unlike in other places, in James Bay European methods never flourished and Europeans continued to be bounded by the hunter's work and, increasingly, the hunter's words. I think it is important here to consider that, while the larger history of contact between Natives and Europeans illustrates how dramatically European work and words reshaped the Native world, nowhere did this happen without a period of cultural discourse and negotiation over the meaning of both. James Bay offers a protracted example of this important phase. Whereas in other places periods of negotiation lasted only a generation or two, in James Bay they were much longer, which is rare if not unique.

We struggle with these periods of negotiation that often occurred in the distant past and that linger tentatively in unclear and incomplete records, with the result that their meaning within the larger history suffers. In this regard, the Cree experience offers a different perspective on the larger process of contact for Native peoples and on their place in the histories of North America. For centuries before the Cree mounted the stage of law and politics, outsiders worked within a Cree context that maintained its local relevance. This is vital: the Cree remained imaginatively robust over a huge geography for hundreds of years, and outsiders moved through that story of the land. The far more radical changes that came in other places, as Europeans adapted the environment materially and conceptually to their own ends, may also help to bring into focus more recent events in James Bay, though the process of paradigmatic change is not a fait accompli. In other words, what's going on today should look familiar in many ways, but because of a very different history, the end result is anything but a foregone conclusion, either for the Cree or the land.[10]

Seeing the huge and lasting landscape of Cree narrative allows us to conceive of Native culture spatially and to acknowledge that there are still Native environments in every part of North America – vastly reduced in size though they may be – and that Native peoples continue to resist the wholesale imposition of Western narratives upon themselves and those places. Part of this resistance is political, and it is worth remembering Momaday's words here: narratives like this one are potentially dangerous in that they represent a powerful aspect of Western politics, and histories are, after all, inherently political and have not often worked in the favour of Native peoples. Historical narrative is probably vital to the Cree in their new legal and political relationship with modern Canada, however, as they now find themselves in the midst of the same negotiations over sovereignty and rights as do other Natives in Canada and the United States. Yet, while it is important to interpret the historical path that led to Eeyou Istchee as a semi-sovereign entity, at the same time it is also important not to conflate Cree politics and Cree culture: they are not the same thing. The larger definition of Eeyou Istchee is still the most important: it is more than a government, or lines on a map, or even a nation (as it is defined in Western political terms). Thinking about the Cree's narrative landscape allows us to range much farther than that.[11]

More to the point, this spatial way of thinking about narrative and culture allows us to get at questions about the processes of cultural interaction, which I think need to be fleshed out more before getting to the actual historical events. This way of thinking helps us get at questions like: What did it mean for widely divergent cultures to come together as they did all across the continent? How did the interaction between these very different peoples change them and the land over time? How, in fact, did they interact as people, and how do they continue to interact within the political and economic structures of the modern world? What should be created at the level of our historical narratives and what are the responsibilities in writing down the history of a people and their landscape? At a more personal level, how should my perception of the vastness of the bush as well as the other different ways it is perceived be incorporated into the story?

Maybe we can begin to answer these kinds of questions by looking at the relationship between human culture and stories. This relationship is central to my way of seeing the process of contact in James Bay because, as philosopher David Carr points out, all people are striving for the position of storyteller in their own lives, in the lives of constituent groups, and in the lives of other peoples. And, as he says, "we must go even further and say that it [narrative] is literally *constitutive* of the group." By extension, it is also one of the primary ways that groups interact. In this competition of stories, "culture is contested, temporal, and emergent" for anthropologist James Clifford, and "representation and explanation – by insiders and outsiders – is implicated in this emergence." So individual people – insiders and outsiders – speaking into a narrative space constitutes one of the ways that culture is created, maintained, and altered. And environment is central to this emergence because vital modes of living and working in nature are always wrapped in words and explanations. We negotiate not only over how to use nature but also over definitions of natural and unnatural, the underlying meaning of nature in our lives, and the relative human position in the hierarchy of nature – again the physical and metaphysical. This is never truer than in the relationship between Natives and non-Natives, where land is the chief subject in that contested emergence both in the past and the present.[12]

But seeing the history of a land as a negotiation over meaning has the potential to get very abstract and rarefied, and it's important to remember that, by definition, environments are also specific places that must be capable of sustaining physical bodies as well as the more abstract cultural soul. There are dynamic tensions here – between individual needs and cultural expectations and between physical nature and storied environments – and these create the kinds of forces that also drive historical change. These are the forces that shaped James Bay, and, in thinking about culture spatially and narratively, I want to see not only how the Cree moved back and forth between their land and the islands of European culture at the trading posts but also how European cultural artifacts, both material and intellectual, were integrated into the act (and meaning) of hunting. Equally important, I want to see those traders, missionaries, scientists, and government officials who moved out into the bush and who depended on their own ability to integrate themselves to some degree within the Cree narrative in order to survive in James Bay. Thinking about language spatially in relation to individual human action allows us not only to take up the idea that the meaning of words buttresses our use of particular places but also to stay grounded in the fact that use is the foundation of meaning. Language is certainly heuristic: its form predetermines what we see and how we interpret it. But these observations and interpretations are then put into practice in the physical world, reshaping it and our modes of observation and interpretation. In many ways, the Cree were prepared to meet the challenges of the last thirty-five years through their prolonged history of environmental and cultural negotiation with Europeans within their own physical and heuristic geography: a place where hunting – in its largest sense – fed bodies and soul.[13]

This interpretation comes first and foremost from the heart of the continent and the history that we have written about it. It comes from a place apart, from Native America – a place that Euro-Americans hardly know because we do not know the languages and the narratives that would enable us to locate ourselves there. Historian Calvin Martin argues provocatively that Europeans and their generations have never in fact reached this Native America, landing instead on a dark and bloody continent that was the product of their own fecund imaginations rather than on the island riding on the back of a great turtle (where Natives had lived for millennia). Trapped within our own cultural expectations and discourse – what he refers to as the ontology of fear – we have never grasped the Native reality that spanned the continent. This is a foundational idea for me, and Martin, as always, rightly reminds us to remember Native consciousness and language as integral to our history. However, I wonder if, in one respect, his analysis is not anachronistic.[14]

Forgetting Native reality seems a present danger – a point of valid self-criticism – far more than it was a danger for those who actually stepped out onto this continent five hundred years ago. It is important to remember that, in one way, narrative is an act of remembering; it can also be an act of forgetting. No matter what they said or wrote afterwards, no matter their forgetfulness, those first Europeans entered into both the material and narrative realities of Native America. They contacted a powerful conceptual reality, an intellectual tradition that challenged what they understood about the world. It was only when they re-entered European space – if they chose to do so – that they began the process of communication and interpretation to which we have access in the written record. The history we tell is in some respects the continuation of a narrative process that goes back almost as far as contact, and this poses a clear danger for those Natives about whom we are writing. Will our history be an act of remembering or an act of forgetting?[15]

Culturally and historically we have certainly and wilfully forgotten Native reality – in many respects we have actively worked to erase it – but those early travellers entered that reality and had to learn to navigate and to partake in the environment that they found here in North America. They had to do this in order to survive. This is one of the larger lessons of James Bay history: Native narrative reality meant material survival in the form of food from the land. Martin is quite right in casting this Native American narrative reality in concrete and geographical terms, but room should be made to differentiate between both the experiences of individuals who entered the cultural space of Native people, and how those experiences were later interpreted within a European narrative space. Narrative spaces, as well as material spaces, are part of the equation, and the historical challenge of Native America is, to a large degree, its continuing existence as a narrative place apart. Contact was not so much a moment in time as an ongoing process through which two culturally different peoples began to live with and speak to and about one another.[16]

All of this discussion of cultural and environmental negotiation, connecting cultural space to physical nature, comes together because, as I have said, the negotiation was and still is largely about the land, that web of relationships the Cree define in opposition to our understanding of real estate. The land was what the Cree went to court to protect when Quebec began to develop the region in 1971, and they continue to try to protect it in their current negotiations with Canadians. This is what all Native peoples are struggling to maintain: the use and understanding of their lands. The negotiation of these narrative spaces continues as the Cree try to work within the legal, political framework of the West. This framework is inherently tied up with historical and cultural writing; thus it is clear that to write responsibly is to write about the past with the realization that one's words have power in the present. Most ominously, because it challenges some of the ways that we have defined Native cultures, what I want to say about Cree hunting and its relationship to the land has the potential to miscarry. So here I want to be particularly careful.

The historical facts are that Cree hunting in the twentieth century was not the same as Cree hunting in the nineteenth century and that Cree hunting in the nineteenth century was not the same as Cree hunting in the past. Hunting in the twenty-first century will no doubt be different still. But are historical change and cultural continuity mutually exclusive? This is the dangerous political question raised by the way in which many Native histories are told. Often there is a tacit assumption that the older practice is always somehow "more Native" and that if Native people have moved away from that older practice then they have somehow forfeited their ability to define their environments and their rights on the land. Many anthropologists see this as an old and outmoded concept, but it continues to have popular and political currency. And it gets reinforced when histories do not connect the Native past with the Native present, thus leaving the impression that "real Indians" dwelt in the former. Sadly, this is an idea that has taken root within Native culture too. I'm reminded of the words novelist Leslie Silko puts in the mouth of the old shaman Betonie:

> They always think the ceremonies must be performed exactly as they have always been done, maybe because one slip-up or mistake and the whole ceremony must be stopped and the sand painting destroyed. That much is

true. They think that if a singer tampers with any part of the ritual, great harm can be done, great power unleashed. That much can be true also. But long ago when the people were given these ceremonies, the changing began, if only in the aging of the yellow gourd rattle or the shrinking of the skin around the eagle's claw, if only in the different voices from generation to generation, singing the chants. You see, in many ways, the ceremonies have always been changing.[17]

Describing a continuity in cultural daylight on the changing landscape of history, as Momaday rightly asks us to do, will help to dispel the idea of changelessness that I carried with me when I first went north. So will a focus on the land and on telling the story into the present, taking care to connect both to recent events.

My own initial disappointment with Mistissini eventually led to my questioning the roots of the popular belief in the static nature of traditional cultures. I was naïve when I first went north, but I was not completely ignorant of culture as a concept. I think, though, that I saw cultures as discrete, as naturally separate from one another, and I believed that Native cultures had only been contaminated by Western culture. This in some ways hearkens back to American anthropology's original mission to "preserve" traditional cultures (which, after contact, were seen as fading away), and it was fed by my assumption that all the modern things I saw in the village had either been forced upon the Cree or were indicative of some cultural lapse on their part. I think my misunderstanding of culture can also be explained by my inability to process the myriad ways that culture has been explained to the public in the years since anthropology moved away from the preservationist model. As anthropologist Clifford Geertz somewhat wryly points out, with regard to defining "culture," anthropology "seems to have asserted almost everything at one time or another." Structuralism, functionalism, Freudian analysis, semiotics – all of these and more have been used as foundational criteria for understanding human culture. Not surprisingly, this has left a somewhat confused picture.[18]

In looking at James Bay, this confusion coloured my thinking for quite a while. Just as on my first visit to the North, the historical record continually presented me with a picture of cultural complexity that challenged static notions of culture. The mythic Indian and the forest primeval are not to be found there either. It wasn't until I came upon Edward Sapir's criticism – made in the early twentieth century – that, in general, anthropological approaches only think "of the individual as a more or less passive carrier of tradition or, to speak more dynamically, as the infinitely variable actual-izer of ideas and of modes of behavior which are implicit in the structures and tradition of a given society," that I found some room for what I was seeing in the record. Sapir's criticism indicates that definitions of culture leave no room for individuality and no mechanism for changing Native traditions other than through the forced imposition of outside ideas. The Geertzian conviction "that men unmodified by the customs of particular places do not in fact exist, have never existed, and most important, could not in the very nature of the case exist," seems true enough; but it is individual people who make and modify cultures, and this is a historical process. What I have come to see is that, with regard to our understanding of Native history, the concept of culture has come at a price.[19]

The concept of culture has helped us to reinterpret Euro-American records in the light of anthropological evidence and methodology, thus enabling us to gain new understandings of the Native past and activities such as hunting. Anthropological studies of Native peoples have discovered threads of culture that run back to a time before white contact, and this has allowed a rethinking of the often pejorative descriptions of Natives and has given new meaning to their historical actions.[20] This has allowed us to find meaning in Native words and actions that those who recorded them saw only as savage and meaningless. But our reliance upon anthropology's tools has limited our thinking insofar as anthropology is not centrally concerned with explaining change over time. It is not that anthropology is ahistorical (this is a common complaint about the discipline and it is one that I do not share); rather, it is that its concentration on group behaviour has led to a totalizing understanding of culture that resists explanations of historical change that, so often, come down to individual choice and action.[21]

I am not suggesting that we impose our modern legal and political under-standing of the individual as a near-sovereign entity onto past cultures, but, in order to understand changes in traditional Native hunting in James Bay, it is important to see individuals. I want to rethink the relationship between the individual and culture, and here, I think, is where Geertz's focus on "particular places" becomes important to understanding culture (just as, earlier, place was important in understanding narrative). Place implies a local geography, a local environment, and it implies individual people fitting into place in some specific and divergent ways. Individuals are cultural in all the ways that anthropologists have described, true enough, but they are also *Homo sapiens,* units of human biology in a physical world in which they have to make their living. Individual hunters, then, are embedded both in hunting culture and in physical nature, and, because they cannot separate cultural self from physical self, they live within a single spatial phenomenon that influences, but does not wholly determine, their actions within it. Historical change is explained because, while various aspects of culture (even traditional culture) and environment may reinforce one another, at times there is a tension between them that pulls the individual in different directions. Thus, Native cultures were changing long before the coming of Europeans, but these changes were exacerbated in situations where individuals entered into another cultural environment, as happened with contact in places like James Bay. The proximity of heuristic geographies offers new avenues for individuals by presenting them with alternatives to their own cultural space, and these individuals, depending on their abilities and desires, can move between environments, testing and changing one space with objects and concepts from the other. This may result in direct changes within the cultural environment, and whereas goods and ideas must be internally communicated (in all the ways mentioned above), they may also be internally redefined in the language of the environment within which they are occurring. In other words, people may understand change without having recourse to outside imposition. Significantly, if it happens slowly enough, change may not be seen at all. All of this requires relative parity in cultural strength, of course; however, as I have noted, this was the case in James Bay for a much longer time than it was in many places.[22]

So rather than defining individuals as separately infused with cultural consciousness – computers programmed with certain software – and also inhabiting physical nature, it is better to see them as moving within cultural environments that are materially and narratively tied together by the presence of those individuals who are constantly negotiating among themselves. We see clearly that culture makes it possible for humans to survive individually in nature, but we should also see that the individual human makes it possible for culture to exist in nature. Individuals survive because culture gives them the tools and concepts they need, but culture recreates itself within individuals through their ability and willingness to communicate with others both inside and outside the group (i.e., to continue the narrative) and their ability to feed, clothe, and reproduce themselves. Individual humans, then, are the nexus of culture and nature and are the engines of historical change within both. Here the meaning of culture connects with the meaning of narrative, and both relate back to the lands of James Bay.[23]

Culture may have determined what was proper for the Cree hunter to eat, but it did not determine his need to eat. Nor could it predict or determine what would happen when culturally acceptable food was absent or was simply the more desirable option to an individual Cree. Individuals made different choices on these kinds of issues and then narrated those choices to others in an attempt to fit those actions within the framework of common understanding. While Cree hunting remained important for survival, it also remained the context of a larger cultural negotiation. Fur traders particularly became part of this context because the fur trade in James Bay was bounded by the realities of hunting food. Two very different systems of consciousness, both of which were internally coherent, met one another in the similar physical hunger of individuals. These individuals helped feed one another, all the while narrating and negotiating the meaning of words and signs. And this continues in a different way today as the Cree deal with their recent integration into the Canadian national consciousness.[24]

If we begin by trying to see the spider's web of words and meaning that clings so delicately to the forests of the North – so often invisible except in the diffuse light of dawn – then we get a sense of the scope and the longevity of this hunter's landscape. In 1914, as a concrete example, white travellers on the Rupert River came upon red marks painted on a large rock by the river; they were glyphs, signs of an older Cree world, and were clearly something outside of Western understanding. The simple explanation given on the spot, that they were "the Devil's Marks," is important, but so is the fact that the paint was fresh and clear, part of an ongoing cultural discourse, literally written on the land – a thread of precontact narrative that some individual Cree were still using to negotiate their place in the world in the early twentieth century. These marks expressed a cultural knowledge about hunting on the land that continued to mediate cultural and political power in the region between whites and Cree as well as among the Cree themselves. This is part of the history of the James Bay environment, and its power must shape how we view the European alternatives that were carried to James Bay, beginning in the seventeenth century.[25]

All of this is to say that words form – or should form – part of the connecting tissue that binds individuals to the land that sustains them. This is part of the power and the efficacy of the words of which Momaday speaks; it is the meaning of change for Silko's Betonie.[26] The play between narratives and their material partners makes it possible to believe in the creative power of words because the Cree engaged them so fully, bending them to their needs and adapting them. The Cree show us something very important with regard to how we think about contact with Europeans. This does not deny the potentially disruptive, even destructive power of narratives' claims to objective truth – particularly the narratives of religion, economics, and politics. The Foucauldian connection between official language, knowledge, and the imposition of political power will be important to James Bay in the end, but only after centuries of cultural interaction within Cree narratives, the most dominant of which is the narrative of the hunt. The hunter's narrative is still being used and adapted.[27]

At this moment the Cree and James Bay have undergone thirty-five years of dramatic cultural and environmental change. Many of these changes have not been for the better, but nothing in the history of the region indicates that this trend need be permanent. Nothing in the history of the region indicates that change, as such, need be a problem for the Cree – only specific changes. Defining the historical context of change and continuity seems particularly pressing in light of these recent events in James Bay. The Cree past needs to be connected clearly with the Cree present in a way that takes the Cree environment into consideration. This is because, when the Cree today appear in court, or at a press conference, or in front of government officials, they are continuing a long negotiation with white culture, and they are trying to explain the meaning of a long cultural narrative about the lands of James Bay. They are trying to explain their environment to us and, in doing so, are attempting to maintain some control over it.

Again, within the larger understanding of Native America, change has often been forced, but it has occurred spatially, and Native cultural environments still exist everywhere. For the Cree, forced change has occurred not only in the form of flooded lands but also in the form of conceptual changes that were brought to the unflooded lands. Through treaties, the Cree have gained a great deal of political control over their villages, but they have lost a great deal of their historical ability to define the lands of the region within their own narrative. The problems in James Bay today come not only from material alterations to the land but also from alterations to the cultural narrative of hunting that, in the past, was meaningful for everyone. This is a process that connects them with the larger story of contact, just as the details of Cree history add texture and colour to the story of that larger event.

Significantly, it was only when political and economic need, along with technical ability, made it possible for Quebec to apply a purely outside narrative directly to the lands of James Bay that change became so disruptive.

This is the last lesson of James Bay: European economic activity could go on for centuries within a largely Native narrative space; the missionary narrative could be controlled and made useful within the material reality of the hunt; an outside narrative of ownership, control, and sovereignty could exist apart from James Bay even as the hunt and its narrative continued because the lands of James Bay were deemed not useful. Only when these narrative lines converged was the effect revolutionary. The significant aspect of this story is the increasing scope and power of an outside narrative understanding of the region and its environment. This is an understanding that was created within a non-Cree epistemology of nature and culture, and it is one that came to challenge the Cree in 1970 and that continues to threaten what philosopher Pierre Bourdieu calls a "dispossession of the instruments of symbolic production" in James Bay.[28]

Over the last thirty-five years, numerous studies have been carried out in James Bay. Environmental impact studies have looked at changes in ecology caused by flooding tens of thousands of square kilometres of land and rerouting major rivers. Sociological studies have looked at how the Cree have been affected by increasing numbers of outsiders (brought in by the new roads), by changes in diet, and by drugs and alcohol. Few would question the connection between environmental change and cultural change, but little has been done to show how they have worked together, how they are really part of the same process of change, and how they are part of a much longer process of change both locally and globally. At the same time, many have romanticized the Cree hunter and the bush, choosing to ignore change in an attempt to hold on to an image that fits well within our own notions of environmentalism and wilderness preservation (an image that omits our own part in this story of change). All of these perspectives fit into a larger picture that involves not only the environmental and cultural issues of the present but also all those of the past. So while I've spent a great deal of time in recent years reading historical records (Hudson's Bay Company documents, Anglican missionary documents, and any others I could find that related to the Cree and the lands of James Bay), and while I believe there's an important story in the region's past, the importance of the present and of staying focused on the land – that great complexity that, in the North, still bounds people's lives – cannot be separated from historical inquiry. This was brought home to me on a recent winter trip made in reaction to the announcement of the Rupert River Project.

I went North because I wanted to see what was going on and to hear how people were talking about it. I arrived in a steady snowfall in the village of Chisasibi, just as school was letting out and people were driving off to pick up their kids. All the four-way stops were backed up six or seven cars deep (another of those ironies – rush hour at, quite literally, the end of the road). Chisasibi is the biggest of the nine Cree communities and a creation of the La Grande projects. In 1980, the old fur trade community on Fort George Island was in the path of the newly increased flow of the La Grande River, and fear of erosion led the government to relocate the people to this new place along the south shore of the river. It was one of those forced relocations all too familiar in the Canadian North, and I know from talking to people that, among the older generation, a great deal of sadness and bad feelings continue to be associated with this move. For the Cree who lived through it, there is a sense of dislocation that will likely never go away; and for the younger generation there is a break with the past – a dislocation in their history as well as their geography. The past is now another place, and while they can visit the island and tell stories about their lives there, it will never again be a truly living place.

I went to the band offices to introduce myself and to ask some questions about the dams and how the land is doing now. I had already received a full dose of the Hydro-Québec version of things that morning while touring the hydroelectric facility, and I wanted to hear the other side of the story. I was a stranger there, and the people I knew in town were away, so those I met were understandably wary about who I was and why I was asking questions. I knew it was unfair of me to drop in unannounced, but for a few minutes there were a half-dozen of us standing in the hallway and a couple of people began to express their unhappiness with the Rupert River project, saying that they wanted it stopped. When I told them that I'd like to stop it too but that the Grand Council had told those of us from the South to stay out of it this time, one young man reminded me that there was still free speech in the world – "for a little while longer anyway." He made a point of telling me that he still used the word "if" when speaking about the Rupert diversion: the thing does not have any physical reality yet, and he will not grant it any narrative reality either. But I saw that many people were very tense; starting yet another fight did not appear to be universally popular.

In the following pages I want to think about the past and present of James Bay in relation to the hydro dams that have already been built but, more important, in relation to the dams that were started in the summer of 2007. It had been seven years since my last trip, and though I'd been warned, I was still astounded by the changes that are happening within the Cree communities and out in the bush due to our use of their land. First, I drove everywhere I wanted to go, something I could not have done even five years ago. And of course, as I travelled, I saw all the other changes that made the roads necessary. Logging is going on all over, and, for the last fifteen years, clear-cutting has been a much bigger problem than flooding. The Cree communities are changing so fast that it's hard to know where to begin to tell the story of how all these changes came about. But in order to understand them one has to go right back to the land itself, back to the human interaction with the land that has been going on for so long. Only by taking the long view do the changes occurring in the present seem understandable as something more than blind, unstoppable decline for both land and people. Only by connecting the history of the land with what is happening to the land today can we find a meaning that will help lead to the future.

2

Imagining the Land

It is really beautiful what he has been saying. He said this whole place is like a garden, because many things grow here, and the Indians are one of the things that grow here. He says the animals were given to the Indians so they could feed their children and old people, and everyone has always shared the food from this garden. He says everyone here will always share. It's always been like that.

— Job Bearskin, 1973[1]

It's the middle of March, 2007, and I'm standing this morning just about midway between fifty-three and fifty-four degrees north latitude, outside of the town of Radisson in northern Quebec. It's snowing now and the wind is cutting, though it was sunny and calm at dawn. The weather is like that year round up here – mercurial, important. My vantage point this morning is the top of the spillway of the Robert Bourassa Dam – part of the world's largest hydroelectric facility – above the so-called Giant's Stairway. Named back in the 1970s by Hydro-Québec construction workers, these eight steps, all of them the width of three football fields, ten or fifteen metres high, and cut into the living granite of the Canadian Shield, are the safety valve for the vast reservoir behind them. The gates below me are used only during extreme spring flooding – every seventy-five years or so – and most of the time the stairs stand dry, a monument more than a functional piece of engineering. Their image is used on local signs and in Hydro-Québec literature not because they are the most impressive thing about this hydroelectric facility but because they symbolize something more than engineering. As engineering marvels, the phalanxes of high-tension towers pushing power as far away as Pennsylvania, the sixteen mammoth turbines spinning under the dam producing 5,600 megawatts of power, and the 66,500 square kilometres of reservoir that feed the eight dams of the La Grande River facility are all more impressive than the stairway.

FIGURE 2.1 *The Giant's Stairway.* The spillway of the Robert Bourassa Dam is one of the most striking and visible parts of the mostly subterranean James Bay hydroelectric facility. This photo was taken from about two kilometres away; each of the steps shown is over ten metres high and the width of several football fields.

But the scope of these other things is hard to capture in a picture, or even in the imagination I now realize, and so, like other symbols, the stairway has become a graspable token of something ungraspable: to Quebec, the stairway means progress.

If I look off the other side of the spillway I see the frozen surface of the reservoir receding into a grey expanse of snow squalls that are pushing through, ebbing and flowing like a tide. The snow is fine and powdery, and under the hand of the wind it recreates a wavy surface, the mask of a human-made lake that now hides the hunting lands beneath. Overhead is the superstructure of steel girders that carries the massive weight of the floodgates when they are needed. They rise about thirty metres in the air and were visible this morning from my hotel room, ten kilometres away. In the grey light of dawn they looked like some pillared ruin, an ancient and abandoned temple on the skyline, and as the light grew I studied their strangeness in this remote place. The sky turned orange and then umber with the coming snow, and when the sun rose behind these hard angles – like the opening of a fiery eye, the waking of some local god who was obviously still very much in residence in his temple – it looked powerful and menacing.

It would be easy to be pessimistic about the future of this land and the people who live here, to say only that they have both been changed and something has been lost. All that is true: these dams and their effects are part of James Bay now. Yet, as I hope this story illustrates, the pessimistic view is not a very good one. It's a view that does not make rational sense if many of the things that the hunter believes about the world are true. And the ultimate goal of this work is to give some outline, some historical weight, to the ways that the hunters of James Bay view their world, to see how their technical and imaginative power shaped a landscape for everyone who lived off the land, and to show how that power continues to shape people's lives today in opposition to this object of the Western imagination upon which I am standing.

It is not enough, however, to simply be struck by the power of Cree words like those that head this chapter, to momentarily lament the fact that much of the garden Job Bearskin spoke of is now under twenty or twenty-five metres of water, and then to move on without trying to comprehend at least part of the context from which those words came. But to come straight at his words may be to risk simply surrounding them with a set of pre-existing assumptions that cloud the issue more than clarify it; too often, in my mind, this is what happens to Native expressions of what the land means to them. Job Bearskin's words express a traditional and profoundly Cree belief, one that is as valid today as it was thirty-five years ago, when he first uttered them; they are also, however, the product of a specific geography and history, the result of many different people's interaction with this land over centuries. The garden metaphor was undoubtedly, at some point in Cree history, a borrowed one. That is an aspect of history, and I say this not to take away from its Creeness but, rather, to illustrate the power of a Cree culture that took one of our more powerful metaphors and turned it to good use: on the one hand, to explain their hunting through the use of a term that we might be able to understand, and, on the other hand, to make something meaningful for themselves. A garden is a complex way of both using and defining the land within Euro-American culture, and it rises very quickly from the physical to the metaphysical – the Garden of Eden being an obvious, though hardly singular, example. This metaphor is just as complex in Job Bearskin's usage, where it is layered with meaning about people's place in the cosmos and comes out of people's interaction with the lands of James Bay. In the end, his garden, too, becomes something akin to a Garden of Eden, albeit a very different one from that presented in Genesis.[2]

So to attempt to get at the meaning of metaphors like Job Bearskin's, I want to go out on the land and look at it from all of Momaday's angles, and some of them, of necessity, will be rather oblique. First, there is the depth of time contained within the rocks and muskeg, and there is the great complexity of its ecosystems. Part of what I want to discuss is the ecology and geology of the region. These are not the most important angles from which to look, but they will help us to triangulate. The other aspect of this triangulation involves seeing the ways that the Cree have used and thought about the land over the course of their history, before and after the coming of Europeans. There can be nothing scientific or exact about this process, though some parts of it may give that impression. I want to give an ethnographic description of the ways the Cree used their land, and the more mundane aspects of Cree hunting feel a lot like science, which is not surprising, as this way of understanding the Cree comes out of the same systems of methodology as do geology and ecology. As we move outward towards what we might weakly call the spiritual and mythological explanations of hunting and the land, however, it is harder and harder to fit them all within one definition of James Bay. An epistemological rift opens between our own expectations of reality and that of the Cree hunter – a cognitive dissonance that is analogous to that sense of irony I mentioned earlier. These perspectives struggle with one another for the right to imagine this region, and I think that the dissonance is worth embracing, mostly because this imaginative struggle is at the heart of the contact experience on this continent.

We can get a glimpse of this kind of imaginative struggle at several levels, even within a Euro-American cultural understanding of the region. It is there in the name "Precambrian Shield," which was given to the northern reaches of Canada by Austrian geologist Eduard Suess in the nineteenth century. Eastern James Bay is part of that Shield, which so dominates Canadian physiography. In that name for the basement rock that underlies and sweeps around James Bay and Hudson Bay in a wide arc, however, something more than geology has entered the vocabulary of the Canadian North. The term "Shield" is more than a simple description, and at different times and places this geological marker has represented many landscapes: the harsh and unforgiving wasteland around which European agriculture struggled on its way west to the Great Plains; the heartland of a continental fur trade; and, today, the modern cornucopia of material resources for the future use of Canadians as, along with the timber on its surface, the Shield also holds valuable minerals (e.g., 90 percent of the world's iron ore has Precambrian origins). Most important for this story, the eastern side of the Shield, the home of the James Bay Cree, has been deemed by engineers and politicians to be one of the greatest freshwater reserves in the world, with a geography seemingly designed for hydro-electric development and nation building.[3]

The Shield has thus been the source of symbolic as well as concrete resources. Boosters and politicians have used the Shield to represent the possibilities of the future: its two great bays have been styled the "great Mediterranean sea of the North America" by those interested in the growth of the Canadian heartland; and its eastern region has been called "a lens" on the future and "The Land of Tomorrow" by those asserting a Québécois identity on the North and seeking the hydroelectricity latent in its rivers. Canadian artists and writers have used the Shield's harsh beauty to repre-sent a uniquely northern, Canadian character, even as they articulated the ambivalence towards nature within that culture, and a more diffuse North American population has seen the Shield's wild rivers and vast forests as a "wilderness" worthy of the challenge. Along with the American West, the Canadian North has been the focus of a great deal of outdoor romanticism and wilderness mysticism since the end of the nineteenth century.[4]

All these various ways of seeing the region are important, but they are aspects of the postcontact human history of the Shield – the narrative of Western culture, empire, nation – that have little meaning within the Cree narrative of the region, anchored as it is in its own imaginative use of the land. Given the nature of Cree material culture before contact, little that is obvious remains of their long physical presence on the land, but their names remain powerful representations of their cultural occupation of this region. Along with those previously mentioned petroglyphs, Cree place names can begin to outline a symbolic Cree interpretation of James Bay not as a peripheral part of Canada or Quebec but rather as something Cree-centred. "Our land is our memory, that is why it is so important to us," former grand chief Matthew Coon Come tells us: "almost every tree out there has a name, almost every rock. Something happened here, some-thing happened there, somebody killed his first moose at that mountain. We know where the bear dens are, the moose yards, the beaver, the otter, the mink. Everything has a story and these are the stories that sustain us." Seasonal hunting camps may have quickly receded back into the forests from which they were made, but what remains are the names that the Cree gave to their land and that represent the anchor points for that spider's web of meaning that is spun of narratives and relationships to that land.[5]

It is hard to be specific about the precontact number of Cree who occu-pied this vast territory – thousands, certainly – but whatever their number, their knowledge of the place was exact, and they occupied all of it both in their use and in their symbolic understanding of hunting. They did this by using the land, naming the land, and also by creating a whole narrative understanding of their place within it. In the words of Job Bearskin and many others, past and present, we hear the narrative of how the land feeds the people and how they reciprocate by being respectful to it and by sharing its bounty. The land and the people here are still one, the gift exchange of food is still the way that people speak of their relationship to it, and this continues to form the larger narrative matrix that helps define people's lives. But it goes deeper than that, involving the meaning that each hunter finds on the land, the meaning that he cultivates to make a living. And this, I believe, goes to the heart of the hunting experience.

Hunting creates personal narratives as well as cultural narratives, and, as anthropologist Richard Preston argues, in Cree life it is the narration of personal events that is the central vehicle by which meaning is placed in the world. Because "ambiguity and unpredictability are more a part of the phenomenal world [in Cree life than they are in our own]," he writes, "man seeks to reduce this ambiguity through precise and sensitive understanding of the whole [narrative] context." At the centre of this is the understanding of life as a complex set of personal interactions involving many other people and beings: real knowledge is equated with the whole narrative context of those relationships, not with overarching rules or natural laws. An individual's competence with regard to giving detailed narrative form to new events and people, and with regard to having knowledge of stories about past relationships, enables her or him to deal with a world whose basic quality is unknown potential. This potential is not chaotic or random; rather, it involves the agency of other beings whom a hunter can ask for help. In this view, these beings are more powerful than humans and, most important, they want to help. A hunter's material competence, shown in procuring a living from the land, is connected to his narrative competence in creating and maintaining these relationships, which amounts to creating and maintaining meaning. Narratives and their meaning, the land and its meaning, are personal to a Cree hunter, and this enables us to begin to outline the very non-Western epistemological view of the world that has shaped the history of this region.[6]

I am certainly not going to presume to try and explain the specifics of Cree epistemology as I have neither the language nor the narrative context to understand it, even if I had the sources. But, while problematic, I think an attempt to catch a glimpse of this set of meanings, to give an impression of what Aboriginal narrative might have related to, is necessary. By definition, this will be an impressionistic portrayal, almost assuredly incomplete and flawed. I mean neither to capture this conceptual environment within our own set of assumptions nor to give access to a complete set of Cree ideas; rather, I propose simply to give some shape and weight to another set of ideas about an environment, a set of ideas that is completely different from that of the West, which has had the power to contain individual people's lives into the present. These Cree assumptions, as imperfectly understood by European visitors to James Bay as by this historian, are as important to James Bay history as are those European concepts and assumptions that we in the present find easier to superimpose upon the past. It is in the play between these assumptions, in their negotiation, that history lies.

Take the very simple example of Waswanipi fur trader John Spencer's decision, in 1835, to call the lake where some Wabanaki (Native trappers from the south) had been seen Wappanakee Sacka Hagun (Lake of the Wabanaki). The name was important during a period (discussed in Chapter 4) when Wabanaki were moving onto Cree land and placing pressure on some hunters. But why the use of a Cree name? The translation is mine – Spencer assumed the reader would understand – so the first explanation is that Cree had long been the lingua franca of the fur trade. Most traders seem to have had some competence in Cree, while few Cree bothered to learn English. It was also the Cree who had seen the interlopers, and it was they who presumably would need to know the name of that place. The fact may be that, though Spencer presents it as his own idea, the Cree gave the name to the place for their own reasons and he entered it in his journal. The name Wappanakee Sacka Hagun would certainly have been important to Chagoshish and his wife, who brought the news of the Wabanaki to the post. It was their hunting land, and the name would have put that place within the realm of narration of new events that were central to understanding and managing their world. The Wabanaki may or may not have been a threat to Chagoshish, but a detailed understanding of the context of where and when they entered the territory would have been necessary in order to create a relationship with them: they were on the land, and so they had to be in the narrative. This was, to a great extent, separate from Spencer's understanding of the name as a marker of an intrusion on his trade by unwanted hunters who would take fur south to his competition. So whatever the origin of Wappanakee Sacka Hagun, its placement happened along a continuum of possible contexts and meanings that represents a much larger negotiation over meaning in the region.[7]

Native names linger all over North America, though they have come to stand for places far different from those they originally represented – major metropolitan areas, states, national parks – and their continued presence is meaningful in a couple of ways. Names like "Ottawa," "Massachusetts," and "Yosemite" seem like ours now because we have forgotten the set of meanings from which they originated. We have forgotten the negotiation of meaning that went on as those names were moved from one understanding into another. We have also forgotten that, at one level, those names became trophies of colonialism and that co-opting existing names is one way of cutting them loose from the web of meaning that anchored them in the environment. This, too, is part of Spencer's naming of Wappanakee Sacka Hagun, and though he was not in a position to impose meaning on the Cree, a review of maps produced over the last thirty-five years witnesses the slow march of French names across the landscape of James Bay. There are still lots of Cree names – even on French signs – but there is a narrative as well as a physical colonization going on with all these names, and this relates back to Spencer and his trading post here on the Shield.[8]

Driving south from Radisson and the Bourassa dam along the James Bay Road, which runs parallel to the coast about 100 kilometres inland, I am reminded of the great variety of landscape that this huge region holds and of how unsatisfying that name "Precambrian Shield" is with regard to expressing this diversity, even within our own cultural understanding of the region. The rocks of the Shield may be Precambrian, but James Bay is not the relic of some former world. During the Precambrian Era this land was similar to a high-altitude desert, or to the emptiness of Antarctica, while now it is a wooded and green world, even at the end of winter. The Shield, in fact, is no different than most of the world's landscapes, all of which experienced many layers of geologic formation after the Precambrian Era; yet, this archaic-sounding name has stuck here because several unrelated processes over the geological sweep of time convulsed the Shield, with the result that Precambrian rocks re-emerged as one of this region's dominant features.[9]

The first of these processes happened roughly 200 million years ago, when a hot spot deep in the mantle of the earth began to push itself up into the crust of the tectonic plate roughly under what is now Lake Garry in the Nunavut Territory. This hot spot, now inactive and lying under the Atlantic Ocean, lifted and disrupted the earth's surface as the tectonic plates that comprise the Shield floated over it. Much of the material that had been deposited on top of the Precambrian rock was cleared away by this process, leaving deposits of newer rock only here and there among the older. One hundred and fifty million years ago, the west side of Hudson Bay was over this hot spot, and 50 million years later, Moose Factory was over it. When the edge of the Shield reached the hot spot, the hills for

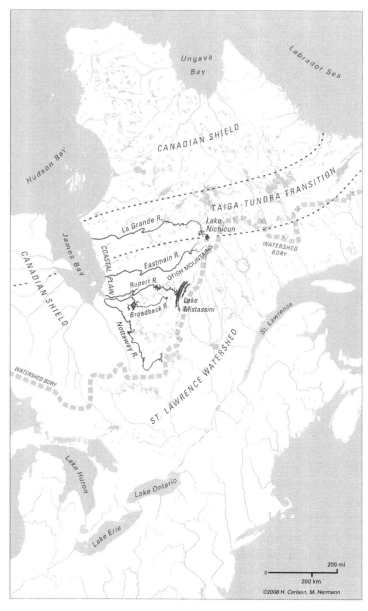

MAP 2.1   *Eastern James Bay geography and hydrology.* The major rivers of the eastern James Bay watershed flow west and north, fed by innumerable lakes and smaller streams, in an area that has more surface water per square kilometre than any place on earth. This region of the eastern Canadian Shield was the epicentre of the Laurentian Ice Sheet, which dominated eastern North America during the last ice age and which today is part of the circumpolar boreal forest ecosystem.

which Montreal is named were thrown up and the Laurentian scarp was formed. The scarp marks the southern boundary to the James Bay region, and the Labrador Mountains (formed by another hot spot) mark the eastern boundary. Together they create a geographic region, rising from north to south and west to east, which is a main determinant of today's hydroelectric geography. The scarp and mountains define the watershed that determines what will flow south into the St. Lawrence and what will flow west into James Bay. From the line of this watershed west, the plateau falls quickly along distinct fault lines, and it is on these fault lines that the massive hydrological head of local rivers is built.[10]

More recently, on a geological scale of time, a glacier ebbed and flowed for several million years over much of the region, and, at times, the Laurentian Ice Sheet covered much of northeastern North America, as far west as Alberta and as far south as Long Island, northern Pennsylvania, and the Great Lakes. It retreated to James Bay only in the last six to eight thousand years or so, where it had begun its existence in the Otish Mountains north of Lake Mistassini. This ice also cleaned away large quantities of soil and moved it off the basement rock of the Shield. The result was what nineteenth-century Canadian geological surveyor H.C. Cooke described as a geology that was "very monotonously granite." The glacier depressed and scraped the land, and the Precambrian rock was shattered and left upended by the movement of the ice. Many shorelines in the region are made up of these scattered slabs of rock, and much of the ground is littered with boulders covered by only a thin layer of moss and soil. These are not the glacial erratics that were carried so far afield by the ice but rather the remnants of rock that sat under the ice for eons.[11]

James Bay remained ice-bound long after the glacier had melted away in other places, and, when the ice finally did melt, the depressed land under what is now James and Hudson Bays filled with the melting waters. On higher terrain, potholes gouged out by the ice became lakes and ponds, and rivers began to cut their way into the rock of the Shield. It is these waters that have always been so important in this area. The region is, in fact, a "hydrological phenomenon" and has more running water per unit of surface area than any other place on earth. The east coast of James Bay receives between 75 and 100 centimetres of precipitation every year, and the fact that much of this falls as snow means that little is lost back into the atmosphere, instead flowing downhill as spring melt into the two bays. This has now changed somewhat as reservoirs hold water in the spring and fall and draw down during high-demand periods in summer and winter. Local hunters know that this change has dramatically reduced the animals on surrounding lands as reservoirs actually alter a much greater area than is immediately apparent on a map or from the air. [12]

What little soil there is in the region contains discontinuous permafrost, depending on the land's latitude, elevation, and aspect towards the sun. This soil is very thin to the north, but towards the southern edges of the region the Shield's rock lays under deeper soils that tend to be a mix of stiff clay and sandy loam, with striking pockets of rocks and boulders intermixed. These can be so regular that some have thought them "done by the work of man's hands," though they are glacial in origin. Another seeming oddity is that, while these hills are often made up of boulder clay, occasionally they are drumlins of pure glacial sand, where lowbush blueberries grow on the warm, well-drained soil. The clay soils in southern James Bay were fertile enough for fur traders to garden extensively at some posts, and this makes a considerable difference when we compare the development of these posts to those slightly to the north, where even root-crop gardening was beyond the limits of climate and soil. This gardening became important for people's subsistence and for the meaning they placed on the land, even though the St. Jean Valley and the area around Val-d'Or, to the south and east, respectively, bounded any full-scale agriculture. [13]

So "Shield" is really a geological term, and all these ancient processes are not nearly as apparent when looking out over the land today as are the trees. Ecologically, eastern James Bay forms part of the boreal forest (known as taiga in its northern reaches) that encircles the polar region throughout Canada, Europe, and Asia, separating the mixed deciduous forests to the south from the northern tundra. Black spruce is the dominant species over most of the region, interspersed occasionally with tamarack and jack pine. The darker hues and the sharp scent of evergreens dominate James Bay, though a vital group of hardwoods is also dispersed throughout different parts of the region. White birch and aspen are intermixed to the south, and alders form large communities along riverbanks and on lakeshores everywhere. All these hardwood varieties are essential to wildlife, especially beaver, and they are important to the Cree as well, forming the raw materials for items such as snowshoes (which they still make). In this region, where the land can only support animal biomass (the total physical weight of animal life) at about 1 percent of plant biomass, all of these plant resources are significant. Ecologically, it takes a great deal of plant life to support the small number of animals and people in James Bay; thus, an important part of the region's history involves the various ways that humans have found to live within that metric. [14]

From an airplane, then, James Bay appears at first as a monotonous mat of trees, an undistinguishable sea of green, but on the ground the forest varies widely. While large areas are covered with continuous stands of closely spaced trees on well-drained soils, these areas are interspersed with muskeg swamps where gaunt, stick-like black spruce grow slowly, sometimes with only small branches flagging their very tops. These so-called "witches' brooms" sit on wet ground covered with sphagnum moss and low bushes like Labrador tea, and these areas, together with the many pools beneath rapids in the many streams, produce prodigious swarms of insects in summer. To the north and east the woodland begins to open, and large tracts are found with the trees spread metres apart and the ground covered in the multi-coloured lichen commonly called reindeer moss. These upland areas, with their thick floors of *Cladonia*, are common winter yards for the small herds of woodland caribou that survive by eating the lichens that have been cleared of snow by high winds. Interestingly, the caribou have been moving south recently, possibly because of the newly opened areas in clear-cuts and power line corridors, where they seem to congregate in winter. In the summer, these herds migrate north to the tundra and their breeding grounds.[15]

The James Bay road rides the tops of glacial eskers along parts of its route, and from these high points you get a good sense of the relatively low topography that the forest dominates. Only low and broken hills delimit the various smaller watersheds within the larger ones, and these comprise, along with muskeg wetlands, a network of innumerable lakes, rivers, and streams that flow to the bay. The density of these wetlands and waterways is comparable to the forest around them and makes topographic maps of the region almost mesmerizing in their complexity. Before the coming of airplanes in the 1920s and roads in the last thirty years, these lakes and rivers were the highways along which humans hunted and traded. Their shorelines still form the riparian ecotones in which much of the area's wildlife lives, larger rivers even producing microclimates by tempering the effects of the extreme cold.[16]

Beaver build lodges and dams by the thousands along the slower-moving streams. In fact, in areas where the initial habitat is suitable, the density of their colonies can be as high as three per square kilometre. The beaver helped to shape the postglacial environment in James Bay, as it did over most of North America, where as many as 400 million of these animals may have existed before contact. Beaver are vital to this wetland because, by changing the channel geomorphology and the hydrology of small- to medium-sized streams, they greatly affect the surrounding landscape both

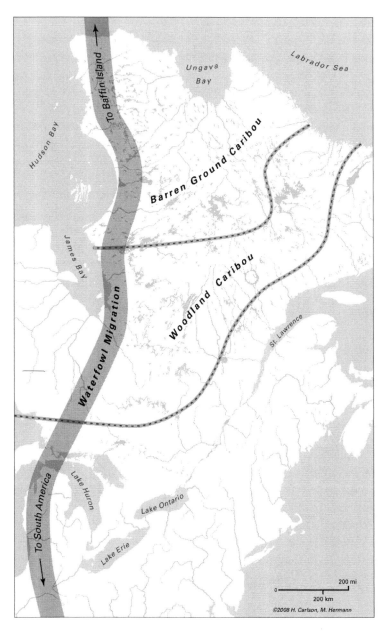

MAP 2.2   *Animal migration routes and habitat.* Eastern James Bay sits beneath one of
the largest flyways for waterfowl in the Americas, and every year millions of birds make
their way along the shores of the bay. Inland, the spruce forests are the home of woodland caribou, bear, martens, and other furbearers; beaver have shaped much of this land,
which is suffused with lakes, ponds, and small- to medium-sized streams.

visually and ecologically. Certainly, everywhere you look there is old and new evidence of their presence. In addition, beaver dams also hold back organic matter and, by creating new wetlands, modify the nutrient cycle of the ecosystem. The vegetation of these riparian zones changes not only because of the wetting of the soils but also because of chemical changes produced by these increased sediments. This modified habitat becomes attractive to a wide range of birds and mammals, and herein lies one major difference between a beaver dam and a hydro dam.[17]

Beaver habitat may have influenced up to 40 percent of the lengths of mid-sized streams in North America, and the effects of these alterations are still visible today, even in areas where beaver have not reintroduced themselves after having been largely hunted out by the fur trade of the seventeenth, eighteenth, and nineteenth centuries. Beaver were nearly hunted to extinction in James Bay several times during these centuries, damaging the whole ecosystem and decreasing the amount of food for the Cree. This also affected the Cree at the level of cultural meaning because, in addition to being central to a web of ecological relationships, the beaver is also central to a set of cultural relationships for Cree hunters, who know him as a powerful friend. What we see in later chapters is that a largely intact cultural web of relationships between the Cree and the animals they hunted helped prevent the extinction of the beaver, thus averting both an environmental and a cultural disaster. But this is getting ahead of the story.[18]

Many other animals, aside from the beaver, are part of these dual cultural/ecological webs. Moose, otter, muskrat, and mink are found in and around beaver habitat, and bear, fox, marten, lynx, ptarmigan, and snowshoe hare are found in the outlying woodlands. There are fish in most of the lakes and streams, with walleye, whitefish, lake trout, and pike being the main species. Many of the fish in these waters are large and old, and even today they are abundant, though again the reservoirs have changed things by altering species distribution and the quality of their food value. With the exception of the fish, all these northern animals are subject to various population fluctuations. Beaver are subject to outbreaks of the disease known as tularaemia, which is thought to be caused by overpopulation, and dramatic rises and falls in the northern hare population drive a boom-and-bust cycle every ten years or so. During the fur trade era there were years when rabbits were stacked in the company stores "like cordwood," and there were others when hardly a rabbit was seen during the course of a whole winter. The same was true of ptarmigan, and since both made up an important component of the subsistence of Natives and traders alike, these fluctuations had important effects. Hares and ptarmigan are also food for many northern predators, those with which humans not only compete but also hunt for their own food value, so these cycles drive others that can have a dramatic effect on the food supply as a whole.[19]

All of these animals coexist within the ecology of the boreal forest, and all of them are tied into the subsistence of the James Bay hunters because of their food value and, more important, because they give the hunter what he needs to feed his family. Like the beaver, all the region's animals coexist within complex relationships of reciprocity that define Cree hunting; thus, as we concentrate on the ecology of the region, it is with an eye towards a greater set of environmental meanings. We can investigate the science of the environment, looking at important features that connect it as an ecosystem, but part of its cultural meaning also lies in the fact that the land is divided into separate hunting territories. Each of these units consists of a unique combination of ecological facts with which the hunter has to interact, and, when this is added to the Cree understanding of each hunter's unique relationship with the animals, the cultural aspects of the James Bay environment become as complex as its many watersheds. Driving south on the road you cross both these James Bay landscapes, and the hunting trails that cross the road at intervals are a constant reminder of this. Maybe it would be better to think of the road crossing these older trails just as it crosses the big rivers that flow to the west: like those rivers, the older trails were here first.[20]

These big rivers are also part of the ecology and culture of the region, and, before it was dammed, the La Grande River was the biggest of these. The Great Whale River lies to the north of the La Grande and, in the early 1990s, was saved from damming. The Eastmain River, just to the south, was dammed along with the La Grande, and its water was redirected north to the hydro facilities. Moving south from there, the road crosses the Pontax River, the soon-to-be-dammed Rupert River, the Broadback River, and the Nottaway River, all of which finish their runs through coastal flats and enter the shallow marine waters of the bay. Here, in the many shoals and reefs, eiders and scoters feed on mollusks, and black ducks feed on invertebrates buried in tidal mud flats. Eelgrass meadows are home to Atlantic brant, and these tidal marshes and waters are exceptionally important as breeding grounds for lesser snow geese and some Canada geese. They also form staging areas and resting places for other geese that migrate though the area, and in the spring and fall huge numbers traverse the James Bay corridor as they move back and forth to their breeding grounds on the tundra. They are another vital source of food, though the Cree are noticing that these flyways are changing for reasons that are not yet clear. Later we will see that these marshes also produced the wild grasses used by Hudson's Bay Company (HBC) men for fodder for livestock, which they raised on the shores of the bay, and so underpin subsistence changes as well as gardening. Here again, aspects of human culture are never outside the environmental picture – indeed, they may be the most dynamic natural forces in this land – but before we allow them centre stage, we must look at two other important aspects of ecology.[21]

Summer fire and spring melt are the two most important non-human dynamics within the eastern James Bay bioregion. Both are annual events, though one is far more random than the other. During April and May each year, snow melt frees billions of litres of water into the streams and rivers of the area. This flooding allows not only a cleansing of the river systems but also a redistribution of nutrients as rivers overflow their banks and deposit silt and mud over outlying areas that are only connected to other waterways and outside nutrients during this brief period of the year, when flooding produces vital refertilization. Areas of erosion and soil redistribution are pioneered by species of shrubs and hardwoods that are prime food for many animals, and silt dumped out over the bay, as river water rides up over the ice, causes a decrease in the reflectivity of the ice pack, thus increasing melting. This increase in solar gain can speed ice-out in James Bay by as much as three weeks, and in a region with so short a summer this is significant. Flooded areas are also crucial spawning areas, especially for pike, and they are areas of new growth when the waters recede. Moose and many kinds of duck feed on these new plants.[22]

Surrounding these areas of flood, the boreal forest is a mosaic of variously aged trees delineated by overlapping yearly fire zones. For example, in 1905 surveyor A.P. Low defined "old-growth" trees in the area as thirty years old and "not very large." Fire is terribly destructive to the forests, but it also acts as a beneficial agent of change. Because of the overwhelming majority of conifers, with their highly flammable needles and cones, fires in the boreal forest are intensely hot and tend to cover large tracts of territory. Fires of over 100,000 hectares are not uncommon. In 2002, a huge fire raged all summer between the Rupert and Eastmain rivers, and there are still huge vistas of burned stumps with new growth interspersed. These fires tend to burn totally, leaving mineral soils exposed, killing seeds along with adult trees. This bare ground means that spruce must reseed from the edges and that other species – like alder, Jack pine, and birch – can pioneer the area. Jack pine actually needs these intense fires to germinate its seeds.[23]

Fire was such a benefit in the northern boreal forest that the Cree were known to burn areas deliberately to encourage the growth of grasses and herbaceous plants, though these human-made fires did not always bring the desired results. When they burned too fiercely, or entered resource areas like rabbit-hunting grounds, they hindered rather than helped the hunter who started them. And during the fur trade era, these fires were often a source of consternation for the traders. Fire improved the land for game animals, but it did not necessarily make the environment better for fur bearers. In 1848, for example, Nitchequon trader Robert Chilton fumed in his journal: "no less than 9 smokes seen today – the Indians will not leave off setting the woods in a blaze – it is burnt enough already." Nitchequon was a marginal northern region for fur as it was, and the Cree were more interested in acquiring caribou to eat than fur to trade. In less marginal areas, traders thought better of the Cree practices of land use, likening the Natives to "skillful gardeners," though even here fire was not seen as wholly useful. These practices were millennia old in Chilton's time, were to a great extent practical, and are a good reminder of how profoundly humans have shaped this region physically as well as conceptually.[24]

Human culture is clearly a third shaping force in the James Bay environment, and a complete investigation must move towards the cultural aspects of the land. This, of course, means that the shaping begins to occur in two directions and thus becomes a far more complex issue to describe. When people followed the receding glacial edge into the area three or four thousand years ago, this was a very different environment from that which existed when Europeans arrived: those hunters were not yet the Cree whom traders contacted. These post-Pleistocene hunters made their living here, on the grasslands that flourished briefly between the ice and the forest, and then they adapted as the tundra receded and the forest moved in along with new animals to hunt. As the world warmed, hunters set about shaping this land with fire, hunting, and stories, and, in the process, they shaped themselves. Historically, the place that eighteenth-century fur trader Andrew Graham described as "a fine plentiful country abounding with beasts and rich furs," and the people he referred to as the "Ou Pee She Pow Nation," were the result of thousands of years of convergence between human culture and the lands of James Bay.[25]

The Cree and their land were born of each other and are unique; this is good to keep in mind as we make generalizations that we find intellectually useful. Archaeology and anthropology tell us that, at the time of contact, the Cree, like other Eastern Woodland peoples, were subsistence hunters, using stone, bone, wood, antler, and tooth to construct tools and weapons. They also point to a narrative culture that is similar to that of other Woodland peoples, both of which we might generalize as hunting cultures. The hunt took on added meaning for the Cree with the advent of the fur trade and deeply affected the Europeans who came to trade. It is a commonplace that the birchbark canoe, snowshoe, and toboggan were used for transportation by both Natives and whites; yet, at least at first, in many other ways HBC men lived "exactly like the Indians." As Andrew Graham points out, they worked "to imitate the customs of the Natives who [were] inured to the climate and extremely dextrous at every kind of business in their way." Traders liked to boast that they "snare[d] rabbits and practice[d] the several methods of hunting used by the Indians," and here we see not only their use of Native technology to further their trade but also their immersion in Native cultural practices to gain subsistence. Of necessity, this involved them in the narrative technology of the hunt, and so, before we can understand the implications for these Europeans, we need to focus on Cree hunting – both its narrative and practical features – in the absence of Europeans. We need to know what Woodland hunting culture looked like in James Bay.[26]

Hunting was grounded in the traditional Cree social organization in which hunters formed themselves into small hunting bands consisting of two or three families that travelled to winter hunting grounds, only gathering with other groups during the summer months at set places along larger rivers or lakes. These small bands allowed two or three hunters to work together, increasing their chances of success and ameliorating the problems of failure. Even today, all along the James Bay Road and the Route du Nord, which runs east to Lake Mistassini, there are Cree camps where hunters work together. Some of the trails I mentioned earlier are snowmobile trails, but it's not unusual to see a group of hunters emerge from the woods with their snowshoes. They are still working in groups, with the hunter who is the tallyman, or steward, of a particular hunting ground taking the lead and letting others share his land. The roads and other technology have changed many things, but the basic relationships of hunter to land and hunter to other humans remains central to how the environment is organized. Some hunters still stay out for the winter, but the ease of travel now makes it possible to visit various communities on a regular basis. This might be seen as adversely affecting the meaning of the hunt, but it may also be seen as connecting those who cannot be in the bush with those who can, thereby enhancing the meaning of the hunt.[27]

In the past, everyone lived on the land. Beginning in late August, families that were going to winter together left the summer encampment, where larger groups had gathered for fishing and socializing. Although those who summered near or along the shores of the bay varied this by delaying their return inland to take advantage of migrating geese. These hunters built "sitting places," blinds of willow brush made into a circle a metre or so high, in which they waited, biding their time making or mending tools of the hunt, sometimes offering tobacco smoke to the geese. Their decoys were fashioned of mud and feathers and placed windward of the blind, and the birds came to the hunters who called to them. This required a deep understanding of the birds that did not underestimate the intelligence of geese and their ability to learn. The relationship between bird and hunter was taken seriously. The hunter was not trying to deceive the goose and hence bring about its death but, rather, he was asking it for its help in his quest for food. The bird's flesh would tie the hunter to his land and, at the same time, tie the community together. "Goose Break" is still an important part of the subsistence and cultural calendar in James Bay, a time for families to gather, though I have heard some Cree question the safety of eating these birds that spend so much time on our polluted land. Apparently, some of them don't taste right anymore.[28]

Whether hunters waited for the geese or not, the trip to the hunting lands could take more than a month as the pace was not as strenuous as it would be later. The trip was made among the labyrinth of lakes and rivers, and, at rapids, the loaded canoes were poled upriver while the women and children walked. Only at the largest rapids were boats unloaded and everything carried. Campsites at these places were long established and used yearly, and, at particularly abundant fishing areas, many groups would stop during the fall spawning season and fish collectively. At places like the first rapids on the Rupert River, fishing weirs were built to trap the fish driven back by the river current. Here, fires were built to dry the fish, which was then made ready for travel by being crushed into powder and mixed with grease and berries. The fish eggs were used to make a kind of bannock. At these places, large tents of birchbark, some as long as ten to twelve metres, were built on either side of the river to house the fishers and their families. In Waskaganish, I was recently shown some pictures of the 2006 gathering on the Rupert River, where the elders showed younger Cree how to clean and cook the fish properly and also explained the meaning of fish. It's hard to say what the stilling of these rapids by the latest hydroelectric project will mean for this important transfer of culture and the gathering of country food; like Goose Break and bush camps, however, this is an important part of modern Cree life.[29]

On the fall journey every opportunity to hunt was taken. When the group reached camp in the afternoon, the men sought big game while the women and children fished or set snares to catch rabbits. Gill nets were made of hide strips like those used for snowshoes, though during the trade era they were often made of twine and dyed with a concoction of boiled pine cones and juniper berries. This multilevel system of food gathering was crucial for, while bigger game was preferred, smaller game and especially fish were used if the larger hunt was unsuccessful. This early season was a time of potential food shortfalls, when the group was not yet established in a permanent camp and had not caught and dried a small reserve of food. This dried food, although its amount was always small, was used when travelling and as a margin during the winter months. The paucity of this food was not due to scarcity but, rather, to the need for mobility. Most traditional hunters see the creation of a large store of food not only as a physical burden but also as a potential burden on their relationship with the animals from which it is taken. Too large a store implies a loss of hope for the future of the human/other-than-human relationship, thereby jeopardizing the hunter's luck.[30]

When the group reached fall camp, more established structures were built to accommodate living and the processing of game. These would include cache racks for the proper and respectful disposal of certain bones as animal remains were never simply thrown away. Most of the animal was used and the parts that remained were hung in trees or placed on racks to keep them from the dogs and other scavengers. All this was done as a general sign of thanks and of well-being in the campsite. Bones were often decorated with paint and ribbons and wrapped in cloth, and, at times, they were reattached to one another (particularly the vertebrae and tail). The camp might also include a sweat lodge for medical and ceremonial purposes.[31]

This camp was located close to a good water supply and good fishing because the group stayed for more than a month. During this period, the men hunted full-time, ranging up to 50 kilometres from the main camp and taking stock of the signs of animals for the coming winter. Full knowledge of the smallest details of the land was crucial to successful hunting over the course of a winter, and before freeze-up, usually in late October, the camp was moved once again to the best potential location. Because it would remain there until the middle of January, hunters sought a location that was protected from the northwest wind, had a good supply of firewood, and was close to the best hunting. Here several weeks were spent to prepare a larger communal lodge; until this time families lived in tents. With camp established and a supply of wood gathered, the normal activities of hunting and gathering began. In the late seventeenth century, with the advent of the fur trade, this period of the winter gradually became more focused on the gathering of furs – beaver, martin, mink, and so on. In early to mid-winter, furs (especially beaver) are at their peak quality; they thin and loosen as winter progresses, which makes them less valuable.[32]

Moving in the bush at this time of year, even today with modern technology, involves a tremendous amount of effort by everyone in the group, and winter camps were full of activity. Women worked at preparing hides and making clothing while men, in the evenings or during bad weather, made snowshoes, toboggans, and the other tools of the hunt. This was the most intensive time of the year in the subsistence economy. In addition to hunting, and the routine checking of fishnets and snares, replenishing the firewood supply and gathering new spruce boughs to replace the flooring in the lodge were regular tasks carried out by the women. Hunting, by providing thousands of pounds of meat over a season, supplied the tremendous amount of energy needed to keep all of this activity going. And the hunt relied on these base camps for success.

As the middle of winter approached, camp was often moved to an area that had not been used during the season. This move was made by snowshoe and toboggans and could take up to a month. With this new camp established, the priority turned to big game hunting. At this time of year, caribou – the main target of the hunt – were easier to track and overtake as they wallow in snow that is often over two metres deep. And, in the northern areas, where the animals were more plentiful, all the hunters worked together to kill a large number. If they were successful, the base camp might be moved to the meat to facilitate processing. Abundant kills like this necessitated feasting in acknowledgment of the generous gift. Historically, while traders sometimes criticized what they saw as the Native's profligate use of food, they also benefited from the hunter's desire to share that food, which had been shared with them by the animals. Today, the results of these winter hunts are often brought back to the communities and shared not only with the hunting group but also with extended networks of family and friends. In this way, even those who are unable to spend a great deal of time in the bush can maintain a connection to "country food," as they call it.[33]

In early April, the group began to move back to the vicinity of its canoes. It was crucial to reach these before the lakes and rivers melted because, after the thaw, travel on foot was tremendously difficult. When the group reached the canoes, it then had to wait for ice-out. Several weeks might pass during which travel was severely curtailed because of unsafe ice, and during this period it was important to have enough food stored away to sustain the group. Fishing at this time of the year, like in the early fall, was important, though the thinning ice – too weak to support a person but too thick to facilitate the use of a bark canoe – adversely affected this activity as well. At this time of year the least desirable, but sometimes inevitable, form of subsistence often came in the form of the ability to undergo periods of hunger. This ability to go without food, for days sometimes, required the mental ability and self-control to sustain oneself during privation. This was much respected among the Cree and is a cultural characteristic that points to the larger relationship between the hunter and the hunted. The hunter trusted the land to take care of him, and the historical record of James Bay notes that the Cree approach to privation was similar to that of other Native hunters. A common historical theme concerns Native hunters who ungrudgingly lived through privations that taxed Europeans to the limit, and this indicates the confidence and hope that they had in their relationship with the land and animals: if it was good, if they were confident and able, then they would eat.[34]

With ice-out, the hunting group could move again. It might wait another week or two to let the spring flood subside, but by the middle of May it was on its way back to the summer encampment. After the strenuous work of the winter, the summer months were spent more leisurely. Men fished and hunted, though socializing was important as it enabled them to make plans and partnerships for the winter to come. With the advent of the fur trade and Christianity, the summer camp probably lasted longer than it had in previous times as there was transport work to be done for the Hudson's Bay Company and a desire to see the travelling missionary. It was during these times that whites were contacted for the longest periods in environments of their own creation, and, although it was the Europeans who kept the records, these times offer important windows on Cree culture in the past. That said, it should be remembered that, prior to 1970, most Cree spent most of the year in the bush living with their land.[35]

The winter rounds were part of a high degree of mobility that occurred not only over the hunting lands but also over the whole Quebec-Labrador peninsula. Hunters had territories to which they returned, while travel for economic and social reasons took them over great distances. In 1843, for example, trader Robert Chilton reported that some of the coastal Fort George hunters had "paid a visit to Petitsikapau Post in summer," meaning that they had been to Fort Nascopie, 400 kilometres to the northeast of his own remote post at Kaniapiskau and near what today is the remains of the mining town of Schefferville. Fathers travelled south to the St. Lawrence "with the view of getting husbands from among the Indians of that place" for their daughters, and "Moravian Indians," from the coast of Labrador, were known to visit James Bay posts from time to time.

Hunters travelled for subsistence reasons too, and, in 1823, John Walford recorded that several Mistassini hunters intended to go "to the country belonging to the Eastward Indians to hunt with them the ensuing winter." These "Eastward Indians" were the Neskapis, who subsisted on caribou, and Walford was not pleased that his fur hunters, as he saw them, were leaving. There was little he could do, however, as they were hoping for an increase in their food supply and were taking the opportunity to rest their own land for a year while living off the resources of another. Movement within a hunting territory and over the whole region was thus a strategy both for subsistence and for socialization.[36]

All of this activity was part of the hunter's journey across the landscape in a quest for food, and, as I have presented it, much of it seems pretty mundane and matter of fact; the danger lies in thinking that hunting consisted solely of this movement from place to place. The Cree word for the hunt, reported by anthropologist Frank Speck as *Nemeckenu*, translates as "my path" or "my road." Hunting was thus conceived as a journey across a personal landscape as understood by each hunter and this was a conceptual as well as a physical path. Physical movement was a strategy that involved the ability to engage different areas over the course of the season and from year to year, but movement through a whole series of possible food sources was another kind of geography that the hunter's path traversed. Hunting relied on the hunter moving within a cultural network, with the result that family, hunting partners, and more distant friends expanded hunting geography in social directions as well. Finally, there are the animals on the land, which can render the hunter's landscape vast and multifaceted all of a sudden – anything but matter of fact. He is intimately connected with the hunted animals – beings of great power and also material manifestations whose flesh becomes food – and this landscape of relationships is the most important terrain that the hunter's path crosses.[37]

To explain this landscape and the various paths across it, the Cree have many stories that have little to do with the explanations I have given above. There are stories of culture heroes mastering the skills and relationships of this complex world, and there are stories of hunters communicating with the Game Bosses (non-corporeal animal chiefs who control the animals on the land), learning their ways and how to offer them the respectful treatment and love they expect. Others tell of the ways that people have lived with the animals in their world, where they live and speak as humans, and of how animals help the hunter when he is trouble. Some of these stories I have heard or read (and there are many others I have not), but to present them here as an alternative to the scientific, ethnographic story does not seem right. For one thing, they are not my stories to use in that way, and, for another, I do not fully understand their meaning. More important, because other non-Cree people will not understand their full context either, they would not have the requisite narrative credibility. They would appear quaint in this context, and they are anything but quaint in the context of the hunter on the land. These stories are powerful, and they locate people within their cosmos. They shape whole landscapes, just as the glaciers did, so we need to find some place for these narratives in our understanding without trying to use them empirically.

Frank Speck, working with the neighbouring Neskapis in the 1930s, called hunting a "holy occupation" and speculated that hunting success was determined as much by a religious relationship to the world as it was by hunting skills. The real hunt happened long before the hunter picked up his snowshoes to go to the bush. It happened when he communicated with the animals and asked for their help in feeding his family; their answer would be based on their knowledge of whether he had been grateful for what they had given in the past. Going out and killing an animal was the consummation of a covenant that had already been made.

Speck's is a powerful metaphor, and it demands a view of hunting that sees it as more than just a physical challenge and response to the material environment – the hunter-as-factory-worker portrayal of subsistence culture that might be inferred from the mostly materialistic explanation of hunting given above. The hunter's cosmos reaches beyond the world of the senses, and hunting is "holy" in that it relies on a faith in the relationship between humans and other-than-humans. It demands love and sacrifice from both sides. It is important to recognize that hunting, for the Cree, exists outside the violent, aggressive evaluation that is implicit in so many Western understandings of the hunt. As Richard Preston points out, "for the eastern Cree, aggression has limited relevance to the hunting and killing of animals. Love, in a sense, is of much greater relevance. Indeed it is assumed by the Cree as both natural and essential to human efforts and goals." Reciprocal to the love felt towards the animals that help maintain human life is the feeling of regret at the necessity of killing them. This is not a conflict-driven guilt associated with the destruction of another being – animals are, after all, meant to give their corporeal form to the hunter – but, rather, the more subtle regret that goes along with the sacrifices that are made in all loving relationships. This is a way of seeing that shows that the hunter's relationship to animals goes beyond the desire to simply fill his belly, and this is important with regard to enabling us to understand why this relationship has been so lasting in Cree culture. All over the world, in fact, anthropologists have recorded these same ideas among hunting people and have tried to understand this way of seeing. The idea of "holy" hunting is still a good one in many ways, though there are some inherent risks in this kind of metaphor.[38]

While identifying the sacred nature of hunting, Speck's metaphor is nevertheless problematic because it leads so easily to equating one context of "spirituality" with another. For me, Speck was essentially right in his assertion, but the use of the term "holy" invokes a Western, religious context, in which there is both a sacred and a profane aspect to the world, and it is clear that this separation of the spiritual and the physical does not exist in the Cree hunter's world. They do not share the Western concepts of Heaven and Earth, nor do they make a separation between the mundane acts of living and the sacred act of hunting. Speck would have been more accurate to say that living itself was a holy occupation for northern hunters.

For the Cree, there is a clear, definable relationship between the physical geography of where they hunt and the larger geography inherent in the hunting lands, and this cannot simply be equated with Western notions of the material world and the spirit. The analogy with Western notions has power as long as it is not treated too dogmatically and as long as the world of animals is understood as both a different place and as directly connected to the human world through the words and symbolic actions of the hunter and through the flesh of the animal. This really demands a different conceptualization of nature and religion, for hunters and hunted could and did move back and forth between these worlds. Hunters communicated with this other world, and, when travelling the human world, these other-than-human beings put on fleshy outer garments, which were shed at the moment the hunter killed an animal to feed his people. This was the gift for which the hunter hoped and for which he had to be thankful.[39]

This is clearly an epistemology that cannot be explained within a Western understanding of the phenomenal world. Yet this epistemology is one that I take seriously on several levels, and this is more than a matter of political correctness. First, the narrative of reciprocity with the animal world is far more meaningful for the hunter than are any anthropological explanations of that narrative, and so it is in a real sense both practical and rational. This way of seeing the world aided people in feeding themselves and in feeding Europeans who came to James Bay in the seventeenth century. These ideas have great historical agency in the story about people and land; not to take them seriously is to miss something central to this region's history. Finally – and this is purely a matter of personal belief – when the hunter tells us that there is far more to the world than we can see and hear in the usual sense, that there is great potential in the world around us and that we should have hope in that world, my experience tells me not to treat this lightly – even if we can't explain it.

The challenge, then, is to talk about this aspect of Cree culture and history in a way that allows us to see its shape and the way it shaped history without simply burying it under a heap of our own ideas. This is best done by starting with something that, though seemingly mundane, is foundational to this view of the world and then to build out from there.

Childhood for the Cree hunter began within the human space of the family tent, either a simple structure of hides in the summer or a sturdier structure with log walls in the winter, and it is here where I want to begin. This world of interior space encapsulated the totality of the hunting world in a young child's life and was a powerful conceptual as well as physical space. In talking to people about their tents, it's clear to me that, in addition to being aesthetically pleasing to them, these spaces open the mind to the bush in a way that a house cannot. Within the tent you are in contact with the earth beneath and the forest outside, even as you are protected from them. You can hear the wind and the scent of wood smoke and, especially, of the spruce-bough flooring, powerfully affects your perceptions of the world outside. The opacity of the tent coverings creates a warm, filtered light during the daytime hours, while at night the fire provides both warmth and light. In a way, the thin membrane that separates the tent's interior from the outside is analogous to the thin barrier between the human world and the world of the animals. The bush is close and all around.⁴⁰

The space inside these tents created continuity as a family or families moved over the land from one campsite to another. Outside space varied while inside space did not. An acknowledgment of this conceptual continuity can be found in Cree narratives that describe the important power relationship between inside and outside spaces, a relationship intimately tied to the one with the hunted animals outside the tent. Inside space is human space, while outside space contains the world of interaction and relationships. Many Cree stories of hunting and other activities in the bush begin with actions conducted inside the human space of the tent (these often include the singing of intentions). Here begins the path of communication. The world outside alters with time, with the actions of all the beings on the land, and can best be dealt with from the firm platform of human conceptual space located inside the tent. The hunting path was thus narrated as a round-trip journey, over the threshold of the tent, into the bush and the realm of the other-than-human beings, and back again to the human living space.⁴¹

This distinction between spaces was often marked by a hunter leaving his take outside the tent so that his wife could complete the process of bringing home the animals. This integrated outside and inside worlds, and emphasized the fact that Cree women were hunters too. For the Cree, the women's role in the hunt completed the process that began when the hunter accepted the outer garment of the hunted animal, because it was the women who unlocked the potential of that gift and transformed it into human food. Significantly, many hunters acted similarly in their trade relations with the HBC. Often they would almost offhandedly mention to the trader that there was meat, marrow fat, or fur outside the post, and it would then be up to the trader to fetch it. Hunters usually related this in a way that indicated that they needed help with the load, even though most loads didn't warrant any. There is no clear statement of how the Cree interpreted these actions: they expressed themselves as simply coming to visit. But Cree hunters were certainly creating a relationship of reciprocity with the traders, and they also seemed to be maintaining relationships with the land by letting traders make the transfer from environment to environment. They were making the traders part of the hunt not only by sharing food but also by sharing a ritual relationship. I discuss the depth of that sharing in the next chapter.[42]

The relationship between inside living space and outside world is made clearer still by the "walking out" ceremony that many Cree children of both sexes still go through soon after they are able to walk. In this ceremony, the young child crosses the threshold of the tent, is led in a clockwise direction around its perimeter, and then is given articles that represent her or his future involvement in the subsistence of the group. The ceremony continues with the child's taking a short round-trip journey into the bush and then returning to a feast, where the whole group hopes for and speaks about her/his future success. The ceremony is thus a small, symbolic representation of the much larger and longer path that the child will follow for the rest of his or her life. The food connects the young child with the land, and with the story of the hunt outside the tent. And while the continuation of this kind of ceremony may seem quaint in the context of a modern Cree community, where hunting is just one of many economic activities, this, I think, is to miss the larger meaning of the land for the Cree. Like the physical space of the tent, which connects them with the land beyond its thin walls, the narrative space created by the ceremony connects them to the same land on a different level.[43]

This understanding of a personal relationship with the hunted leads to an understanding of the environment as a personal event and not simply as a geography of resource options. Environment becomes a personal geography of individual and reciprocal events and relationships, and a process of negotiation becomes the hunter's main activity in the act of living on the land. When Rupert's House trader Joseph Beioley noted that his hunters did not think it "politic" to kill too many beaver, he was speaking very precisely about these relationships.[44]

With this in mind, we can go back into the historical record and see the communicative pathways along which people move and the narrative energy they put into travelling. The simple, respectful treatment of the animal's carcass, which fed them and clothed them, has a story behind it that explains the hunter's negotiation. In 1841, Yihitshin, a hunter at Fort George, expressed it this way: "when I kill a deer I take off the skin very carefully, and then dress it very well, as well as I can, and then put some vermillion on it, when it is dry, I spread it out by my tent, and say I know that you are very good to send me these things to kill and I show you this to let you see that I am thankful, that is the only way Indians know of to show that they are thankful." Yihitshin told this to Reverend George Barnley, who took him to be talking to the "Great Spirit" when he gave thanks. In Chapter 4 we will see that this may be true, but we will also see that his treatment of the hide indicates that he was addressing his thanks and respect to the hunted as well.[45]

Feasts were a communal way of addressing thanks and respect to the hunted. Recalling her time at Rupert's House, the wife of a Moose Factory trader talked of how the hunters would have feasts after a big hunt, when the men came in with deer meat on their sleds. "An old woman would walk by Mrs. Moore's house," she remembered, "with a cane decorated with beads and feathers" to announce the event. Then, "two old Indians would first sit down at a big cake of deer's fat, smoking their beaded pipes and discussing the details of the hunt. After the feast, a drum was beaten, speeches made, and Indian songs sung." The hunt was thus wrapped in words that recounted not only the actual events but also the cultural narratives of song and story that acknowledged the gift that had been given within the larger context of the hunt. Everyone had to share in these events, and the whole gift had to be eaten if the exchange was to go on. And it did go on. "The Annual Duck Feast was held at the Post," noted Waswanipi trader Fred McLeod in 1944. "The usual custom at an Inland post, the first Ducks must be eaten together, and everyone at the Post must eat his share, the bones being tied together and hung upon a tree after the feast, if this is done the hunter's luck will hold."[46]

In a similar way, beaver were brought into camp and treated as honoured guests at these kinds of feasts, as was the bear. "The Indians think a great deal of a bear," wrote Reverend William Walton in 1894, "especially of the black bear – I was almost going to say that he used to be their god, still he was not very far short of it. They have numerous superstitious ideas concerning him ... Some think he does not sleep all winter, but simply retires to meditate. It is a common belief that he understands when they speak to him and some believe he has a soul like a man." In 1899, trader William Arthur recounted the hunter Sha sha ganass's belief "that when a man goes out to hunt bears in winter, when the bear is in his den, that he knows the very minute that the man leaves [from inside his tent] on the hunting expedition and endeavors to bewitch and prevent the man from finding him, by some wonderful performance inside the den." "Bewitch" is a pejorative term, implying something adversarial, but what the ethnographic record implies is more a relationship of negotiation and a hope in the friendship that might be made. The bear was willing to make the gift, but only to a hunter who had proved himself capable, first in his mind and then later in the bear's den. The hunter had to find Bear in the larger geography of the hunt and become his friend, before he could find the bear on the land.

In all of this, one central idea keeps reappearing in both the historical and ethnographic records that knits this material and narrative landscape together and gives the kind of shape and weight to Cree hunting that will help us to interpret James Bay history. Here we have a world characterized by a basic quality of contingency. In place of a system of natural and predictable laws – the Lockean and Newtonian understandings of empiricism and causation that underpin the modern Western perspective – there are a series of relationships with other-than-human beings. These relationships are not random but, rather, conform to a rational system of thought that centres on the concept of hope. I began by talking about hope out there on the land, and there have been hints of this idea along the way, but I now want to show how I see it as a central theme in the hunter's world. And I also want to talk about the power I see in Calvin Martin's ontological argument. When the idea of hope – hope as the Cree seem to define it – is placed at the centre of a system of thought, many things change with regard to our perception of the ways that people relate to their land and those on it.[47]

"The Indian is very much like a fatalist," wrote Reverend Walton in 1904, "he is forever saying when in sickness or danger of any kind 'Cha etiwana nititaetan – my idea is to see what'll happen to me' and they think we are hard-hearted if we try to get them to fight" against adversity and impose some end upon a given situation. Walton interpreted this seemingly fatalistic Native attitude as an abandonment of hope, but in Cree terms it was more likely a manifestation of a specific kind of hope in an aspect of the world that Walton did not accept. Hope for the Cree is not a passive emotion related to pessimism or to giving up, as it often is in Western culture where we fall back on it when all active means have failed. It is, instead, an active emotion – *speyum* is the word – through which an effective relationship with the environment can be created. Hope and luck are related to one another, and hunters are always speaking of being lucky or unlucky, something we think of as random chance. But hope is a vehicle by which the hunter impresses his will and ability upon a contingent world of individual relationships, and his luck is a representation of the effectiveness of his hope. In terms of hunting, this means that, if the hunter is successful in his hopes, the animal-beings will know his mind and will allow themselves to be found, thereby making him lucky. Part of this Cree ability and will is the individual's appearance of self-control. Thus, what Walton perceived as Cree fatalism was more likely a very active hope in the land expressed as self-control in the face of adversity.[48]

Other outward manifestations of this way of thinking were found in the simplicity of material possessions (which also aided mobility) and the expression of good nature in troubled situations. Eastmain trader James Russell wrote of the hunters there as "being contented ... when they are possessed of a hatchet, a kettle, a gun and other little necessities requisite for procuring their food," while naturalist Olaus Johan Murie described them as "always cheerful and good natured. You might come into a camp that has been fasting for several days for lack of food, but you would not guess the fact from their countenances. I have never seen a people so contented and happy in the face of adversity and so filled with gratitude." This was more than simply good nature or a propensity to be content with simple belongings; rather, it was a way of thinking and acting that related the hunter to the hunted, and it was expressed in terms of hope, or faith, understood from within the land.[49]

The nature of hope is important in connecting the hunter's stance of respect and humility towards animal-beings with the internal logic of the hunt. Humility and happiness with simplicity are the outward, active expressions of a hopeful attitude towards life in that they express a faith in something beyond the human world. To give up hope is an act of great hubris – maybe the first and greatest act of hubris. In order to be without hope one must presume to know the end result of any situation with certainty, to be, in a sense, omniscient and, ultimately, by giving up, to be in control. In a contingent world where many factors shape reality, not the least of which are the actions of other beings, hopelessness can be equated to irrationality in that it expresses counterproductive, counterfactual, and even counterintuitive beliefs and actions. In reality, hopelessness only makes sense within a worldview that assumes laws and rules that allow the foreseeing of final outcomes. This is not the world of the hunter, and, while we will never grasp the complete inner meaning of this worldview, I think we can at least approach its internal logic when writing the history of the hunters of James Bay.

For the Cree hunter living in a world rationalized around active and individual hope rather than on passive reliance on natural law, pathways into the geography of the hunt can be made in a number of different directions. Through his songs the hunter can express the hope that he has in the relationship between himself and the other-than-human beings upon whom he relies. "He comes – He comes – I see him, I see him – He is dressed so very fine," ran the caribou hunting song recorded by James McKenzie in 1808. "When I hunt caribou, I feel as though they are standing still even if they are running away from me, I feel as if they are standing still. How easy it is when I go to kill caribou," was the way that George Head expressed the same sentiment in song to Richard Preston in the 1960s. These are expressions of hope, unconnected to pessimism or fear of failure, spoken to the hunted to show faith in the relationship between them and the hunter.[50]

Through dreams, too, the hunter can map out this geography and the resources that are available to him to partake in the relationship with other-than-human beings. Knowledge and power come in dreams, and, like songs, dreams are an expression of hope, which shapes reality as the hunter tells others what he has dreamt. Here again the narrative quality of hunting speaks to the importance of words with regard to the material success of the hunt. Given this, it is not surprising that many Natives were wary of making their dreams and songs known to whites. "They do not like to tell their dreams, especially to a white person," wrote R.C. Wilson in 1891, "for they think that if they do, everything will leave them." Given the Cree understanding of how different the expression of hope was within white culture, opening up their world to white narrative scrutiny could not help but damage their hunting.[51]

We can gain a further understanding of hope or, more specifically, loss of hope if we look at Cree ideas about cannibalism, a subject that has troubled anthropologists in their studies of Native cultures. The acceptance of privation has been noted above, but at times individuals succumbed to both hunger and loss of hope and became cannibals. The Cree feared these people, they feared succumbing themselves, and people were often put to death to rid a group of even a suspected cannibal. No doubt we can understand the physical hunger that might drive one human to eat another, but the cultural repercussions of that decision are extremely complex. The Cree response to privation might, as Richard Preston points out, be explained in terms of hunger anxiety, using Clyde Kluckhohn's theory that, in their rituals and myths, all cultures express anxiety over some aspect of life. But while there is a clear and continuing consciousness of hunger in Cree culture, according to Preston the application of this kind of broad theory does not fit the ethnographic record. And it does not fit the historical record either. The Cree did not express anxiety about hunger, but they did express anxiety about cannibalism and its connection with both insanity and a loss of humanity and hope.[52]

A great deal has been written by anthropologists about Algonquin "windigo psychosis." Much of this has involved an attempt to describe cannibalism as a very specific kind of mental disorder affecting certain individuals. Within this "culture-bound psychopathy," individuals are taken with the desire to kill and then eat human beings. There was certainly a cultural interpretation involving insanity and cannibalism for the Cree, but attempting to fit it into a clinical, psychological framework is no more satisfying than is speaking of structural anxieties. The historic and ethnographic records do show some first-hand examples of people displaying a kind of "psychotic" behaviour directed towards harming other people, but the Cree interpretation of this was not a medical one. For the Cree, the concept of windigo was closely tied to aspects of the cultural environment related to the loss of self-control, but its meaning within Cree culture remains unclear. Within the Cree environment, cultural expectations were applied to specific disorderly behaviour, but individuals also used these concepts to understand their own feelings and behaviour. Windigo was, thus, a semiotic and narrative category connected to the larger subject of hope, and cannibalism might be explained more as an ontological crisis than as a psychological one.[53]

For the Cree, the term "windigo" (also known as *witigo* or *atoosh*) referred both to a creature that roamed the woods feeding on humans and to a person who had been possessed by this creature after having resorted to cannibalism. John Horden described *atoosh* as a "semi-spiritualized body assumed by a cannibal which rambles through the country but is seldom seen; it is of an immense size and the print of its feet, which are often seen, are of a size corresponding to the bulk of its body." This was how the creature was described to him, and he recorded what he heard, not with complete acceptance but, significantly, without quite being able to dismiss the idea either. These beings lived alone in the bush and lost their humanity in very specific ways. They lost their appetite for human food; they did not shelter, clean, or clothe themselves properly. People possessed by them became other-than-human, thus threatening the cultural relationships between people and those that they hunted. And, I think, these people gave in to the irrationality of pessimism – the ontology of fear.

There are disturbing historical cases of such behaviour. At Nitchequon in 1857, for example, Mark Eshkacappo told Robert Chilton that he had come upon a hunting group whose members were starving and eating moss in order to survive. The wife of one of the hunters told him that another hunter in the party had not been bringing food home to the tent but was eating it out in the bush, even though people were sick and needed his help. According to Eshkacappo, this strange behaviour was directed towards others outside the group as well. The hunter had gone to another tent and had demanded that members of that party build a fire for him, "which they did for they were afraid of him as he looked so frightful." He then half-boiled his rabbits and partridges and ate them without removing the fur and feathers. For the Cree, the context of insanity is not only the threat of violence but also the loss of expectations concerning humanity, reciprocity, and their relationship with food and the environment. All these people were giving up hope in this relationship, becoming greedy and violent.[54]

People also interpreted their own internal struggles with reference to cannibalism. In 1845, the hunter Metaweabinau came and asked Mistassini trader William McKay if he could stay at the post, but McKay refused him. In fact, he hurried him along, giving him a gun and a canoe to speed him on his way. "He is the worst fur hunter ever I knew," he wrote in his journal, "and I am really at a loss to know what to do with him. The Indians who have been mostly in his company think that he will turn out to be a cannibal some time or other. He generally goes about by himself." Metaweabinau came back the next day complaining that there was too much wind for him to leave, but McKay again moved him along as quickly as he could. Several days later, Robert Watt and James Moar, McKay's servants, brought word that Metaweabinau's canoe was up the lake and that they were not sure whether he was there or not. McKay went to investigate and found Metaweabinau under the boat, hungry, and without a fire. He said that he was sick, and McKay, relenting a bit, told him to come to the post for food the next day. When he arrived, however, he had his gun with him, and when McKay asked him why, he replied that he did not know. He said that he had not meant to bring it but had grabbed it as he left his campsite. McKay, obviously feeling threatened, took the gun from him and gave him food: "I do not think the above Indian is quite sane. Before he went to bed he told me he was afraid that he would get bad sometime or other – what he meant ... is that he will lose his senses and do mischief to others." For the next few days local hunters reported Metaweabinau's actions and movements to McKay. Clearly, they were also worried about his behaviour; yet, if anything happened later, it was not recorded. There are many examples in the record of individuals, both Native and white, losing their senses for periods of time in the bush and then suddenly recovering them. It is possible that nothing came of the incident. It is also possible that the locals took action and that McKay chose not to record it. After all, acceptance of local decisions was a part of living in James Bay.[55]

Accounts of insanity and cannibalism continue into the ethnographic record of the twentieth century, and the loss of self-control and the blurring of the distinction between the human and other-than-human worlds seems to be a consistent theme in stories concerning *atoosh*, as does the implied loss of hope. In the end, that may be as much as we can know with regard to specifics. Like songs and dreams, the issue of cannibalism shows the complexity of the Cree understanding of their world, but it does not mesh cleanly with this kind of narrative. Analysis tends to place Cree stories and concepts within a cultural geography with which we are familiar, a four-dimensional physical space involving linear time that follows certain constant laws. Here these things always lack weight because, as I said, they do not fulfill the expectations of narrative credibility. And this is true of one last important feature of hunting as well.[56]

Traditionally, what have come to be known as shaking tent ceremonies were a part of the human relationship with the land and animals. As we have seen, all hunters communicated with other-than-humans, but some chose to enter into a much deeper shamanic relationship with that world. The shaking tents were another tool for those hunters (it seems to have been a minority of them) who chose to become *kwashaptam*[57] and to form a relationship with a *mistabeo*.[58] This was a reciprocal relationship, again much like that between two friends, and, like friendship, it could be both helpful and problematic. The hunter who chose this relationship neither controlled nor was controlled by his *mistabeo*, and yet there was an obligatory bond between the two beings that was dangerous for either to abuse or to break. Significantly, the power that one gained by practising this kind of a relationship could be aimed in a variety of moral directions: the power of *kwashaptam* might be used to harm others, and men who entered into it were both respected and feared.[59]

Historically, and in the narration of myth, preparations for entering the *kwashapshikan*[60] involved lying face down on the ground without food for a number of days, during which time one had dreams and visions. This does not seem to have been the case in a number of more modern *kwashaptam* performances recorded by ethnologists, but deprivation is a fairly universal means of preparing for shamanic activity. The *kwashapshikan* was constructed of a number of saplings driven into the ground in a circle about two metres in diameter. These were bound together by two hoops, a large one midway up and a smaller one at the top of the three-metre-high structure. This was covered tightly by tenting material, and the hunter entered by crawling in under the edge. As the *kwashaptam* began the conversation with his *mistabeo*, the top of the tent would begin to sway back and forth and the voices of all of the beings, those of other *mistabeos* and those of animals within the tent, could be heard by those listening outside when the ceremony was carried out in public. The physical manifestations of the *mistabeo* and the other beings that came could be seen, and the hunter, "during the process, without boldly looking up, [caught] glimpses in the same plane as the top most hoop of the lodge of a number of objects like little stars." These were *mistabeo*, and, in conversation with them, the hunter received information and/or expressed his will. Given that these performances were often conducted in front of audiences, the *kwashaptam* was narrating his will and the will of the other beings into the cultural environment, and communicative pathways opened up in several directions.[61]

The shaking tent, and the much larger geography of hunting the land to which it allowed access, brings us finally to an intellectual impasse. But even as we allow that the shaking tend cannot be assimilated into our systems of understanding, it remains part of the historical world of James Bay and it was an aspect of Cree culture with which outsiders had to grapple. Here are the words of twentieth-century fur trader J.W. Anderson:

> The willow frames of conjuring tents were to be seen on most of the portages on the river route and occasionally a séance would take place right at the post, usually in the autumn when all the voyageurs had returned from the coast and all were at the post prior to departure to the trapping lands, it is difficult for the white man to understand what brings about these séances, for they seem to happen spontaneously. The conjurer, or medicine man, begins to beat on the drum and very soon the whole tent village is electri-

fied. The actual conjuring is hidden from view inside the conjurer's tent, and sometime is carried on for an hour or more. It is an eerie sensation indeed to have an Indian come up to you and, pointing through the dusk, ask if you can see the Wabinakae, or bad man! In surroundings like these – in any vast vacant quiet – the senses play uncommonly queer tricks with their possessor. The very air seems to be astir with sounds and shapes on the edge of revelation.[62]

Anderson was not only faced with the fact of these ceremonies but also, seemingly, with their power. He chose to think of them as resulting in "uncommonly queer tricks," but he was affected by them nonetheless. They may have lacked credibility afterwards, but at the time they seem to have moved him, and the historical record offers a great deal of evidence regarding the efficacy of Cree thought in relation to contact with Europeans. This does not come from understanding those narratives but, rather, from seeing how they affected individual action.

What we believe, in the end, about the reality of the Cree hunting world is a matter of philosophy or religion, and answers to such questions are not found in the historical record. What is found in the historical record is the fact that Cree hunters spoke and acted within this worldview and, in their interactions with Europeans, made some of it a part of the outsiders' worldview when they came to live on Cree land. The Cree negotiated the nature of the world with these outsiders, adapting themselves even as they sought to change the outsiders. This larger cultural process is clearly visible in the events in James Bay over the last several hundred years.

Let's begin briefly, in 1818, when an HBC trader named Greeley was sent inland from Rupert's House by Chief Trader Alexander Christie to set up a new post at Waswanipi Lake. He only made it as far as a place called Big Lake before winter set in, and, in the spring, the Native Cammitachiset brought the news that, with one exception, all of Greeley's party had starved to death. Only William Langston had not starved, and he had been put to death by Cammitachiset's partner Amooshish because he had resorted to cannibalism in order to survive. Christie understood the meaning of cannibalism. "It is common amongst Indians to put to death even their nighest relations," he wrote, "when they know of their having been seduced to the dreadful necessity of eating human *Flesh*." When Christie asked Cammitachiset why he had not helped Greeley before the tragedy occurred, the hunter replied that "some time around the middle of January he went to the house in purpose to persuade Mr Greeley and party to leave the house and goods and go to live amongst the Indians ... as at that time he had a tolerable stock of food at his tent. Mr Greeley unhappily did not comply with the wishes of the Indian or had he done so, in all probability, both him and his party would have been alive to this day."[63]

This is the end of the incident. The above entry was included in a long district report for Rupert's House, so the HBC was duly informed, but no action was taken, or even suggested, against Amooshish. Certainly, Amooshish did not come to Rupert's House, where he may have put himself in danger by entering a cultural environment in which other concepts of cannibalism might have held sway. Christie's decision not to take further action on this matter is also partly explained by his having neither the personnel nor the legal mechanisms to do so. But there is more to it than that. Christie was scornful of these practices among some of the hunters, and he questioned their definition of insanity, calling it "very improbable"; but there was a grudging acceptance of their action. Greeley "unhappily did not comply with the wishes of the Indian," who knew best how to live on the land. He should have taken food and assistance when it was offered.[64]

For whatever reasons, Greeley did not want to enter the hunter's camp, and he paid for that decision by starving to death; on the other hand, the killing of Langston and Christie's acceptance of it shows clearly that the party was deeply embedded in Cree space, whether it left its own encampment or not. Cultural relationships with the environment that enabled people to feed themselves and assumptions about the nature of cannibalism were necessarily accepted. The future success of the fur trade in the interior of the James Bay region would rely not only on the Cree's ability to move back and forth between the bush and the fur trading posts but also on the traders' ability to do the same. In order to do this successfully, traders needed to be able to navigate the Cree environment both physically and narratively. This negotiation of material and narrative environments is what constitutes the history of James Bay.

All of this revolved first and foremost around hunting and food, and there is one Cree narrative that I want to use in spite of what I said above. It is handed down in the oral record, and I think it serves as a bridge between narrative traditions – between myth and history, if you will – and also points towards the central issue that I take up next. It concerns the first encounter with white men and hints at what was important to the Cree beyond the trade in furs and European goods. The story begins with the culture-hero Chakaapash (Cha-Ka-Baish). One day Chakaapash is travelling along the coast of the bay when he sees boats out on the water. Being curious, he gets into his canoe and goes out to them and discovers that they contain white men. There may have been trade goods, but, more important, the whites give Chakaapash some food as a treat. He likes it very much and is so taken with it that, in return, he gives them a haunch of squirrel, which is his own favourite food. Historically significant is the narrative's ironic touch: this one small haunch of squirrel weighs down the entire side of the ship, almost to the gunwales, and feeds the whole crew. Chakaapash, the Cree, fed the white men, and the power of the hunter to provide food shaped the relationship between Native and white in James Bay for centuries.[65]

According to both our traditions, it was somewhere in Rupert Bay, somewhere around the village of Waskaganish, that Henry Hudson met Chakaapash – metaphorically speaking. Here is where it all began: the trade in fur and the sharing of food, the long narrative negotiation over the land. Today Waskaganish is a community of slightly under two thousand Cree that sits at the site of one of the first fur trading posts in eastern James Bay. The original post was on the bluff, where the Anglican church now sits, and the HBC had warehouses down by the shore, where the lodge and restaurant are today. It's a quiet town, though it has changed dramatically in the last thirty-five years. It was only recently connected by road, but the hydro projects brought changes to all the communities that were once HBC posts. With the new band office building and all the new houses being built, it's a little hard to think of this place as having been connected with the HBC and the fur trade, but the history is here. Interestingly, it is less difficult to connect this village with the Cree world I've been describing in this chapter: all you have to do is have a cup of coffee in the restaurant and listen to the Cree being spoken or talk to people about the land and the animals. It's all still very much in the forefront, and what I want to do in the following chapters is to connect these Cree villages with the hunting camps out in the bush, both in the past and in the present. We've come part of the way in our attempt to understand the meaning of Job Bearskin's words, but there is still a way to go.

3

Inland Engagement

*Dear Sir I wish to leave this post and to stop down at the coast –
as I am afraid of perishing here for the want of food unless I am
better supplied in provisions from Rupert's House. Altho I buy a
great quantity of eatables I am not fit now a day to labour hard
for my living here.*

– *Robert Chilton Jr.,* Nitchequon
Post Journals, *1862*[1]

Lake Nichicun lies by the northern foot of the Otish Mountains and is part of the headwaters of the Eastmain River. It is almost as remote now as it was when the HBC canoe brigade rushed to complete its yearly journey to Rupert's House and back to Nitchequon Post in the relatively short window between ice-out and freeze-up – a practice that lasted into the twentieth century. The area is part of the northern taiga, and the trees are small and widely spaced. There's a feeling here that the forest is opening up to the north and the tundra beyond, that, though the forest continues from here, it's losing its momentum. Today the old post is abandoned and sits next to a government airstrip that was built in the 1940s for a weather and communications station. It is kind of a ghost town, though the Cree have not forgotten it. The Nitchequon Post was first opened in 1816 by trader James Clouston, and, after a couple of false starts, it ran nearly continuously until the 1960s, when, for business reasons, the HBC closed it permanently. Those hunters who traded and summered there turned mostly to Mistassini Post at that point, and the Mistissini people claim Nitchequon Post as part of their land and heritage.[2]

Today, all but three of the Cree villages sit on or near the sites of former HBC posts. As mentioned above, Chisasibi was built in 1980 after the La Grande project threatened the old island post of Fort George at the mouth of the La Grande River. Oujé-Bougoumou was built belatedly, in 1993, to compensate for land taken around Chibougamau after the Second World War, and the new village of Nemiska sits north of the old fur trade post on Lake Nemiscau. The settlement at Nemiscau was abandoned in 1970, when the site was slated for flooding, but since this aspect of the project was abandoned, some of the people have moved back to the old site as a summer encampment, and a few live there year-round. The other modern villages, as well as a number of places where posts were abandoned in the nineteenth century, were areas that the Cree gave over to the use of traders – coastal areas early in the eighteenth century and the rest when the HBC began its move inland in the 1780s.

In a way, these places became contested ground, although, for the most part, the contestation was not overtly confrontational. The proximity of the traders was a benefit to the hunters in some respects, but the posts were an outside intrusion into their environment. And, while the Cree ceded control of these small areas, they also continued to involve themselves in creating meaning both inside and outside the new posts. As I noted earlier, under the provisions of the 1975 James Bay and Northern Quebec Agreement, the treaty that let the La Grande project proceed, these communities are now the places where the Cree have greatest control: it is out in the bush that the intrusions are happening. This is an inversion of the history of the last two hundred years, and it is an important part of the modern story of the Cree. To understand the modern Cree struggle to maintain some control over the land beyond their communities, it is important to investigate the process by which, in the past, hunters engaged with these trading posts and tried to integrate them into the hunt.

I mentioned above that there was still an HBC trading post in Mistissini when I first went there and that I was surprised that it didn't look very different from the hardware store in the town in which I lived. There were certainly things there that I wouldn't have found at home – bear traps, ice chisels, and so on – but for the most part it looked the same. I don't know exactly what I had expected on that first trip, but I was certainly caught up in the aura of romanticism that surrounds the HBC – the Company – even today and that belies the real history of how people interacted and moved into the present. That modern store was the product of a long process of adaptation on the part of both the HBC and the Cree, and, by the time I arrived, the HBC really was the local hardware store (so to speak). It was a part of the cultural landscape of that twentieth-century Cree community, and the way that it became part of that landscape has a lot to tell us about culture and nature in the James Bay region.

The HBC's move inland to places like Mistassini Post came after nearly 150 years of marginal contact between the Cree and Europeans. This was important contact, in the sense that trade goods were exchanged on a seasonal basis, but only a limited number of Cree actually interacted with Europeans, either French or British. Few Europeans ventured into the interior of James Bay before the end of the eighteenth century, instead being satisfied to wait for the Cree to bring the trade to them. As in other regions of North America in the sixteenth century, so in James Bay through much of the eighteenth century, Europeans lingered on the littoral. A few French traders from the St. Lawrence traversed the eastern fringes of the watershed shortly after Jesuit missionaries visited in the 1660s. And it was, in part, a circumvention of this St. Lawrence trade that led the now famous Radisson and Des Groseilliers to deal with the English. Des Groseilliers led the English ship *Nonsuch* to the eastern coast of James Bay in 1669, and the next year English investors established the Hudson's Bay Company. Under a royal charter from Charles II – given in true European monarchic fashion, with little understanding of what or who was being given – the HBC was granted a monopoly over much of what we now call the Shield. HBC traders began to set up posts along the perimeter of James Bay, and a small blockhouse named Fort Charles was built at the mouth of the Rupert River at what is now the village of Waskaganish. In a very small way, this was part of the larger rivalry that unfolded across the northeast before 1763. The French and English both claimed sovereignty in James Bay, as they did elsewhere; yet, unlike in other places, the conflict in this region was small, short-lived, and, significantly, did not draw the Cree in (unlike what happened to Native groups to the south).[3]

In 1679, Louis Jolliet travelled into the James Bay area from New France and brought back news of the scope of the English presence on the Eastmain (the historic name for the eastern coast of James Bay). The need to counter this move was obvious, and, in 1682, the Compagnie du Nord was formed and the French moved north. A post was established first on Lake Nemiscau, inland from Fort Charles along the Rupert River, and soon after on the coast nearer the English. Joint occupation lasted for several years, but in March 1686, the Compagnie du Nord sent a party of 105 men overland and took three forts at the bottom of the bay, leaving the English with only Fort Nelson on the western shore. With this the French seemed ascendant, but the HBC regrouped, sent a hundred men of their own, under Captain James Gilpin, and drove the French from

Hudson Bay in 1693. The retreating French destroyed Fort Charles, and, while it was just getting going across most of eastern North America, the imperial conflict was over in this region. Strikingly, the several hundred men in the two respective forces represent by far the largest number of non-Natives in the region until the 1970s.[4]

In James Bay, the struggle lasted roughly a decade, involved a relatively small number of men, and, in the end, gave the British only nominal sovereignty over the bay. There was no real occupation of the territory, the country remained under the monopoly of the HBC, and the few traders along the Eastmain were a tiny presence in that vast country. After the destruction of Fort Charles, in fact, there were no permanent buildings erected until 1719: the few traders to visit the area chose to live seasonally aboard ship. Even with the building of another permanent post in 1724, only eight men wintered on that side of the bay. There was no real need for the English to occupy the territory farther inland as their rivals remained at a distance.[5]

The French did not abandon the fur trade in the region, even after the Treaty of Utrecht confirmed British possession of eastern James Bay in 1713, but they largely remained on the St. Lawrence side of the watershed and let the hunters come to them. The post at Chamouchouane, near the watershed, was used heavily by a small number of free traders from the St. Lawrence. For its part, the HBC was satisfied with the situation – or, if not satisfied, not sufficiently motivated to act further. To increase the Company's seasonal trade, Eastmain House was established as a permanent post in 1724, Moose Factory in 1730, and Rupert's House in 1776, all of them attracting and maintaining certain hunters who became associated with them in the company records. This was an HBC bookkeeping designation, and hunters attached to various posts worked together during the winter within their own networks of family and friends, though some became more attached to these new places within the environment of the hunt.[6]

Some hunters chose to come to the posts independently, but, increasingly, many came in gangs of four or five canoes under the leadership of a so-called captain. Throughout the eighteenth century, this system grew as these trading captains led larger groups downriver after the spring melt. In many ways, this fit with the Cree practice of seasonal gathering, though it was also an adaptation of this practice. These men who brought other hunters down to the coast were rewarded by the HBC with gifts and clothes, much of which they redistributed among their fellow hunters. The way goods were redistributed by these captains highlights the Cree concept of *uuchimaau* – the idea that giving is integral to leadership. The Cree word *uuchimaau*, which is usually translated as boss or chief, derives from the verb "to give away," and ethnologist Colin Scott argues that, historically, this reciprocal kind of relationship was the basis for all social and political relations among the Cree. This reciprocity was naturally transferred to traders when they arrived, and the trading posts created new arenas for this power relationship within Cree culture. But how this played out beyond the posts is not clear.[7]

Traders – and historians after them – used the term "captain" to describe these leaders, but it seems clear that this was a position of limited, informal authority quite unlike the formal hierarchy suggested by the title. These captains were not always the best hunters out on the land, but they were valued by the HBC because they brought other hunters, and they were valued by the latter because they took on the burden of dealing with the HBC. What is safe to assume is that captains had personal skills in dealing with Europeans that helped their fellow hunters who were not as able or willing to do so; for this they were given a leadership position in the trading season. These mediators, negotiators really, were able to communicate with and understand European traders and, maybe more important, were able to make traders understand the hunters in some limited way. In a world predicated on reciprocal and variable relationships with all kinds of people and beings, these skills would have been highly valued. These men – we will see women playing this role in a related way later – assumed an identity that made it possible to deal with the Europeans within their spaces, and this certainly benefited the group. It's interesting to consider that today Cree politicians, especially those who work in Ottawa or Quebec City, play an analogous role for their constituents who stay in the bay.[8]

This system of captaincies flourished because of the need to counter the increasingly organized activity of Scottish, Montreal-based entrepreneurs who began to operate after the 1763 defeat of New France. These new merchants incorporated as the North West Company (NWC) in 1779, and their organized, aggressive competition prompted the HBC to begin its own move inland. Building on the old French fur trade, and benefiting from the labour and knowledge of French *couriers du bois* who remained in Quebec after the Conquest, these new rivals began to challenge the HBC monopoly across the North. That they were not led by the French and were part of the British mercantile world made little difference to the HBC; they were, in fact, more of a threat because they competed for English markets as well as colonial resources. They also moved aggressively across the whole continent, through the old *Pays d'en Haut* around the Great

Lakes and into what is now western Canada. Their practice was to engage hunters directly, seeking them out rather than waiting for them to come in. They challenged the HBC monopoly all around Hudson Bay, and, in eastern James Bay, this meant moving inland from the St. Lawrence, setting up posts nearer to the hunters, and giving rewards and captaincies of their own.

The direct rivalry in eastern James Bay lasted until 1821, when the HBC succeeded in a corporate takeover of the NWC, and for decades there were duelling posts at many places in the region. During this period the two companies used whatever means they could, including a great deal of liquor, to get hunters to bring in furs, and this free-for-all had negative consequences for both people and land. Beaver were certainly diminished on the land, and it seems clear that other animals suffered too. Food and fur became scarcer, and there is some evidence of struggles over hunting territories as hunters tried to maximize their hunts. Some hunters seem to have been motivated by their desire for more trade goods, including liquor, and we will see in a later period of increased trade rivalry how territorial encroachment led many to over-hunt in a pre-emptive attempt to stave off food shortages. This was probably the case in James Bay during this period as well, and, had the rivalry between the companies gone on longer, this downward spiral might have led to the disastrous results that we see later in the century. The roots of the later crisis are probably here, though the link is not certain.[9]

Alcohol took its toll on individual hunters, and there is evidence in James Bay of lives lost and ruined because of it. This is a complex issue within Native history and one that has political resonance today. There is no getting away from the fact that fur traders used alcohol all over the continent to induce hunters to bring in more fur because, unlike other trade goods, it was a commodity with a seemingly limitless demand. The addiction to alcohol had dramatic and tragic consequences for many Native communities both in the United States and Canada, and it is emblematic of many dark aspects of the larger history of contact between Natives and Europeans. There are plenty of entries in the HBC journals in James Bay of traders using liquor to get furs and of hunters going into debt to get liquor. Whether this was "to drink dull care away," as one trader put it, or to mask the pain of the confrontation with outsiders and the confusion of the trade rivalry, individuals and their families were hurt. It has to be said too, however, that, in addition to these stories of harm, there is a good deal of evidence that some hunters turned their backs on this aspect of the trade. One hunter explained to Missionary George Barnley that, when he had begun to dream about how liquor was destroying him, he had made the decision to stop drinking. And there were many others who either turned away or avoided the problem altogether.[10]

Putting alcohol into its proper historical context during this period in James Bay is difficult. It was an important part of the wider strain placed on the relationship between hunters and their land, but the worst of the liquor trade ended with the merger of the two companies. Liquor, along with disease and warfare, was a force that rent the fabric of Native societies in other parts of the northeast, but the Cree seem to have been spared the worst of it. Some rum and brandy were traded until the HBC banned them in 1851, and, while this did not eliminate all problems from the region, it did seem to dramatically reduce them during the rest of the nineteenth and the beginning of the twentieth centuries. This action was paternalistic, but it seemed to give Cree culture the space it needed to cope with a chronic problem. With regard to the nineteenth century, other aspects of cultural exchange and engagement were more relevant, while liquor has resurfaced as a current problem.

Limited amounts of liquor were brought in by individual free traders after the 1851 ban, but until after the Second World War only the HBC had the ability to bring in large amounts. Ease of transport is what connects the problem of liquor with the present and with some of the social problems that the James Bay Cree are facing today. I said above that this issue has political resonance for Native people in general, and this is true for the Cree in particular. In the last thirty-five years, both because of the stress placed on communities by rapid development and the ease with which drugs and alcohol can make their way into the region, addiction and abuse have become serious problems, especially for young people. Whether they do it to escape from their hopelessness or as a self-destructive protest against the changes we have brought to them, all of the Cree communities are, to some extent, having to deal with the trauma of substance abuse. Most important for this investigation, many in these communities are coping with this problem by taking people back to the land to find the cultural strength with which to heal themselves. This is part of a much larger and longer process in the region; it is an aspect of Cree history that has outlasted the fur trade but that harks back to it.

The move inland and the rivalry between the two fur-trading companies were intrusions, and they brought many negative things in their wake – not the least of which was liquor – but, in a larger way, they simply made it necessary for the Cree to engage with newcomers. This cannot be presented as being exclusively a benefit to Cree culture, yet it wasn't a destructive process either; it meant negotiation, acceptance, and change on both sides. The fact that traders from both companies needed to convince hunters to trade with them meant that, while hunters were not always adept at driving hard economic bargains or avoiding pitfalls, many of them could and often did drive hard cultural bargains. Hunters at times were swept away by the trade, but traders were also swept away by hunting culture as they tried to solicit friendships and partnerships with hunters not only for their furs but also for food. After more than a century of occupying small beachheads along the coast, the company men began living in James Bay in an entirely new way, and for the traders and hunters this was a new level of engagement – economic on one level but, far more important in the long view, cultural on many levels.

Beginning in the 1780s, then, what had been small coastal outposts became the launching points for fur trade forays into inland regions and clearinghouses for both fur coming out of and supplies going into the bush. The yearly ships still arrived from England with trade goods and limited preserved food, but now transport infrastructure had to be developed to make sure that those supplies made it inland in time for the winter. This was a labour-intensive proposition, and Native participation was vital. Over the course of those decades, as post were established in farther-flung places, the big, west-flowing rivers – La Grande, Eastmain, Rupert, Broadback – became highways for HBC canoe brigades that moved goods and furs during the summers. The HBC continued this inland engagement after the merger because, for reasons not entirely clear to the traders in James Bay, the HBC began to lease what were known as the King's Posts to free traders from the St. Lawrence after they gained control of them in 1831. These were the old French posts south of the region, and for much of the rest of the century they continued to give hunters options that, for many, were good alternatives.[11]

All of this had the effect of making coastal posts larger as they tried to meet the needs inland, and traders became focused on managerial tasks. Their journals are all business, and it is easy to get swept away by their priorities as they looked out into the bush and thought about getting fur off the land. In reading these journals, it is easy to think that the most important thing going on in James Bay was the fur trade; if one thinks about the Cree and their land, however, one realizes that it really was not. Trading furs was part of their lives, but the narrative context in which they lived was not predicated upon it. That was the world of the trading posts: some hunters became wholly taken by the fur trade, but Cree culture did not. Avoiding this preoccupation with trade, moving out

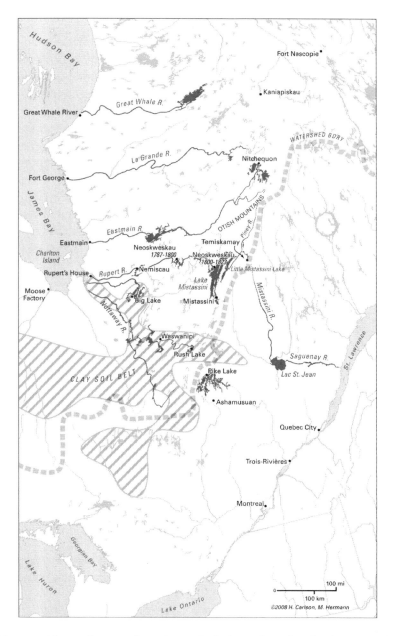

MAP 3.1   *Nineteenth-century fur trade posts.* In the late eighteenth and early nineteenth centuries, fur traders of the Hudson's Bay Company moved inland and set up trading posts to be closer to the supply of fur. These posts were located both where the Cree gathered traditionally during the summer and along the watershed boundary to try and prevent hunters from travelling south to trade.

into the bush, and following the hunters as inland traders did brings an entirely different perspective on how people engaged each other and the land that supported them.

When, in 1862, Robert Chilton wrote from Nitchequon Post that he was "afraid of perishing here for the want of food," he was not new to HBC service; he had been involved with the company for forty years in eastern James Bay, most of his time having been spent at northern inland posts just like Nitchequon. He was the son of Robert Chilton, Sr., and a Native woman who may or may not have been the daughter of a mixed marriage herself. Her name and her history are unclear, but her son went to England in 1812, when his father retired as one of the HBC's schooner captains. Robert Chilton returned to James Bay a year later, rejoined the HBC, and married a woman named Betsy, who was herself a "Native of the Country" – the local term for a child of mixed parentage. He went to Nitchequon first in 1820 as a company servant under James Clouston, was there as a trader from 1835 to 1837, and then returned permanently in 1844, having run other posts in the years in between. He was a successful and long-time trader, and he had a clear understanding of his situation in 1862. He died the next year at the age of sixty-seven, worn out by a life lived in an environment only marginally suited to supporting the trade and its posts.[12]

Chilton's life spans the period of greatest inland expansion by fur traders in eastern James Bay, and it mirrors those of others who worked for the HBC in the region. And this is never more true than with regard to the struggle to acquire food. On a yearly basis, traders like Chilton worked constantly to keep themselves, their families, and their servants provisioned. They caught and salted fish in the fall, gathered and cut firewood throughout the winter, and hunted game seasonally. In addition to the traders' efforts, the Cree hunters who brought furs to the traders brought food as well, and this complicated the understanding of the trade. While the HBC in London could look on the trade as a simple trade in fur, men like Chilton had to see it within a much larger context. For them, the Cree were suppliers of meat, and, if the trader in James Bay wanted to avoid starvation, he had to learn to adapt to a world in which Native hunting was central to everybody's survival. At one level this meant that starving – that is, going without food for days as Natives often did – was, by definition, a regular part of Robert Chilton's life and one that he had learned to accept. It also meant that real starvation – the threat of imminent death from hunger (which he had faced on several occasions) – had to be kept at bay. It was this daily concern that, in one way or another, tied everyone to the Native subsistence cycle. It was this, too, that, at another level, tied the conceptual world of the hunter to the trader's survival.[13]

Establishing a new post was a delicate process as traders had to rely not only on their own skill and Native help but also on their luck in an environment within which there were many contingencies. This was a land that could shrug off even the most concerted human effort with ease, and well-founded plans did not necessarily come to fruition. After struggling for several years, with a good deal of Cree help, posts were usually able to stabilize themselves. They were even able to begin to reciprocate, helping hunters who found themselves facing privation, and this began the much more complicated set of interdependencies that changed and evolved for the next 150 years. As these men moved farther and farther into the Native environment, as their lines of supply became more and more attenuated, their trade grew far more complex, and trade items became interwoven with a whole set of personal relationships.

In the summer of 1825, to use one post as an example, Alexander Collie and three men travelled up from Mistassini Post, through Little Mistassini Lake (Lake Albanel), up the Piney (Temiscamie) River, and over the portages into Temiscamie Lake. When they arrived at the south end of the lake they set up a base of operations "Our guide Nepenappaw went off," wrote Collie, "paid him for his services with rum and tobacco, and sent by him for Indians a gallon of rum and tobacco to induce them to visit." Here is an example of the use of alcohol, though gift giving was a common practice at all times during the fur trade as Native hunters almost universally resisted a strictly economic interpretation of their relationship with traders. For them, it was a matter of exchanging gifts, one friend to another, and so the rum and tobacco made some sense, especially for hunters who probably did not need other items at that point in the year. It also helped set a precedent for gift giving that would come to include a great deal of meat.

Thus the post began. Word spread of the trader's arrival, though this was more difficult than might be imagined, given the size of the region and the small number of hunters. Temiscamie is one of those places where the trading post did not become a Cree village, and its land is still hunted by Mistissini people today. Until recently it was an isolated place, a couple of days from the watershed portages at Coldwater Lake and surrounded by relatively high hills. Not long ago a road was pushed through and logging began. The road follows the Mistassini River, just over the height of land that flows south to Lac St. Jean, and logs are now driven down the same river that, in the past, the Cree used to carry their furs south. The post was placed here to prevent hunters from making this relatively easy trip down the Mistassini River, not because it was a traditional gathering place.[14]

Collie immediately sent the HBC men out to find food, and by mid-October he was writing regretfully that they could "hardly catch so many fish as is necessary for their subsistence," so he sent them instead to the falls at the outlet of the lake to fish. It was late in the season, however, and, while they found some fish still spawning, they did not catch very many. This may have been due to their lack of skill as well as to the time of year, but whatever the cause, the lack of fish was a serious matter; the food that they had been able to carry from Mistassini was limited. All they could do was keep trying their luck with the nets and keep an eye out for Native hunters coming to the post. It proved to be a prolonged wait. In early November the hunter Stenicimaw arrived and reported that he had been hunting on the borders of the "King's Domain" – the eastern watershed – all summer but that he had not seen any of the Mistassini hunters that were supposed to be in that area. On November 13, the hunters Sacatchunappu and Nepenappaw arrived, and neither of them had seen any others during the summer. Although he regretted this, Collie still "engaged Nepeneppaw [sic] to come in the month of March to go as guide to the borders of the Kings Domain in search of the Mistassini Indians." He was still trying to focus on trading fur, but food was becoming of primary importance as the season progressed.[15]

Before the end of January 1826, Collie had to send a letter to Mistassini relating the poor fall fishing and hunting and the fact that he had not seen the hunters he had expected to see. He worried that, even though the few hunters who had come in were looking for those others, they did not think that any other bands had been there for some time. "I am unable to give any information about any of the Indians that are gone in that direction," he wrote, "as it appears to me that they have altogether left their lands on the Mistassini waters." Collie requested food from Mistassini as none of his visitors intended to return until late spring, but on February 27 the men arrived with only a bit of oatmeal and flour. They had a letter from James Clouston, which said that he had three families of Natives "starving" and that "the families of the list men – Robert Chilton and Robert Thomas – at a tent little better." He could send nothing more to Collie.[16]

On March 21, 1826, Thomas Moar, tired of going hungry, left the post against orders to go to Mistassini. According to Collie, "He had not provisions off with him but the flesh of one fox – nor was there a single mouthful of anything that was edible in the House. This is the second day that I have not tasted a mouthful of food." Moar made it to Mistassini, but he got little to eat there. Finally, late in March, the hunter Camatut arrived and brought four to five kilograms of venison to Temiskamay Post, as it was then known. He had killed several deer and offered to provide more if Collie would go back to his tent. This was an easy choice and the next day Collie tried to walk the 32 kilometres to the camp, but he was too weak and had to turn back. Camatut went on without him, and a couple of days later his partner Wechimaugen arrived to again attempt the trip with Collie. This time he brought more meat with him for the journey, and, the next day, Collie closed the house and went off, coming back several days later with 80 kilograms of venison. When he arrived he found a letter that Chilton had brought from Clouston and a little more oatmeal, which was all that Mistassini could spare. The postscript of the letter read: "Hope this letter finds you in existence." Clouston knew the hardships of inland trade.[17]

Collie and his men survived to see the summer, with the help of local hunters, and it was a season of relative plenty in fish and game. It was also a season of greater travel. The word spread about the new post, and the next year there was much more activity, with hunters coming to trade on a more regular basis. Early in the winter, Collie was even in a position to help several hunters who had had bad luck with hunting. In January, however, Collie was again complaining that "the fishing here is very bad"; from six nets, in an entire week they had taken only enough fish to serve each man one meal. "We are living almost totally upon flour," he wrote, and though "I supplied Sanderson with a weeks flour and with nets and ammunition and sent him off to a place about 16 miles from here to endeavor to procure a part of his living, he did not however succeed and was obliged to come home." The man's failure was a hardship on all the people at the post, and throughout January and February Collie's journal contained only brief daily weather accounts and a weekly account of work. "Variously employed during the week," he wrote, "but principally in hunting and attending the nets." At the low point of the year one week's tally of food was twelve fish and three partridges, but, as the winter progressed, the hunting in the area slowly improved and the men's luck got better. The hunter Amitoegam brought in meat, and the traders, in turn, went with him to his camp to get more. With the help of Native hunters and small amounts of food transported from the coast, the post slowly created a subsistence level of survival.[18]

After several years, Collie was replaced by James Robertson, who, along with his son James Jr. and their wives and children, spent the next thirty years at Temiskamay until it finally closed in 1861. The Robertsons and those like them mark the most successful adaptation of the HBC to the environment of James Bay, and the long tenure of a single trader's family is a pattern that stands out at most of these inland posts in the first half of the nineteenth century. The Robertsons are an example of how one family made itself a home in the local environment and developed relations with the local population. These people lived closely with the Native world, they married Native women, and, significantly, both Robertsons, like Robert Chilton and Thomas Moar at Waswanipi, and William McKay at Mistassini, were children of *marriage à la façon du pays*. Here, again, we see the mediating of cultures but at a far deeper level. It is worth noting here that the term "Métis," or "half-breed," has limited significance in James Bay. We will see that some of these Natives of the Country became more involved in Western activities, but many of them also became hunters and re-entered the Native world: identity in eastern James Bay was always more about how and where you lived than about blood. Yet this fluidity over generations does not mask the cross-currents within these people's cultural identities. They, like their posts, were the creation of two worlds, and, to some extent, both are a measure of how those worlds interacted and changed over time.[19]

When Temiskamay and other posts were begun, they resembled Native camps far more than the coastal trading posts that spawned them. Thrown out onto the land, the HBC men lived in log-walled tents and shelters covered with bark, much as the local hunters did. Except for the stockade walls that most posts erected, it would have been difficult to differentiate between these early posts and the Native encampments in the region. Yet these posts were not like Native camps, which moved over the landscape, and all of the HBC posts quickly began to take on the outward appearance of European settlements, distinguishing themselves clearly as places apart. In all locations traders soon built log houses for themselves and other log buildings for storage and livestock. In the northern parts of the region, at Nitchequon and Kaniapiskau, for instance, these buildings were low, with double-walls filled with moss and sand to mitigate the effects of the wind and cold. In southern locations, like Mistassini and Waswanipi, some two-storey buildings were erected, and, as the nineteenth century progressed, these buildings were often replaced with timber-framed structures with windows of parchment or glass, clapboarded on the outside, and plastered mud on the inside. Ovens and ice houses were erected as well as more permanent byres and henhouses, complete with fireplaces to keep the animals warm. All of this went a long way towards differentiating these posts from the bush and the camps of the Cree.[20]

Within the first several decades of the nineteenth century, the effects on local environments caused by these HBC posts were striking as resource use was sustained in these permanent locations. Wood for construction came from the surrounding forest year after year, and more striking still was their prodigious use of firewood. Posts burned dozens – in one case seventy – cords of firewood during the course of a winter, and soon the local woods were cut clean. This not only made firewood difficult to bring in but also further exposed the posts to the wind, increasing the need for fuel. Rafting firewood along the various lakes became a common practice as well as hauling wood by dogsled and even ox sledge. "It is such cold weather," wrote Robert Chilton in 1849, "that I cannot get a stock of firewood on hand altho some days I would chop up 1 3/4 cords – for the houses are so cold and standing in such [a] bare place." Chilton's situation at Nitchequon was doubly difficult as the trees there were so naturally sparse. All these locations were given a unique appearance in the boreal forest not only by the buildings but also by the bare landscape that surrounded them.[21]

This more intensive and sustained use of forest resources is mirrored to some degree in the production of food and the unique subsistence cycle that delineated traders' lives at these posts. They settled into a yearly rhythm, like that of the Native hunters, and this had layers of effectiveness that we can peel away and examine. Take, for instance, the 1831 entry of James Kellock: "We procured 1600 fish at Waswanby last fall and rabbits have been plentiful there throughout the winter, but partridges have been uncommonly scarce. Our crop of potatoes was but a trifle of 23 kegs." Kellock thought his prospects, if not abundant, were at least good that particular year, even though he knew that all his other food options, mostly flour and salt meat, were limited by the constraints of canoe travel. He thus put fishing to use, and salting kegs of fish became primary to subsistence at all the posts. This was unpalatable food, but it was reliable if a good spawning place could be found, and it offered a base level of subsistence for the winter. Partridges and hares made up a second layer of subsistence, and here local hunters were more central. Traders often hunted small game for themselves, but they relied on gifts, too, and, with the Natives, they had to ride out the cycles of scarcity. Finally, there was big game, and here traders relied most heavily on the generosity of Natives for their survival. Despite their own hunting, it was the steady flow of venison from Cree hunters that they needed and anticipated.[22]

The coastal stations at Rupert's House and Eastmain House were a little different from those inland. In addition to having easier access to food brought by ship, they had recourse to the seasonal migrations of game birds, which were supplied by local hunters. Like fish, these birds were salted down in barrels and kept for winter use; the HBC had early on tapped into this traditional Native resource. A small group of hunters that had lands near the coast became more closely attached to these posts, both by making frequent trips for supplies and by working seasonally as goose hunters. These "homeguard" Natives, as they were known, fed the traders in an important way; because the coast could be better provisioned by ship, however, the food relationship between trader and Native was not as pressing and so not as evident in the record as was the case inland. Traders at these posts did not spend much time writing about food, and this was also true of the more northern whaling stations further up the coast at Great Whale River and Little Whale River. The contrast with the inland posts, where traders spent much of their time thinking and writing about food, is striking.[23]

August, September, and October – the spawning season – was the time to put away as many fish as possible. At Mistassini and Waswanipi the spawning grounds were relatively close by, and Wachenichi Lake near Mistassini was a consistently productive ground, as were the rapids that fed into Lake Waswanipi. For other posts the work was harder. Temiskamay Post never produced any quantity of fish locally, and the men were forced to travel to Little Mistassini Lake (Lake Albanel). This was a trip that took several days and required that the fish be carried over the Assini (Boulder) portage, which was, as one trader complained, "two miles long and one end of it for about the space of 60 yards there is nothing to walk upon except Large round Stones which are so loose with one another that a man is in Danger of Loosing himself every step he takes." It is still a long, hard portage, and even this kind of effort did not always bring success at Temiskamay.[24]

At Nitchequon no reliable fishing grounds were ever found, and the yearly supply of fish had to be collected from a number of less productive fishing places. "Nitchequon is the most miserable place for fishing," wrote Chilton, and, on another occasion, he wrote "Thank God" next to the total of forty-one kegs of fish for that year. That he was thankful for a diet of salt fish illustrates how vital this food was for mere survival; yet, he often complained of being sickened by it too. The vitiating effects of salt fish were common and sometimes seemed life-threatening. Living solely on this preserved food, another trader complained bitterly, "I fear I shall not see Spring again," adding, for the benefit of his employers, that, "in spite of fast failing health from exposure and food to which I have not been accustomed – if such trash can be called food – I still work away like one of the men. 'Needs much when the Devil drives.'"[25]

Fish clearly provided only for survival, and the traders were always eager to supplement them with something more tasty and filling. Throughout the year, hunters visited the posts to transact business, or just to visit, and food was usually part of the ritual. At times they traded rabbit and partridge for European food – likely a welcome change of pace – and at times the traders exchanged goods with widows or the elderly as a form of relief. At other times, the Cree simply gave this food to the traders, though this was also very much part of the bonds of social interaction. These small exchanges added up to a considerable amount of food over the course of the year. In the years between 1828 and 1830, for example, Natives brought 956 rabbits and 1,444 partridges to Mistassini Post. In 1844, at Pike Lake, more than a thousand rabbits were brought to the post over the course of the winter, and in March 1851 James Robertson cheerfully wrote that "the Indians is walking with the partridges today" – hundreds of them were brought into the post soon afterward.[26]

Finally, large game hunting, particularly caribou, brought in the most bountiful and welcome subsistence; not only the meat but also the marrow fat, and bones were eaten with great relish. Traders were hardly ever matter of fact about the arrival of hunters with venison, and they recorded combinations of relief and happiness, depending on their current need. As I have noted, especially during the winter months food was discussed in correspondence between the inland traders. Indeed, letters were rarely completed without a wish for hunting success or by a happy acknowledgment of it. "I was glad to learn you were under no apprehension of being in want [of] provisions during the winter," reads a typical postscript. The daily cant of the journals during times of privation illuminates this preoccupation: "nearly starving for want of fish"; "starving for want of fish"; "cannot make out a living"; "cannot get a sufficiency of fish – nor venison – for our subsistence"; "*No Fish*"; "nothing to *eat but flour – no fish!*" The urgency is justified because ordinary privation could quickly devolve into something more serious. As situations worsened, the hides, skins, and sinew of animals had to be boiled and eaten to stave off weakness. This, too, was part of Native strategy. These hides were a loss to the company, but the necessities of subsistence always drove the needs of trade. In still worse situations, even inedible bulk filled empty bellies and calmed pangs. "Rockweed [reindeer moss] is a part of our living and it is so scarce to be got the rain has covered them with ice," wrote Chilton during one very hungry March.[27]

These kinds of situations could quickly become ones of real starvation for the traders, and deadly privation could happen anywhere. Pike Lake, in the southern part of the region, was in bad straits for food in 1836, for example, when, for lack of food, John Corrigal was "found laying dead on the ice about 3 miles from house, it is supposed that he was not able to reach the house from weakness." Similarly, James Clouston and James Robertson returned to Nitchequon Post a year earlier and reported that they had "found Robert Chilton apparently at the point of death – he was so *feeble* and *emaciated* from absolute starvation – that he could not walk – nor indeed he could not – without assistance – raise himself from a reclining position. He had not seen an Indian since last Fall – consequently got no venison." He had not seen an Indian since last Fall – consequently got no venison: this is the crucial nexus.[28]

Native hunters played a pivotal role in keeping the trading posts from reaching a state of starvation, and they clearly understood the importance of this. More than simply bringing food when it was convenient, they rearranged priorities and schedules in order to do so. William McKay, for instance, noted with approval that the hunter Etapai was delayed coming from Pike Lake because he had killed five deer on the way to Mistassini and turned back to get the Pike Lake men so they could come for the meat. He knew how hungry they were and thought it important to make the journey. The Pike Lake journal for those days notes how eager the traders were to walk the 20 kilometres to help Etapai with the load. Similarly, when the hunter Duck sent his two sons to Nitchequon for a winter resupply of ammunition, he sent 55 kilograms of dried meat for Chilton rather than the fur he had at his tent. According to Chilton, Duck "told them not to take their furs now – as the venison would be the needfulest at present – as I was almost perishing for the want of food [at the same time] last winter." Later, when the hunter Peeshus came in, he lamented that it was "with furs and not a mouthful of any eatables."[29]

With regard to day-to-day living, the meat that the hunters brought in was of far more importance to the traders than furs. It was better when they arrived "with very poor [fur] hunts but a very opportune supply of venison" than it was when they arrived with fur but no food. It was good, too, when a hunter like Maskemoot arrived at Temiskamay with only a small number of furs but a welcome invitation to James Robertson "to come to his tent for some venison." Robertson gladly went off with the hunter, helped him dry meat for two days, then returned to the post with sledloads of the stuff. More hunters arrived four days later with furs and the dried meat of seven deer. In early April Robertson was travelling again, and this time he went to the hunter Fox's tent, where he got two more sledloads of meat. Late winter was the prime season for big game, and if the Natives had good luck, then so did the traders. These joint activities grew over time, and reciprocal needs and obligations centred on the Native supply of meat.[30]

The question is, what was the meaning behind all this Cree effort to keep traders fed? Having trade goods close at hand may have motivated some hunters to feed traders, but the sheer weight of meat seems to demand a better explanation than this. Basic humanity also has something to do with it, and not wanting to see others suffer affected hunters and traders alike at times; but this, too, falls short of the mark. In trying to explain this I am reminded of the modern stance of many Cree, who feel the need to keep interacting with governments and corporations even when they are fighting them in court over issues of land and resources. When it is suggested that they cut off negotiations until the courts make a ruling, the Cree say that they see this as a form of disrespect towards the land, which deserves every form of effort on their part. It is clear that hunters saw these HBC posts as an intrusion as well as a source of goods, but this did not eliminate the need to interact with traders in all the ways that humans were meant to interact with one another. Today, many Cree feel that love and generosity, shown even to those who are doing harm to them and their land, is part of their relationship with their land: it is important to show not only love *for* the land but also love *on* the land. This aspect of the Cree philosophy of engagement and reciprocity is applicable to the actions of hunters in the past as they dealt with these newcomers on their land, and it also shows how traders engaged in a reciprocal relationship around meaning as well as meat.[31]

Part of the meaning of food was tied to the fact that hunters themselves sometimes needed help, and this required that traders and hunters engage in a reciprocal relationship. Most traders seem to have taken this to heart, at least while their own need lasted. When the hunter Chiashamanbi and his family came to James Kellock for help, he noted: "starving and miserable looking creatures they were – being merely living skeletons." He was truly sorry not to be able to help. "I have got very little to give them," he wrote, "except some flour – as we catch so few fish – that we have not half enough to eat ourselves – and Indian visits here with venison are *few and far between*." He understood that he was not meeting an obligation, though the group did not hold this against him as he had nothing to share. But it was understood that, if he had been in a position to help, he would have done so. Often this willingness to help made good business sense for the trader, but one can overlook neither the fact that they owed a part of their living to these well-known hunters nor the bonds of friendship and compassion that grew between some traders and hunters. "Cheshannew and his family came in starving and I am glad that I had plenty of Provisions to give them," wrote James Robertson, Jr., in 1847, without any mention of trade or what Cheshannew might have done for him in the past.[32]

Hunters also used trading posts as places of refuge for the old, the infirm, or the sick – those who had become a liability to the band's quest for food – though this was not an option that all people wanted to exercise. Traders were more often than not willing to take individuals into their care, even extending invitations to certain people, as when William McKay, on hearing that one of his hunters was sick, sent for him to be brought to Rupert's House, "where every possible care should be taken of him." The hunter was brought to the house and spent a week recovering from the effects of sickness and hunger, though, significantly, he wanted to leave for the bush as soon as he could. The posts offered options; still, just as not all traders were successful living inland, where they had to be so much closer to the Native world, so Natives were not always successful living at the posts. Some simply chose to die on the land rather than resort to the posts, while others held out until they had no other choice. When Andrew Moar invited Canashish to come to Rupert's House to recuperate, the hunter refused for more than a month before finally relenting.[33]

Some individual Cree clearly had trouble with lengthy stays with the traders, yet groups of hunters increasingly used the posts for gatherings, and this was yet another level of engagement. Though beaver and bear were not often hunted specifically for the posts' food supply, they were often brought in for feasts and ceremonies in which Native drumming and singing were the centre of ceremonial activity, and traders were expected to share in this. Traders also came to be expected to share European celebrations with hunters, and New Year's and other holidays became occasions for Native feasting that displayed a fascinating combination of traditions. Most traders took it for granted that their hunters would visit them at these times, and many of them looked forward to it. Various admixtures of culture swirl around the central act of feasting in James Bay, and there is a sense of both conviviality and cultural negotiation: "a very happy X-mas was enjoyed by all and in the evening, to the tune of the violin and the tom-tom, a lively dance took place only interrupted now and again by some old hunter singing his praises to the Bear or Lynx." There is not only celebration here but also the continuation of the serious business of living on the land.[34]

FIGURE 3.1   *Mistassini bear's feast, circa 1900.* This picture of a bear's feast taken at Mistassini around 1900 shows both the cultural adaptation and longevity that marks so much of James Bay history. At the table to the left sits the Company employees and their families and to the right on the ground sit the hunters – "each to his custom" as one trader put it. In the centre stands a hunter displaying the drum, which was central to the ceremony. *Library and Archives Canada*

Clearly these posts and their traders meant many things to the hunters in James Bay, engaging them on many different levels. What we see is that reciprocity involved not only hunters using the posts for a variety of short and long visits but also traders living with hunters for extended periods of time. In January 1853, for instance, James Robertson, Jr., was glad to accept a hunter's invitation to go to his camp to hunt: "And I intend for to comply with his wish as I have very little provisions at the place. Perhaps if we can hunt for ourselves a while from the House [this] will save what provisions I have at the place." In this case, his strategy did not work and he was back at the house in less than two weeks badly in need of food. At other times, however, traders were able to stay for longer periods with their Native hosts. In March 1836, the hunter Mitupuesh and his partners, having brought nine sleds of venison to Nitchequon, told Chilton that they had been to Kaniapiskau in mid-January with some meat but that James Clouston and Thomas Beads were not there: "For they had gone toward the North to some Indians in that quarter – they had followed an Indian that had come to them – he likewise informs me that they had been scarce of food." Clouston and Beads had been just making it on salt fish and partridge and had had to leave the post and move onto the land with Native hunters in order to survive. They were away for nearly a month.[35]

These long stays had many implications, and, as has been noted, many inland traders married into Native families, fathered children, and intertwined themselves with local hunting bands. Indeed, many of them were children of these marriages, though such unions were frowned upon by the HBC as being detrimental to its business and to discipline. This, however, does not seem to have modified behaviour. "I have to inform you that Joseph B. Aideeson has thought proper for to take an Indian woman for a wife and T.J. Beads has done the same," wrote William McKay to his superiors about a breach of company rules, "this is a thing they have done entirely without any permission from me whatever – indeed I never expected that any thing of the kind would happen in such a manner." His shock at the men's behaviour is somewhat disingenuous, given that he himself married a Native woman, and the fact is that, over time, sanctioned or not, most HBC servants and traders became involved with Native women in eastern James Bay.[36]

There were all kinds of reasons, having to do with the requirements of trade and subsistence, for these men and women to marry and set up households. We know the men had to rely on their own hunting and that these marriages were part of this need. Having a wife who had the skills to aid in subsistence was certainly vital as women netted snowshoes, sewed moccasins and clothing, and prepared food. This would seem to have been a motivation for all men to find wives, especially since many of them trapped fur and would have relied on women to prepare these catches. Wives also created a network of relationships with their families, and this helped HBC traders in their quest for furs. The traders that these women married benefited by their subsistence labour and their trade connections; in return, the women lived under somewhat physically easier circumstances than did their counterparts in the bush. All of this is pertinent, but there are other reasons why hunters would have seen these marriages as important.[37]

Individual women became attached to HBC men and HBC posts, but they did not leave the Native environment permanently as they, like their husbands, travelled back and forth and, at times, lived with them in the bush. In this way, Native gender expectations affected the traders out in the bush, providing yet another reason for the need to be married to a Native woman. As we have seen, gender roles were important with regard to the relationship between the animals and the hunt. There were powerful assumptions regarding how and by whom the hunted would be turned into food, and traders were no doubt pressured by the imperatives of these Native spaces. Everybody's luck depended on behaving properly towards the animals, and a fur trader without a wife would have been a cultural liability when he came for a prolonged stay in the bush. The human and other-than-human worlds were in a precise relationship, and when the trader became a hunter, he had to work within the framework of the Cree relationship to the land. Marriage to Native women certainly aided the trade, gave alternatives to Native women, and eased the work of the trader within the post environment, but it also maintained the balance of the hunt out in the bush and tied the posts and bush more closely together than ever.[38]

All of this added up to hunters' having a great deal of leverage in their interactions with the posts, and though I said earlier that confrontation was not the norm, it was in moments of confrontation that we can see how clearly these men understood their position. We can also see how exasperated some traders became as they tried both to survive and to do the HBC's business in a relationship that could be neither avoided nor controlled. James Fogget, for instance, fumed impotently at one old hunter, complaining bitterly that

> all the rest of the Indians went off except the Great Captain Caumuscasse who I could not get off, he says 'tis his ground and he'll not go away for me. He is one of the most useless Indians I ever saw [i.e., he did not put a priority on fur]. He don't kill 10 beaver in the course of a winter and the summer he'll plant (if possible) his tent close to the gate, carouse and drink with every one that comes and tell them the master gives nothing to the Indians and why do they come here to trade. The Canadians [the NWC] are coming here soon then we shall get everything for [the] asking.[39]

The flavour of the scene is near comic, with Caumuscasse having not only a clear understanding of trade independence and the rivalry between the whites but also a pretty clear sense of land rights and personal independence. Fogget was out of his depth and needed to heed the advice of more experienced traders. "I do not think they are disposed to admit of any right which a European can possibly have to control them on their own grounds," wrote Joseph Beioley, "much less do I suppose that – if intimated to them – they would submit to any assumed authority to remove them from their lands to others against their own wills." In many respects, nothing has changed, and both these sentiments might easily be paraphrased in the mouths of Canadian and Québécois politicians today as they seek accommodations from the Cree. And the Cree continue to balance powers against one another to maintain cultural independence. Clearly, the long history of negotiation is still going on.[40]

The first thing to note is that, for hunters, the most basic way of maintaining their negotiating position was simply to concentrate on hunting food before hunting fur and to maintain the fundamental understanding between human to other-than-human as they dealt with the otherness of the fur trade. "Really I do not know what to do with my Indians," wrote Chilton, "for they do not hunt as much furs as to buy their mere necessaries which occasions me to supply them ... which involves them in such debt." His hunters were hunting food but still wanted goods, which he could not deny them because he needed food. Putting these goods on the books as debt did not guarantee that the fur would come in later. This was the other side of the reciprocity ledger, which was vital to Chilton but could not be justified to his superiors. The balance between food and fur was easily disrupted, as Erland Erlandson found when he induced his hunters to trap martins in the early part of one winter. "Subsequently some of them were starved [went very hungry]," he wrote, "which they blamed on me, saying, that I enticed them to hunt furs when they could have killed abundance of deer – they then came to me, not only expecting, but demanding food which I was unable to supply them." Frustrated though he might have been, there was little he could do, and both his trade and subsistence suffered through this mistake.[41]

The fact is that it was not within the trader's power to push hunters farther than they wished to go. This was not only because of the trader's need for food but also because he had to balance his actions against the hunter's other trading options. James Clouston, for example, reported that the bad conduct of the trader who had been at Neoskweskau before him was compromising his own position there. The hunters were, in fact, avoiding the post. They had paid their debts the year before but had not received the usual presents from Alexander McElwin, and so they were now planning to go down towards Lac St. Jean. The effect of this was not only a great reduction in trade but also a shortage of food for the men at the post. Clouston had to actively convince the locals that things would change, and, of course, actions speak louder than words. The same held true in 1825, when the hunter Chiptapewit told James Robertson and Robert Chilton that he would "not go to Waswannipie again, because [he had been] ill treated the last time ... and could not get nothing. The master having gone down and locked up the goods and taken the key of the store away." Chiptapewit was not upset because the trader was absent but, rather, because the store was locked so that he could not serve himself. There is much evidence of hunters' taking things on the honour system, and Chiptapewit clearly felt offended by the actions of this particular trader. It was only after some talk that Chiptapewit gave his furs to Robertson. He told Robertson to bring a gun and ammunition to Rush Lake in April and that he would later make up his mind about going back to Waswanipi.[42]

What was really problematic for the traders was the fact that, despite some protests, it was characteristic for most hunters to react to problems in an understated manner that was more than likely expressed in quiet actions rather than in words. Early on at Neoskweskau, for example, John Clarke looked forward to a bad year's trading because "the Indians went off last spring much dissatisfied, so much, that some of them took their furs back and went off toward the Canadians." There were no hard words or displays of anger, but this was a truly confrontational thing to do, and Clarke clearly knew the strength of the hunters' feelings. When hunters at Mistassini were only allowed necessities in advance of payment of their furs "they never expressed any dissatisfaction," wrote John Walford, though he had "not seen them since." Most hunters did not get mad or even express displeasure; they simply created new relationships at Lac St. Jean, across the height of land, until they had made their point and things at the posts were changed.[43]

Neither Walford nor Clarke stayed long at their posts, and such person-nel changes were tied to an aspect of the fur trade story that we have already seen – the ability of traders to adapt to local expectations of friendship and reciprocity. When the hunter Otaspaupan came to visit Nitchequon, purposely without his furs, and found Robert Chilton in charge rather than John Spencer, he came back a day later with forty Made Beaver[44] worth of trade. He told Chilton that he had intended to go south to the St. Lawrence until he found that Spencer was no longer in charge and had been replaced by his friend. On another occasion, William McKay went after the hunter Catspitsway to bring him goods that he knew he needed because the trader had been away from the post when the hunter came in for supplies. There was a friendship between the two men, and McKay travelled 190 kilometres to catch up to him, partly to avoid committing the kind of offence I mentioned above. While he was at Catspitsway's camp he stayed and helped with hunting deer – "to please them for the sake of drawing their attachments toward the Honorable Company's Servants" he told his superiors, though he also took a good share of the meat back to the post. He had many things on his mind, and undoubtedly Catspitsway did as well: trade, food, friendship all played a role in the negotiation.[45]

There are always multiple aspects to these interactions, and it is interesting to watch a negotiation like this unfold over a prolonged period. In 1861, for instance, the hunter Toopass informed Mistassini trader Angus Macleod that he was going to Lac St. Jean to get a double-barrelled gun from the post there. Macleod was not pleased by the news, writing reluctantly that, "so long as he paid the advances ... I would not place any obstacle from following the bent of his own Inclinations." There were in fact few obstacles Macleod could put in his way, though, interestingly, it took Toopass two years to actually get around to making the trip for the gun. Macleod seemed to think that Toopass was seeking some kind of blessing for his trip, but it was more likely that he was trying to make a point. In 1862, Macleod and Toopass were still talking about whether or not the latter should go, and Macleod used all his rhetorical skills to get him to stay. He tried to point out how badly off the hunters in the south were in comparison to those attached to the HBC. Toopass thought those concerns unfounded, as he did Macleod's argument that the HBC gave better presents. Macleod wrote that the hunter "said it was very true that 'they got large presents yet those presents will fall very short of what I would get for my furs on the other side tho I would receive no premiums.'" He pressed Macleod to consider how he treated his hunters, but Macleod would not budge. The next June, Toopass made his decision. He visited Mistassini briefly but left his furs in the bush and travelled south during the summer, arriving back at the post on July 13, 1863, with his double-barrelled gun, cloth, tea, and sugar. After this successful trip, Toopass was far less willing to listen to Macleod, telling him "'you want always to keep me from going to where I can get more for my furs ... look at this (pointing to his double barrel gun) for this gun I did not give quite four female martins and to get it such a gun from you I would have to give you Eighty of them or forty male ones' of course [said Macleod] there was no answering such statements."

The strain between Macleod and Toopass speaks to a changed and less meaningful relationship between the two,[46] and the trader's unwillingness to listen or be moved is telling. Macleod, who seems to have been an outsider (he never married and travelled frequently to the coast), had replaced William McKay at Mistassini in 1855. He was free to travel and try to change the trade relationship with his hunters because, by that point, Mistassini had become far more independent thanks to gardening. Most hunters, like Toopass, fought against this change, but their leverage decreased over time as these posts succeeded in creating part of their subsistence by means other than the hunt. This change in the traders' subsistence had been evolving for decades and had reached maturity by the middle of the century.

For the HBC traders, using the environment meant salting fish and storing game, but it also increasingly meant working to grow small crops around the posts. The record shows that hunters worked to include these places within the conceptual world of the hunt; but agriculture, more than any other activity, changed the environmental relationship wherever it was successful and worked against that inclusion. Traders were practical in their thinking and writing about crops; they were not terribly conscious of the conceptual aspects of this activity, but gardening changed the seasonal rhythm of life around the posts and was the foundation for some of the cultural differences that mark them as places apart. Here, as with so much about the James Bay region, both the limits of European activity and the slow process of development give us a window into the various ways that cultures worked on each other and their surroundings.[47]

Gardening was tried everywhere but was never sustainable in the north or east because of the lack of soil and the severity of the winter. To use Temiskamay Post as an example again, Alexander Collie attempted to plant a small garden on the first of May, 1828, but a hard frost in early July froze the crop solid. The next spring James Clouston, then in charge of the post, ordered 15 litres of seed potatoes from Mistassini, noting that they should "be brought with care without having them injured by frost." They arrived safely but to no great end. By the fall of 1830, the next trader was only able to collect a bushel of potatoes, the largest of which was "the size of a musquet ball." These are only passing mentions of horticultural attempts recorded in daily journals that recount how hard the men worked to catch fish and to hunt for themselves. For the thirty-five years that the post remained at Temiskamay, food had to be gathered off the land or hauled upriver from the coast. The same was true of Nitchequon, Neoskweskau, and Kaniapiskau posts. At these places little mention was made of any gardening, and then only to report its failure. One October, when Clouston was at Neoskweskau Post, he shovelled snow from his garden only to find most of his small crop dead and blackened from the cold. And even as Robert Chilton was asking to be relieved from Nitchequon Post in 1862, he was trying to grow potatoes there with no success. Thirty years earlier, James Kellock had summed up the farming possibilities at Nitchequon in one brief sentence: "from the shortness of the summer in this quarter it must prove unfarmable to vegetation – and there is very little probability of potatoes coming to maturity."[48]

Circumstances were different moving west towards the coast of James Bay and south towards the watershed with the St. Jean Valley or Ontario. Here, in places, there was good clay soil along with wetlands and tidal hay fields. There is a marked contrast of soil types approaching the height of land, and, as Surveyor J.M. Bell noted later in the nineteenth century, the trader at New Post, to the south of Moose Factory, was able to grow not only potatoes but also sweet corn and pumpkins in his garden. Where "the soil is nearly all clay," Bell concluded, "the advantages of the country passed through today would be in its agricultural possibilities." Bell was overly optimistic: nobody in the area expected real farming to take hold, but gardening as a supplement to other activities was a practical idea.[49]

From the eighteenth century onward, HBC traders exploited limited agricultural potential. At Eastmain House good potato and turnip crops were grown in the sandy soil, which added to the abundance of strawberries and currants as well as to the rhubarb that was cultivated. By the 1790s at Rupert's House and Eastmain House there were not only crops but also a large number of cattle, which had been imported and bred in the country. With the use of local hay, large numbers of cattle could be kept on the coast. By 1822, there was a full-time cattle keeper at the post, and Rupert House had fifteen cows, which Joseph Beioley reported as being too many for the existing resources. By 1877, however, Eastmain House had fifty-eight cattle, thirty-eight sheep, and one horse, and Rupert's House was also counting animals in the dozens. As early as the 1820s, the summer season on the coast came to revolve both around the trade with the Natives and the agricultural cycle. Not only potatoes but also barley, cabbages, turnips, onions, and radishes were being grown there, and gardens were fertilized with animal waste. The traders were even burning and slaking lime for fertilizer.[50]

Inland the development of agriculture lagged, but crops and livestock were eventually successful at Mistassini, Pike Lake, and Waswanipi posts. At smaller posts, like Big Lake and Rush Lake (both of which were closed shortly after the merger with the NWC), gardening also succeeded. At Pike Lake, gardening succeeded until the post was closed in 1860, when Thomas Moar was ordered to abandon the house (but not, so the orders stipulated, before digging up the potatoes and bringing them down to Waswanipi). Men worked hard to establish gardens and to bring crops to harvest, and even if the trade at a post was abandoned, the potatoes would not be.[51]

Traders struggled for years before getting their crops to grow. Gardening at Mistassini Post was attempted repeatedly from 1816 to 1822. Bringing up seed potatoes undamaged from the coast and keeping them unharmed by

frosts over the winter was the first challenge. In 1823, John Walford successfully raised three bushels but reported the next September that "the Frost
has completely spoiled most of the Potatoes and as for the turnips most
of them have not grown at all – Altho the weather has been very warm
latterly the nights have been cold with slight frosts." The chief traders on
the coast at Rupert's House were ever mindful of the potential boon of
potatoes and urged continued attempts to grow them in order to lessen
what they perceived as the "enormous quantities of grain" they had to ship
in annually up from the coast.[52]

Cold and frost were not the only obstacles to gardening in this marginal
area as the soil itself offered its own kind of trouble. It was a mixture of
clay and sand, which could be productive if tilled, but that was the difficulty: it was difficult even to sink a spade into the ground, and, as John
Walford complained, "all the ground about the house [being] full of half
decayed stumps of trees ... there is infinite labor and trouble in clearing
it and preparing it for cultivation." All the traders worked hard to establish their small plots, and they regularly pointed out this labour to their
superiors. In his 1827 annual report, James Kellock chose to underline an
entire paragraph describing the effort he put into getting fifty-six bushels
of potatoes. But by the 1830s, thanks to hard work, Mistassini Post was
raising a hundred bushels of potatoes in a season, and this would remain
stable for the rest of the nineteenth century. The periodic infestations of
grubs were a continuing problem that could hurt the year's production,
but once the soil was tilled and fertilized it remained productive. Cows and
chickens produced manure for the gardens as well as providing a limited
supply of meat. At Mistassini Post it is difficult to ascertain how many
animals were kept over the course of the nineteenth century, but it seems
to have been far fewer than were kept at Rupert's House or Waswanipi
Post. They also seem to have been brought to Mistassini Post only in the
1850s and 1860s, whereas at Waswanipi Post they were clearly established
by the 1820s.[53]

The soils at Waswanipi Post were even better than were those at Mistassini Post. Early on, Jacob Corrigal optimistically assessed the potential
potato crop, calling the ground "excellent for that invaluable vegetable."
In that same year, he reported that he killed two of his six cattle for want
of winter fodder, thus adding to his meat supply. From the early 1820s,
both cattle and gardening played a vital role in the trade at Waswanipi
Post. This was both because the post was close to the coast and because, in
many years, the growing season started at the end of April. By the 1840s,
work at this post came to revolve around the fertilizing, planting, fencing,

Year	Fish (kegs)	Potatoes (bushels)	Hay (bundles)	Beef (pounds)
1821	16			
1822	28			
1823	13		100	"*little*"
1824	28		1,500	300
1825			750	230
1826				
1827				
1828		7.5		
1829				
1830				
1831				
1832		51		
1833		31		340
1834				
1835		102		
1836				
1837	21	30	1,600	600
1838				
1839			1,830	
1840		119		
1841	45	155	1,846	
1842		33	1,960	
1843			2,014	
1844	45	77	1,150	418
1845	40	64	1,935	
1846		34	2,020	
1847	42	50	2,630	
1848	32	61	1,700	588
1849	37	38	2,192	
1850	35	59	2,040	300
1851		60	1,863	
1852				
1853		168	3,310	
1854		230		300
1855				662
1856	42	204	2,534	
1857	45	232	3,260	
1858	50	98	3,290	709
1859				
1860	56	368		596
1861	63	285	3,000	756
1862	59	207	2,400	306
1863	80	234	3,582	
1864	64	248	3,229	164
1865				
1866	60		3,733	800
1867				
1868				
1869	33	219	4,578	295

TABLE 3.1 *Waswanipi farming output, 1821-69.* This table shows the increasing amount of agricultural surplus being produced at Waswanipi in the nineteenth century; this upward trend marked an increased self-sufficiency at the post, which was similar to other posts in the southern part of the region. After 1825, the journals record that all these products were being produced on a yearly basis, though in many years no numerical accounting was made; this production continued to the end of the century and into the early twentieth as well. *Library and Archives Canada, Hudson's Bay Company, Waswanapi Journals, MG 20, B227/a, vols. 1-53*

and harvesting of the gardens, and each fall saw both fishing and the collection of wild grass for cattle fodder. Hundreds of bushels of potatoes were grown and thousands of bundles of hay were cut and dried each year at Waswanipi.[54]

By then the cattle at Waswanipi Post, which James Kellock called a "tolerably certain resource," were also providing hundreds of pounds of beef on a yearly basis along with valuable fertilizer. The meat was lean, "the poorest beef ever I saw," he reported, but when the most salt pork that could be expected from the coast was four or five barrels for the winter, even poor beef was desirable. The cattle were kept on an island during the summer, and fodder only appears to have been a problem in years when high water flooded the wetlands where the wild grasses grew. In times of shortage, cattle were fed willow tops and even cedar brush in order to keep them over the winter. Slaughtering was carried out yearly, but some animals had to be wintered over as the only way to get new ones from Rupert's House was to send the young up in the yearly canoe – an intriguingly tricky business.[55]

Agriculture thus created another layer of subsistence at posts where it was successful. Nowhere did it eliminate the desire for hunted food, but the need was softened. Bad gardening years and bad hunting years rarely coincided, and so traders had not only food for themselves but also another product that could be given in times of real need. Agriculture did not eliminate the reciprocal food exchanges between the traders and the Cree hunters, but it did begin to change the meaning of that relationship. By the 1860s, aspects of a relationship that had begun in the eighteenth century were changing, and, for many, the agricultural calendar was now just as important as was the hunting cycle. Over the course of the late nineteenth century, these changes would relate directly to challenges faced by Cree hunters in James Bay.

Particularly on the coast, and at the more agricultural posts inland, some Cree became part of the local workforce and did not make long forays into the bush even in the winter, even though this could have serious consequences if the local food supply failed. Most hunters, however, continued to make a seasonal trip to the posts and some stayed away far longer. In 1857, the hunter Nahnepahnew came to Nitchequon Post for the first time in five years, not having been to any post for the previous two years. This was not uncommon, though during these absences many of these hunters were undoubtedly still living in the general region, quite possibly trading goods with other Natives rather than with the HBC. Clearly, they were maintaining their independence by continuing both

FIGURE 3.2   *Waswanipi Post, circa 1920.* This picture of Waswanipi was taken in the 1920s, before the region was accessible by plane. Notice the fenced gardens around the main building, which were important for potato production. The building in the background with the white door is the Catholic Church; the others are the bunkhouse and various outbuildings for animals and storage. The post had likely changed little in the preceding seventy-five years. *Library and Archives Canada*

their hunting and its cultural narrative away from the trading posts. But things were changing for these people too. It was not so much that hunting culture was changing as that the hunters' ability to engage with traders was changing. Agriculture never reorganized the landscape in James Bay as it did in so many other places in North America, but it did free traders from some of their dependence on hunters.[56]

What's interesting in looking at agriculture in this setting is how disconnected it is from so many of the cultural expectations that usually surround it. Fur traders did not think of their gardens as a way of reshaping their economic relationship to the land or as the foundation for a new kind of community. This was a new application of technology that created different food and allowed traders to change their relationship to hunters in the bush; yet, they never echoed Reverend E.A. Watkins' declaration that potatoes were "a luxury" and a clear link to a more civilized way of life. For Watkins there was an obvious connection between the application of agriculture to the land and the narrative of a Christian life. He was not alone in thinking this, but in James Bay these two things were never connected in any real sense. Christianity is, however, important to the history of the region and the Cree relationship to their land. I have intimated that changes were in the making for people and land in the region, but before any discussion of that change, another aspect of life here must be addressed. Watkins' Christian narrative is important as it not only relates in some ways to the discussion above but also has its own relevance to the people and land of James Bay.[57]

Earlier, I used Robert and Betsy Chilton as examples, and perhaps this is a good place both to end this discussion of early fur trade posts and to begin a discussion of the more narrative aspects of change in James Bay in the nineteenth century. Robert Chilton had gone to England with his father, presumably to be educated as some other Natives of the Country had been, but he chose to return to the James Bay region and to take up a place close to the hunter's world. And he was not alone in this kind of choice. He had been criticized in his youth for being too interested in socializing with Cree hunters, and he seems to have remained close to their culture throughout his life. Betsy Chilton, for her part, chose to live as a fur trader's wife, but her siblings lived in the bush where she visited them, and it is hard to say that she made a clear choice to leave Native life for life at the post. The lives of both Chiltons were lived between two worlds that existed side by side and that invested each other with meaning. Both husband and wife seem to have found meaning in both places. A final story serves as an illustration and as a bridge to the topic of religion in James Bay.[58]

In the latter part of August 1851, Betsy Chilton came back from Rupert's House to the post at Nichicun. She was originally from Rupert's House, and she was in the habit of visiting her family at the bay during the summer when the trade went down to the coast. Those who went to the coast in the summer often came back with sicknesses that, each year, ran their course in the small community. That year Betsy became so ill that she was convinced that she was going to die. When she came to that realization, she asked her husband to put up a tent into which she could move to spend her final days. In his journal, Robert Chilton simply recorded, "self and two Roberts made a billet tent for poor afflicted Mrs. Chilton for she would rather stop in a tent than in a house." She moved into her tent and asked to see her brother Thomas Beads. When he arrived they visited and talked for an extended period of time within that Native space. Betsy Chilton did not die that September: she lived at least until 1877, when Robert Bell of the geological survey met her when she was living once again at Rupert's House, but her retreat into a Native tent was a significant act. Her decision to do this provides us with an entry into a cultural environment that existed outside of the fur trade posts, even for someone who had chosen to live her life within the stockade walls of that hybrid world.[59]

Betsy Chilton found some meaning within the context of the Cree environment, and the continued meaning of this cultural space – both physical and conceptual – is an important part of the story of James Bay. At what she thought was the end of her life, Betsy found meaning in the physical surroundings of a Native tent and in the company of part of her extended family. The fur trade post had offered her a quality of material life that she would not have had had she chosen to live in the bush; still, it seems that it did not offer her anything meaningful when it came to facing death. But what of her involvement with Christianity? She and Robert had taken up Christianity in the previous decade, and, on her trips to Rupert's House, she probably held hopes of seeing the missionary there. Unlike the fur trade, Christianity could offer meaning to someone facing the end of her life. If Betsy Chilton did look to Christianity in her sickness, and it would seem likely that she did, the fact that she did so within the context of her Native surroundings would make her emblematic of other Cree and their interaction with this Western religion. Christianity is the next facet of life in James Bay that needs to be examined as it had and continues to have a great deal of meaning for the Cree in the region. Like the trade with the HBC, Christianity both shaped the hunters and was, in turn, shaped by them. It, like the trade, was something that brought new people and new ideas into the region and forced the hunters and their families to find ways of dealing with change. Unlike the trade, however, it was a powerful narrative force that was concerned with shaping the Cree's relationship to their conceptual world.

4

Christians and Cree

*Ooskidae told me that when he could get nothing for food that
he did not forget God and when in distress he always found how
good it was to call upon him, as by doing so he was enabled to
keep him[self] from despondency and was likewise certain of
finding something or other.*

— *Reverend John Horden,*
Horden Journal, *1853*[1]

By definition, any discussion of Christianity and missionary activity
among Native people occurs on contested and worried ground
both with regard to the history of contact in North America and
with regard to present-day politics. This fact is far more a part of the Canadian popular consciousness than the American as, in Canada, abuse in
government-funded and missionary-run Native residential schools has
reached the same level of scandal as have abuses committed by Roman
Catholic priests in the United States. Americans ought to be far more
aware of the abuses in their past – the legacy is long and shameful on both
sides of the border – as residential schools attempted to strip Native children of their cultural identity (clothing, language, religion) and remake
them into whites. "Kill the Indian and save the man" was the motto of
Pennsylvania's Carlyle School and the sentiment was nearly universal. This
kind of program, which like so many other sad parts of history was
mostly carried out by otherwise decent people, left generations of wounded children who had trouble fitting into either world. And, of course, not
everyone involved was an "otherwise decent" person: many children suffered physical, sexual, and psychological abuse in these schools in addition
to cultural dislocation. Neither Canadians nor Americans like to think
about their societies being involved in this kind of cleansing, but it is part
of our respective histories.

I don't want to turn away from this issue in discussing eastern James Bay as many Cree, along with Native people all over Canada, are seeking reparations for what they suffered in these schools; I also do not want to make it the focus of my discussion of religion in the James Bay region. In the history of the Cree and their land there are far older and more lasting features to their interaction with Christianity than those associated with residential schools, and I want to focus on the meaning of the former rather than the tragedies of the latter. There can be no clear separation between the Cree and the missionaries as my window into this world is almost exclusively through the journals and letters of missionaries; they – their actions and desires – must be considered, even if they are not the focus of the story. For the Cree, residential schools are a twentieth-century event, an aspect of their history; but Christianity was a part of their history long before this, and it is a part of their present as well. Both these facts must be borne in mind.[2]

I was in Mistissini recently, and I happened to be there on a day when people were making ready to greet members of the community who had been on a winter journey in the bush. Out behind the police station two big, lodge-sized tents were set up, and people were gathering to cook moose and caribou while they waited. Everyone was welcome, even the white guy who showed up just in time for a free meal – some things never change – and the atmosphere was upbeat and expectant, even though it was spitting snow and the wind was a little cold. Someone had a boombox going and it was playing religious music. Some of it was pretty corny – "I'm drinking from my saucer Lord, 'cause my cup has overflowed" – but it was a genuine part of this scene. Many of the people in town are devout Christians, and while this sort of song may not be everyone's cup of tea, the expression of faith is accepted. When the walkers arrived, they were taken into the larger of the two tents and given food and ceremonially welcomed home. At the start of the ceremony, one of the elders was asked to give a prayer, which he did, with both the usual soft-spoken Cree inflection and a great deal of emotion. It was in Cree, and I only caught a few words, not enough to get a sense of what the prayer was about, but I was struck by how well it fit with the setting, which was such a mixture of old and new, of "traditional" and "modern." This expression of faith did not seem to be imposed on this ceremonial meal of food from the land, and, in talking about Christianity in this region, I want to find some historical foundations for that prayer and its meaning within a modern setting.

As with the discussion of the fur trade, so with the discussion of Christianity: some basic points are important. First, missionaries were never more than a token presence in eastern James Bay. Christianity helped to shape this region and its people, but it was not imposed by missionaries. The record is full of moments of cultural imposition, but they are not the most meaningful moments. Second, Christianity is clearly still a powerful force in Cree culture. Many Cree are still Anglican, but many are now Pentecostal, and if the goal is to connect past with present, then something more sophisticated than an argument about cultural hegemony is required. I want to keep the words of Native author Stan MacKay in mind when he equates Natives with Old Testament people who also came out of an oral tradition. In his estimation, Natives have internalized Christianity, making it their own. "We, like Moses," he writes, "know about the sacredness of the earth and the promise of land. Our creation stories also emphasize the power of the Creator and the goodness of creation. We can relate to the vision of Abraham and the laughter of Sarah. We have dreams like Ezekiel and have known people like Pharaoh." He is speaking about the modern Christian Native experience, but, in many respects, his words are applicable to the past as well. The fact that missionaries were scarce and that Christianity was important to the Cree helps to redefine some of the usual perceptions about religion and Native people.[3]

Shortly after his arrival in the James Bay area in 1853, John Horden recorded the hunter Ooskidae's profession "that he did not forget God." Horden was pleased by this seeming faith in God's ability to provide; thanking God for one's daily bread – a powerful cultural metaphor – was, after all, one of the more important expressions of his own faith. He did not believe that this made Ooskidae, or any of the Cree in James Bay, truly Christian, but he did believe that they were a well-meaning people who desired to be led to Christ. He had come to do just that, and over the course of his nearly fifty-year career in the region, he worked diligently with a small group of others to attempt the religious education of the Cree. Like fur traders before them, missionaries had to find a place in James Bay from which they could work. They had to stake out some territory within the Cree environment, and, for them, this was more a narrative than a geographic location. The nature of their work was conceptual and was related to a reality in the bush that they often found disturbing, and it involved them in a negotiation with the Cree over ideas rather than over the mundane aspects of trade. Of course, the Cree engaged in a fair amount of negotiation over meaning with traders, but their negotiations with missionaries were on a more abstract plane and concerned core beliefs.[4]

Missionaries related more peripherally to the Cree hunt for food than did the traders; they were often fed by the hunt but rarely did they involve themselves directly in hunting. They related differently because they had not come to take away furs and use the Native economy but, rather, to bring a new narrative of humanity's place in the cosmic order. They thought of themselves as part of a larger story – Christian missionaries spoke of a world within the greater context of God's dominion – a story into which the Cree could be written if their work and faith were blessed and their hearts could be opened to the story's truth. This was largely a process of changing individuals, and much of what the missionaries desired for the Cree has all the usual overtones of cultural imperialism. The Cree provided a symbolically sophisticated audience for these new storytellers, however, and none of the parties, or the story itself, remained unchanged.

Ooskidae's expression of faith was not likely as simple as Horden believed it to be, nor were the Cree as simple in their beliefs as the missionaries thought. Ooskidae lived with the land and its potential in ways that Horden did not at first understand and that, when he did begin to understand, he was not pleased by. Ooskidae – expressing hope in God in order to hold off despondency regarding the hunt – opens a small window onto some of the ways that Christianity might have aided the hunter, might have bolstered the hope and personal control that the hunter had to maintain in relation to his lands and the animals upon which he depended. This was a reinterpretation of the Christian message, largely beyond the missionaries' control or understanding, and central to the historical meaning of Christianity in the region. This reinterpretation is important to understanding the meaning that Christianity continues to play in many Cree people's lives today because, if many Cree became Christians, it is likely because Christianity, in its turn, became very Cree.[5]

"I have spoke to him [God]," a hunter told missionary George Barnley, "I speak to him in Indian." Whatever words were spoken to or about God in James Bay were spoken in Cree, and Christian ideas and meanings thus fit within a pre-existing narrative web. This man was interested in Christianity, but he was also interested in Barnley's teaching one of his children to read and write the Cree language. Indeed, the importance of literacy to the Cree is another central aspect of our examination of religion in James Bay. Many Cree grasped immediately the potential power of both the Christian message and the written word, and this led them to set about establishing a relationship with the missionaries. They understood too that, like all relationships of power, the missionaries might be friends and allies, but they might also present problematic demands. This was a different, albeit analogous, set of problems to those of the fur trade, and the solution was a similar form of cultural negotiation in which the Cree language and Cree concepts were central.[6]

Reverend William Walton saw the centrality of Cree concepts. Speaking of his years in James Bay, he wrote that a successful missionary had to "readjust his own mind to the mental attitude of his Native charges. For his preconceived notions just don't fit in." A simple problem involved the Cree habit of ignoring those who could not speak their language. But it was more than this. "The missionary," Walton continued, "must not only learn the language of his charges thoroughly; he must go deeper – find the various connotations which they attach to certain of their words. Lacking this knowledge, he is likely to fumble broken-heartedly for years." Walton's comments show a cultural sophistication that sounds almost modern, though he did not accept the validity of these Cree interpretations – only the need to understand them. The Cree idiom was as vital to the missionary effort as was the Cree language because the goal was to change that idiom. This posed the largest challenge to missionaries who were trying to transfer Western religious concepts into a complex system of thought. Simple answers would not work.[7]

"It was chiefly by signs that I elicited most of what I learned from them," wrote a breathless F. Hamilton Fleming in 1859, "and this was a most difficult thing to do correctly, on account of the many different ways in which signs, to which they were unaccustomed, might be understood by them: when I wanted to tell them how the Saviour died – that he was crucified, I had first to obtain their word for cross." Fleming wanted the Cree to see the meaning of the crucifixion, salvation, and redemption, but even communicating the material meaning of a cross was difficult: "this I strove to do by picking up off the floor two bits of stick and placing them together in the form of a cross." When he asked them what they would call it, "they gave [him] the word for a bit of stick." Undiscouraged, Fleming struggled for basic definitions while trying to communicate the larger, abstract symbolism of crucifixion for he had faith that, if simple definitions could be made clear, then the larger message would follow. He showed the Natives two sticks, placing them together repeatedly, and then asked what they would call that figure. This time they dutifully gave him the word for "putting together." When he got a piece of chalk and drew a cross on the wall, they gave him the word for "chalk marks." "I at length obtained the word for cross," Fleming concluded, "by first getting the word for *figure* which I did by drawing the likeness of a man. I then got a nail and told them how wicked men had crucified Jesus, and at the same time strove to make it clear to them that he bore it willingly to save them and all men from the bad fire and take them to live in heaven with himself. I am sure they understood me and that God was blessing my poor labours."[8]

The cognitive leap here is comical, and it is difficult to imagine the Cree interpretation of this exchange, though if the Cree had as wry a sense of humour then as they do now, I can guess at it. Local custom would have demanded trying to help the stranger, generally trying to agree with him in order to avoid any conflict; but, despite Fleming's faith, there was clearly a failure to communicate. The Cree were tolerant of outsiders who did not speak their language, but they did not go out of their way to communicate outside of their language either. From trader and missionary alike, they demanded at least competence in Cree, and Walton's emphasis on the Cree idiom is clearly understandable in light of Fleming's experience. Missionaries always had to come to grips with the meaning into which they entered, and this meant a solid grounding in the language.[9]

In this respect, missionaries had to interact with Native culture on an intellectual plane that traders did not. The trader, embedded in Cree culture though he may have been, was involved in subsisting and reshaping fur-hunting behaviour while the missionary was involved in something more conceptual. Consciously or unconsciously, missionaries tried to change Cree behaviour to match their own notions of humanity's proper role in the world. This is something the traders did not do. When Natives came to visit the missionaries, their actions were interpreted through an outside lens that was more powerful than that used by the HBC men. Traders described Native behaviour while missionaries more often tried to explain it and fit it into their narrative understanding. They were far more likely than were traders to try to see Native actions as part of some larger divine plan or as a test of their own faith and desire to serve God.

This is not to say that missionaries were disinterested in changing subsistence behaviour. In the beginning, missionaries hoped in vain to bring some kind of settled agriculture to James Bay, building on the traders' limited success. David Lofthouse, the first bishop of Rupert's Land, noted with some hope that Moose Factory was "more like an English village" than any other place along the Eastmain coast, even while admitting that there was little hope for real settlement even there. "And yet," he wrote, "I am convinced that the work will be more permanent, and the gospel take deeper root, when the people are settled with something to bind and connect them with the soil." Lofthouse found it difficult to separate his religion from the environmental relationship that supported it, and he did not recognize the meaningful bonds of the hunt. He was based in the

Red River Colony, where the changes he sought were bearing fruit, and he, like Watkins in the last chapter, made a deep connection between the Christian faith and agriculture, even as he bowed to its impossibility in James Bay.[10]

Agriculture, nevertheless, was a part of the missionary narrative, and hunters picked up on this in some ironic ways. After preaching to a group of hunters at Moose Factory in 1853, John Horden quizzed them on what they had learned. He asked one older man what Jesus had done on earth and, to his great distress, the man told him that Jesus had "tilled the ground." The hunter had missed or ignored Horden's explicit religious message, but he clearly understood the implicit cultural message. Horden presented agriculture as the ideal – at bottom he believed that nomads could never really be Christian – even as he held no hope of turning the Cree themselves into farmers. It is interesting that, for these hunters, Christianity's meaning needed some local connection with the land and by the time Horden and others arrived it had already been made. It is impossible to say, but the meaning that Job Bearskin gave to the garden metaphor may have already been developing by then, though Horden and his fellows were not equipped to see it.[11]

By Horden's arrival, Christian ideas had been loose upon the land for generations, and, while the early chronology of Christianity in James Bay is vague, its longevity is important. Protestant missionary involvement began in 1840, with the arrival of Reverend George Barnley, and he was the first to live here year-round. Barnley, however, did not bring Christianity to the Cree, nor did the HBC traders. Moving widely, as they did, over the whole of the Quebec-Labrador peninsula, the Cree were in trade contact with distant regions prehistorically, and it is likely that some hunters would have had contact with Jesuits from the earliest period. Certainly, by the middle of the seventeenth century the Cree knew of the Christian fathers in New France, and they, in turn, knew of the Cree.

In May 1661, Jesuits Claude Dablon and Gabriel Drueilletes travelled up the Saguenay River, through Lac St. Jean, to the height of land and a lake they called Nekouba. This was close to Lake Chamouchuane, though it is not clear if the latter was yet a place of trade. The *Relation* of 1660 intimates that the *Kilistinons* – one of several names given to the Cree – had come south and invited a missionary to travel back with them and that Dablon and Druceilletes had planned a trip as far as Hudson Bay. This, however, was the period when the Iroquois were still struggling with massive, disease-driven depopulation and were raiding even their distant neighbours for captives to replace the dead. The presence of Iroquois in

James Bay that year forced the fathers to turn back. Despite this setback, the Jesuits spent many days with their hosts at Nekouba at the edge of the James Bay region. In 1671, Charles Albanel became the first priest to reach the shores of the bay, and he travelled among the local hunters for months before he was taken prisoner by the English and removed from the region. Even with his removal, the Roman Catholic presence on the eastern edge of the region continued.[12]

The 1730 "Relation of the Saguenay," written by Pierre Laure, speaks to a full knowledge of the Cree who lived within easy reach of the watershed. The "Mistassins," he wrote, derived their name from "michta assini," the great rock with its petroglyphs that sits near the outflow to the Rupert River. The Cree venerated this rock, Laure thought, because they believed that it affected the weather on the lake, and they attempted to placate the power associated with it by leaving food or tobacco for the Manitou when travelling by it. Interestingly too, he wrote that this rock was where the Cree believed the great canoe had first landed after the Flood. Already Christian narrative had made its way into the landscape of the James Bay region, and new stories were finding a place in the local environment. By 1895, when trader Charles Gordon recorded the story of "The Indian Deluge" from a hunter at Rupert's House, it was believed that the flood had been caused because a man had killed too many fish and that all the local animals had been rescued. The story's resolution came with the active participation of these animals, who dived to recover the ball of earth from which all the land was recreated. The narrative sounds familiar in many ways, but the setting is local and the trope of hope and reciprocity is very Cree. Missionary J.A. Mackay rightly believed that these stories had been adopted from outside Cree culture long before the full-time missionary effort began in this region. He was less attentive to just how Cree these stories had become.[13]

With the end of the Jesuit mission in the 1760s, it becomes difficult to track the movement of Catholic missionaries in the region until the middle of the nineteenth century. It is known that occasional itinerants did still come through, and the Cree travelled south to trade and to see the priests on Lac St. Jean and the St. Lawrence. Their continued presence and importance was recognized when, in 1850, the HBC allowed Catholics to set up a seasonal mission at Waswanipi because so many of the local hunters were attached to the church and the people who represented it. In the nineteenth century Waswanipi was always marked by a large cross planted on a nearby hill by early priests. Later in the century, Catholics set up a mission at Fort George, and there is still a Catholic presence in James Bay.[14]

The first Protestant to arrive in James Bay was Wesleyan George Barnley, who came to live in the region in June 1840. He spent much of the next seven years in James Bay, but his work ended badly, with a psychological breakdown and nearly open warfare with HBC traders. Barnley is a fascinating character, but his story serves mostly to illustrate how cultural isolation resulted in failure. Barnley's failure to learn Cree or to gain knowledge of the daily meaning of hunters' lives left him isolated and unable to effect change. The Cree were interested in his spirituality; his Wesleyan zeal and his personal asceticism were compelling to them. But they seem to have been unable, in the end, to make a meaningful connection with him. To a great extent, Barnley was on a personal spiritual journey that never really included the Cree or had any relationship with James Bay.

It was Anglicans who came and stayed, developing a long relationship with Cree hunters. The Church Missionary Society (CMS), founded in 1801, began contemplating involvement in Rupert's Land almost immediately after the HBC merger with the NWC, and it was very critical of what it saw as the Church of England's complacency with regard to mission activity. The CMS wanted to use a more involved and emotional method to reach Natives, and booster Benjamin Harrison wrote to the society in 1822, insisting that the time was ripe for missionary work. "Opportunity is now afforded for every exertion," he told them, "and all the parties who have influence in that country appear ready to render their cordial cooperation in the plans under consideration for the extension of religious instruction, Civilization, and Education, over this immense extent of country." On the eastern side of Hudson and James bays this proved to be an overly ambitious expectation, and it took decades to organize. The HBC was in business for profit and had difficulty seeing religion as beneficial to that end. When it acquiesced, it saw the missionaries more as additional customers than as wards and did not hesitate to profit from their dependence.[15]

An Anglican mission finally arrived in the summer of 1851, and John Horden came to Moose Factory in June. He was only a catechist when he arrived, and his mission seems to have been rushed into existence to counter the Catholic Oblates at Waswanipi. Nevertheless, he spent the rest of his life in the region between Fort Severn and Little Whale, struggling constantly against a lack of resources and personnel. Even after Horden became the bishop of the newly created Diocese of Moosonee in 1872, eastern James Bay was often neglected, and the region became a missionary backwater within the greater world of Christian proselytizing. As late as 1898, Jervois Newnham, Horden's successor as bishop, complained that he needed another man to travel the region if any advance was going to be made in the mission. He offered to pay for another missionary out of diocese funds, and wrote somewhat bitterly that "the real facts seem to us to be that you can not spare a single man from the East [Asia] for our missions, except when you have one that seems hardly up to the full standard. 'Anything will do for N.W.A. [North West America]' is a statement that I have not seldom heard attributed to the minds of a good many of the committee." All this is important with regard to how Christianity developed as Native populations were smaller and more scattered than the missionaries had expected, and missionaries from England were always scarce.[16]

By 1900, there was only one English missionary left on the east side of James Bay from Great Whale River down to Moose Factory. Even at the high points there were never more than a handful of missionaries at any given time. Horden and E.A. Watkins began in the 1850s, with Horden at Moose Factory and Watkins at Fort George, but Watkins did not stay. E.J. Peck worked for several years to the north of Fort George during the 1880s, while Jonathan Keen worked for a few years to the south. William Walton began his thirty-two-year stay in Great Whale River and Fort George in 1892, and a small number of others worked for a year or two throughout the end of the nineteenth century. This lack of personnel can be explained because, as early as the 1850s, even as Horden was setting up in Moose Factory, missionary societies began to re-evaluate Native interest in conversion and the expense of the North American missions. African and Asian missions were far more successful, and a lack of tangible results in North America made it hard to raise money. This lack of money, of course, made results harder to achieve. By the late nineteenth century, many missionaries had shifted to getting aid from Ottawa, particularly as treaties were signed across the west. It was hard to get government money for this region because there was no treaty with the Cree; Ottawa thought it was Quebec's responsibility and Quebec was not interested either in taking the time or in dealing with the expense. Here – and not for the last time – the lack of a treaty between the Cree and either the federal government or the provincial government helped to shape events.[17]

Given all this, Horden understood from the beginning that he would have to adapt to local circumstances if he hoped to make any change. And, in looking back to George Barnley and drawing lessons from his failure, Horden clearly demonstrated that he understood that local culture would play a part in this change. He had met Barnley before leaving England, and, in his opinion, Barnley's manner had "produced much ill feeling without producing any good." He would consider carefully his stand on issues like

marriage à la façon du pays and Sunday work for these were some of the
points "among many which caused that serious misunderstanding between
Mr Barnley and the Company." He was determined not to repeat those
mistakes, and he was determined to connect with the Cree in a way that
Barnley had not. Horden set about learning Cree immediately, and from
the beginning he tried to comprehend the complex and dynamic situation he had entered, even though, in the end, he never fully grasped the
complexity of the spiritual world that surrounded him. In part, this was
because he could never fully accept the Cree's traditional belief in the land
and animals, but it is also because he would not give credence to the local
tradition of Christianity that had developed long before he arrived.[18]

In addition to the presence of Jesuits and other Catholics in the region, the fifty or sixty years before Horden's arrival had been eventful
decades. Part of the reason for this was the inland migration of the fur
trade posts and part was the introduction of new ideas into the region. In
1840, Methodist missionary James Evans, working among the Rice Lake
Ojibwa, developed a system for writing Native languages known as Canadian Aboriginal syllabics (commonly referred to as syllabics). The speed
with which syllabics were taken up by the Cree is provocative, and they
have been a lasting and powerful tool for Natives across Canada for nearly
two centuries now. In 1842, Barnley noted with amazement that a hunter
coming to trade at Rupert's House requested "a beaver" of writing paper
from the manager for his personal use. He gave no explanation, though
it had nothing to do with Barnley, who had never seen the man before.
What this man's purpose was we do not know, but syllabics were taken up
wholeheartedly by the Cree, and they taught the system to one another
across the region for both religious and practical reasons. Syllabics were
adopted for everything from business information within the fur trade,
to love letters left on portage trails by Cree suitors, to letters written to
London by dissatisfied Cree hunters. More to the point, the Cree used
syllabics to communicate songs and prayers across the same wide region
that they travelled for trade and social reasons.[19]

Barnley first noticed this among hunters at Albany House who were
taking notes in church on birchbark with their thumbnails; he later noticed
it at Moose Factory, where he was shown more writing. He commented
that it was "the work of an Indian who has not seen a missionary till his
interview with me on Monday last. The subject was a hymn and the
characters employed those of Rev Evens [sic] invention. Some of the York
Indians had obtained the original document of which this was a copy from
Norway House, and by them it had been communicated to the Severn

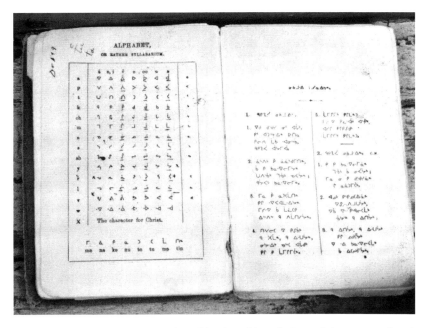

FIGURE 4.1 *Pages from a Cree syllabic Bible.* This Bible with Cree syllabic text was found at a campsite in the late 1960s and is an example of the Bibles, hymnals, and Psalters that had been produced by missionaries since the middle of the nineteenth century. The syllabics, invented by missionary James Evans in 1840, became central not only to the Cree interaction with Christianity but also to any number of communications across the region. This syllabic alphabet is still used by the Cree and is a powerful tool for keeping their language vibrant.

Indians." Apparently, two hunters had spoken to Evans, and, when they met others, they spent a day "in recounting the wonders they had been acquainted with." There was a vital, regional discussion of Christianity going on within Native culture at James Bay. And although this was fed in some part by Evans, Barnley, and other missionaries, it was sustained from within.[20]

In the 1840s, and no doubt aided by the power of this new written text, Natives all across the North began to interpret and experiment with Christian religious concepts. At York Factory during the summer of 1841, a man named Abishabis, claiming that he had visited heaven and hell, began to proclaim a new religion for the local people. The cult attracted adherents for a short while but ended abruptly when Abishabis began to demand first tribute and then other men's wives. He was driven out, fled to Severn House, and was eventually killed by a hunter who burned his body – the usual remedy for dealing with a person taken by the spirit of an *Atoosh*. As he had produced a map of the path of his heavenly travels that each of his followers copied, Abishabis' religious ideas lasted for a brief while; but, like much of the religious creativity going on in the Second Great Awakening to the south – a creativity that borrowed heavily on Native ideas and myths – it did not last.[21]

The full extent of Abishabis' cult on the western side of James Bay is outside the scope of this work, but the religious creativity that it implies, along with the speed of communication and the power of new ideas within Native culture, is important to the Cree story. Horden met with a similar experience at Rupert's House soon after his arrival, when he spoke to a man who claimed to have visited heaven and who planned to follow the same path again.[22] His vision did not become a movement, though he urged others to follow the path he had found. This speaks to the Cree's continued experimentation with Christian ideas and how they adapted them to a context in which communication beyond the material world was a necessary part of life. The fact that these experiences were spoken of as a "path" is also provocative. As already noted, the hunter's life is a path by which he gains his subsistence and upon which he encounters many powerful beings, and his responses to the unknown potential of these beings and this world have to be creative. Indeed, creativity in situations like this is almost a necessity. Half a century later, William Walton wrote: "I found certain of my Indians claiming that queer ideas they were spreading around had come to them directly from the Holy Spirit. And when I challenged them they pointed to the 14th chapter of St. John's Gospel – 'But the Comforter, which is the Holy Ghost, whom the Father will send in my name, He shall teach you all things.'" Walton tried to argue that those words had been spoken to the disciples and not to the Cree so that they could "dream up" their own ideas. To his chagrin, the Cree continued to think it perfectly proper to express their revelatory dreams to one another.[23]

Another aspect of the dynamic nature of the years prior to Horden's arrival is the presence of other Native hunters on Cree lands. Beginning in the 1830s, Natives from the St. Lawrence and as far south as Maine began to enter the region both to trap fur for themselves and to trade with the locals as agents for independent traders. This lasted fewer than twenty years as a generation of southern hunters looked to mitigate pressures on their own land; and, while the HBC simply felt threatened by these incursions, for the Cree they comprised a more complex set of relationships. As I have noted, it was the Cree who encountered the Wabanaki directly and it was they who had to negotiate this cultural encounter. Despite many attempts by HBC traders to intercept these strangers, they rarely did so; and what they knew of them they learned from their own hunters. The biases of the traders made it difficult to comprehend the meaning of these new hunters as different Cree seemed to have held differing opinions of them.[24]

Wabanaki were first reported travelling through the area of Waswanipi, Pike Lake, and Mistassini in the early 1830s, but their presence becomes clearer in the middle of the decade. In 1836, for instance, the hunter Nottaway and his wife came to Mistassini complaining about Wabanaki from St. Maurice having killed a great many beaver on their lands. This did not seem to be a perennial problem as it was not until 1839 that Nottaway again came to complain about outsiders. For him, the eventual solution was accommodation. By the early 1840s, he had created some kind of personal relationship with these Wabanaki, and they were spending winters with him on his land. When William McKay asked him why he was letting them stay, he told him that "the trappers being so kind, [he] could not say anything against them." He told McKay that they did not kill many beaver now and that they gave good trade, better than that at Mistassini, in fact. The trade was no doubt important, but the control over resources that Nottaway had regained by accommodating the Wabanaki presence was vital. Drawn into a personal relationship – a daily living arrangement it seems – the Wabanaki had been managed by the hunter. This is not very different from the way that traders were dealt with on the land. Local hunters continued to engage with these Wabanaki and, it seems, actively worked to prevent the HBC men from meeting them. In 1839, for instance, James Robertson returned to his post and reported that he had seen only one sign of the Wabanaki. They had marked a date in June on a tree, but the day of the month had been rubbed off by local hunters. These hunters had apparently rendezvoused with some of the Wabanaki and then had destroyed the evidence of their presence.[25]

Given these circumstances, it is difficult to interpret the Wabanaki as a constant problem for the Cree, but, over time, subsistence seems to have been an issue for some. John Spencer thought that the Wabanaki were simply taking all they could find and bringing hardship on local Cree hunters, who located animals in summer only to come back to find them gone in winter. This disrupted local environmental understandings, he thought, "for in this quarter each family of Indians has a certain range of country which he conceives as his domain and which is considered sacred amongst them." Yet, as discussed in Chapter 2, his naming of Wappanakee Sacka Hagun may have reflected a Cree accommodation of the presence of the Wabanaki, or it may have served to mark the point of entry of unwanted strangers. It may, in fact, have done both, for, like the whites in their midst, the Wabanaki could be interpreted differently at different times. How long the name Wappanakee Sacka Hagun lingered on the land is not known; still, as we saw in J.W. Anderson's report on shaking tent ceremonies at Mistassini, the name "Wabanaki" lingered in the upland areas as a vague menace into the twentieth century.[26]

The Wabanaki certainly disrupted some local hunting and brought some hardship and confusion. They were skilled hunters, and, being well supplied from outside, they could choose to ignore the effects of their hunting on the land and the local people. This foreshadows events in the late nineteenth century – and, like the fur trade rivalry, the roots of that later crisis can probably be found here – but this is not what is important about the Wabanaki presence at this point. In addition to the changes that they brought, which necessitated that local hunters respond creatively, they also brought with them another interpretation of the Native hunt and of relations with Europeans. For more than two centuries, the Wabanaki had seen their world radically transformed by European economics and politics. They also had a long history with Roman Catholicism, and there are hints at connections between their presence and the Catholic priests who came up from the south. We will never know exactly what those Cree who spent winters with the Wabanaki exchanged with them at a cultural level, but for these hunters having an understanding of who the Wabanaki were and where they came from would have been vital. The Cree would have engaged the Wabanaki as thoroughly has they did the HBC men, and this clearly added to the cultural complexity of the regional situation in James Bay when Horden arrived in 1851. Religious agency, individual revelation, the rapid communication of spiritual ideas through written text, the new inland fur trade posts, the trade rivalry, and Natives other than the Cree all added to the narrative mix at this time.

If Horden did not immediately recognize this complexity, and it seems that he did not, he did understand that the region's small population would need a special kind of missionary presence. Rupert's House consisted of only Chief Trader Gladman and his family, along with five employees. Horden estimated that it, along with Mistassini, Waswanipi, Pike Lake, Temiskamay, and Nitchequon posts had only 135 hunters and their extended families – this in an area of hundreds of thousands of square kilometres. Fort George could boast 150 hunters who came seasonally to trade, and Horden concluded that only it warranted a full-time missionary. Knowing that the Cree could not be gathered into sedentary villages, he determined that it was necessary to have men who were capable of travelling the land. Native religious agency and syllabics became central parts of Horden's mission as he struggled to spread his faith over the immense and empty territory in his charge. He would never be completely satisfied with the compromises involved in negotiating both the vast physical geography and the religious landscape of James Bay, but this was the only option open to him.[27]

Horden took up the idea of using Native teachers, and E.A. Watkins, who began his duties in 1852, also came to believe that "nothing of a permanent character could be accomplished for the good of these poor people till a Native agency be at work." Native men – Thomas Vincent, William Wapatchee, Redfern Loutit, the Iserhoff brothers (Robert, Joseph, and Charles), John Gull, Edward Richards, Jacob Matamashcum, and Second Bearskin – came to make up this local agency. These itinerants were subordinate to the English missionaries – sadly, most left little written record of their movements or their understanding of their missions – and they moved more often and more freely through the environment of James Bay than did their white counterparts. They related to Cree culture on their own terms, all of them were hunters living on the land, and William Wapatchee at least was well known around Waswanipi for his personal power and relationships with the other-than-humans of the hunter's world.[28]

Using local agents for missionary work meant that Horden was using hunters, and this brought a set of problems with which he struggled until the end of his time in James Bay. When he laid out plans to educate these men, he emphasized that they should "speak[ ] only their own language" and support themselves from the land. They, "who are really Indian in thought, Indian in occupation, and entirely Indian in speech," he wrote, were vital to the cause of the mission, for only they could spend extended periods of time with people who had to keep moving across the land. Because of their lack of formal training, he thought they should be no more than deacons in the church, "after which they should return to their present mode of life, obtain their livelihood by hunting, at the same time superintending and watching over the brethren of their tribe." Significantly for the mission, they could trade in fur as well as preach, thus saving money while staying in cultural contact with their fellow hunters.[29]

Horden saw the value of these men, but he really only wanted them to function as a conduit for religious messages; he did not want them to be independent interpreters of those messages. Men like William Wapatchee, however, were not simple conduits; rather, they were spiritual thinkers in their own right. Wapatchee was, in fact, a rival of the Waswanipi priest, who could not speak Cree. Wapatchee, known locally as *aiamie okima*, or "prayer boss," hunted and interpreted religion in Cree terms for whoever cared to talk to him about it. This disturbed the local priest, who found himself shut behind not only a linguistic but also a cultural barrier that he could not overcome. Horden, even though he shared the same nominal brand of Christianity, was no less challenged by Wapatchee and these other men. He never really had control over the message they delivered, and this never ceased to make him uncomfortable.[30]

Some of his concerns revolved around the then-current thinking in Europe and North America, which increasingly viewed the world through a racial lens, interpreting cultural difference as something essential to race. Most of Horden's missionary agents were Natives of the Country by birth, though they were hunters by occupation and, increasingly, by culture. He thus worried about "the declension of the European intellect in the second and third generation" of fur trade children. He saw this as a serious drawback to his mission but also had to be careful with this kind of thinking because the missionary effort was predicated on being able to raise people up. Still, he was troubled by the behaviour of his Native agents. His interpretation was one of intellectual decline, but of course his descriptions were of men becoming more Cree in their behaviour and attitude towards life in the bush. He never mentioned any loss of interest in the religious message, only in the way that it was delivered. And, of course, the prejudice that he harboured with respect to his Native missionaries was mostly a self-imposed restraint on an effort that already had many other challenges to overcome.[31]

Horden claimed not to want to create a caste system, which he thought did "not, and should not exist," although J.H. Keen held that "lighter skin [was] universally recognized as a claim to superiority" in the region. This may explain why even Thomas Vincent, who rose to be archdeacon in the diocese and whom Horden often praised, fell short in his eyes. Horden trained Vincent himself and first sent him on a missionary trip to Rupert's House in 1857, calling him "an excellent missionary for his poor benighted countrymen." He rose higher in the church than did other Native clergy and was well known across the region by hunters from Albany to Mistassini. He worked and travelled extensively, but, despite the training Horden gave him, the relationship between them was never free of cultural tension. When Vincent took over during Horden's extended trip to England in 1868, Horden was ultimately dissatisfied with his conduct. Upon his return, he wrote to the CMS that Vincent did not "possess the weight

of character for so important a position as that which he occupied here."
Horden did not specify his complaints, but he was upset with Vincent's
actions rather than with any lack of initiative in leading the diocese. Vincent had a strong personality and his own views of the faith, and this raises
questions about those unnamed specifics. Horden's questioning regarding
whether or not "the Native character ha[d] become more solidified" in
Vincent hints at the problem.[32]

Vincent was a Native of the Country who made a significant, if sometimes troubled, place for himself within the larger structure of the missionary effort. Clearly, too, he traversed the many cultural spaces that were
part of a Native catechist's life. Vincent was a hunter as well as a preacher,
and he spent much of his time in the bush with a gun or tending fishnets.
To a large extent, he supported both his mission and his family through
these activities, and he travelled extensively throughout the region both
by canoe and dogsled, moving and supporting himself in a way that the
English missionaries could not. He was known in the region as "Praying
Chief," and he took both aspects of this epithet seriously, looking after
people's spiritual and material needs. In both preaching and feeding his
people, he demonstrated and gained power through the *uuchimaau* principle, which governed relations within his culture.[33]

Vincent was an advocate for his people as well as an advocate for God,
and this, in the end, may have been the real source of tension between
him and Horden. He wrote to the CMS committee in words that were
very much in the missionary tradition, but he referred to the Cree as "my
people" and "my Indian Brethren." Well known for taking hunters more
seriously than non-Natives, he felt no need to please his superiors. As one
eulogist noted, "for the same reason he was not particularly popular among
the white people in the country, he was pre-eminently the missionary to
the Indians. His heart, his talents, his strength, his life, were given to the
cause of the Indians, and they rewarded him with all the devotion and
faithfulness of their reserved nature." He likely challenged his fellow Natives on cultural issues too, but his loyalty was to them. And, in the end,
this cost him the promotion to bishop upon Horden's death in 1892.[34]

Horden and fellow missionaries were faced not only with the beliefs
and actions of their Native deacons and catechists but also by the whole of
Cree culture. This was true when Horden first arrived, and when Reverend
William Walton sat down to write a friend in England about the state of
his mission in 1902, he was troubled by this same fact. In twelve-and-a-
half years, he told his friend, he counted both successes and failures, but
for three or four years he had truly believed that he had been "gaining

ground." Hoping "to influence one or two, here & there, to carry on the good work in their respective hunting grounds during the long winter nights," he was now disturbed by recent evidence to the contrary. He was suddenly faced with the apparent failure of his attempts to convince locals of the role of the church in their lives and of his authority.[35]

Recently, Nero, his Native helper and lay preacher at Great Whale River, had come to him in much distress over a personal situation. His sister, who was married to an HBC man, had left him for another partner. Within the Cree community the separation of the couple was not an issue, but for Walton and the church it was a grievous sin. "I thought the testing time for poor Nero had come," Walton wrote to his friend, as usually Natives would not "denounce a relative no matter how wicked, but Nero – thank God – was true. She is the only close relative he has left." He loved her, but he denounced her before the community. The situation was resolved when the young man with whom Nero's sister had been living moved back to Fort George, in what Walton alone saw as a state of disgrace. Nero's sister remained in Great Whale River, apparently did not go back to her husband, and did not face any repercussions for the incident. It was Nero who faced a number of troubles. When he finished his work, Walton wrote, he "went off to the north himself for he felt so ashamed and grieved he thought it best to go off for a while." Nero was in distress about what he had done to his sister, and it was he who faced the disapproval of the Cree community. The record is not clear regarding how long Nero stayed away from the village – he did eventually go back to work for Walton – but for a while, on his own out in the bush, he found some relief from the tension between Cree and English demands. Walton lamented that "whoever strives to live differently from the old way is often times discouraged by the people saying 'Ska ne opimanaik- owa!' – how he sickens me." Given the circumstances and the general tolerance of Cree culture, it seems more likely that the disapproval came not from Nero's personal beliefs but, rather, from his trying to force those beliefs on others.[36]

Walton was further upset when he went to Fort George several weeks later and found that the Natives there were not treating the adulterer with any of the moral outrage that he thought appropriate. In fact, they were ignoring the whole business. A local hunter, wrote Walton, "who has always been looked upon as a sort of catechist to me – was most bitter in his cruel opposition." Walton wanted the adulterer banned from the church for a year, but this man and the community would not listen to him. "They do not *hate sin*," he wrote his friend. They went to church, he explained, and were excited about his printing religious books in the Cree syllabic text – and this was true even of an old man whom Walton called "a *real* Indian" (by which he meant he was not a Christian) – but they did not have the "courage to stand up for religion." Walton was discouraged not only because the Natives would not condemn the behaviour of the adulterer but also because they would not condemn the behaviour of those who practised older beliefs involving the relationship with a *mistabeo*. Sadly, he concluded, they would not even listen to him when he told them that they should not drink tea or dance on New Year's Eve. Exhibiting both independence and humour, they told him that dancing was not a sin; they had even known ministers to enjoy it from time to time.

Clearly, here, too, there were many cross-currents in the religious and cultural worlds of the bush and the posts. Some currents flowed in channels that are by now well known. Nero's sadness and shame at condemning his own sister in order to live up to the expectations of his religious mentor show all the cultural disruptions seen in other Native communities in relation to the missionary effort. Walton and other missionaries certainly had a cultural as well as a religious effect on some individuals in James Bay. Some Natives, like Nero, took up not only Christianity but also the cultural assumptions of the ministers, and, also like Nero, they lived uncomfortably in both the world of the missionary and the world of the hunter. But the Cree world was still evident not only in the defiant continuation of local custom surrounding marriage and various forms of celebration but also in Nero's retreat into the bush to find solace and space from the world of the mission. The bush still offered not only an environment in which to escape the tension of the trading posts but also an environment in which a different set of conceptual relationships held sway and whose power continued to move people's behaviour.[37]

The bush did not mean the abandonment of Christianity, but it was a place apart both materially and symbolically, and the reality of this was evident to the Cree, though for the most part missionaries seemed to have missed the power of Christianity to adapt to this hunting world. When the Cree left for their hunting grounds in the fall, Walton thought,

> they as much as give up hopes of being better [i.e., becoming Christian] after they leave the trading post, as if no one is thinking of them out there. They say they do believe in what they hear in church, and know that it is quite true, and yet they don't follow it because their old habits have such power over them. They say it is so different when they are off from the place.

Walton interpreted their explanation as apostasy, but the situation seems to have been more complex than that. Certainly, the demands brought by the missionaries did not fit the environment of the hunt, and when hunters re-entered the bush, they re-entered another material and symbolic environment in which other beings helped them to survive. These beings had to be spoken to and spoken about in order for people to live, and one can guess that, even as they talked to Walton, they understood that his insistence upon separating spiritual reality from material reality might work at the posts but that it would not work in the bush. The solution to this was not necessarily apostasy, however, only adaptation.[38]

Walton might have related to this for the missionaries found themselves in a similar, if less pressing, position to that of the Cree. Missionaries worked to create some cultural connections with their local missions, but they also maintained a connection with the wider social world of the Church as well as with English friends and family they left behind. It was this connection that gave their work meaning and that gave them the ability to try to impose their set of social and moral values on James Bay. They, too, struggled with this double life. They often expressed loneliness and a longing for contact with a cultural narrative that explained their work in the bay. Horden assuaged his isolation by seeing his church as corresponding "with those of the earliest ages; the liberality of Xians [Christians]; the persecution of the heathens; the sun shining brightly; the cloud, the storm, the tempest coming." He thought of himself as part of a wider narrative world, a world connected with distant places and ideas that put James Bay not at the centre but, rather, very much at the periphery of his narrative geography. Surviving at the narrative periphery was only possible because he and other missionaries were maintained by their mission societies and by the HBC. Thus, their remaining at a distance from the narrative of the hunt did not lead to starvation. And this was something that hunters, who made their living from the land, could not endure.[39]

Being on the narrative periphery made James Bay a lonely and isolated place for the missionaries, and all of them suffered from it. Horden remarked somewhat sardonically that Moose Factory was "a place of confinement for Europeans much more secure than Pentonville Prison," and inland posts seemed even more remote. For Horden, Mistassini was "a very lonely place" that made "one fancy he is at the end of the world." Waswanipi was isolated too, but its more agrarian appearance gave it "not the dreary, lonely appearance" that was Mistassini's. In comparison, Waswanipi was better, but on returning from England fifteen years earlier he had lamented leaving that "land of plenty, the pleasant land" for James Bay, which was "the dreary land, the land of want." Henry Nevitt also thought the region the "end of the earth" and Mistassini a particularly "lonely place." The perception of James Bay as being at the edge of the world strengthened all of the missionaries' perceptions regarding the spiritual isolation of the place in which they had to work. Watkins addressed the society secretaries as having "the good providence of gracious God" to promote "the glorious work of the Lord in the wilderness." Horden, too, saw the Cree as "sheep in the wilderness," where "wilderness" meant not only isolation but also the unsettled hunters and the belief that nomads could never be completely Christianized. This narrative of isolation, of seeing James Bay as being at the end of the world, was fairly innocuous at this point, but in later chapters we see the growth of its historical significance.[40]

The need for Natives, even Native catechists, to hunt for a living challenged the religious geography that saw James Bay as peripheral, just as the environment challenged the missionaries' belief that Christianity was inherent to sedentary agriculture. They struggled with what to do about these circumstances. Early on, Watkins at Fort George wrote to the secretaries of the CMS that lack of provisions was putting a damper on his mission and that his students had to hunt at least part of the time to make their living, thereby losing valuable hours of education. He had tried to hire a hunter to supply his students, but he feared that he would not bring in enough and that the demands of the HBC would likely call him away from his work for the mission. He requested that the CMS supply him more adequately, but this was no more viable an option for him than it was for the HBC men. He and other missionaries did not get involved in actual hunting, nor did they spend winters in the bush, but they were every bit as bound by hunting as were others in the region. While they tried to keep their attention elsewhere, they were constantly brought back to the basic reality of subsistence, both for themselves and for the people they hoped to change. There was tension between the fur traders' desire for fur and their need to eat, but this was a tension between two aspects of essentially the same activity. For missionaries, the tension was more abstract, being that between what they saw as two very different activities and narrative explanations of humanity's place in the world. This perception that hunting and subsistence were distractions from religion continued to distance them from local meanings of Christianity. As we have seen, and as we will see later, missionaries were not blind to this local interpretation; they seem simply to have been tone-deaf with regard to its importance.[41]

In 1858, Horden worried that "the Inland Indians from Rupert's House can yet say, No man careth for my soul"; just like Walton, he saw his absence as an absence of religious activity. He did not hold communion at Mistassini until 1869, and, for the next fifty years or more, a missionary presence was all but non-existent away from the coast. In 1876, Keen visited Mistassini and Waswanipi for a few days each, and he spent a short while at Rupert's House. Everyone wanted to see him, and he knew that they would not have a chance to do so for another year. In fact, the wait was longer because his arrival at Rupert's House was delayed the next year, and many of the hunters had already left. They would have to wait for his longer trip, in 1878, when he had to fit four hundred people into only three weeks. Horden felt that this kind of disengagement was a failure of his mission, whereas, really, this distance and lack of pressure was a powerful stimulant to local activity. Horden may have believed that missionary absence left the members of his flock lost in the wilderness, but they did not live in a wilderness.[42]

Christianity was alive and at work at these inland places whether missionaries chose to acknowledge it or not. Native catechists were a part of it, but, beginning in the 1840s and 1850s, Christianity also became an increasingly important part of HBC men's lives. Just as we saw with Robert and Betsy Chilton, other traders and their families, particularly those inland, began to form autonomous religious communities during this period, and, over the years, they had a profound effect on the way in which Christianity was practised. As these traders took up Christianity their posts became centres of religion as well as places where hunters came to trade and socialize. Hunters, in part, practised Christianity intermittently from within this framework. Significantly, too, these HBC men were beginning to include themselves in the European cultural narrative even as some tried their hand at agricultural subsistence. They began to speak of themselves as culturally connected with the wider Protestant world in a way that they did not in the past.[43]

At Mistassini Post, William McKay first read prayers to the servants and Natives in the spring of 1842. It is not clear if this was a result of meeting George Barnley at Rupert's House, though the timing seems more than coincidental. McKay read prayers and then explained parts of them to the hunters present "as well as I could." He wrote, self-consciously, that he found this "to be no easy task owing to [his own] want of a good education." He felt poorly qualified – maybe he felt the weight of his background – but quite motivated and resolved: "I will do all I can to get them to understand every opportunity I have." By the 1850s, he was making regular note of

Sunday services and stressing the meaning of a day of rest whenever it was possible. He even made special note of his pleasure one Sunday when a hunter named Taikosin had a bad hunt "as he need not go on such business – this day." Food was still of primary concern, but, particularly in the summer months, McKay often noted that he spent Sundays with "most of the Indians in the house whilst I was reading prayers."[44]

The pattern is similar at the other posts in James Bay. At Nitchequon, Robert Chilton began recording Sunday prayers in spring 1844. He, too, stressed the need to hold Sunday as a day of rest, writing pointedly on one Sabbath: "the Lord forgive me I employed the men to pack up the furs." They had needed to move them across the lake before the ice went out and that had outweighed his feelings of religious obligation. Chilton had not expressed religious tendencies in his journals prior to this, either at Nitchequon or at Pike Lake, but for the rest of his life he continued to hold services when he could. By 1852, James Robertson, Jr., was also recording prayer services at Temiskamay, and, as noted, Roman Catholic services were beginning at Waswanipi at that time too. Traders also began performing other religious duties. Robert Chilton married Joseph Iserhoff to his daughter Caroline, noting a bit uncomfortably, "I read the Matrimony of England to them so I am thinking that they are almost lawfully married until they get married by a minister here after." The next year his servant Moar asked that one of his daughters to be baptized, and Chilton again "read the ceremonial law of England" and baptized the infant as Elizabeth. Fur trade posts became centres of seasonal marriages and baptisms, along with all the other roles they filled, and these ceremonies were followed by feasts to which all were invited. This was a standard pattern well into the twentieth century, and these strong connections to the trading posts affected many people's lives.[45]

The underlying quest for food cannot be forgotten, though. At the posts people's daily subsistence needs affected the ways Christianity entered their lives as much as it affected other aspects of local culture. In February and March 1855, for instance, when Chilton and his family were starving at Nitchequon, brief Sunday prayers were immediately followed by members of the group splitting up to go in search of food; it takes no great leap of imagination to guess that those prayers involved the success of that search. On March 26, when the hunter Neck sent much-needed meat to the post, Chilton wrote fervently, "the Lord be praised for sending us great deliverance in the scarcity of provisions, Amen" and made special note in early April that it was "the first Sabbath that we have not laboured for food since 14th Jan last." Hunting and Christianity worked together for these isolated people and clearly bolstered their hope in challenging circumstances. In some ways, the Christian faith connected James Bay to the wider world and prayers to God connected the hunt to the wider narrative of Christian spirituality, but in specific ways that made them both very local. Christianity had a local narrative in James Bay, and this narrative was related to but distinct from that of the missionary, involving, as it did, everyone's search for food.[46]

It should also be mentioned in this general discussion of Christianity that there were plenty of people who denied the Christian faith. Most denial came in the form of apathy or absence, but in death some confronted the missionaries directly. In 1842, a hunter named Kesekonene, a noted *Kwashaptam* in the community, lay dying while Barnley tried to attend him. As he died he chanted what Barnley called his "threats of conjuring" and physically turned away from the missionary even as he symbolically turned away from his message. He was closing out his life within the wider world of the hunt and had no need for words about heaven. Nor did an old woman, described by Donald Grant several decades later, who denied the ministrations of the priests at Waswanipi. While she was dying, Grant wrote, "I believe the priests were endeavouring to administer extreme unction to the departed spirit tho without success." The old woman would have none of it, and the "gentlemen in the black gowns departed" in defeat. Both these individuals were defining and structuring the ends of their lives in ways that comforted them and connected them with the whole of their lives. Many others came to church only to assuage the minister and took little interest in Western religion. Horden bemoaned the fact that there were "those who will not speak at all [of religion], and those who ward of everything you can recommend by telling you they have already got it." When he confronted an old hunter for chuckling at his preaching, the old man "told [him] that his sons could learn these things, but that he was too old." Horden hoped that he was somehow touched by the faith, but his sons told him that the old man never talked of Christianity or prayed when out in the bush.[47]

The negotiation of old and new ways of defining life and death continued even at the end of the nineteenth century. After nearly fifty years of work, Horden had to admit that the Rupert's House districts included "a sprinkling of utter heathens and others who are almost heathen, hardly even seeing a missionary." What is striking in this situation is not the pejorative implication of "almost heathen" but, rather, the fact that many Cree seem to have fit Christianity into their environment without eliminating other aspects of their world that they found necessary and desirable. In Horden's words they were "almost heathen," but what does this really mean? The presence of missionaries, changes in the location and culture of the trading posts, and the more formal training of Native teachers changed the Cree's relationship to Christianity, but keep in mind how creative people were in their beliefs. Keep in mind E.A. Fleming's report of a "former" *kwashaptam* who came to him "with a very great manifestation of zeal in the new religion." He brought three figures painted on a deer skin to share with the missionary and told Fleming how he had been hurt and how they had healed him: "what was my horror to hear him call the largest God, the second Jesus, and the third God's wife!" These kinds of healing figures were an aspect of an older tradition and the man had adapted them. His adaptation of God and Jesus was not unlike the adaptation that occurred when many other symbols from pre-Christian Europe blended with Christianity during the Middle Ages. In this particular case, Fleming was at something of a loss with regard to engaging this hunter in religious dialogue. What the man had done was beyond Fleming's ability to accept, and he fell back on lecturing him, with the expected result – silent, non-confrontational disengagement.[48]

These kinds of encounters were not unusual, and failures like Fleming's created a kind of spiritual malaise between hunters and missionaries as the former tried to engage the latter in their quest. As early as 1853, Horden wrote of receiving an apparent insult from a hunter who came to the house and, after exchanging a few words, sat quietly for only a short while before changing his mind about being there. When Horden went out of the room momentarily, the man left without a word. Asked later about his behaviour, the man said he had wanted to go to see his daughter, but Horden put more meaning into the act: "this is the first instance I have known, where an Indian turned his back on the Gospel." The hunter seems to have been turning his back on Horden rather than on the gospel, but Christianity did fail the hopes of some, leaving them saddened and somewhat lost. The hunter Oolekitchish confessed to Horden that he had been very sad over the winter thinking of his friends: "I once thought that on receiving Christianity our life would be much lengthened, but now I see that all my friends are gone and I am left alone; I felt depressed and unhappy; I know it was wrong, very wrong, but I could not help it." The increase in deadly disease is something I take up in the next chapter, but in this case Horden had to admit that he was faced with an indifference to his faith that troubled him.[49]

Reactions like these are hard to interpret, and failures to connect with Natives (remember Nero's pain) need to be considered fully, as do those hunters who ignored the innovations of Christianity. But what of the continued meaning Christianity has for many Cree in the present day? How does all this history relate to that? Like the trading company that helped support it, Horden's Church was yet another corporate entity in the region with which the Cree had to negotiate in order to get what they desired. Like the goods for which the Cree exchanged fur, Christianity was also a set of goods that was taken out into the bush and interpreted within that world. There seems little doubt that the Church meant something to a good many hunters who came to see the catechists and ministers during the summer, but most of their year was spent away from the posts and the missionaries. Horden worked with the material at hand – a hunting economy, Native Cree who were already involved with Christianity, Native teachers who interpreted his faith according to their own lines of thought, and the Cree language. He did not always do this willingly or to his best advantage but the result was a negotiated notion of the Church that some hunters valued even as they worked to shape it to their own tastes.[50]

As noted above, Horden set about learning Cree immediately upon his arrival, and this was a first and necessary step in negotiating a church with the hunters. Within a year, the Cree were complimenting him on his skills, though he worried that there were "many parts of that curious language" that he had been unable to fathom. Understanding Cree, whether imperfectly or not, was something Horden demanded of all the missionaries in the region, giving them only a few weeks after their arrival to begin reading prayers in it. Language was the key feature of his mission, as it was for most missions in the nineteenth century, but it was a double-edged tool in many respects. It allowed the missionary entrance to the religious conversation, but, as Walton later saw, it was a conversation carried on within the Cree idiom. We can gain some insight into historical processes by looking at language, which posed some interesting problems. We can also gain some insight into why so many missions abandoned Native languages and began to demand the use of English.[51]

Horden and his men produced a number of religious translations for the Cree, and, thanks to the syllabic system of notation, the Cree and their neighbours were able not only to read what was produced for them but also to communicate their own ideas. For those who were interested in Christianity, these printed works appear to have been the most valuable item that the missionaries offered, and they were willing to buy them in multiple copies. It is possible that some used these books like charms – certainly, many Christians around the world do the same – but it seems clear that others used these books, in true Protestant fashion, to gain access to a set of powerful ideas. After all, there was nothing new or mystical about the written language by 1850. As I mentioned, by the time Horden arrived in the region, the use of syllabics had already been internalized, and "many of the Indians," he wrote, knew "something of the syllabic characters." Even many of the inland Natives could use the syllabic writing system thanks to trader Gladman's daughter, who had been teaching them. Horden was taken by how keen they were to learn.[52]

Horden took up syllabics and began the long process of translating religious material into Cree. He received a printing press in 1854, though he only used it until 1859, when, because of time constraints, he started sending his translations to England to be printed. The Cree were pleased with the books in their language, and Horden spent most of the next forty years translating the whole New Testament, the Anglican Book of Common Prayer, and several hymnals into Cree. These were printed by the thousands, and, at Rupert's House in 1878, for instance, prayer books, hymnals, and Psalters were selling for half a Made Beaver, while the Gospels were sold for a whole Made Beaver. By the turn of the century, according to William Walton, the Cree were wearing these books out over the winters in the bush faster than they could be replaced. So much a part of Cree life did writing become that Walton had a typewriter made in England with Cree characters so that he could produce periodic bulletins and other materials in Cree, like the almanac he produced in the early twentieth century.

There are several interesting things that should be noted about the use of syllabics that are important to its cultural meaning in James Bay. First, even English words tended to take on a Cree sound when put into this Cree context. This was something that bothered Watkins when he arrived. He wanted to change the system so as to prevent such things as "Joshua" being pronounced as "Choshu," "David" as "Tayit," and "Joseph" as "Chosip." He was bothered by the blurring of linguistic and cultural lines, but there was little that could be done; Cree is not the only language that shapes these kinds of pronunciations. The second problem involved bad or inadequate translation – both literal and idiomatic. At the prosaic level, Horden was vexed at a passage in a previous translation of Isaiah 28:13 – "therefore the word of Yahweh will be to them precept on precept, precept on precept; line on line, line on line" – where "line on line" had been translated as the meaningless "piece of string on a string." There were seemingly endless such problems that took a great deal of effort to correct, but there were more serious idiomatic problems too. Horden took years to find translations for idiomatic passages, and Walton struggled with the same problems in the early twentieth century. Frustrated by the phrase "lift up your hearts" – all he could think to use was *oopinamuk*, which means to physically lift up your heart – Walton was ecstatic when one of his parishioners supplied him with *oopikootowook Chi-tayewowa*: let your heart go upward.[53]

It was situations like this that made Horden and others so conscious of the Cree idiom. To fit Christianity into the Cree language was to fit it into the Cree narrative of culture and to negotiate a relationship based on words. It is difficult to imagine how many passages in the Bible, with its emphasis on paternalistic and agricultural order, could be placed into an idiom and narrative structure that would have meaning for hunters in the bush (though, no doubt, in here somewhere is part of the history of Job Bearskin's garden metaphor). It may be less difficult to imagine how those hunters would react to "behold, I will send for many fishers, saith the Lord, and they shall fish them; and after will I send for many hunters, and they shall hunt them from every mountain, and from every hill" – though maybe we should be wary of easy fits. Here, seemingly, is a larger idea that might be more easily translated for the Cree hunter than some others; still, we have no way of knowing how it was received or used. What is easier to know, and what bolsters the inference that a more conceptual negotiation was going on, is the Cree reaction to the structure of the Church in more mundane matters. Here it is interesting to see the Cree interpretation of religion and society coming to bear.[54]

When the Cree interacted with missionaries, both individually and in congregation, this Cree interpretation becomes clearly visible. Early on, Barnley observed "a considerable unwillingness to kneel before the Lord and Maker," which he took for stubbornness or ignorance. Given what was going on at the time of his arrival, neither of these seems likely, and the Cree may have been reacting to Barnley himself, who appears overbearing even in his own writings. Certainly this was the root of his problems with the HBC men – particularly the Catholics – and his isolation, to which I alluded earlier. Many hunters may have also felt that public prayer was more responsibility than they wanted to take on: remember the public performances by powerful men in the shaking tents and the public preaching of men like Abishabis. Again, we are left to draw inferences about their specific reasoning, but the deployment of a Cree understanding of propriety seems clear enough.

Cree hunters were also in the habit of registering their feelings by reacting to Barnley's sermons. Like any good congregation, they expressed their level of pleasure: "good words, good words" when they liked what he said and silence when they did not. He and other missionaries were not sure if this was proper, but there was little they could do about it. Horden was similarly confused about the propriety of women participating in prayer meetings. He wondered if it should continue, "connected as we are with the English church," though he knew that allowing women to participate had kept some Cree from turning to Catholicism. In some cases, he thought it should continue as "opportunity is thus afforded the Indians of expressing their want in the congregation, which was crucial to their participation," but this was a compromise for him. Here is a sentiment not too different from that shown by HBC traders who worried that their hunters would take their fur south if they were offended, and thus Native services were organized around a number of Cree beliefs. When services commenced, Fleming noted, members began "to crowd in and take their seats, the women on one side, the men on the other and in the center aisle, and the children around the communion rails, until every seat and place for standing room is occupied." Then the doors were opened and others stood outside. He could certainly find much there to remind him of his own understanding of what church should be, but the members of his congregation were also defining and gendering space for themselves.[55]

The Cree continued to define for themselves other aspects of culture that the missionaries felt should be dictated by the Church. Many hunters still had multiple wives, and couples separated amicably when these marriages did not work. This left missionaries in a quandary over how to react. "How are illegitimate children baptized," wondered Walton, when they were accepted by the community but not within his Christian understanding. Changing practice meant moving individuals, but this had to be done carefully and without upsetting the group. Walton's and Nero's failure to impose an outside interpretation on marriage illustrates the power of local understandings, and this was true even in less charged situations. Horden faced a more humorous kind of frustration while questioning betrothed couples about their commitment. "Do you love each other? Are you happy?" he asked them. Some said yes, but many seemed to think the questions irrelevant. They replied, "More generally, 'yes we love each other a little, we have a little regard for each other.'" And here, thought Horden, "the sharp corners of individual character had not been yet entirely rounded." More frustratingly, he recorded that, while performing the marriage ceremony for these couples, "and asking the usual questions, one of the women, on my saying 'will thou obey him?' taking a retrospective view of the case replied, 'I do sometimes, not always.'" Horden hastened to write that he thought she would try hard in the future, but he made no further mention of obedience.[56]

Finally, of course, Cree hunters had to negotiate their relationship with the Church within the context of the hunt. When Horden asked for a subscription to be raised for a church at Rupert's House, some hunters told him outright that they could not: "We can give nothing, we are too poor, we have to go to the wood and there hunt for furs and food, and sometimes we get nothing for our pains, so we can give nothing." Horden took this as an outright refusal to participate in his plan and as a rejection of the church, so he was somewhat taken aback when these same hunters came to him and contributed quietly to the church project. Significantly, the Cree wanted no great ceremonies or declarations of wealth. Hunters were always circumspect in talking to traders about their success, and here also they wanted to be circumspect for fear that giving a subscription would disturb their relationship to the hunted. Building a church when the missionary provided food, as happened later at Mistassini, was far less problematic than building a church while demanding food from the local environment. They could partake in both the hunt and the church, but only on carefully negotiated terms.[57]

Clearly, from the beginning missionaries knew that the Cree were a spiritually active people who carried out their beliefs in private as well as public, and they tried to engage them in this. They encountered a people who had not only a clear interest in Christianity but also a strong sense of their own beliefs. In James Bay, Christianity added something to Cree culture, even if, from the missionaries' perspective, many parts of it were ignored or poorly understood. Many Cree were changed by their relationship with Christianity, as was their language and its context. But the analysis can go further, and, as with the fur trade, equal intellectual space should be given to how Christianity was changed within the Cree environment. It seems clear that Christianity was modified to fit to the local geography.[58]

Anthropologist Frank Sun, in the 1960s, noted this continuance of Cree-ness. At Paint Hills he described a Native service, with women sitting to the left and men to the right, and the Cree catechist doing most of the talking for the missionary – in Cree. He described the nature of the belief system as consisting of Cree and Euro-North American layers and as something that continued to evolve as it was practised. Cree spirituality – which sees the world in terms of human and other-than-human – and the Christian notion of heaven and earth were negotiable, he thought, and made it possible for the Cree to understand Christianity in their own way. He also argued that the Cree transformer/trickster/culture hero Chakaapash was, for them, comparable to Jesus. This, too, made it easier for the Cree to take up Christianity, and all of these factors made Christianity in James Bay a syncretic creation. If Chakaapash and Jesus are comparable within a Cree-Christian context, then we can maybe get a sense of how Christianity evolved here. But even while Chakaapash is a powerful figure, he is often mischievous and very funny. Again, I think we should be wary of overly literal analogies. The syncretic process is what is important.[59]

More central to my concerns, ethnologist John Long, also working in the 1960s, argued that Christianity added to the personal power of individual hunters, thus aiding in the gathering of food, and that this allowed the Cree to use this belief system to their own purposes. He rightly noted that hunting was the most important issue for the Cree and that their understanding of Christianity was tailored to fit the needs of life in the bush. This was also important for the ethnological work of Richard Preston as he explored the nature of hope within Christianity and how it related to the nature of hope within the hunting world. Active and effective hope within an indeterminate hunting world is the key to the environmental and historical significance of Christianity in James Bay. And, while Christianity changed the Cree, the Cree actively worked to change Christianity to fit with the environment and their understanding of it. It was here, where material need met conceptual need in the individuals in James Bay, that Christianity's meaning played itself out most fully.[60]

In the end, hunting must be connected to Christianity in some meaningful way, and, given that hunting occurred out on the land and away from the missionaries and the traders, it is almost impossible to find this connection in the written record. There are clues as Cree hunters did sometimes express the power of Christianity with regard to their quest for food, but these are often statements transcribed by missionaries and interpreted as an abandonment of older beliefs. This abandonment of older beliefs and conversion to a "pure" form of Christianity was their hope, but historical facts belie much of that hope. Here we can return to the epigraph with which this chapter begins: "Ooskidae told me that when he could get nothing for food that he did not forget God and when in distress he always found how good it was to call upon him, as by doing so he was enabled to keep him[self] from despondency and was likewise certain of finding something or other." Here we have a hunter calling upon God in time of need but expressing himself in terms of fending off despondency. Calling on God was an active form of hoping and fit well with the other ways that hunters had of expressing themselves in the world of other beings. The "something or other" – the vague and powerful potential of those words – is significant too. The unknown potential of the hunt and the hunted could be compared to the unknown potential of God. Calling on God, keeping up hope in Him, not being too deterministic with regard to what that hope might achieve: all of this was a Cree profession of faith in both a Christian God and in the land.[61]

In James Bay, Christ may have become, as he did in the medieval European tradition, the hunter of men's souls, actively pursuing his prey with the same hope for their salvation that the hunter cultivated in finding his prey. More provocatively, that same medieval tradition carries stories of Christ as the hunted other – a saviour disguised as prey – revealing himself to those in need at the moment of the kill, saving their lives and their souls together with his gift. Again, these are only analogies, but they open up space for Cree analogies and for a consideration of what they might have looked like. The Cree symbolic world continued to be supported by and concerned with the hunting of food on the land, and hunters and their families fit Christianity within that matrix. Christianity did not replace Cree beliefs any more than the fur trade replaced the hunt for food, but both affected Cree culture and were affected by it. This, in part, explains the sense that I got during that prayer in Mistissini. There are still Anglican ministers in many of the Cree communities, and, as I have said, the Pentecostal Church has been very influential over the last thirty years. Yet, for those Cree who are practising Christians, this is also part of a "traditional" way of life.[62]

There is one last thing to consider with regard to the effect of Christianity and the fur trade on Cree culture. Christianity brought a powerful narrative innovation to Cree culture, but it did not mesh cleanly with the innovations brought by the fur trade. As I said earlier, missionaries knew the combined power of Christianity and agriculture – the history of North America bears witness to that power – but the fur trade could not help them create a unified vehicle for change. The missionaries' understanding of humanity's natural place, on the one hand, and the fur traders' modes of making a living, on the other, could be engaged separately by the Cree and adapted to circumstance in the bush. This would not be so different from how the Cree used their ability to trade with NWC traders in order to maintain their leverage with HBC traders. This separation of narrative and action will continue into the late twentieth century, but from now on we must be aware of both the events in the region and the narratives that are growing outside James Bay. In the end, they work together in a way that missionaries would have understood, though in the decades after 1860 the changes happening in the region take centre stage.

In trying to illuminate some of the historical meaning of Christianity in eastern James Bay I've stepped away from the chronology of events, pulling material together from across more than a century. This stepping out of the landscape of events and into the landscape of ideas helps to show how the Cree negotiated the meaning of a new religious presence on their land, but it is now important to get back to the events that occurred after the 1860s. Religion was involved in these events, but so were environmental factors and the developing political history of Canada and Quebec. A sensitivity to the narrative contexts within which people lived, and to how those contexts changed over time, will ensure that this era of Cree history takes on a significance that goes beyond that of a dismal tale of increasing physical hardship, starvation, and death.

5

Marginal Existences

He arrived yesterday – his wife died this spring, he has no fur, so as far as we are concerned it would be more profitable were he also to die soon as we will almost have to give him more supplies this fall.

— *Trader James Bell,* Mistassini
Post Journals, *1937*[1]

D riving along the James Bay road or along the Route du Nord, the road that traverses the territory west to east, the intrusions of the outside world are everywhere. The road itself is an intrusion poignantly illustrated by the number of dead animals and the living ones who just don't know to get out of the way yet. Along the road there are clear-cuts and "borrow" pits – a wonderful euphemism suggesting that the gravel will be paid back someday. There are also the phalanxes of high-tension towers buzzing and crackling at 750,000 volts. The scale of this intrusion is monumental in comparison to what was brought about by a few fur trade posts, but, as I drive the road, I think about the three or four decades on either side of 1900, and, for me, there are some analogies to be drawn between those decades and the present. During both periods there were dramatic changes on the land, and the Cree suffered from those changes; during both periods it was, in part, the intrusion of outside economic forces and people that were at the root of these changes. What is different today is that the challenge now is not continued physical existence but continued cultural self-definition. The Cree today are not starving and poverty-stricken – nor are they as rich from their treaties as some would have you believe – but they are faced with a reorganization of their way of living with their lands. This reorganization has been forced on them by our resource demands in James Bay as well as by our cultural expectations of them as a people. This is a unified process – a reshaping of land and the narrative of the land together – and it ensures that the changes of today are on a different scale from those of the earlier decades (although there was a reimagining of the land going on then as well). For now, my focus remains on events on the ground in the decades before and after the turn of the nineteenth century, but the larger forces so dominant today were there to see even then.

Beginning even before the Confederation of Canada in 1867, and increasingly thereafter, more and more people began coming north and with them came severe and often detrimental change. Because of them disease, death, and environmental degradation became more and more a part of Cree life. Some of this was simply the terrible, coincidental convergence of the Cree with new people who more frequently carried sickness into their territory, but trappers from outside the region also moved more frequently across the region in the decades after 1870, stripping the land of its resources. Some of these trappers were whites from southern Canada, though it is not clear whether they all were. They used new trapping methods, including poisons, and, like the others before them, they put stress on the local environment. The difference was that, given all the other events of the late nineteenth century, the Cree were less able to absorb these trappers or to mitigate their effects than they were in earlier decades. These were extractive hunters in a way and to a degree that had not been seen; they brought with them both new technologies for hunting and a more market-driven fur hunt, which changed the behaviour of some Cree hunters.[2]

Many of the other new arrivals in the region were extractors too, though in other ways. Bureaucrats, scientists, and even tourists came to take something from the region without necessarily connecting with it or with the people who lived there. Rather than extracting fur off the land, they came to learn things about the land, to expand an outside body of knowledge, or to find something symbolic in James Bay. They all placed the region into a context of understanding and meaning that differed from that of the Cree. In other words, the process of "discovering" James Bay had truly, if slowly, begun within the larger culture to the south. What happened in James Bay was hardly a new phenomenon in North America – simply the pushing out of a cognitive frontier that had lingered at the edges of the region for centuries. The "discovery" of the Americas, after all, came not with the fishers and whalers who had visited for centuries but with the first European explorers who claimed sovereignty and began to fit the new land into an existing body of European cultural and political knowledge – inaccurately, as it happens, but with remarkable effect.

In the same way, information began to flow out of James Bay in the later nineteenth century, many narratives were begun, and the bay was firmly placed within the larger cultural environment to the south. Missionaries were part of this process across the North as many of them became proto-anthropologists who helped inform the larger culture; bureaucrats began to redefine the region as being within their jurisdiction and scientists began to analyze and explain both environment and people within their paradigm of understanding. Slowly, too, recreationists, steeped in romantic notions of wilderness and driven by the growing urban, industrial reality of modern life, began to include the North within their narratives of adventure and conservation. James Bay was a small part of this larger process, and, for the time being, all these narrative creations had little relevance to everyday life in the region, but they were the start of the more unified process that is happening today. It was the material effects of greater outside contact that began immediately to reshape the James Bay environment, but narrative divergences from local understanding began filling a reservoir of words that would flood back onto the lands of the region a century later.[3]

Traders had always taken fur from the region in the name of an outside profit motive, and missionaries related deeply to an outside commitment to Church and religion. But when missionaries and traders came to live in James Bay, all were drawn into a reciprocal cultural relationship with the Cree and their environment. To a great extent they were forced by the Cree, and by their own need for subsistence and cooperation, to incorporate themselves into local understandings and to interpret James Bay with those understandings in mind. Newer arrivals were freer to interpret the region independently because they did not depend on it nearly as much as had the older arrivals. This ability to live at a distance from Cree subsistence and to interpret the region apart from any Cree context only increased as the environment degraded, as sickness increased, and as the Cree were less able to feed themselves from the land. This, in turn, threatened the Cree's ability to interpret their own material and symbolic surroundings, and they became increasingly dependent upon government aid, outside food, and a cash-driven market economy. By the turn of the century, this had become an increasingly downward spiral for both the Cree and the land, and things reached a true crisis in the late 1920s and early 1930s, when the fur trade was deeply affected by the Depression. In James Bay there was no Dust Bowl; rather, there was a land stripped of beaver – the animal that had created an environment for the Cree and for other animals – but the causes were not dissimilar: a land pushed beyond its capacity by market-driven use. As one reporter described it, by 1930 "the Indians were starving. Their fur catches were pitiful. There was nothing left but grass covered dykes, long abandoned slit dams, and dried up holes."[4]

The James Bay region, then, saw dramatic changes between 1870 and 1930, and these changes were increasingly influenced by what was going on outside. Outside understandings of the region were an increasingly important part of its story, though for the Cree, who were still hunting for their living and existing with their land as best they could, local meaning was still the context for local events. When J.W. Anderson wrote about the Mistassini shaking tent ceremonies in 1916, and about "the Wabinakae, or bad man," he was writing about something that was just beyond his reach, hidden behind the veils of ethnocentric perception – a culture using all of the tools at its disposal to maintain a context for understanding change. That the Wabinakae had transformed into some kind of bogeyman is provocative, though we are left to guess at the full meaning of this. Anderson lived closely with the Cree and may have understood more than he chose to write about when he sat down to chronicle his fur trade life in the 1960s. Maybe it was harder to believe at the physical and temporal distance from which he wrote. It's hard to say.

In many respects, the life Anderson had lived in Mistassini was just as enmeshed with the Cree as that of his predecessors in the hundred years or so since the trade moved inland. He gardened and fished and waited for hunters, just like they did. He interacted with the hunter's world on a regular basis. At the same time he lived with greater ability to communicate with the outside – he and his hunters listened regularly to the news from the European Front on a shortwave radio during the First World War – and at a time when travel to and from the region had been greatly eased. He also chose to become a writer after leaving the bay and so became an interpreter of the Cree and their land for the outside world during a time when interest in the North and its occupants was growing in the South. Anderson was a part of both the internal world of James Bay at the turn of the century and of the story later created by outsiders about the Cree and their land. In his own small way, he was like those early explorers who lived with Natives and then tried to explain the New World to a fascinated European audience. But this is getting ahead of the more mundane events on the ground.

In the late nineteenth century, at the level of subsistence, the success of agriculture at the posts in the southern parts of the James Bay region drove changes in the relationship between traders and hunters. Changes in food supplies altered the local food reciprocity that had developed earlier in the century and allowed some traders to pull back from Natives to the point where they seemed more like strangers to one another than people engaged in a long-negotiated coexistence. It is not coincidental that this occurred at posts where the margin of agricultural output allowed the traders to rely less on the hunted food brought in by the Cree. From the outset, these posts had sought independent subsistence, and their greater success, coupled with the stress placed on Native hunting, altered the cultural balance. In some respects, this created a self-imposed isolation. "I am left alone with old Etap," noted James Vincent one late fall, after all the hunters had been given their winter supplies and had left for their lands. It had been agreed that Etap would make short hunting trips interspersed with working stints at Mistassini that season, though Vincent was anxious to have even him gone as soon as possible. James Vincent, the brother of the missionary Thomas Vincent, shared his brother's connections with white culture but seems to have had none of his compassion for, or understanding of, the local way of life. He had a Native wife who took part in the local culture, practising many of the traditional chores of a fur trader's wife, but he remained aloof from his surroundings and alienated from his local environment. He does not seem to have been a hunter like his brother and, for all intents and purposes, wrote himself out of the local narrative, longing for some outside reality.[5]

"Oh dreadfully dull," reads a much repeated journal entry in October, 1874, "oh for the YMCA room." James Vincent longed for a world outside James Bay that he had known in his younger days, and his local existence held no appeal for him. He did not care for the people that surrounded him or for their habits. "William Boy unwell from gormandizing himself," he wrote sardonically when a hunter came in looking for medicine. Feasting was going on somewhere in the area, but Vincent was not a part of it; in his journal he seems to take some satisfaction from William Boy's distress. Not surprisingly, the locals left him alone most of the time, though they insisted on coming for New Year's Day, when tradition demanded visiting the house, feasting all day, and dancing at night. They came, but Vincent took no interest in any of their celebrations. In fact, he took a walk alone in the woods, abandoning the post to them for a short while. He continued to do this sort of thing on other occasions. "Had a long walk for nothing," he wrote later that spring, "angled a trout." This was not travel for the sake of work or net fishing for subsistence but, rather, recreational walking and sport fishing. This was something new in the region: subsistence independent of Cree hunting as well as physical and cultural isolation from Cree hunters.[6]

James Miller, Vincent's replacement, was even more disdainful of his surroundings. He, too, had a Native wife who involved herself in the local social network even while he became increasingly unfriendly towards

Cree hunters. In December 1885, for instance, he went so far as to set up
a tent for holiday visitors, explaining in his journal that he expected a lot
of "scamps this year" and wanted to keep them out of the house. They
might come to use the post, but he did not want to be part of it, and,
unlike Vincent, he chose not to go walking in the woods. He became
more adamant in these dislikes as time passed, feeling himself harassed
by the demands of hunters who wanted to trade before going out to their
grounds. He begrudged all the talking and ceremony that surrounded the
act of trading, understanding neither the hunters' concerns nor their way
of doing business. Business should be transacted as quickly as possible
without any socializing, and the hunters should then leave, as far as he
was concerned. Similarly, in the spring he waited impatiently for them
to come back with their furs. "The Scamps of Indians is not coming in,"
he wrote petulantly, and their continued refusal to cooperate with his
schedule made him dislike their behaviour even more once they finally
arrived.[7]

As time went on, the relationship between Miller and his hunters became almost hostile. The next summer, he again recorded his satisfaction
when all the hunters were gone from the post: "good to get clear of them
for awhile now as they are troublesome set of scamps as ever was on the
face of this earth." That September, again waiting for hunters to come in
with some furs, he fumed that there was no sign of them: "let them stay
off and be hanged." One hunter finally came in, only briefly; the others
remained at a distance, happy to leave the trader be. In the years that
followed, in his journal Miller began to refer to all the local hunters as
"strangers," a term that had traditionally been reserved for hunters from
outside the bay, while locals were almost always referred to by name. For
Miller, the term "stranger" now applied to even to those attached to his
post, and though he must have known their names for his record keeping,
they were mentioned less and less.[8]

By the turn of the century, harsh expressions of alienation had given
way to the loss of the trader's ability to understand the nature of the hunt.
Early in 1900, for example, Miller reported a very snowy spring. "I hope
none of them will starve for want of food," he wrote, but his concern was
not for them so much as it was for their fur hunts that spring. A few days
later, he commented on the snow, thought about how bad the weather
was, and presumed that his hunters were living on rabbits. Hunters were
indeed relying more on small game than they had in the past during this
period, but absent from Miller's words is any understanding of how valuable the deep snow could be for tracking and catching larger prey. He was

genuinely surprised to report that John Bowson was not starving, that he had killed eight deer that winter, and that he was doing well because of the snow. Significantly, Bowson had "not brought a single bit to the house" and apparently felt no need to share his success with Miller. Mistassini during his time received a very limited amount of shared food, and locals clearly felt little obligation to feed Miller either.[9]

Food had been the foundation of the relationship between Natives and traders, but with the growing stress placed on the food supply and the diminishing number of beaver, this changed. At Mistassini, reciprocity broke down because of the traders' attitude, while at other posts it was replaced by a dependence on the traders' charity. Waswanipi had an even more productive agricultural sector by the end of the nineteenth century, and traders there could survive on fish and potatoes if they wished to do so. Unlike the traders at Mistassini, they remained more charitable towards Native culture and tried far more to help in times of need; still, while charity may seem more laudable than the hostility described above, it, too, had the effect of distancing traders from hunters. The meaning of food and the power of the hunter diminished in some respects, and bonds of interrelation changed from meaningful reciprocity to well-meaning charity. Only at places to the north, like Nitchequon, do the journals show that the traders suffered real privation along with their hunters. After Robert Chilton's death, his son took over and ran Nitchequon into the 1880s with seemingly no change in its cultural patterns. The traders and hunters had no agricultural options and had to continue to rely as best they could on the old reciprocity in a time when hunger and disease were becoming increasingly deadly to the Cree.

Colds had always been a part of the yearly routine of contact with the HBC ship, but the length of time needed to cross the ocean and the limited contact in the area had kept these to a minimum. Older, slower transport had been a poor vector for diseases, which ran their course by the time the crew reached the bay. By the late nineteenth century, better and more frequent transport had brought the region within the disease frontier of large outside societies. Faster ships and the proximity of trains meant that more sickness could make the leap, killing people in greater numbers, and disease and hunger reinforced one another. Hunger made Natives more susceptible to disease, and disease reduced their ability to feed themselves – hunger pushing hunters towards the posts even as disease made them wary. Increasingly, diseases spread out into the bush, despite the efforts of hunters to stay away from the posts when things were bad, and by 1902, the Rupert's House district report warned ominously that "epidemics of sickness it is feared will now become more or less a feature of the Indian trade as civilization extends toward the North and travel through the Indian country becomes common." This was probably in reaction to the recent measles epidemic that had swept the region, but epidemics had really already become a deadly feature on the land – for half a century at that point – and had already become a part of the equation of life and death there. That this report describes 1902 as some kind of novelty may mean things were getting worse at a faster rate, but we cannot avoid the evidence that disease had been affecting individuals and the culture at large for a couple of generations.[10]

As we have seen, the most common ailment was a head and chest cold that travelled into the region with the trade goods, both by ship from the coast and overland from the St. Lawrence. It was one of these yearly colds that afflicted Betsy Chilton, making her seek the solace of her tent. Even these simple ailments had been causing serious disruption for quite a while. In 1827, Kellock, for example, was troubled when only one of the annual canoes arrived at Mistassini; the other was at the head of the Rupert River, and a cold had left the men too sick to travel any farther. He sent men for the cargo, but, distressingly, they reported back that the sick men had eaten much of the winter supplies brought up from the coast. That same year, at Pike Lake, Robertson had no men to fish, and his own voyageurs were on the Rupert River, also eating winter supplies. While these outbreaks were sometimes deadly, there were also serious consequences that played out over a whole season having to do with food.[11]

Disease could run wild in the isolated populations of the posts and surrounding areas, causing weeks of disruption for both hunters and traders. In late January 1848, the hunter Etap and his family brought one of their boys, who was very sick, to Mistassini, "not knowing what to do with the child," as McKay put it. The boy had a high fever, and by early February two more of Etap's family were also very ill. In late February, McKay wrote that most of Etap's family was sick and that one of his own daughters had caught the disease. By the end of the month, most of those at the post and the general area had taken ill. He was forced to give them flour and oatmeal as they could not hunt or even stomach fish or rabbit. He concluded that it was not the usual cold: "I think it is the Typhus fever that they have – most of the people at the place is affected with it – more or less." No one recovered for another week. Out in the bush this same outbreak caused problems for others, and, in late April, the hunter Cheechaiwash told McKay that his brother's family had been sick for two months during the past winter. "By what he says I think it is the same disease that Etapai's family had," concluded McKay. The hunter Wapatch's family, it turned out, had the same fever in their camp. No one was reported as having died from this outbreak, and it is not even clear whether the outbreak was actually typhus, but its virulence and the fact that it afflicted the local area for most of the winter foreshadowed events in the coming decades.[12]

It was in the 1850s that greater contact and shorter times needed to reach the bay increased the frequency and seriousness of diseases. Whooping cough broke out all along the Eastmain coast in 1858, and F.H. Fleming, when he returned to the Moose Factory late that August, found to his dismay that the epidemic had left twenty dead. "The whole island looked like Rachel weeping for her children," he wrote, "it has been a sad, sad time for us all." By October, Horden recorded that ten more had died in the space of only a few weeks, bringing the total to thirty out of population of less than two hundred. This, he wrote, "caused a great gloom to hang over the place; I was deeply moved the first time I entered the graveyard to see so many new graves, at the head of many of which stood a member of my congregation weeping over the loss of her offspring." Children had faced the brunt of the outbreak here as well as at Albany and Rupert's House, which had epidemics of the cough as well. Eighteen-sixty was another bad year for whooping cough, many more died during that outbreak, and, in 1866, Rupert's House reported that eight out of eleven sick Natives brought into the post had died. "It was a touching spectacle to hear the lamentations of the poor Indians," wrote Angus Macgregor. Thomas Vincent reported that year that, during his sermon, there was so much coughing that, as he put it, "I found it difficult to hear my own voice." Though whooping cough seems to have started as a sickness in children, it had moved into the whole population by the 1880s.[13]

Surveyor Robert Bell reported it as "a sort of influenza" that rapidly spread through the settlements on Hudson Bay on a regular basis, and John Horden lamented that Rupert's House, once the "gem of Moosonee," was in dire straits, sickness and starvation having "more than decimated its hunting population." In 1884, there were twenty-nine deaths, in 1885, twenty-four. A devastating, unnamed sickness hit the post again in 1891, and as many as 20 percent of the population died that year. In 1898, the community suffered an outbreak of scrofula, a form of tuberculosis. The situation was nearly identical at other posts, and, because Rupert's House was the hub for supplies in the region, the network of outlying posts suffered both the effects of disease and the disruption in transport. At Waswanipi in 1890, for example, the trader Gordon worried about his supply lines. "I shall endeavor to take down as many canoes as I am able to man, but I imagine I will find great difficulty in inducing the Indians to voyage. The sickness of last year coupled with the insufficiency of men will no doubt prove prejudicial for another year." The next year several women had to be employed as voyageurs at Mistassini because so many of the men at the post were sick. Things got worse.[14]

As the nineteenth century continued, the list of diseases grew and continued to kill: one chronicler estimated that bronchitis and pneumonia caused 35 percent of deaths; scrofula, 30 percent; rheumatism, 10 percent; infant "convulsions," 10 percent; and various other causes, 15 percent. By the early twentieth century, tuberculosis increased and measles also became a chronic problem, and, at times, so many people were dying that those who remained healthy seemed to spend most of their time making coffins for the dead. Like other Natives before them, the Cree were more susceptible to diseases than were Europeans, but while this may correlate to their pre-Columbian separation from the Eurasian disease pool, it points at least as much to the deterioration of their food supply. Increased exposure is part of the explanation, but hunger and reduced resistance are surely also at play.[15]

It is impossible to say how many Cree died from these diseases, no reliable population data exist for the region, but it is clear that, beginning in the mid-nineteenth century, the effects of disease on the population increased dramatically. Waves of diseases continued to wash over the region, and, as late as 1935, the *Waswanipi Post Journal* notes occurrences like the arrival of Charlie Gull and George Diamin in the morning and their quick departure in the evening as they tried to "get away" before they got sick. Everyone at the post that year was sick, and while no one was yet dead, the interruption of hunting caused increased hunger. That March, another hunter came to the post, having walked five days, and reported that his family "too are in poor health, and not the best for provisions, and worst of all short of matches." He, too, left quickly, as anxious to get away from the post and the sick people there as to get aid to his family. The death rate was, on average, between 10 percent and 20 percent of the populations of these small posts.[16]

The quantifiable data are sketchy, but the psychological effects were palpable. Surveyor Robert Bell described a kind of "epidemic mania" that resulted in some individuals being locked up due to their violent reaction to grief. Self-control and hope slipped away from some as they were faced with increasing numbers of deaths that could neither be controlled nor explained. The sweep of these deaths was region-wide, touching every post and every hunting family. Most simply continued to try to hunt and survive – little else was possible – but ethnological studies conducted in the 1950s and 1960s indicate a sense of oppression in the memories of those who survived this period. We are thrown back on our imagination and a shared sense of humanity to try to comprehend what these times meant for people, but there is a sense that, at times, the disruption of hunting due to disease and death led to social breakdown.[17]

There was no organized medical presence in James Bay in these years, nor was there even any official knowledge of the area or study of its medical conditions. For many decades after Confederation, Department of Indian Affairs reports did not mention specific conditions in the area, though they do claim an unchanging demographic stability that is completely at odds with the facts on the ground – clearly the numbers were copied from year to year without knowledge of what was actually happening in the bay. This lack of knowledge existed because there was no government presence in James Bay that concerned itself with the Cree. Disease was a problem internal to the region, thus traders, missionaries, and hunters had to find their own solutions – and there were none. A combination of Native and limited European remedies were available, but neither had much effect given the scale of the problem. This may, in part, explain the alienation of traders from hunters; it certainly explains the increased need for charity towards many hunters who could not make a living.[18] Sadly, the end of the nineteenth century was also a time that saw the degradation of hunting resources – a failure of food on the land. Southern areas, in particular, experienced a decline in beaver stocks, the cause of which was not completely understood. It may have been due to the increased use of the resource by hunters and outside trappers, or there also may have been an outbreak of tularaemia. This bacterial disease regularly infected rodent populations, and outbreaks were common across the North. The effects of this shortage of food were mitigated to some degree by a shift in the international fur market, first to muskrat around the turn of the century and then to marten and fox. The cash market for these furs allowed the substitution of European food to make up for the loss of country food, and, while expedient at the time, this shift to outside food and the money economy that paid for it left Cree hunters vulnerable to market vagaries. This proved to be nearly disastrous later. Even at the time, "English" food did not meet nutritional needs as well as did country food, and people were weakened by it.[19]

The 1880s seems to have been the worst period in inland areas around Mistassini and Waswanipi, though it continued to be difficult later, even as hunger and poverty reached a peak along the coast. Just before his death in 1892, John Horden wrote to his superior and warned of the failure of the beaver and the HBC's troubles in James Bay. He foresaw disaster if the resources on the land did not recover. Despite all the death and suffering in the last decades, Horden believed that the worst problems would occur if the beaver did not reappear. These fears and worse were realized over the next few decades as the Cree were reduced to living only on fish, rabbits, and partridge. The increased pressure placed on these secondary components of the Cree subsistence system created a strain that made any changes to the cyclical nature of smaller game even more dramatic and the effects of hunger even more widespread. In years of decreased populations the Cree suffered greatly; in better years they were forced to use these resources beyond their capacity, making the low years even more frequent – another downward spiral. In 1893, the Rupert's House Journal explained the deaths of seven hunters in simple terms: "the total disappearance of Rabbit, Partridge, & Fish." Over the three subsequent years, twenty-one hunters, and it must be presumed their families as well, starved because of this loss.[20]

In the northern part of James Bay, the late decades of the nineteenth century were equally difficult. Food shortages in upland areas along the verge of the tundra were caused by a decline in the caribou herds during the 1880s and 1890s. This was due, in part, to massive forest fires that drove off the herds. These fires may have been caused by hunters overburning in an attempt to create new habitats that would draw the herds to the young growth. It was also likely due to a natural shift of the herd to the north. Caribou migration is still not completely understood, but patterns of migration do change over time. Hunters adapted to shifting patterns in the past, but in doing so they fell back on other resources. What happened in the 1880s and 1890s speaks to a declining set of resources, not simply to a shift in the migration patterns of one hunted animal. Whatever the ultimate cause, during the winter of 1892-93, as many as 150 people died of starvation in the northern regions of the bay because of the lack of caribou. These hunters always had less access to fur and, even with rising prices, were far less able to buy food. They suffered greatly and, by 1900, the hunters around Rupert's House, despite their own hard times, were of the opinion that the northern hunters were by far the poorest in the region because they were still unable to find caribou in any great number. The first thirty years of the twentieth century in the northern part of James Bay are obscure, but the environmental situation clearly did not improve. Cree reliance on relief from the HBC grew there as it did in other areas.[21]

By the end of the nineteenth century, both trade and subsistence were being shaped by environmental changes (associated with both food and sickness), and cultural changes followed. In the 1891 Rupert River District Report, W.K. Broughton observed the cumulative results: at Rupert's House two Natives had died of influenza and four from starvation, and, in addition, four hunters had gone down to Abitibi to trade in an attempt to get higher prices. With an increased need to use "English" food came an increased need for money: one had to trap as much as possible in order to make the best profit possible. The same report noted that, at Mistassini, an epidemic the previous summer had caused a great deal of disruption, and opposition traders from Saguenay were making inroads, trading liquor, and getting fur from hunters at the post. The same was true to the north. At Nitchequon Post that year it was unclear whether two hunters had gone down to Bersimis to trade or whether they had died during the winter, either from hunger or disease. At Eastmain, Broughton believed that strict business practice demanded the post be shut down but that it could not be abandoned because the locals were in such need of food. In short, the whole district was, he concluded, in fearful shape. He guessed that 20 percent of the inland hunters had starved, and he urged the HBC to seek government assistance for the people to keep things from getting even worse.[22]

Beginning in the 1890s, after Broughton's dire report, the HBC brought the matter of hunger to the notice of the Dominion government in the hope "that they might feel it incumbent upon them to provide relief, as they [had] already done in the case of Ungava." In 1894, government assistance in the form of a grant to the HBC helped to some extent, but, more important, the Cree experienced a relatively good year even without aid. In fact, 1895 through 1898 were all relatively good years for country food, and the HBC spent none of the government's money; 1899 was hard for both food and fur, however, and the HBC began to give out aid, first from the 1895 government grant and then from their own coffers (for which they were reimbursed with further government money). Hunters were now allowed relief at the company stores, and this continued for the next thirty years. The relationships between Cree hunters and traders were changed by the former's increased need to ask for help without any countervailing force in the social equation. Reciprocity and mutual need was giving way to increased dependence, and, in order to stave this off, Cree hunters were pushed to use their land more intensely. Urgent productivity meant more demands on people as well as on the land, and increasing death and environmental stress led to adaptive cultural behaviour aimed at preserving families and communities.[23]

The effects of an increased death rate within Cree culture are as difficult to find in the record as are all the other aspects of the Cree world, but there are clues that, in the face of all this turmoil, behaviour changed to allow the maintenance of hunting and its environment. Some of these changes involved the continuation of older practices, whereby unproductive group members (i.e., the old and the sick) were left to die or were put to death by their families. When Horden charged two hunters with killing their mother during the winter, they readily admitted to it, telling the minister it was her wish to die. "It was only at her repeated request that the deed was done," they told him, and both agreed that it had been expedient, though they were saddened by the necessity. This was a culturally acceptable act for some, and, though in Horden's mind the fur trade post offered an option, as we have seen, living with non-Natives was not acceptable to many Cree, and the old woman was not interested in this. These kinds of incidents appear to have increased during this period, but this may have more to do with the frequency with which missionaries (as opposed to traders) commented on it.[24]

In addition to these kinds of decisions about the living, hunters also seem to have had to alter the relationship between the living and the dead. Traditionally and historically, death meant moving in order to assuage both personal grief and the power of the dead that lingered on the land – a disengagement from the scene of death and, often, engagement with new people through a sharing of grief and news. If they so chose, the spirits of the dead could detrimentally affect the land and the hunt for food. The attitude of the living also affected the relationship with the hunted, and this had to be controlled. Grief, like pessimism, was problematic with regard to the quest for food, and dwelling on death and loss quite literally affected a person's environment. Hunters did not like to hunt land upon which a death had recently occurred, and many opted to spend the winter with another hunting group, letting their own lands be for the year. Hunters might also choose not to take fur but only to hunt food, thinking that they would not be lucky because of their sorrow and the spirits of the dead. As the hunter Woppunaweskum explained to Robert Miles, his group had "not killed a single fox" as they had refused his bait since there had been a death in his family. The relationship with the hunting lands was out of balance, and he told Miles that they were proceeding inland "being according to Indian custom desirous of leaving their usual residence, after the fatality which has happened." When death came, it demanded certain symbolic responses, but material needs made their own demands: with a declining hunt, no time could be spared to let land lie fallow, allowing the dead to occupy it. Ceremony was necessary, but traditional practices had costs.[25]

It seems clear that burying grounds came to be used to clear the land of bodies and spirits that affected the hunt for food, in addition to the uses that we normally associate with them. Graves at the posts certainly had significance to people and were, in part, an aspect of the growth of Christianity. Indeed, they may be the best evidence we have of how important Christian ideas were as far back as the late eighteenth century. George Barnley had commented on the burial ground at Moose Factory when he arrived, in 1840, noting the "wands stuck in the ground to mark their resting places decorated with ribbon and having pieces of tobacco suspended on them." In the early nineteenth century, gravesites were mentioned in all the journals in relation to local hunters. For example, Hamlet Henry Hawthorn noted the death of a child at Rupert's House in the spring of 1806 and commented on the "men and Indian digging the grave." Stockades were put around the graveyard in 1809, and all the journals mention the placing of stockades around graves, particularly those of children. But if Christianity played a role here, these burials were also used to meet an evolving Cree need. As mortality increased throughout the nineteenth century, increasingly hunters and their families began to bring the dying and the dead into the posts or come themselves when they felt that death was near. One hunter sent word to William McKay that he was coming "as he thinks he will die soon being in a very poor state of health, and prefers being buried at the house, than any other place." This hunter may have had a variety of personal reasons for wanting to be buried at the post, but he did not want to die on the hunting land, which would have forced the group to change its hunt. This one act in itself might have many explanations and might not be provocative, but it fits into a larger pattern – one that increased as hunger, disease, and death grew.[26]

Hunters began to bring the bodies of relatives for burial more frequently, and it is the actions of those left alive that are most interesting. When the hunter Shayeyew believed he was dying, for instance, he asked his nephew to bring him to the post, where he died several days later in the care of his mother and sister. Significantly, after the man died his female relatives immediately left the post in order to tell the rest of the party that the old man was gone. The body was left to be attended by Thomas Beads and his men; it was important for the group to know that the man was dead, but the body and any funeral seemingly were not. This pattern was repeated throughout the nineteenth century. Cree hunters and their families would bring in the bodies of their relatives and leave without ceremony. The HBC would then build coffins and bury the dead, so not only the posts but also the company men were used in this process. The 1909 journal at Rupert's House noted that "Reuben's sons came in today his mother is dead and his father wants the body buried at the post. So word was sent to the sawyers to haul it up." Here, as at other times, the trader went so far as to fetch the body to the post, thereby relieving the hunter and his sons of transferring it from one environment to the other. None of these mortuary services seem to have been primarily about the post or religion but, rather, about the lands outside.[27]

As the resources of the hunt declined over the latter half of the nineteenth century, the ability of hunting parties to leave land alone after a death became less and less. Death and its consequences for the hunt were vitally important, so trading posts, along with people who dealt with dead bodies, became a mechanism for clearing the land in an appropriate way. Hunters were adamant about this on many occasions. When Gunner (later John Gunner) and his partner came to Nitchequon Post and told Chilton that the hunter Mistappew had gone out of his mind with sickness and hunger and wanted to come to the house to die, Chilton told them that they must not bring him because supplies were very low. If they came, everyone would starve as the people at Nitchequon were already boiling sinew and bones to survive. One of Chilton's own men was suffering from headaches and bouts of irrational behaviour caused by hunger, but still Gunner brought Mistappew. Both men eventually succumbed to hunger and were buried at Nitchequon. Gunner went back to the bush immediately and continued to hunt, relieved now both of the burden of the living man and the burden of dealing with his death.[28]

The use of trading posts as burial grounds speaks most basically to the intensification of land use that was ongoing in James Bay. The removal of bodies allowed continued hunting and eliminated the forced periods of environmental recovery that were a part of the Cree's long-term success. This necessary adaptation played some part in the overall decline of hunting during this period. People were trying to maintain a relationship with the land and with each other, but by the turn of the century things had reached the point where hunger was a year-round problem, and one trader noted almost as a matter of fact that he had advanced the Indians some food "to keep them from starving for a few days Enyhew [sic]." That winter, Peter Gunner and his five children, along with two other hunters, starved to death in the bush. In July 1905, geologist A.P. Low, working in the Chibougamau area, recorded that he met six canoes full of starving Natives to whom he had given flour in order, as he put it, "to tide them over for a day or two." Later in the month, when he reached Mistassini, he found many hungry people there as well. He gave them as much pork, flour, and tea as he could spare, but this could not solve the situation. Even summer did not bring relief, and that May the Mistassini trader wrote of the poor fishing: "cannot get enough to keep us going it seems to be wars then [sic] winter."[29]

Hunger and disease were further exacerbated at the turn of the century by new factors that built on earlier environmental degradation and loss of cultural control. In 1900, the Quebec government ended a short-lived moratorium on the non-Native beaver hunt, and the district report warned ominously that "competition from that corner is to be looked for" again. The ban had been largely unenforceable due to the lack of local or provincial authorities, and, while trappers had done a great deal of damage in the nineteenth century, their increased number had an even greater effect in the twentieth. By 1905, the grim forecast had come true: the price of fur was on the rise and more people were trying to get in on the profits. By the 1920s, some whites were flying in from the Toronto area and setting up for the winter on Little Mistassini Lake to the north of the post. Others came from Ontario by train and then overland, and others seem to have arrived over the height of land from Lac St. Jean. Before this, the post journals from the era do not refer to white trappers, but they do refer to the fact that a greater number of Lac St. Jean Natives were visiting the post. The Lac St. Jean journals show that, by the second half of the nineteenth century, the majority of the hunters on the register had French names, and it seems reasonable to think that, while later writers have characterized these trappers as white, the people in the bay may have seen them as Native because they were trapping for a living. There was as yet no real legal distinction between white and Native. But no matter their origin, these trappers supplied themselves from the outside, were not dependent on the land, trapped areas completely, and did not worry about the long-term effects of doing so.[30]

Competition from outside trappers was further increased by the advent of the French Révillon Frères Company. This Paris-based company, controlled by a New York branch run by Victor Révillon, established posts at Moose Factory and Fort George in 1903, and, by 1904, Révillon Frères also had posts at Mistassini and Rupert's House. Both the Révillon Frères and independent traders like Jack Palmquist and George Papp (who set

up at Fort George and Great Whale, respectively) offered new trade opportunities to hunters and disquieted the region as the HBC once again
competed more aggressively for their furs. The HBC's rivals were willing
to pay much higher prices in cash to get hunters to trade when, in 1912-13,
world fur prices began to rise dramatically. The First World War caused
a lull, but the 1920s saw another boom in fur production as the raging
economies to the south increased the demand, particularly for luxury furs
like fox, mink, and lynx. Many options were open to individuals now, and
this moved some Cree to hunt more extensively for profit. William Walton
worried about the implications of rival trade. He saw lying and cheating
increase, among both hunters and traders, to the point where the whole
community was disrupted as each company competed for a dwindling
supply of fur. "The poor Indian does not know what to think," he wrote
to a friend as the two companies began to slander each other in the attempt
to bring Natives to them. To people used to negotiating their way through
various power relationships, this new situation forced them to mediate
between both sides even as they strove to understand this outside force.[31]

Not since the NWC/HBC competition a hundred years earlier had
hunters had to deal with this sort of thing on their land. The Révillon
Frères and the HBC were now competing with cash rather than with the
brandy and rum that were used in the earlier period, but the corrosive
effects were not dissimilar. The greatest disruption to the local hunt seems
to have involved individual hunters' loss of control over their territories.
The evidence is only anecdotal, but more and more it seems that hunters,
both white and Cree, were willing to range over as much territory as they
could to get as many furs as they could. There has been a great deal of
debate as to whether or not these hunting territories were a pre-contact
phenomenon – a debate to which I can add nothing useful – but in James
Bay throughout the fur trade era these family hunting grounds had been
part of local tradition. As I have noted, there is some evidence that this
tradition began to break down during the HBC rivalry with the NWC,
but during the Révillon Frères/HBC period it is clear that Cree culture
began to lose control of the land in the face of the free-market economy.
This powerful new idea of people's relationship to the land was reshaping
the territory and leaving many people hungry.

As the prices of certain kinds of fur went up, some hunters were able
to make enough profit to make up for the lack of country food, but this
was a temporary solution to the problem of hunger as neither the world
market nor the James Bay environment could support that kind of behaviour for long. Even during this time of a booming market and increased

prices, the growing poverty of many can be seen in the amounts of transfer payments that were being made from the government to the trading companies. Hunters who experienced unsuccessful years were not able to feed themselves off the land and so had to take more and more credit from the traders. Sometimes they had good years and paid off their debt, but often they did not. From 1900 to 1930 the numbers show not only an increase of relief money being given in individual communities but also, eventually, the steady inclusion of all of the Cree communities. To make matters worse, in the first two decades of the twentieth century, along with outside economic pressure, there were again huge fires that forced some land to be abandoned for years. Hunting small game became the only means of survival as, over huge areas, overhunting had killed off the beaver almost completely. Before the First World War, the combination of large fires and overhunting also decimated the caribou herd, and the Cree narratives of this period focus on how, under ever more difficult circumstances, hunters tried to maintain control of the material and conceptual context of their lives.[32]

In 1926, an inspection of the district found $5,000 in unpaid debt in James Bay, above and beyond the payments made to relieve hungry hunters.[33] In the winter of 1928-29 there was a complete absence of both rabbits and partridges, leaving Hurley at Mistassini Post to write that, "although people around here have snares out all the winter, not a single rabbit has been taken so far – not one [partridge] has been seen all this winter." At Rupert's House that winter only four beaver were brought in to trade. Writing about the winter of 1929-30 at Waswanipi, Angus Macleod emphasized the lack of country food, noting, in an attempt to be hopeful, that a few hunters had arrived and that "most of them paid their accounts." This was not a sign of overall prosperity though, and by November he was busily looking for signs of rabbit as he was "getting hard up for fresh meat." He had "never experienced such a poor year for fur and fresh meat," he noted, and, on December 25, he commented that "we had to be content with salt fish and potatoes for our X-mas dinner." In fact, there was massive starvation in the Rupert's House area that winter, and it spread quickly. In March, Joseph Capisisit and his family came to Waswanipi and told Macleod that they had been eating moose hide in order to survive, and, as the world economy tumbled into chaos, so too did the situation in James Bay.[34]

Amidst this economic and environmental confusion, communities tried to maintain the normal rhythm of social interaction that had become traditional in the bay, but this had costs too. In the late spring of 1931 at Waswanipi Post, Bishop Anderson's arrival and the killing of a bear was

	Eastmain	Ft. George	Mistassini	Rupert's House	Waswanipi	Great Whale	Nemiska	Neoskweskau
1903	148	309	17	885	39		No Aid Given	No Aid Given
1904	172	889	30	523	100	31		
1906	200	541	21	469	109	41		
1908	176	286	66	929	208	46		
1910	290	617	14	1,170	365	264		
1911	70	310	135	785	207	89		
1912	245	679	35	948	308	347		
1913	129	564	no data	1,624	no data	93		
1914	342	1,973	174	2,908	642	4,311		
1915	450	3,319	583	1,685	325	2,647	0.81	
1916	423	7,513	355	1,691	353	1,317	110	
1917	1,244	5,302	383	1,875	no data	4,985	1,046	
1918	3,290	9,843	429	2,520	495	5,494	946	75
1919	915	2,559	377	2,809	230	2,000	431	110
1920	2,976	10,730	630	3,785	257	8,009	1,539	no data
1921	530	3,986	no data	1,518	no data	2,752	184	no data
1922	1,671	14,655	300	2,956	405	4,802	895	214
1923	2,244	9,379	399	5,710	271	3,834	1,184	156
1924	1,696	4,028	475	1,467	56	4,872	741	134
1925	1,634	10,049	584	3,226	919	7,827	1,001	162
1926	1,747	6,028	601	2,509	615	6,406	568	195
1927	4,173	9,733	2,318	4,753	850	10,370	2,283	532
1928	4,085	7,624	1,163	2,316	1,157	6,327	2,560	1,294
1929	1,781	4,981	539	1,857	1,456	1,986	1,685	377
1930	7,156	8,614	955	4,663	1,881	2,160	4,033	1,763
1931	3,251	3,212	841	307	2,418	1,838	2,947	1,627

TABLE 5.1 *Government relief for Cree hunters, 1903-31.* Between 1903 and 1931 an increasing amount of government aid was given to the Hudson's Bay Company to relieve the poverty and hunger of the Cree. The apparent peak in 1927 28 is likely due to the increased poverty of all Canadians after 1929 rather than a reduction of Cree need. Despite the increasing dollars spent, the Cree continued to suffer from lack of game and fur on the land. *Library and Archives Canada, RG 10, Annual Reports of Indian Affairs, 1864-1990*

the cause of a bear feast. "A short speech was given by the chief and his councilors then a dance was held later on," Macleod observed; and moose feasts were held five days later and again in July, when hunters brought in meat to share with the whole band. Interestingly, Macleod noted on July 11 that "there is very few of the Indians that are getting enough to eat these times." Clearly, the feasts were not about food. Still, the hunters remained at the post for another ten days for the wedding of Alfred Miller and Elizabeth Grant. The couple were "lucky enough" to get two moose for the celebration, but the hunters started to leave for their land soon after: "as they are poorer than usual they are anxious to get away from the post where they can store up food for their winter's use." These hunters had, in fact, expended a good deal of their own subsistence in order to partake in important cultural activities at the post – a very difficult thing to do by the 1930s.[35]

For the Cree, bad debt and hunger continued into the 1930s. In 1932, W. Jeffreys at Mistassini Post recorded $900 in unpaid debt to the post. "It is a terrible business to collect debt this spring," he wrote. White trappers had flown in and set up on Little Mistassini Lake that winter and had taken much of what little the hunters had been counting on. Nineteen thirty-four and 1935 saw $919 in unpaid debt, and 1935-36 saw $1,200. In the spring of 1935, Macleod wrote at Waswanipi: "our hopes seem to be shattered with regards to fur collection." None of his hunters had brought anything to speak of, and they were, by that time, living largely on fish and other small game.[36]

By the mid-1930s the federal government was sending some direct aid to the Cree, although, given Ottawa's limited response to the needs of all Canadians at the time, federal funds were extremely small. It was during this time, however, that a limited band government was set up to deal with the federally appointed Indian agent. Created under the Indian Affairs Act, these band governments had very limited power over the loosely organized groups of hunters around the trading posts. The Cree were still not under any treaty, and the band governments could only hold so much power within this new kind of relationship between the Canadian government and the Cree, but it was something new to the region. Church groups in Canada were sending clothing to be distributed by the missionaries, but, again, the need was great across the whole country, and this did not change the fact that Cree hunters were starving. In the depths of both a world depression and a local depression, a trader at Nemiska recorded somewhat desperately that "things have been bad enough so far this winter, but right now they have reached a point which all but brings us to our wits end."

At Nichicun that spring the same trader noted: "I have never seen such poverty among Indians." Everybody at the post was underclothed and hungry.[37]

And still, despite all this poverty and hardship, in March 1939 Matthew Ottereyes brought two sleds of moose meet to the post at Nemiska to relieve them temporarily. Given the opportunity and resources, old patterns remained and reasserted themselves between hunters and the trading posts. It is also clear that these hunters were maintaining a relationship with their land as well. The environment had undergone massive change in the previous fifty years and would never again be what it was, but many had not given up hope in the land and its ability to maintain Cree culture. In fact, the environment of James Bay and the Cree hunting culture were about to rebound, allowing the Cree to again feed themselves largely off the land. To understand the context within which that resurgence took place, however, as well as what would bring it to a premature close, we must look at another aspect of the late nineteenth and early twentieth centuries in this region. There were other people in James Bay during the period I have just described, and, though their presence seemed limited with regard to local meaning at the time, in the end their effect would be profound.[38]

Even as tragic events were unfolding within James Bay during the nineteenth century, an increasing awareness of the region was developing as outsiders travelled the area, experienced it, and carried their knowledge southward. These travellers were the vectors for some of the immediate change in the region (e.g., that due to disease), but they were also vectors for a much slower kind of change. As they defined what was important to them about the region, they developed many intertwining narratives that related to James Bay. These had little to do with the story told thus far or with the internally defined environment that had shaped people in the past. But though this may appear trivial in light of what was happening to the people in the bay, these various perspectives, augmented by others over time, would eventually form the lens of conceptual and narrative understanding through which Canadians and Americans would see the bay and its people. That lens, its size and its shape, defined what would be seen – and, more important, what would not be seen – by everyone to the south. What we know and don't know about the Cree and their land has become crucially important to them, and that knowledge has been shaped by both our ability and inability to see.

Prior to 1870, outside knowledge of the James Bay region was sketchy at best. Andrew Graham's 1768 *Observations on Hudson's Bay* was the only history and natural history of the region. Graham drew together information that he had gathered during his time in the western portion of the HBC's territory. The book was political as well as investigative and had been written in response to criticisms raised by those who disliked the HBC's monopoly and had pointed out how ignorant the company was of the region even after a hundred years of occupation. Graham's book was meant to prove how much the HBC did know and how much it valued its domain in North America; but, while his knowledge of the west was rich, he devoted only a superficial paragraph or two to the Eastmain. No maps of the area existed before James Clouston began to draw its interior in the 1810s, and even these well-drafted documents were largely route maps that did not attempt to capture the geography of the region. In the early to mid-nineteenth century, the Royal Society in London and the Smithsonian Institution began specifically to collect information and specimens from the traders, asking them to preserve animals and to fill out questionnaires about species and their habitat. The HBC men accommodated these requests, but, when fit into their trade and subsistence activities, the amount of information sent out of the bay was limited.[39]

Likely the first real scientist to visit James Bay was Sidney Coolidge from the Harvard Observatory in Boston. Coolidge was a young and well-known astronomer – a grandson of Thomas Jefferson, who himself spent much of his life investigating and documenting the continent. It is unclear from the record whether Coolidge was working for the observatory in his travels to James Bay or for himself, but in the summer of 1857 he spent an evening at Mistassini Post. He lied to William McKay for some reason, telling him that he was travelling only to improve his health. Records at Harvard indicate that he was there to speak to the Cree and to acquire local knowledge about the region. He arrived from Lac St. Jean seeking linguistic information, but, as an astronomer, he was most interested in the Cree understanding of the stars and the heavens in general. He apparently spent much of the summer there, though sadly, if he kept records of his time in the region (and it seems certain that he would have) they are not extant. Coolidge's visit to the bay is fascinating, made all the more interesting by its opacity, but maybe this only serves to illustrate how little was known about eastern James Bay at the time.[40]

Despite the slow start, the pace of investigation picked up markedly with the creation of the Dominion of Canada in 1867 and the ceding of all HBC land to the new country three years later. The combination of political sovereignty and scientific inquiry was a potent and effective force for gathering knowledge, and, after Rupert's Land was transferred to Canada, the Geological Survey of Canada began to seek a more fully developed understanding of the region's resources. Founded in 1842, the survey sent a number of scientists to study the geology, hydrology, and forest resources of James Bay beginning in 1877. These surveyors were looking for precious metals as well as for more mundane resources such as iron. The many quartzite outcrops in the region, so important for Paleolithic tools, also hinted at diamond and gold resources (these are only now being developed in the early twenty-first century). The timber and agricultural resources were also of interest, though, except for some overly optimistic reports by Robert Bell – one of the few committed boosters of the region in the nineteenth century – few saw great reason for exploiting them.[41]

Bell travelled the coast in 1877 and went into the interior in the 1890s. In the 1880s and 1890s, A.P. Low made more extensive surveys of the James Bay region, and in 1901 the geological survey crews mapped all the coastal waters for navigation, travelling the Eastmain coast and sounding the travel lanes and the harbours. At the turn of the century the rough survey work had been done, though eastern James Bay still held the single largest amount of unexplored land in Canada's North, and most would have agreed with W.J. Wilson's 1902 assessment that "the country as a whole is of little value at present." This continued to be the general opinion, and with few exceptions James Bay had little use and little meaning within the cultural environment of the South, though there were important foreshadowings of how this would change in the future.[42]

A.P. Low's 1902 expedition was paid for by the American Dominion Development Company, which was looking for resources valuable to private industry (though the information was also passed on to the geological survey, with which Low was still associated). With an eye on future development, Low was interested in the region's massive hydro potential. Even at the mouth of the Nastapoka River, to the north of Great Whale and far beyond where the needs or the technology of the time would have placed hydro generation, he was struck by the potential. At that site he took photos "of the water power, gullies, and lower level ground to show the ease for development," concluding that there was "water enough to develop 100,000 HP." Megawatts were not part of his calculations, but the region had exponentially more hydro potential than that one river, and he made note of others despite their remoteness. In the next few decades Quebec would begin the development of its southern water resources, and hydroelectricity would, from then on, be connected with the province's future. It is interesting to note that, like so much of what has been developed in Canada's North – fossil fuels, uranium, hydroelectricity – James Bay

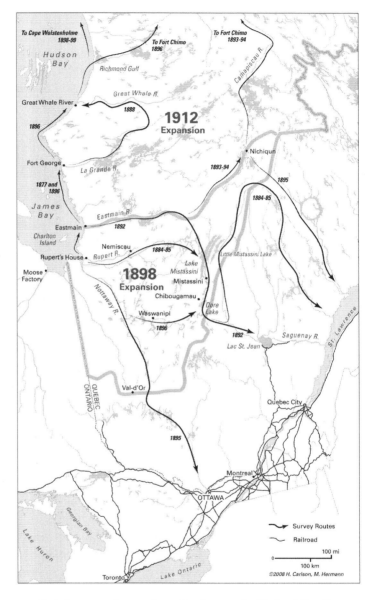

MAP 5.1   *Geologic surveys of eastern James Bay.* In 1870, the Hudson's Bay Company
sold its holdings to the new Dominion government, and the region became part of the
vast Northwest Territories of Canada. In 1898, jurisdiction was given to Quebec up to
the Eastmain River and that was extended to Ungava in 1912. Shortly after this land was
purchased, geological survey teams began to map and study the area in an attempt to
put a value on its resources. Eastern James Bay was of little value to either the province
or Ottawa before the 1970s.

would require both twentieth-century technology (to make development possible) and twentieth-century needs (to make it meaningful). In 1902, James Bay was still neither useful nor meaningful to most people, but the information was being collected.[43]

It was the survey crew's overall job to begin cataloguing the resources of the area and to construct an understanding of James Bay that was related to the needs of the new country to the south. On a day-to-day basis, their activities relied primarily on Cree work and Cree knowledge to fulfill the larger task. Survey crews used Native guides to find their way through the new country, and, to some extent, they also used the local environment to survive. An entry from Low's 1902 journal told an old story, noting that the men were working as hard at finding food as they were at surveying the land. Low's crew spent a week or more that spring salting geese for summer provisions to supplement the small supply they had brought, and the next winter they continued hunting and trapping their way across the land. In December, he noted that the men were going away on a weekly basis to visit their traps and that he had sent one of his men and a Native to set a net under the ice on a lake 16 kilometres from their camp. One of his men had become lost on one of these excursions, and, consequently, he gave orders that none of the men was to go far without a Native companion: "it is the simplest of things to get lost."[44]

The guides and their families were also supplying Low and his men with food when they could. In January, he noted with satisfaction that four families went inland "to hunt deer for us, some were quite successful and in consequence we obtained a good stock of venison and fat." In some ways, these crews simply recreated the system by which the fur traders had survived for centuries, but there were important differences as these hunters were supplying more than just food: they were supplying information, particularly about geology, all of which was recorded and sent south to add to a growing body of knowledge. All the survey men appreciated how well these hunters knew their land and tapped into that resource to aid their fact finding. Importantly, there was little reciprocity, though the flow of information was slow enough at first and its effect was unnoticed in the region.[45]

At the same time that the Geological Survey of Canada crews were working in the area, rail lines were being pushed north from both Quebec and Ontario. Part of the survey crew's mandate was, in fact, to judge the geography and resources for these lines. These rail lines had a more immediate effect on the local environment than did the surveyors, although throughout the nineteenth century the rail never got closer to James Bay than ten days' canoe travel. Even this was a vast change from the weeks of travel required before. The Lac St. Jean Railway was completed in the 1880s, and by 1886 the Canadian Pacific line reached its northern limit south of Moose Factory. Chibougamau, less than a day from Mistassini, was being supplied by rail by 1910, and by then Waswanipi was also within easy reach of the rail line. In 1923, Ontario premier George Howard Ferguson announced to the press that there would be no Toronto and Northern Ontario rail line north into James Bay. "To go to James Bay would be building a considerable time ahead of necessity," he said, but though the Toronto and Northern Ontario line did not reach the shores of the bay at Moose Factory until 1932, the overall effects of rail in the region were already being felt.[46]

Even limited rail service allowed access to the region for more casual visitors, particularly in the late nineteenth and early twentieth centuries, when canoeing and camping became a part of American and Canadian recreational culture. Tourists from Europe and New York City found their way to James Bay beginning in the 1890s. People wanted to traverse what they perceived as a last wilderness and to meet Native people whom they supposed still lived as had their ancestors. The stories of Leonidas Hubbard and others highlighted the fact that the Quebec-Labrador peninsula was one of the last great tracts of unknown country left in North America. And while the North American western frontier was closed, the North was still open to adventure. Thus began a tradition that continues today. In August 1938, for example, American boys from Keewaydin Camps on Lake Temagami came through Waswanipi, "a dance was put on for them which they all seemed to enjoy," and other boys from Keewaydin received the same kind of welcome at Mistassini in 1935 and 1939 as they made their way down the Rupert River to the bay. The Cree and James Bay have become an important part of Keewaydin's culture, as well as of the cultures of many other camps in New England, and the rivers of James Bay are well known to wilderness canoeists. These summertime visitors were a novelty and provided a welcome distraction to trader and hunter alike, but their presence marked yet another conceptualization of the region that was being created from the outside. This was the story that first brought me to James Bay, and, like its scientific cousins, the romantic notions surrounding James Bay and its people would have practical effects only later in the twentieth century.[47]

All these new encounters with James Bay saw it either as an objective, scientifically knowable environment or as a sublime northern wilderness harbouring exotic Natives. Neither of these narrative creations had much local meaning, and readers were free to imagine a region where "large areas [had to] be represented on the map as blank spaces – unexplored," or so wrote a young Olaus Johan Murie regarding the anticipation he felt at going to James Bay. "Hudson's Bay became a reality to me," he continued, only after he had lived there a while, though the reality of the region eluded him in many respects. His time there did provide him with much detail, but what he observed and what he wrote, both then and later, had far more relevance outside the region and in the future than it did then and there. In some ways, Murie's narrative is similar to the missionaries' narratives of Christianity, but the scientific and romantic understandings of the region that he helped to shape became far more important in relation to the political, technocratic narratives that would follow than did anything the missionaries had to say. These understandings would resonate with popular political understandings of what the region should or should not be in the future.[48]

Murie first wrote about James Bay in the fall of 1914, at Moose Factory on the southern shore of James Bay. From 1914 to 1917, shortly after graduating Pacific University, Murie was field naturalist for the Carnegie Museum in Pittsburgh. During this period he made two expeditions to Canada: to James Bay and Hudson Bay (1914-15) and across the Labrador Peninsula (1917). He travelled extensively during his years in the North, collecting ornithological specimens, eventually, by dog sled, going as far north as the Hopewell Islands. For Murie, this was the beginning of a long career with the wilds of North America, and he would spend most of that career in the US Biological Service and, later, the Park Service. Significantly, in 1935 he, along with Aldo Leopold, Robert Marshall, Benton MacKaye, and others, co-founded the Wilderness Society, and together they would shape much of the environmental thinking about wild North America in the twentieth century. Both Americans and Canadians would discover an aesthetic resource in their wildernesses, and, for Murie, James Bay was foundational to this discovery.

In addition to his scientific work in James Bay, Murie left a diary, a composite narrative written at the time, and a reminiscence written shortly before his death in 1963. Northern Quebec was Murie's first encounter with wilderness, and the memory of the place and its people remained an important touchstone for him and his thinking. Murie saw James Bay as largely untouched by the outside world, and he struggled to comprehend his surroundings and their relation to the Cree; even his reminiscence fifty years later attests to the many questions that, for him, remained important and unresolved. He never seems to have quite located himself in that place or with the Cree.[49]

When, in the summer of 1914, his party's canoe floated away when he was having a lunch break on a rocky island, Murie's immediate and panicked reaction – jumping into the icy water of James Bay and swimming after it – was nearly fatal. His guides, after pulling him out, calmly built a raft of driftwood, retrieved the boat, and then took him to his destination after nursing him for several days. Reflecting in old age on the near-fatal events of that day, he still asked, "how can one understand such things?" The men's actions seemed superhuman to him, and years later he continued to be astounded by those Cree hunters, seeing them as inherently attuned to their wilderness surrounding, their natural state. For him this had been an encounter with raw nature, and he had been saved by the equally natural skills of his guides. These memories across half a century belie the subtlety of his encounters in 1914-15. He had been saved by men who were part of a long historical process and part of an environment that included other-than-human beings upon whom they may have called for help in this very dangerous moment. This is conjecture, but there are many stories of how animals have helped men in similar situations. For Murie, this was hard to fit into a coherent story. Viewed through his cultural perceptions, all the individual reality of James Bay's history was filtered out, leaving only his generalized perception of the Cree and their land.[50]

In place of local understandings, Murie came to the bay carrying his own cultural toolkit, which he put to work in relating to both the local environment and the Cree. He was a scientist first, and identification, cataloguing, and analysis were his main occupations in the region. He created a large catalogue of bird species, duly killed and preserved, so that they might be studied later. And in this work he was clinically objective in both his method and his results, both of which are illustrative:

> Saw also a small flock of *cedar birds* and got four specimens. Took an adult *Wh. Cr. Sparrow*. Shot a male *downy woodpecker* on a cottonwood. Mr Todd [Murie's superior until the end of summer, when he returned home] got a *hairy woodpecker*. Shot a *hermit thrush*. I saw a *hawk owl* on the top of a spruce tree at the edge of a high back. I took a shot at it but missed. It lit again, flew and perched again in the top of a high spruce. As I approached it flew again turned and came right toward me and I shot it. Shot a *Wilson snipe*.[51]

This expression of scientific, material objectivity speaks to a specific conceptual relationship with the environment, one that was likely incomprehensible within the Cree cultural environment. Taking animals was a part of their daily routine, but the Murie's act and the Cree act seem almost completely unrelated, given the widely divergent conceptual frameworks that surrounded each. Murie's rationale made perfect sense, but only outside of the James Bay region.[52]

Interestingly though, for all the difference between Murie's perceptions and those of the Cree, his physical activity was comprehensible to them. In James Bay, Murie was a hunter of sorts. His material relationship to the environment was understandable to the Cree, even if his cultural motivations were not, and their own systems could easily mesh with his. Young boys became one of his best sources of specimens and information as they practised their small hunts around the settlements. They were paid for their work, mostly in food, and became enthusiastic workers and informants. In some ways, this was simply a small translation of the fur trade carried on for so many generations by their parents and ancestors, and yet the value of their exports was now in knowledge and not money. One can only guess at what the Cree thought of Murie's preserving and stuffing his samples, but he was working with skins, which they understood well, and they watched him intently.[53]

Cree hunting was meaningful for Murie, as he saw clearly that "the Cree Indian is primarily a hunter and nothing else," but he was less clear as to how to interpret their lives in relation to the wilds around him. Murie saw the difficulty of Cree life at the time. "Hunger," he wrote, "is not rare, [and the Cree hunter] has not learned to hoard or lay up something for a rainy day. This is not so much the fault of the Indian as of circumstances." The Cree, he thought, were dependent on an environment that was hard at best, particularly at this time, and he knew that "the depleted game supply of the Labrador Peninsula [was] of variable quality, unreliable and deceiving." He saw real privation, and he interpreted this as being the product of a static environment that had hunters at its mercy. It worried him and, on occasion, filled him with foreboding.[54]

At other times, he saw things very differently and articulated a romantic idea of that same nature. On his way home from a day of collecting in the bush, he could look out on a purple sunset and the moon rising over the snow-covered spruces and be moved to write: "there was a feeling of purity about the whole thing, as if I was in a holy place, so much so that when I heard someone shout to his dogs in the distance it felt painful, like a discordant note in music." From the cultural distance of ninety years, it is hard to see how discord arose, not between his dispassionate collection of birds and this romantic, almost religious sentiment, but instead from a man shouting in the distance. This is especially true given that the dog-driver, almost certainly a Cree, was so much a part of the region – hardly "discordant." But the driver represented another reality and jarred Murie out of his self-constructed environmental reverie, though later he recovered his sense of inspiration, writing: "in such surroundings a man feels elated, no task seems too big and all evil thoughts disappear." He was inspired by his surroundings, but his sense of discord in the presence of human action – the imposition of the mundane upon the holy – speaks to a separation of humanity and nature that is emblematic of Western thought but does not fit the history of the bay.[55]

The Cree environment was something beyond Murie's scientific and romantic parameters, something whose meaning he did not fully comprehend. "This evening, before dusk, I heard excited calling outside and went out to see what was going on," he wrote that fall, "I found that *wavies* were going up the river flock after flock.[56] At first it was only a babble of voices coming out of the darkening snowfall, but soon I made out dim lines of birds flying by in the distance, one after the other. It felt strange to see these birds flying off for the distant South, drifting off with the driving snow as if a part of it." The calling voices of the geese were part of the scene that so captured his imagination, but so too were the delighted Cree cries of "the wavey's are going, the wavey's are going!" that had drawn him outside in the first place to see the ducks flying south on that snowy November night. Unconsciously it seems, his phrasing connected the calling of the geese and the excited calling of the Cree, but again he was left guessing at a different knowledge of nature and of people's place within it: an old relationship between the hunters and the geese, that he never got to the point of seeing clearly.[57]

Entering only occasionally into the Cree world of subsistence hunting, Murie never made a foundational material connection that might have connected him to the Cree and their land. He did not rely on the land as others had done, and so he remained somewhat at a distance and continued to fret: "my visit in camp impressed on me the uncertainty of the Indian's precarious life. He is not many meals ahead and depends largely on hunting in a land where game cannot be depended upon. It gave me an uneasy feeling and made me think of my own source of supply. What if that too should fail!" Given the state of the environment at the time, this fear was understandable, but it speaks to a pessimism about Cree prospects that the Cree themselves would not have accepted as reality.[58]

Murie's fear was increased by his own desire to share food with Cree children. Sharing food made him feel a part of the community, but while he did not doubt the Cree's willingness to share in return, he doubted their ability to do so. His understanding of the hunter's world left him alienated from its possibilities, and he found limited meaning in things like the decorated bear skulls that he saw hung in the trees. He was never forced to grapple with the day-to-day needs of hunting, though he feared he might have to, and so the conceptual geography of the Cree remained largely unreachable because it lacked practical meaning. He never learned that the reciprocity of food sharing was founded on a larger environmental reciprocity between hunter and hunted: to share was to be part of the Cree cultural environment on both a material level and a conceptual level.

Instead, Murie tried to associate these notions with his understanding of Native religious ideas, perhaps with his own too, but they remained unclear:

> William says they hang up all the bear bones in this way, wrapping them in a cloth. They will lay a bear on a blanket when killed and often put beadwork or tobacco on its breast. Several old Indians will sit around it often and smoke. Certain parts of the carcass are eaten only by women, other parts by men. A young boy is not allowed to eat any of the "arm" of the bear. William says they think it is bad luck if they fail to observe any of these customs and they will not get another bear. I have been unable so far to learn the true religious significance of their customs, possibly it is only a matter of "luck" in the Indians mind now.[59]

It was, in fact, a matter of "luck," but as the Cree understood the term, not as Murie understood it. Entering only briefly into Cree cultural space, Murie was left confused and could not understand "luck" in its Cree context. The scientific delineation of specific actions did nothing to give him access to their meaning.

Much of what Murie saw intrigued him, but, as he began to sort things into conceptual categories, he relied upon patterns of Western thought. He was somewhat confused by the fact that the Cree enthusiastically participated in Christianity even as they held to "traditional" beliefs. He was bothered by their Western clothing and their sometimes European features. He was amused by meeting hunters sitting on a cliff playing checkers while watching for game with a telescope. These patterns of thought and categories of meaning are important because he and others took this carefully catalogued information out of the bay and used it to create meaning for themselves and others who were interested in the region. This collecting and filtering process can be seen as Murie writes about his encounters with the Cree.

On February 18, 1915, Murie was travelling to the north and visited the camp of the hunter Swallow. This was an intriguing experience for him: "I had been disappointed in the Crees, with their un-Indian features and ill-fitting 'civilized' store clothing. But here in this camp was something a little more interesting." Outside the camp children were "coasting" on a small toboggan, and, when he started to photograph one boy in his new rabbit skins, he soon had the whole troop along with their mothers surrounding him and studying his camera. After some time the women went back to hauling logs for firewood, which they were piling carefully around the tent, and "a little later in the afternoon the men came in, one by one," from their hunts. The men left what they brought outside the tent so that the women could make the transfer of food from the outside environment to the inside environment, and here, too, Murie crossed the threshold into a different space.[60]

He entered their large square "tee pee," which was covered with snow for insulation, and, as he passed the threshold, "something rattled overhead as [he] rubbed [his] head against it." The bones of the hunted decorated the ceiling, along with the pelts of several foxes. Two stoves heated the space, which was shared by ten families, and the atmosphere was warm and close. Goods were arranged around the sides of the tent, defining gender and family space in a way that Murie would not have understood at the time. Spruce bows covered the floor, padding it and giving off a fresh, clean scent. Hanging cradles kept the young children away from the stoves, and women sat and wove rabbit skins into robes and blankets when they were not preparing food. They were also boiling spruce cones in a large pot, and Murie did not know why; certainly not for food, he thought. Murie spent an uncomfortable night with Swallow and his band, and this was as deeply embedded in the Cree environment as he ever became. The children were noisy, both awake and asleep, and space was tight. There were obviously rules that enabled these people to share a tight space, and Murie, a cultural stranger, was out of his depth: "this was the winter home of the Indian, picturesque, but rather unsatisfactory, I thought." He did his best to fit in but was relieved to conclude his time there and move out into the bush to continue his work.[61]

Olaus Murie's scientific work was valuable, but other scientific know-ledge brought out of the region had more effect on the future. What is more important is that Murie brought home with him a narrative under-standing of wilderness with which he continued to work for the rest of his life. I don't know for sure how the Cree affected Murie's growth as an environmental activist and thinker, but when he sat down to consider the meaning of environmental change in the United States late in his life, it was to the Cree that he turned for an analogy:

> While writing this account of experiences with Indians in the Hudson Bay country back in 1914, I am interested now, in 1962, by the necessity of examining critically some bills currently in Congress aimed at laying waste some of the beauty of our outdoors – with huge appropriations for the purpose. And I wonder: can we compare the hectic, unethical motivation in our vast effort to change the face of the earth, with the simple, honest motivation shown by those Indians facing coexistence with fellow creatures in their environment? Which is the more worthy, from the standpoint of human, spiritual progress? We can smile at primitive beliefs, but it is the human motivation behind them that counts.[62]

A half-century had clearly nuanced his understanding, though there is still a romantic haze in his view of the Cree. It is ironic that the massive, state-sponsored Central Arizona Project was Murie's concern in the above passage as, in less than a decade, the Cree themselves would be faced with precisely this scale of development, and they, too, would have to question the meaning of progress. Most important here is the fact that, when the Cree put forth their claim to rights in the region in opposition to that of the Province of Quebec, the legal and political systems in the South looked for their understandings of the region in the narratives of science and romanticism. Then the Cree, too, had to learn these narratives and deal with the changes that they had brought to their land.

Murie is important because he had a foot in both the scientific and the romantic understandings of nature and also because he became such a powerful voice for wilderness and environmental preservation. He is also, however, emblematic of a larger process of narrative understanding that grew up around the James Bay region in the early twentieth century. He experienced James Bay at a time when some of the worst of what I described earlier was happening, but he also created a lens though which the region could be seen from afar. In this he is much like J.W. Anderson, even though their experiences and narratives were quite different. To tell the history of the bay now requires grasping not only the internal events and realities but also the external ones. These different versions remained apart for the early decades of the twentieth century, but, as hunting continued into the middle decades, and as Canada and Quebec developed during and after the Depression and the Second World War, they began to converge on the Cree lands.

Beginning in the 1930s, and continuing until the hydro development in the 1970s, a series of reserves were created on Cree land, and this helped the environment to restore itself while allowing hunters to return to feeding themselves and their families. What was created on the reserves was clearly not the same subsistence hunting that had gone on in previous centuries, but it was still subsistence hunting. While these reserves were a government creation, they were also, in their way, very Cree expressions of the Cree place in the world – a new articulation of tradition. The long thread of hunting was not broken by the events of the late nineteenth and early twentieth centuries, and the Cree began a new relationship with both their environment and the governments of Canada and Quebec. This occurred even as those governments began to reshape their own relationship with each other and as both began to re-evaluate James Bay.

6

Management and Moral Economy

We do not originate anything. We merely recognize their system and adapt ourselves to Indian custom.

— *Hugh Conn,* Fur Conservation Report, *1943*[1]

Walking around Waskaganish (formerly Rupert House[2]) and thinking about the hardships of the early twentieth century, I find myself looking for the name of James Watt. He was the HBC trader here in the 1920s and 1930s, and I know that there used to be a community hall in town named for him. It was built in the 1940s, so I'm sure the building itself is not standing anymore, but I thought there might be something else. My search doesn't last that long, as it's a bitter and windy day, and I don't find his name. I ask a couple of people, and they haven't heard of him, so it seems as though maybe Watt is not well remembered. I've heard on a couple of occasions that, in the post-hydro political atmosphere, some people in town found the idea of that dedication offensive and wanted it removed. That's not surprising, given the circumstances then and now, though Watt and the Cree tallymen with whom he worked are an important historical bridge between the past and the present and really should not be forgotten. This is not so much because to forget Watt is unfair as it is because to write him out of the narrative of the region is to risk losing the history of something that is of vital political significance today – history and politics, entwined as always. Watt and a good many other people, both inside and outside of James Bay, had a hand in creating what the hydro development ended so abruptly, in 1970. And, if we are going to understand the full meaning of what happened thirty-five years ago, then we can't forget that. Watt was not some great white father who saved the Cree (he has been portrayed this way more often than not, and this is as bad as forgetting him altogether); rather, he was a fur trader involved in a cultural negotiation, just like his predecessors.

But he was a fur trader in unusual times, and this made the outcome of that negotiation unusual as well.

From the time that Watt took over Rupert's House in 1922, he was frustrated and disturbed by the situation at the post and the state of the whole region. The fur trade, as he saw it, was in serious trouble: the beaver were all but gone and the other fur-bearers, those still profitable in the 1920s luxury market, were also quickly disappearing. The beaver had been a commodity; they had been food for the hunter and, maybe most important, had created an environment within which other food could grow. Their disappearance impoverished both the ecosystem and the economy. As far as Watt was concerned, the cause of this disappearance was simple: competition from other traders had created a cash market for goods and food and that had put fur hunters in a precarious position. The debt structure that had been built up in the free-for-all of the preceding decades was now crippling what little fur trade was left. "This putting the heavy pedal on the debt," as Watt put it, while it had been started to hold on to HBC profits, was now resulting in his being short of hunters as they were going south and trying to make a living there. Five had left the post in the previous year alone, seeking work for cash to the south, and, under the circumstances, there was little likelihood of the trend reversing itself. People were impoverished and hungry, and they had few choices left to them. Watt was convinced that preserving the fur trade, which meant, first and foremost, preserving the beaver, was the only hope for the Cree as well as for the HBC.

The question was how to save and maintain the beaver, which were nearly extinct in the region, and to revive the environment of the hunt. Watt had some ideas. They were ill defined and not very feasible for the region, yet they were the seed crystals for a much larger structure of preservation – one that changed the region dramatically over the next forty-five years and that served as the foundation for several generations of cooperative efforts between the HBC, government bureaucrats, and Cree hunters. It was between these three groups that a system of beaver reserves on Cree lands was negotiated. This system was sanctioned by the provincial and federal governments and then shaped by the hard work and ideas of Cree hunters, all with the goal of protecting Cree hunting. The ecosystem of James Bay recovered remarkably quickly during these years, and the Cree returned to living largely off the land within a redefined subsistence system that matured remarkably well itself. While the hunt was not precisely the same as it had been before, it was understood by the Cree and others to be part of their long hunting tradition. The reserves were a new legal structure on the land, and those hunters who had responsibility for individual traplines within Cree culture were now legally designated as tallymen. They supplied the government with information about the land, but regulation was largely self-imposed, and working with the government did not change the Cree's traditional cultural role as stewards of the land.[3]

There are still tallymen who have stewardship of all the traplines in James Bay, and, for the Cree, they are a vital connection to the land in the political process. It is they who keep track of what is happening to the land in relation to all the resource extraction, and it is they who take it upon themselves to speak for the land. What was created in the reserve system lies beneath a new organization of the land, and, like the underlying geology of the Precambrian Shield, it helps shape the landscape. The reserve system was not perfect, but, because it met Cree needs and expectations both economically and symbolically, it became a part of Cree culture. Thus, these reserves may be unique in North American history. Under the reservation/reserve policy of the United States and Canada, respectively, Native peoples have never been given enough viable land, or enough control over it, to make a go of the situations in which they find themselves put. Here in James Bay, for a while anyway, a whole region was set aside for Cree cultural use, and they were given wide leeway to organize it as they saw fit.

This was a two-edged process, however, for while Cree remained the language of the hunt (which found new meaning in James Bay), the Cree also became an ever-larger conduit through which information flowed out of the region to the various levels of bureaucracy that had begun to take a greater interest in them and their land. This was subtle in the decades around the Second World War but knowledge gathering begun in the previous century was now strengthened by the creation of reserves, and the potential control of the governments to the south was increased – another extension of discovery. Practically speaking, this meant that the Cree hunters had to fit their hunting within official understanding, and the relationship between the provincial and federal governments became increasingly important to the region. For the first time on Cree lands dissonance arose between provincial control over resources, granted under the British North American Act, 1867, and federal responsibility for Native peoples. And this, too, would later have a great effect. At the same time, James Bay and the Cree remained outside any treaty, either with Ottawa or with Quebec City, so even as the official narrative grew, it had no overarching legal structure to inhabit – yet.

The outside understanding of the region that developed, then, had some immediate consequence: the land was more clearly defined within the framework of Canadian government, and the Cree were more clearly defined within the larger context of Native/white relations. More important, as the reserves became successful, James Bay became a place that politicians could point to as being both a cultural and an environmental success. A new narrative began in official literature and the popular press – one concerning the place and meaning of James Bay within Canada. The North and its people also entered the popular consciousness during this period – authors like Farley Mowat hectored the government over Native policies – and James Bay became a valuable success story. Even as the hunt remained central to Cree life, as did the evolving traditional narrative surrounding it, this traditional understanding also became of interest to politicians, the press, and anthropologists, all of whom, over the decades, defined it in different ways and made various uses of it.[4]

All this is important with regard to understanding the decades that led up to the development of hydroelectricity in the bay. The investigation of resources and, to a large extent, the narratives of wilderness had left the Cree on the periphery of the larger culture's perception. Now, as conservation and Native cultures became a part of popular, intellectual understanding, Cree hunting became more central to the narratives of conservation, government action, and academic study. The Cree were supplying information to scholars and bureaucrats not only about their land but also about themselves. Just as when they had supplied food, they attached meaning and reciprocity to this process of exchange, so in the reserves they found a platform upon which they continued to build hunting culture. But the interchange was different and more abstract than it had been before, and the Cree had no control over what those in the South made of their ideas and information. This had also been the case with what happened to beaver pelts, but now the product they were exporting was resulting in a new definition of James Bay and the Cree – a definition that could and would reshape the region later in the twentieth century.

The reserve system is most important for understanding James Bay in this period because it was the aspect of white activity that the Cree chose to and had to engage with in order to ensure the continuation of their cultural connection to the land. Other non-Native activity was important, but these programs were distinctly unsuccessful, carried out by a relatively small number of poorly funded and poorly organized people that were disconnected from the hunt. After the Second World War, nursing stations were planned for many remote locations in the North, but funding in the mid-1940s was lacking, and years passed before anything of the kind came to the bay. Various economic schemes were also planned for Natives living in or near the communities, but sturgeon fishing for a New York market or craft production for a souvenir trade never came to fruition. The 1946 "Report on Crafts" put it rather pointedly when it noted that the Cree were not interested in making crafts (like moccasins) to sell because they had too many things to make for themselves: they were still hunters and would remain so into the foreseeable future.[5]

Even the official attempts to educate Cree children were often ad hoc and fragmented. The government found it difficult to act on issues involving the Cree (because of their nebulous legal status), and even giving missionaries permission to build privately run boarding schools was problematic because no clear title to land existed in the region. These schools were eventually built, and some Cree children went to them (most of these children were under twelve and were not old enough to fully participate in hunting). Some children, particularly in the 1950s and 1960s, were sent to boarding schools in the South, and individual lives were shaped by all the cultural trauma referred to above. Still, it has been noted by many that, though some Cree were injured by these schools, the understanding of white society that they learned there, along with the network of Native friends from other bands that they developed, became invaluable to them in the 1970s.[6]

My focus on the reserve system and the meaning of hunting culture is not meant to marginalize these individual experiences or to downplay the intrusiveness of bureaucratic programs, but it was hunting and beaver preservation that galvanized and moved Cree cultural action in the decades after the Depression. This is where they chose to engage with non-Natives in all the ways that they had used before. James Bay remained a Cree world because of hunting, and the reserve system was foundational to this. In reading through teachers' end-of-season reports, I was struck again and again by the fact that, in order to teach anything, they had to change their curricula to make them apply to hunting. Subjects only resonated with the children when they related to the animals out in the bush and how people related to them. One first-year teacher summed up this cultural staying power best when she concluded, "I am afraid that my pupils have learned little English, but I have already learned quite a bit of Cree." The Cree have been tenacious in the maintenance of their language and culture, in their connection with the land and the animals, and it was through the beaver reserves that they continued to shape the environment of the hunt after James Watt and the Rupert House hunters began their program.[7]

In the mid-1920s, Watt began pushing what he thought of as "beaver farming" to people both inside and outside the HBC. "I have been amusing myself with a little farming with highly gratifying results," he wrote to Ralph Parsons in Winnipeg, using the "tropical" growth in his potato garden as a metaphor for the beaver cultivation he hoped to begin, with the company's sanction. Hopeful in all endeavours – though he did admit that there were numerous logistical problems – Watt considered the environment of James Bay to be well suited for a fur farm, and his original plan was to use a peninsula near Rupert House called Ministokwatin. The peninsula was 18 by 8 kilometres and nearly cut off from the mainland by muskeg. Being only 40 kilometres from the post, he believed it would make an ideal location for a beaver and fox farm tended by the Cree. He had learned that "several years ago when Indians kept possession of what they considered their own hunting lands, Beaver were always found on Ministokwatin, but during the past number of years Indians have been hunting where ever they please and have entirely exterminated the Beaver on the peninsula." What made him hopeful was that he had been in contact with a man who had been farming beaver in the United States since the end of the First World War, and he had assured Watt that the animals were quite fecund if left alone. Watt wanted to stock the peninsula with beaver and muskrats as he had learned already that these two animals had a symbiotic relationship. This would re-establish the possibility of fur trading, but it would be on what Watt thought of as a scientific and predictable basis.[8]

He thought that his numbers – he included charts in his letters that showed expected increases – were corroborated by the experiences of local hunters, several of whom had "formerly always had beaver permanently on their land" and who had told him "that beaver often increase at a higher rate. One old man had a pair of beaver in a lake known only to himself; in three years he killed 17 beaver, small and medium; the following year someone else found the lake and killed the old ones." Watt felt sure that, had the old hunter been able to continue his conservation, he would have been able to trade furs on a yearly basis as well as to feed himself. Taking this information, he wanted to begin an experiment that would produce those results within a controlled setting. He had only a small farm in mind on Ministokwatin, only a small crop of beaver for food and fur, and his immediate concern was "how to prevent beaver from migrating out of the concession, which is too large to fence."

He was not thinking of a regional solution, but his interest in Ministokwatin led him to encounter the local environment and its history in a new way and to see that the old hunter mentioned above was not an isolated case. For "while questioning Indians as to the best locality for establishing fur farms," he wrote, "a fact came out, which although I have known it for years did not strike me before as being the principal factor in the extermination of fur bearing animals." He wondered why, with so many old beaver houses on Ministokwatin, there were no beaver: "The answer was that now-a-days the Indians do not respect each other's hunting lands as formerly, and consequently kill everything in sight, knowing if they do not do so, some other Indian will come along and do so." Watt was beginning to see that the breakdown in the local environment was a matter of culture as well as overhunting. There had been an organizational understanding of the land in the past, and though people remembered it, they were driven by circumstances to ignore it.[9]

The crisis had its roots in the behaviour both of some hunters and of whites in the region. "Up to about twenty years ago each Indian considered his hunting lands as his private property," he noted, "and handed them down to his family; this right was respected by all the Indians, with a few exceptions, also, the Hudson's Bay Company having more power than at present, enforced this right, and punished those who infringed on the rights of others by refusing to give them advances." With the coming of the Révillon Frères Company, the HBC had lost the ability to reinforce these practices or to control white trappers from the South. According to Watt,

> while I was in charge of Manawon Post, St. Maurice District, as it then was, this right was still respected (although commencing to be infringed owing to white trappers killing game everywhere) and the Indians could tell when taking their advances approximately how many beaver they intended to kill. To take Ministokwatin as an example; this land used to be the hunting ground of old Katapaituk, who to [all] intents and purposes was a beaver farmer and when killing beaver on some particular lake on his estate, always tried to leave sufficient breeders to restock the lake.[10]

Watt's understanding of hunting as a kind of farming did not involve the Cree notion of reciprocity between hunter and hunted, though the end result of both was preservation. This was not the garden that Job Bearskin talked about either, but there was room to work together. The divergence in conceptual frameworks, however, meant that Watt's plan would need to be flexible in order to succeed.

Certain aspects of the plan seemed straightforward enough: "From a long discussion I had with several Indians on this subject it would appear that were it possible for a hunter to uphold his right to certain hunting lands it would do more to conserve beaver" than any other action. He concluded that, because civilization had "made very little inroad in the Labrador Peninsula," there was "no reason why the country should not support the many thousands of beaver it formerly did." He believed a plan could be put into place whereby hunters could stake claims on the beaver, much as prospectors staked claims on gold, and take only that to which they had rights. Here he uses yet another metaphor to conceptualize how hunters might increase their stocks, though, like farming, prospecting appears somewhat inappropriate, given the past use of territories and the fact that the Cree still remembered who had responsibility for what land.[11]

Watt was also conscious that conservation had been tried a hundred years earlier by the HBC, and "so far as I have been able to learn," he wrote, "the method adopted was to maintain the Indians rights to his particular hunting ground and to limit the hunt of beaver in proportion to the number of beaver on the 'land.'" In addition to upholding land-use rights, Watt was also aware that, prior to 1850, the HBC had started a reserve on Charlton Island, its purpose being to stop the alarming decrease in the fur supply brought on by competition with the NWC. He assumed that the HBC had imposed this system of enforcement, though it is likely that some system of hunting lands was well established in Cree culture before these HBC regulations. He noted that the system had continued for many years after the HBC had lost the power to enforce it and that this showed that it must have had some kind of meaning for the Cree. He wanted to go back to these old ideas, "with certain improvements," and he hoped the HBC would back him in his efforts. Interestingly, while Watt knew of the HBC's nineteenth-century beaver preservation work, he did not seem to know the specifics of the process at Rupert House. If he had, he might have seen how vital the work of Cree hunters would be to his own plans and how little the process would resemble farming.

In the early nineteenth century, Chief Trader Robert Miles was in charge of Rupert's House, and it was he who took up the idea of re-establishing the beaver in James Bay. In February 1838, Miles sent the hunters Kennawap and Caue-chi-chimis to survey Charlton Island, 32 kilometres off the coast, for the purpose of starting a beaver reserve. They brought back a map that they had made showing sixty-one lakes in which beaver could be placed and many smaller ones that the animals would be able to find on their own as their numbers increased. Several years later, a similar map was drawn of Ministokwatin and other likely places along the James Bay coast, though the record does not mention any beaver having been transplanted there. There were already, in 1838, a few beaver being kept at Rupert's House: the hunter Matoowishe had brought one in late in December 1837, and the hunter Governor and his sons had brought in a female in April 1838. Governor's involvement is particularly interesting as Miles referred to him as "the Indian I have named one of the rivers at Charlton after in consideration of his being the Indian who first communicated to me the great conveniences of the island for a beaver preserve."[12]

Miles pronounced the "Charlton Beaver Preserve established" as of April 1838, noting that its inhabitants would "be happy to receive as many more settlers as our friends [the hunters] are willing to supply." Over the course of that season, more beaver were brought in from Nitchequon and Mistassini, and the traders and Cree began the plantation effort in earnest that spring. "Father George," a large male beaver and "a lusty fellow," was the appointed patriarch of the new colony on Charlton Island. He and four other beaver were taken to the island in late June 1838, and Miles noted with satisfaction that the animal was a worthy sire. The hunters thought so too, and they made sure to impress on Miles that Father George never received food without sharing it with the other beaver and making sure that they ate first: he was a fitting leader. With this initial success, Miles planned to put more animals in the same spot the next year "and afterward [to] put others in places as pointed out by the Indians." By the following April they had a beaver pen built, were successfully breeding the animals in captivity, and took a total stock of ten to the island that spring. Though little more is said of the reserve in the Rupert's House records after this energetic start, as late as 1844 the men at Mistassini were capturing and breeding beaver for transportation to the coast. McKay reported that in June one of the beaver gave birth to three pups, which he reported as healthy and likely to do well. The reserve on Charlton Island was operated until the turn of the century, though its significance seems to have been overshadowed by other events. That it never grew into the larger system that came in the 1930s has everything to do with the conservative nature of the HBC, which continued into Watt's era, but it also had to do with the fact that, until the twentieth century, there was no other legal framework upon which to build. For all the negative things that can be said about governments and bureaucracy, their presence in the 1930s was necessary if preservation was to work.[13]

Watt in some ways, then, revived an old system, though he has received credit for creating the modern idea of the reserves. Credit is surely due for the time, energy, and personal funds he put into the plans; nonetheless, the historical roots of his action run back to Miles, Governor, and the other

Cree hunters of the territory. And just as Miles' plans were influenced by the involvement of his hunters, so the revitalization of the environment in the twentieth century grew as much from Cree hunting culture as it did from Watt's ideas of farming and individual rights to resources. The two were inextricably linked, as were bureaucrats representing Ottawa and those representing Quebec City, and whether influenced by a real belief in Native practice or simply by a lack of desire and/or the means to impose any other solution, Watt and these bureaucrats helped the Cree to modify and preserve an internal definition of hunting culture in James Bay. With their efforts, preservation became regional, covering hundreds of thousands of square kilometres and encompassing most of the eastern James Bay watershed.

At first, Watt paid out of his own pocket to buy the individual live beaver from hunters in order to keep and breed them. This, in turn, enabled the hunters to live on store supplies, and, by July 1932, Watt had twenty-five animals at Rupert House ready to transplant when and if the reserve was created. By this time, his plan had evolved into the protection of a large area of hunting territory, into which beaver could be introduced and left to their own devices. There is no mention of when he changed his strategy, but his discussions with hunters over the hunting lands of which they were still the stewards within their culture would seem to have been what influenced this change. He had been writing and lobbying the HBC for three years at this point, it being the only authority with de facto power to parcel out land for the project. But trying to convince the HBC that it was a "new era" in the fur trade was a nearly hopeless task. Though he cajoled the company ceaselessly, saying that, if it would only act, its decision to do so would be equal to "the small beginnings here in 1668," the HBC was not interested in investing in the region. Fiscally conservative to its core, it would not spend money on environmental conservation.[14]

Frustrated by inaction, Watt moved at last to create the reserve himself, sending his wife Maud to Quebec City to get the provincial government to act directly. Maud Watt, born and raised on the south shore of the St. Lawrence River, spoke French fluently and believed as strongly in the project as did her husband. She went to the provincial capital and met with L.A. Richard, deputy minister of Fish and Game, and worked out a compromise whereby she was named the holder of a lease on a large tract of land near Rupert House. This left both the HBC and its employee James Watt off the record and was a nod to the expediency of provincial politics of the time. On the one hand, Quebec had sovereignty over the region, while, on the other, Ottawa was responsible for Native affairs. And while the HBC was helpful to Ottawa in dealing with the Cree, it was a threat to Quebec. Giving the lease to Maud Watt, an ardent supporter of Quebec political rights, circumvented the issue.[15]

It was still not an easy decision for the province, and Richard had to use his political skills to achieve even this compromise. Reminiscing ten years later, he wrote to Maud Watt, "I cannot forget likewise that you were the instigator of a system of conservation which will enable our Indians to earn a living. There is no doubt that if we finally granted a lease, after much shilly-shallying, it was greatly due to the masterly way you convinced us." There is no doubt either that Maud Watt was, in the words of Hugh Conn, federal fur supervisor for much of the next three decades, "very fortunate in finding, in the person of L.A. Richard, a man with vision and imagination enough to grasp the possibilities of the idea." "A man of lesser calibre," he concluded, might have dismissed the idea "as a wild pipe dream." The future of Cree hunting was being influenced by the actions and the vision of outsiders in both Quebec and Ottawa, and, while it benefited them, it also increased the de facto and imaginative control that those outsiders held over the bay. If, over the decades, this has become a story of white paternalism, then it is here that it began to be told.[16]

The reserve was created at Rupert House after the political issues were sidestepped, though not without tension between Watt, his employer, and the Quebec government. Watt's intention was not to finance the operation permanently but, rather, to push the HBC to take action. He knew he could not afford to run the reserve on his own for long, but he did want to hold the HBC at bay long enough to demonstrate, as he put it, "what can be done by discarding antiquated ideas and running the fur trade on entirely new lines." The company, after 250 years of control over its territories, did not react well to an employee's freelance activity or to the interference of the provincial government, which had only gained jurisdiction over the area in 1898. Company officials immediately began to lobby Quebec for a change. For its part, the provincial government was worried about the perception that it had granted another kind of HBC charter, an ironic replication of Charles II's 1668 grant. There were Quebeckers who saw the potential in the North and who did not want to see any possible development closed by HBC activity. Quebec's north was not yet as politically charged an issue as it would become in later decades, but issues of provincial sovereignty were already contentious. In the end, the HBC received its lease, and Watt was made its manager, though while he was paid by the company, he was responsible to the government for his actions as fur manager. This became the new official jurisdiction in the Cree hunting lands.[17]

Yet hunting and the Cree remained the central focus of Watt's concerns. Watt had emphasized the monetary issues to his superiors, arguing that no company could profit if the Cree were poverty stricken, but clearly he understood the importance of Cree cooperation and the Cree emphasis on food. He wrote that "all the Indians with whom I have discussed this scheme, are very much in favour of it, but they all say, it is too bad it was not taken up before" they became so poor and hungry. He had sounded a number of them out on the matter because, without Native cooperation, he knew that these new rules "could only be enforced by an army of Game Wardens." Even if the HBC refused to buy furs from them for a number of years, the Cree would continue to kill beaver for food if they were hungry and did not see it as being in their best interest to cooperate with the conservation efforts. Watt was correct in his belief that the hunters supported the idea, that they would work to make it happen, and, by the late 1930s, the beaver reserve system was proving to be such a success that it was a point of pride for those outside the region.[18]

Conservation proved Watt's contention that James Bay could be one of the greatest fur reserves in North America, and, in 1938, the HBC's R.H.G. Bonneycastle went so far as to provide an overview of the James Bay system to the Third North American Wildlife Conference, which was held at the American Wildlife Institute in Washington, DC. It was an interesting explanation not only because of the pride he took in the effectiveness of the system but also because of the historical narrative that he created to explain it. He began his talk by making explicit the damage done by white trappers through their use of poison on the fur bearers of James Bay. He maintained that Natives, when "overrun" by white trappers, would not conserve in their usual manner. He argued that, "when subjected to intense competition of the white trapper, there is only one thing for them to do and that is to get their share of what there is before the white man gets it. The result is obvious." He believed that placing restrictions on white trappers was helping to restore the moral economy of the Cree. The government, he noted, was learning that restricting white trappers did more than conserve fur: the project on the Eastmain coast, "once a paradise of beaver," was also truly helping the Natives, who had been "reduced to poverty with consequent deterioration of morale and independence." When the projects were started, Bonneycastle went on, "we enlisted the help of the Indian," who made it possible, and "they entered into it heart and soul. Woe betide anyone who molested a beaver, and even though suffering great hardship themselves, they would sooner starve than touch an animal." He concluded that, because of this program, "the Indians are a changed people, their morale is restored."[19]

This story was repeated in many speeches and newspaper articles for the next twenty-five years, and, though there is a great deal of bureaucratic self-congratulation in these accounts, not to mention an oversimplification of the situation, there is a great deal of compelling evidence behind it as well. The real problem was that any internal understanding of how the hunt was developing was not captured as part of this outside narrative of conservation and management success. The Cree were helped immensely by the protection granted to their land and their way of life, and perhaps something like an old moral economy was reinvigorated, but it was not the erasure of hundreds of years of history as this new narrative of the beaver reserves began to imply. The Cree had asserted a great deal of intellectual as well as physical effort in order to make this plan work; yet, while Bonneycastle acknowledged the need for Cree to patrol the land, he failed to understand that the beaver reserves were also a success because the Cree worked to conceptualize them within Cree culture as it existed in the 1930s. The reserves were an internal redefinition of the Cree relation to their lands that, as anthropologist Frank Speck noted, existed "in great explicitness in the minds of the northern Indians, a state which we are totally unable to describe for the want of adequate means ... in respect both to cartography and to knowledge of actual conditions." He might have added history to this list as well because outsiders were also unable to see how hunting was changing to fit the new circumstances and how it was continuing an intellectual tradition into the twentieth century. All this started to be flattened into the story of a museum piece: ancient tradition reborn on Cree lands.[20]

On the ground in James Bay, reserves were the development of something new, and their negotiation began, in fact, when Watt first addressed the hunters of Rupert House and told them about the formal creation of the first one. He used paternalistic language, placing emphasis on their need, but he was clearly bargaining with the Cree for their help. He told them that the government was making laws to protect beaver between the Rupert and Eastmain rivers and that the law must be obeyed: "all the government has to do is send in a few White Game Wardens to enforce the law" if the Cree did not want to cooperate. He knew this was not the case – the Cree surely did as well – and that without their help the project would fail. Still, he told them that he had had to lobby the government to use them as trial wardens and that they needed to live up to his expectations. Because they had left so few beaver alive – there is no mention of white trappers here – this only required a few men, but the number of Native wardens would increase if the beaver increased. Again, he emphasized that they had "already killed off nearly all the beaver so ... [could] not say the government ha[d] taken anything away from [them]." The government, he reminded them, owned all the land after all "and [that it] recognized no one's right to it, neither white man or Indian." This, too, was wishful thinking, given the lack of formal treaty, but the hunters were being asked to buy into both the reserve scheme and the assertion of government authority.

The government was helping the Cree and their children, Watt pointed out, and this would cost "more money than [they could] count"; therefore, in the future, beaver would also be the property of government. The government would set quotas as well as prices, and it would have the right to turn any Native off the land if its rules were not followed. In addition, he told them that the hunters who had left the region had no rights and could only return with RCMP permission. Like his comments on white game wardens and government ownership, this was a dubious argument. Again the hunters were being asked to accept government authority, but the lack of any way of backing up his rhetoric highlights its real meaning as a bargaining position. The Cree genuinely had to be convinced of the promise of his plan for it to work, and, in the end, Watt had to take up the cultural language of James Bay in order to do this. Nothing was guaranteed, he told them, and those whose lands were not protected at this time and who did not receive warden's pay must "remember that all Indians do not get the same amount of furs, even when they try hard, and they must just think in the meantime it is not their 'luck.'" They must not give up hope, he told them, they must not be discouraged. Even though it was not their "luck" to be on the reserve selected by the government, this trial run was important to all because more beaver would come and then they might get a chance. Things were not certain.

The government also had hope in the Cree and their situation, Watt told them, as they had shown themselves willing to work in other endeavours. The government had decided that James Bay would be a good place to attempt the restocking and conservation of the beaver. "Now I want your opinion of this way of doing things," Watt told them, and they needed to decide for themselves if it was good. He emphasized that the plan's chief end was to feed not only them but also their children and their children's children. He then asked them to discuss the issues and, if they agreed with him, to sign a paper he had prepared. What they were gaining was the protection of their lands from outside use and the ability to continue their hunt, and, in return, they were being asked to agree to the application of another outside narrative of James Bay's place in the order of things. The story of government control and that of the timelessness of Native culture are tied closely together, but that fact and its meaning were not readily apparent. The hunters at Rupert House signed on to the reserve system because it was the right thing to do for the land.[21]

It appeared that all parties were getting what they wanted with this seemingly easy solution to poverty and environmental degradation. A.F. Mackenzie, the secretary of Indian Affairs, was convinced that exclusive Native hunting and trapping would not only materially "assist the Indians to earn a livelihood, but promote true conservation" as well. The only questions came from W.L. Tyrer, the Indian agent in the region, who liked the plan but was concerned with its legality. He pointed out that the Cree were under no treaty and wondered whether the lease of their land was legal. He wrote a letter to his superiors that foreshadowed the momentous events that followed the announcement of the hydro development in 1970, as did the response he received. He was told in no uncertain terms that the Cree in James Bay had no Aboriginal title to the land and that the lease was legal: it had begun on January 3, 1933, and would run for fifteen years, and that was the end of the matter. The answer left no room for further questions, but government assuredness was sustainable only while Quebec and Ottawa manipulated James Bay on paper and while the Cree did not raise questions of their own. For now, the narrative of political sovereignty did little to affect the region from within, though the Cree had agreed to hunt within this framework of Canadian laws. The way in which they hunted and interpreted hunting was still within the context of regional traditions, but from then on James Bay existed as both a locality, internally defined, and as a legal region of Canada, externally defined and only vaguely connected with local understanding.[22]

Within the region, hunters reacted positively to this initiative. Clearly, they were not without their doubts about white commitment, but the plan was sound, and, over the course of the next thirty-five years, they adopted the idea. The beaver reserves became part of the environment of James Bay, and the concept was adopted by other Cree village bands in the area. In July 1933, the chief of the Waswanipi band wrote to the federal government to draw attention to the fact that something had to be done very soon on their hunting lands or there would be no beaver left. He suggested that the hunting and buying of beaver pelts be closed for at least three years as this would allow the beaver to increase, "where as now they are decreasing every year." This kind of petition, written in Cree and translated by traders or Indian agents, became a part of the legal process for creating further reserves and would help to provide political and legal justification for them outside of James Bay. They would also help define these reserves within local culture as something locally created and sanctioned. Here is another unique event in North American Indian policy.[23]

Like the Waswanipi band, hunters at Rupert House wanted another reserve created south of the Rupert River to take in the remaining Rupert House hunting lands. They voluntarily stopped hunting beaver, and they pressed Tyrer on the subject, asking for twelve more beaver guardians to be assigned. Despite his earlier legal concerns, by the end of 1933 Tyrer had been won over, and he passed on the Cree sense of urgency to his superiors. If saving beaver were to be successful, he told them, it would require "the enthusiasm and cooperation of the Indian population, who take the greatest interest in the operation of the sanctuary." He emphasized that the hunters south of the Rupert River had been protecting their beaver, "hoping that a similar operation might be started in their territory," but that if something were not done soon, "they [would] be greatly discouraged." Most of the hunters in this area had left the beaver alone for two years but were afraid that, if there was no reserve to protect them, white trappers would be back if the market rebounded. They were also not being paid for their effort, which made it more difficult to leave this vital food source alone. The hunters had been presented with a possibility, however, and they were pressing the government to back them. If beaver preservation and the independence of the local population were both important, then the Cree were acting to give the governments what they desired in exchange for protection of their land, food supply, and way of life. The government response to both these requests was to delay until the evidence was clearer, but the hunters kept pressing.[24]

The proof of the program's success, evident to the hunters immediately, was borne out in numbers by the end of the decade. In 1933, the Cree beaver guardians counted only 162 animals in the whole of the 18,000 square kilometres of Rupert House reserve land. Yet, with the hunting ban, this increased steadily, doubling nearly every year. A 1936 report, written by Indian agent George Patrick, noted that he had "held a discussion with five or six of the prominent Indians and they are very pleased with the results of the beaver preserve." One hunter told him that it was "like putting money in the bank for our children," and by 1937 the tally reached 1,545 beaver. Putting money in the bank is an interesting phrase; it raises questions regarding whether the hunter was using an analogy that he knew would work for his audience or whether he was actually thinking about beaver in terms of money. It may be that Patrick made his own idiomatic translation, but whatever the meaning for that one hunter, others continued to explicitly express their desire to preserve hunting as a negotiation between beings, as an exchange of gifts between partners in the hunt. James Bay continued to be a place rich in ideas and cultural exchanges that gave meaning to the actions of Cree hunters on their lands.[25]

Cost, along with efficacy, was another governmental concern because the HBC also wanted the reserve south of the Rupert River, but it did not necessarily want to be responsible for it. It told the government that it had spent $5,000 a year creating the first reserve and that, while this probably cost the company less than paying assistance to hunters who could not find enough to eat, it did not want to take on more expense. The major cost of the reserve involved paying the guardians for their work, paying them to count beaver and not to hunt them, and, though some in Ottawa thought that this outlay could be cut, the HBC warned the government not to do so. The HBC thought the federal government should take on the burden of future reserves and that it was "essential" for Ottawa to "secure the good will and cooperation of the Indians for without this, it is very difficult to obtain adequate control." If the HBC paid its guardians and the government did not pay its own, it would "be construed by [the Cree] as injustice," and they might not cooperate. The hunters wanted the reserves and the HBC wanted to see the government "helping [the] Indian to help himself," but the Cree could forego their hunt only if they had money to buy food until the beaver returned.[26]

The real issues for the government were not the validity of the idea of beaver reserves, or even the expense, but the nebulous legal state of the James Bay Cree and the need to include Quebec in the process. Despite their firm assertion to Tyrer earlier, there was, in fact, real concern about how the Cree fit within the bureaucratic, governmental framework. The Cree were governed under the 1876 Indian Act, but the territory had been given to the province in 1898. Unlike in the United States, in Canada public lands are a provincial concern, so things like reserves involve several levels of government. Quebec was required to sign treaties with the Natives when the land was ceded, but it had not. Added to this was the Department of Indian Affairs' surprising lack of information regarding the number and location of the Cree: one report could only conjecture that there was a band somewhere "at the South end of Lake Mistassini, one at Waswanipi, and possibly one at Chibougamou [sic], in addition to the band residing at Rupert's House," but no one in Ottawa was sure. The HBC had a better idea where the Cree lived, but the company's legal status was unclear in the region. Quebec clearly resented HBC jurisdiction in the territory and did not want it increased in the form of new reserves. Rupert House had set some precedents, but there were details that still needed to be worked out.[27]

The Nottaway reserve was eventually created by Quebec in 1938 under a new comprehensive plan. The lease was given to the federal government, with the stipulation that Natives would be used as guardians and given exclusive use when the reserve was opened. The HBC would manage the reserve in the name of the federal agency, and the lease would last for fifteen years at a rate of ten dollars a year. The lease, however, could be cancelled at any time if Quebec had need of the territory. Harold McGill, director of Indian Affairs, did not foresee any problems, but he, too, foreshadowed future events. "The region is too remote and unsuitable for colonization," he conjectured, and "apparently the only eventuality that might change the situation there, would be the discovery and intensive development of resources, and of course in that case the province hardly could be expected to allow the lease to interfere with the larger public interest." The seeds were planted for a conflict between provincial interests and those of the Cree, but potential conflict did not stop the further creation of reserves in the region.[28]

In summer 1941, the hunters north of the Eastmain River requested that a reserve be created for them as well. Four chiefs met with Hugh Conn, now superintendent of fur for the federal government, and brought him maps and all the other organizational information about the hunting ground that should be included in this new reserve. Conn reported that "there are about four hundred Indians at these points and they have been practicing conservation for some years," but they, too, were afraid that, without protection, a reopened hunt could spoil their work. The hunters of Eastmain petitioned Conn to try to secure their internal effort within the legal framework of a new reserve, and he was sent to meet with L.A. Richard to discuss the details. Clearly, despite the federal government's perennial lack of extra money, the demand of the Eastmain hunters was driving bureaucrats into action. Within a week of their meeting, the principles of the reserve were laid out and Quebec created the Old Factory Preserve in 1941. The speed with which the plan was approved shows how convinced Richard had become of the efficacy of the reserves. The next year he wrote to Charles Camsell, at the Department of Mines and Resources, "like you, I have been won over by the sanctuaries. It is probably the best way of paying off our debt to the Indians for the harm we did them in the past."[29]

The details of the new reserve were given to the hunters in August 1942, and Conn reported that he had appointed the tallymen and spent a day "deciphering maps and giving instructions for the beaver count," though they already knew what to do. The new reserve covered 39,000 square kilometres between Eastmain and Fort George. Divided into three areas – Fort George, Old Factory, and Eastmain – the land within these divisions was then separated into family grounds. Conn was not involved in this final process and simply sanctioned what the hunters told him. Some of the area was not very productive, but he was hopeful that the forest fires in the inland area would provide good beaver food in a few years.[30]

Just as the cadastral pattern on the maps conformed to family territories, so the use of the reserves began to conform to the Cree perception of who it should benefit. When the Old Factory reserve was being created, Richard requested that "authorized missionaries" also be allowed to trap furs in order to add to their small incomes in the region, reasoning that they would make only small demands on resources. C.W. Jackson at the Department of Indian Affairs worried that this would set an unwanted precedent and that many others would also want the right if the door was opened. This would destroy the hunters' confidence, he argued, and he warned Richard that, "if any step along the lines suggested are to be taken it should be only after consultation with the Indians and full explanation ... any white, as we see it, must agree to conform with Indian custom," and this meant getting Cree permission to trap on their grounds according to their rules. Cree custom was the rule of the country, he maintained, and "our officers, in organizing a fur preserve revert to the ancient family system of land tenure, which predates the discovery of this continent." This was imperative for Native cooperation, he warned, and "any place where this system has broken down can be traced directly to white encroachment and the over crowding which inevitably follows." Preservation required Cree cooperation, which depended on their controlling not only their relationship with their environment but also white action.[31]

By 1942, the program had succeeded to such a degree that Conn was reporting that some families who had been driven south to La Sarre by hunger and lack of game were moving back to Rupert House. Some had been in trouble with authorities to the south, and he was a little worried at their return, but still he thought – despite Watt's contention of RCMP control – that it was up to the hunters at Rupert House to decide if the families should be allowed to return. In 1942, there were, in fact, enough

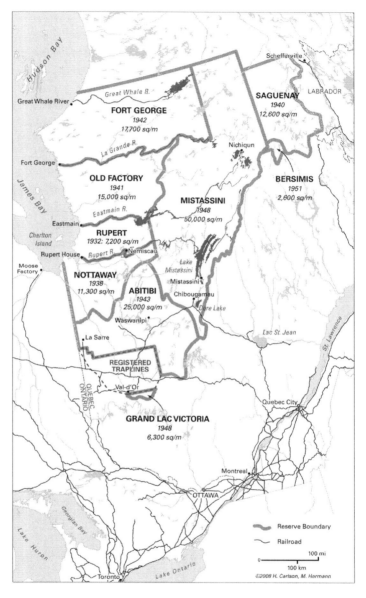

MAP 6.1 *Twentieth-century beaver reserves in eastern James Bay.* Beginning in the 1930s, the governments of Quebec and Canada worked with the Hudson's Bay Company and the hunters of James Bay to create beaver reserves where the Cree were given exclusive hunting and trapping rights. In exchange for protection, the hunters agreed to count the beaver on their land and follow government quotas determined from the information given by the hunters. Except for the yearly meeting with the fur supervisor, the hunters were left largely on their own to manage their land.

beaver to give the hunters larger quotas, and Conn enthusiastically reported that, upon hearing the news, one hunter exclaimed: "we can't eat all those beaver." This was an expression of happiness, certainly, but it was also one of genuine cultural concern over treating the beaver with respect. They had fur quotas now, numbers they had agreed to trap, but they also had to need the food. Families on the reserves readily invited those whose lands were not on the reserves to come and share their luck because hunters still felt the obligation to eat what they had trapped, and sharing was a matter of family and personal connection to the land. Bringing those people who had been forced to go south back to the land was also part of this equation. Family and community structures were being put back together by hunters who again had the material foundation of the hunt to build upon.[32]

Successful and popular as it was, the program was not without problems. In February 1941, Indian Agent Hervé Lariviere reported that the hunters whose lands abutted the Nottaway reserve south of the Rupert River were reporting a good stock of beaver and wanted to protect it. Another reserve seemed the logical solution, but access to the rail line and the surrounding country would continue to make reserves in this southern region less successful than those to the north. In most places this simply had to do with the proximity of poachers and private traders, but around the mining town of Chibougamau, which is today about an hour's drive south of Mistissini, hunters and their families were being moved off their lands to make room for the copper-mining operations that started at the beginning of the Second World War. These were hunters who had traded at Rush Lake, Pike Lake, and Mistassini, but whose principle gathering place was around Dore Lake, near town. Over the course of the next four decades, they were forced to move four times for mine expansion, and, by the 1970s, the community was nearly lost: many were living in shacks by the road. They were not part of the reserve system, and, by 1975, they had lost so much community cohesion that they were not included in the treaty with Quebec. By the 1970s, this kind of dispossession was no longer acceptable, but these Cree were already following a different path into the present.[33]

Despite the real and potential problems in these southern areas, by 1943 Hugh Conn was also pushing to create a new reserve west of Chibougamau, finally taking in Waswanipi and the La Sarre region. Noting that few Natives were poaching there, he knew that whites were pressuring them and he wanted to apply "the well-known ounce of prevention before the pound of cure [became] necessary." Several factors complicated any new development for the federal government. First, preservation was an internal political matter, and it was not a universally popular idea, though by 1943 those who wanted reserves seem to have created some consensus on the matter. Conn was clear that the fur program only expanded when "Natives demand[ed] it," and this was a difficult matter in southern areas, where the benefits of preservation were less certain. The land was not yet the political issue it is today, but government action was beginning to affect the internal control of the region. Another issue was that the HBC held trading leases around La Sarre that stood in the way of government action, though, in the face of the legal complaints of free traders and the resentment of the local Natives, the company was easily convinced to release these claims to the Department of Indian Affairs. And, again, an issue had to be resolved with Quebec. The province now had firm plans to open some of the lands in the area to colonization by the end of the Second World War, which, by then, was being anticipated. The province was not averse to the idea of a new reserve, but the proposed boundaries had to be altered to conform with provincial plans as well as Cree need. Conn and others knew that the reserves in James Bay were working because they had not yet been pressured by outside development and that this new area would not benefit from that kind of isolation. A reserve was created, but its lack of success is illustrative.[34]

The Abitibi reserve was begun in 1943, covered 65,000 square kilometres, and was run under the same tallyman system as were those to the north. Conn noted that the "Indians were familiar with procedure on a fur preserve from conversations with participating Indians," and the hunters duly presented their sketch maps to him showing the location and number of beaver on their lands; they worked out the details together. The Native attitude in the new area was, Conn thought, "sceptical, but willing." He knew this scepticism came from the confused administrative history in the area as well as from the proximity of white trappers, the availability of higher fur prices, and the presence of free traders. More formalized law enforcement would be needed on this reserve, he thought, and Native sanction would not be enough to keep the situation under control. Consequently, hunters in the Abitibi region would have to bring their furs in and show their provenance to the provincial and federal authorities. Pressures on this southern reserve also kept RCMP in the area closely involved with the hunters who brought furs out, and there were always problems. The combined pressure of more whites, more roads, and a larger local economy limited the control over individual actions within Cree hunting culture, and hunters who had their lands on the edges of the reserves sometimes had them trapped out by Native hunters from the La Sarre area who took advantage of the local black market. Conn pushed the RCMP to do its part in upholding the rights of those within the reserve system, but in the end most investigations were inconclusive and nothing came of them.[35]

To the north, where pressures like this were less severe, the practical regulation of the reserves was much easier, though the definition of beaver preservation was still in flux and more subtle problems were arising. The Cree were using the reserves to reinterpret hunting within the new system, but, at the same time, they were participating in the creation of outside interpretations of reserves and preservation that were markedly different in both purpose and explanation. In the language of official reports and news reporting regarding conservation, a reasoning and a narrative continued to grow that highlighted how intellectual control of James Bay had begun to reshape the Cree and their lands. "The agreements are really tri-party," wrote Conn in one of his many reports, because Quebec and Ottawa cooperated in the legal framework and "because the Indians agree[d] to stop trapping beaver during the period of development." He emphasized many times that only the Cree could manage the land for conservation and that, if they had not agreed, it would have failed. He thought he could explain their cooperation easily because "once the white man's practices of leases and agreements are disposed of we adhere to Indian manners of procedure and pattern our organization after their sound, well established custom. The plan of organization used on our fur preserves is an adaptation and elaboration of the aboriginal plan of land tenure that from time immemorial has served the Indian population." By the mid-twentieth century in James Bay, everyone thought the tallyman system was traditional. While it was a new articulation of tradition for the hunters, for Conn and others it had become a restored cultural artifact and an extension of the natural moral economy of the Cree.[36]

According to Conn, while beaver were the sole prerogative of the tallyman on his land, other resources were shared with members of the band freely. This might necessarily extend to members of other bands if "they were traveling to or from one of the periodic pow-wows these having a claim on [the] hospitality of the tribe they were visiting." Family connections between bands were a factor in this system as well, and this was all part "of the recognized moral and economic code of the Indians" of James Bay. The history of the region shows that there was a great deal of truth to what Conn wrote, but this cultural system was not as natural or as easy as he believed. Cooperation existed, as he suggests, but so did tension. One only has to look at incidents like those at Mistassini in 1829 to see

FIGURE 6.1   *Fur Superintendent Hugh Conn and Rupert House hunters.* Hugh Conn, federal fur supervisor through much of the 1940s and 1950s, is seen here going over maps with hunters on one of the reserves. This picture, from an unidentified newspaper clipping found in a government file, was part of the many journalistic stories that came out of James Bay in the 1940s and 1950s. *Library and Archives Canada*

this. That year the hunter Nosipitaw sent word that he was sending his furs in with his wives or children because they had few and it was not worth his coming to the post. Richard Hardisty did not care who brought the fur but thought the truth of the matter was that they were "afraid to meet [the hunter Cheemooshoominiban] here in consequence of some disagreement which took place between both parties last summer and which is [sic] likely will again be renewed when they meet – as Nosipitaw was hunting upon [Cheemooshoominiban's] lands last summer and fall and intends to hunt there again this spring. This Nosipitaw calls paying himself for Cheemooshoominiban having seasonally hunted upon his for several years past." The moral economy was real enough, but it was one that was in constant flux as individuals moved through the land and negotiated relationships.[37]

Another aspect integral to this moral economy, as Conn interpreted it, was that the hunters had had a system of conservation in the past and that they had left areas untouched, letting them lie fallow for years at a time in order to let the beaver stocks grow. The system had worked well and would not have failed but for the intrusion of whites on the land. The implication is that hunters were essentially conservationist game managers in the manner that Conn would have attributed to more enlightened whites. To some extent fur traders caused the weakening of the system, as did the advent of settlement and farming to the south, but, in Conn's eyes, it was specifically white, independent trappers who had caused the complete failure of Native land use. Conn labelled it "their depredation," and he emphasized that "the term depredation is used deliberately because no other term can describe the results." These trappers disturbed the animals, along with the Native system, and hunters could not "continue the practice any more than a farmer [could] leave livestock in a field continually raided by rustlers," though at least farmers had recourse to the law. The hunter had no system to fall back upon when faced with this threat. Conn praised the Quebec government's "recognition of Indian practice," noting that the large growth in beaver stock was "the result of natural Indian conservation without supervision and under the effects of the handicaps caused by unscrupulous fur traders and the partial breakdown of the family holding system" due to encroachment. "We do not originate anything," he maintained, "we merely recognize their system and adapt ourselves to Indian custom."[38]

Again there is nothing inherently untrue here, just the same simplification of historical events, the truncation of the story – really, the elimination of historical change. Conn's words imply that the Cree and the lands of James Bay remained unchanged until the coming of white trappers in the late nineteenth century – that both had remained since time immemorial, little affected by two hundred years of European activity. Most important, his interpretation clouds or even erases the historical power of Cree hunting and Cree hunters in negotiating with Europeans, and all the changes that this negotiation brought – both good and bad. "Indian practice" became for him something essential and ahistorical. There is a tension here between what Conn saw happening on the ground in James Bay and what he felt was the "nature" of the Native. Beaver reserves were an extension of ancient practice certainly, but they were also a new tradition in the bay. Agreeing to count beaver and report those numbers to conservationists was a dramatic concession to the cultural desires of the whites, and, as in the past, the Cree engaged with conservationists to create a relationship in which they could shape change. His romanticism about the Native past, as well as his conservationist desire to use that as a tool, shaped Conn's view and the view of others who looked at the region.

The Cree engagement in this negotiated historical change can be seen in Conn's own reports of his annual visits to the bay. They provide a window into the cultural exchange that continued to go on in James Bay with regard to conservation. After the business of these trips had been taken care of and the Cree had given their information about their lands, the last night of the visit was devoted to the "Beaver Feast," which was a tradition in all the communities, as we have seen. On these occasions, speeches were given from both sides of the cultural watershed; conservationists expressed their thanks for Cree cooperation and band leaders expressed their gratitude for being able "to restore their ancient custom." Here, as with the use of petitions, a certain familiarity with white discourse was needed, but this was part of the reciprocity. At the beginning of the reserve system the feast was in name only, but even then Conn wrote, with hope, that soon there would be an end to "Shaganash Didjim (English grub)" and that there would be beaver at the Beaver Feast. The feast was integral to the system from the Cree point of view, and it built on the long tradition of feasting. When Chief Malcolm Diamond made his request for the Eastmain reserve in 1938, he asked specifically that the government provide a beaver feast for the band. This was to replicate the one that the HBC had given historically and that was still a tradition at Rupert House. Feasting and the system of preservation went hand in hand in the region, and Conn thought this a good idea. He suggested that the agency do the same at Waswanipi. As a matter of politics he thought that the government should provide for the one at Rupert House as well. He understood the power of reciprocal giving in the region, and he thought that Ottawa should benefit by it rather than the HBC.[39]

In the negotiation over the cultural interpretation of the reserves, "ancient custom" as well as modern accoutrements and procedures mixed together. The tallymen received a small stipend for the work they did and also a cap, badge, and uniform windbreaker that became highly prized within the communities. In his 1943 report, Conn mentioned rather wryly a hunter who had come in wanting to be counted as a tallyman, even though he was now old. Conn learned from Watt that the old man wanted the windbreaker as a badge of status. He was adamant even when Conn warned him that if he took the money for being a tallyman he would lose his old-age pension. Conn was struck by the old man's determination: "The old man replied at length giving details of previous hunts, the loads he had carried over portages, and the enormous distances he had snowshoed in a single day and finished up that he was still a pretty good man and was therefore entitled to a hunter's rating." Tallying was a job that Conn needed done, but this was an issue of identity for the old hunter, and within the new model being a hunter was associated with certain accoutrements. In the end, they made him an honorary tallyman and he got a badge and coat to wear. Later that evening, he addressed the gathering at the feast "to extol the virtues of the Amik Okima (beaver boss)." The report does not make clear whether the old hunter was referring to Conn, the federal "boss," or to *Kitchekisamisk*, the old beaver boss who shapes the hunter's luck. Quite possibly it was to both.[40]

All the wordplay within this negotiated conservation, even the foreshadowing of the power of those words, does not take away from the fact that, both in terms of the country food supplied by hunters and in terms of beaver ecology set out by bureaucrats, the reserves were perceived as successful. Between 1942 and 1948, the population of beaver on the lands north of the Eastmain River and south of Fort George increased from 500 to 13,880, and a new reserve was proposed in 1947 for the upland areas, which were not yet under protection. Again, some of the hunters on the new lands had been practising conservation on their own but, as always, were anxious to have it made official. To gain legal protection for their hunting practice, bands and their leaders used the legal and political means at their disposal to engage white culture on its own terms. Like some whites, who saw the efficacy of Cree practice without understanding the power of the narrative Cree traditions, some Cree may have used white laws without being aware of the larger context or the potential future meaning of so doing.[41]

At Mistassini Post on July 5, 1947, the leaders of the band government sent a letter to the Indian agent stationed there. "Dear Sir," it read, "Further to general meeting of the band as regards fur conservation, we have decided to make the following demand, and wish that the same be considered within the least possible delay." Mistassini was the last part of the region left unprotected, and the letter shows how useful the language of reserves had become. The hunters at Mistassini asked for specific protection: "that the BEAVER SEASON be closed on all territory covered by the Mistassini Indian Band" and "that no white trappers be tolerated in future like at present." They also asked "that any Indian who may have to trap beaver during the close season, to protect his life and of his family, such pelts be surrendered ... that the proceeds be used to restock areas depleted." In return for protection, "during the close season period, we agree to take 'inventory of our grounds,' and submit an animal report, to establish the number of houses in view that when a good number is found, that if there is sufficient beavers in the area, that we be given permits to trap, on a quota basis." The quotations around "inventory of our grounds" are fascinating – a nod to the outside understanding of the hunt for beaver or maybe a self-conscious note on the part of the translator as he moved across cultural borders. The letter had been written in translation by the agent, and the marks hint at the complexity of translating Cree action into white discourse. It is important to note the same kind of hard bargaining language in this letter that Watt had used in his attempt to get the help of hunters at Rupert House at the beginning of the reserve era. The letter goes on to "demand" the protection of mink and marten as well as of beaver, and it concludes with the assurance that these decisions had been made in consultation with the entire band. Only four hunters south of the lake had dissented, and they had no beaver on their lands.[42]

The agent forwarded the letter to Ottawa, along with his own inter-pretation of the band meeting at which the petition was presented to him. The residents of Mistassini, he told the bureaucrats, had been watching the reserves to the west and felt that if beaver could be restored that, in the future, they would again be able to make a living from the land. He strongly recommended that they be given the closed season in all areas, including those not presently organized under the system. Moreover, he suggested that the demand be rushed to Quebec City. He emphasized that the Cree had proposed this themselves, explaining that the new chief, Isaac Shacapie, had been elected on the "'promise' [to] do something worthwhile for the future." To this end, the Natives would act as though the ban was in effect and hope that the province would legalize their decision. Clearly, the matter of preservation at Mistassini, as at Waswanipi, had become a matter of internal politics, and this was a change in environmental concep-tualization that government action would strengthen. Some hunters saw conservation as a good means towards the end of protecting hunting, but others, likely for a variety of reasons, did not. It should not be presumed that all those opposed necessarily wanted a free market kind of hunting as there were plenty of aspects of conservation that some hunters might have found problematic (like the "inventorying" of beaver).[43]

On July 14, 1947, a deputy to Conn met with Isaac Shacapie and agreed to close all of the North, and, in late 1947, the organization of the last reserve in James Bay was begun in the region around Lake Mistas-sini. Passed into law by Quebec in 1948, it consisted of 130,000 square kilometres of territory to the south and west of the lake, and it was again set up under the tallyman system. There were hardly any beaver left in this vast territory (they were only found in boundary areas, where they migrated in from the reserves to the west), but the most important issue with the Mistassini reserve involved the confusion over legal and family boundaries. These needed to be negotiated in order for the new reserve to succeed. With its creation, and with the mapping done by the Natives, a discrepancy between the Cree family system and the government leases for the Rupert House and Mistassini reserves became apparent. The leases had used the seventy-sixth and seventy-third meridians as the demarcating lines of the old reserve, and these had no relevance to the Cree understanding of hunting grounds. Conn informed the HBC that he had "instructed George Jolly to meet with his Nemiska relatives during their winter hunting operations and to settle among themselves the dividing line between their respective trapping grounds." When this was done he would go to Quebec and make the legal changes to the reserve leases; when the changes were made the reserve would then adhere as closely as possible to the band hunting system, and "the only difference between the organization of our preserves and the Indian system [would be] one of phraseology." The new interpretation of James Bay was certainly more than just a matter of phraseology, but for now the solutions did seem to be fairly straightforward.[44]

These kinds of issues could be worked out easily, but the success of preservation brought other challenges to the Cree relationship with conservationists and their understanding of "Indian custom." In the same year that Mistassini was requesting a reserve closure, the members of the Eastmain community were requesting that an adjustment to the timing of opening their reserve at Old Factory be made to take into account their need for food. They appreciated the reserve system, but country food was very scarce, and they wanted to start taking beaver like the hunters to the south in Nottaway, whose reserve was older and therefore more mature. Until the reserve had matured in the mid-1940s, the food situation at Rupert House had been precarious for the hunters and their families as well, and, even with government help, the lack of country food had caused malnutrition, especially among children. In 1947, they had, as Conn noted, "just emerged from a more than ten years' deficiency ... of country food." The Eastmain Cree now faced the same problem, and when they saw their neighbours benefiting, some judged the time ripe for their lands as well and so started a limited hunt. The hunters requested legal changes, but, given their sole control of the resources and their need, they would not stand on ceremony when it came to using their land.[45]

The increase in resources made it possible for the Cree to change their communities as well as to feed themselves, and this required change and compromise with regard to the understanding of hunting. In 1948, hunters at Rupert House requested that the quota on the reserve be raised from fifty to two hundred beaver so that they could use the extra money to build a community hall. Conn thought the request high and consulted with Maud Watt, who still lived at Rupert House, to find out how much money was actually needed for the project. Maud Watt and the hunters had already, in fact, agreed upon the number of beaver, and she supported the idea of a centre for the band. She wrote to L.A. Richard asking him to approve the hall (which, as I mentioned earlier, was named for her husband), and he agreed without hesitation, telling her that his fifteen-year interest in Rupert House had made him eager to accede to the community's wishes – particularly since his having been made "a member of the tribe." He also saw it as a step towards some notion of civilization; perhaps he and Maud Watt had a compelling point. Here again we see a riffle of politics in the relationship to the land, but this was also an instance of the people of Rupert House using the resources at their disposal to reassert a claim to territory that had been ceded to the HBC in the seventeenth century. In a real sense, they were threading their way between the progressive notions of Maud Watt and Richard, on the one hand, and Conn's notion of "Indian Custom," on the other.[46]

The beaver reserves were an adaptation to both the needs of Cree hunting and the restoration of the James Bay environment, and they succeeded in both areas. On a day-to-day basis, they left much of the region in the hands of Cree hunters, though, in a number of important ways, they marked a conceptual reshaping of it. In a limited way, we see the development of an internal political process surrounding the land at the band level. Hunters had negotiated land use in the past, but now the bands were involved in petitioning for reserves and in creating the political consensus needed. Many hunters wanted the reserves but clearly there were some who did not, and they had to be persuaded. Many of the white bureaucrats involved thought of the system not as a political creation but, rather, as the restoration of something natural to the land and the people of the region. The historical process of change that had been going on in the region for centuries was largely forgotten to make room for a romantic image of the Cree and their land. Finally, and most important, there was the overarching conceptualization of conservation and scientific regulation. For the hunter on his lands, neither the romantic nor the scientific understandings of his actions were meaningful, but, as I said earlier, when they worked in concert they were tremendously powerful, and conservation was part of this shift.

I discussed the limited scientific work of the nineteenth and early twentieth centuries in the last chapter, but, like so much of the development of the Canadian North, real change in James Bay began with the Second World War. The mapping of the whole Quebec-Labrador peninsula was carried out during the war with the use of high resolution aerial photography, which was then interpreted in order to map the geography and the vegetation of the region. These were the first maps to really attempt to show the area's complex systems of forests and hydrology and to visualize the northern biosphere. The maps were at first designed for military purposes, particularly in the areas of Labrador that were of strategic use, but soon after the war they became invaluable to scientists working in the region. Kenneth Hare, one of the biologists who had helped the military interpret its data for mapping, in fact went on to found the McGill Subarctic Research Station in Schefferville in 1950. The research station has been an invaluable facility for understanding the northern bioregion, but this kind of knowledge is redolent with political power.

Across much of northern Canada, science and industry began to push out into the hinterland, and, as the land began to be understood and developed, it needed to be managed. Much of the science was aimed at understanding the land so that it could be developed to meet the needs of the growing country. Like Americans, Canadians worried about the health of the postwar economy and looked eagerly for new sources of material for industrial use. The discovery of oil in Alberta and uranium in the Northwest Territories was dramatic, but the more mundane resources (like iron) were also in great demand. Schefferville was, after all, a mining town first and a base for scientific research second. In many respects, it is surprising that eastern James Bay remained outside of this dynamic for as long as it did: until the 1970s, only the mines around Chibougamau and Val-D'Or influenced the region.

From the standpoint of scientific conservation, the most serious issue that arose during the reserve era was the disease known as tularaemia, and here the interaction of bureaucrats and hunters illustrates a more conceptual negotiation than that we have been discussing. Tularaemia was a fatal illness that could potentially destroy whole beaver colonies and spread rapidly throughout a region. It was, many thought, part of the reason for the depletion of the lands around Rupert House in the 1920s and early 1930s, although this was never proved. The disease can also infect humans, and some of the symptoms are not unlike the "influenza" described in the late nineteenth century, though nothing was proved here either. In 1944, there was another scare in James Bay; a beaver had been found dead, and conservationists did not understand beaver pathology well enough to be sure why it had died. Conn wrote uneasily, "what little is known of Tularaemia among beaver, bears out the old Indian's contention that it is caused by stagnant water and that it spreads from stream to stream by infected beaver," but he did not know if this particular beaver had died of the disease. He did know, however, that the disease could ruin the whole conservation plan if it was left unchecked. Luckily, the disease did not gain a foothold in James Bay, though Conn's fears were not without merit. By the mid-1950s tularaemia had caused a great deal of damage in the western provinces of Canada, as well as in Minnesota and other parts of the United States, and people inside and outside James Bay continued to worry that it might spread east. An aide reported the gravity of the situation to Jean Lesage, then a Member of Parliament, in clear terms: "Cette maladie n'a pas encore fait apparition dans notre province et nos graigons for que l'epidimic se propage chez-nour egalement, et ce serait un desastre si notre industrie du castor etait ainsi effectee"; "le bien-etre de nos Indiens particulierment en souffrirait d'une facon desasteuse." The Quebec government was worried about both the welfare of hunters and the economic effects of the disease.[47]

Conn attended a meeting held in Winnipeg in November 1953 to discuss tularaemia, which was then causing heavy losses in Saskatchewan and Manitoba. In Ontario and the western provinces, Indian Affairs had told the hunters to trap out heavily utilized areas. In James Bay, the government issued orders that the Cree should be sure to meet their quotas of beaver: "it is *better to over trap than under trap*," read the federal report. Conservation and management were constant necessities for those in charge of the reserves, but so was the Native understanding of the situation, and many were not comfortable with overhunting the beaver. The beaver were not simply numbers to them but one of their main sources of food; this tied them historically to the memory of hunger and culturally to the environment, and they could not view the land the way that Conn and others wanted them to, so they worked for a compromise.[48]

No record of Conn's discussions with Cree hunters in eastern James Bay exists, but the situation in other areas of Hudson Bay was similar. In 1955, the *Globe and Mail* ran an article that illustrates the kind of interaction that went on between the Native hunters of the North and conservationists. Under the headline "Indians Kill Only for Food" ran the story of a Fort Severn meeting between western Cree hunters and W.J. Harkness, chief of the Fish and Wildlife Division. These hunters, like Cree to the east, had approved of restricting white hunting, and now Harkness also wanted them to prevent whites from killing too many geese. "'It is good. It is true' they murmured," reported the *Globe*. Restricting white hunting was a point that was easily agreed upon, but the article related an issue that caused the hunters great concern. Cam Currie, a game management officer who spoke fluent Cree, next asked the hunters to kill more beaver. They had backed off trapping, and he wanted them to make more room: "but the Indians could not see this reasoning. 'No, no,' protested a trapper, 'you must leave the beaver so there will be more next year. Kill them and there will be no more to trap!' 'But,' reasoned Currie, 'if the beaver does not get enough food or eats poor food it gets sick.' 'That is so' agreed another Indian, 'So' continued Currie, 'if you leave too many they will die of disease.' The Indians nodded dubiously, looked around at each other until at last one of them spoke up. 'What you say is true, but ... but we just cannot kill as you say, for we fear no beaver will be left. Then what would we do?'" The hunter stood at the nexus between two systems of environmental logic, and it was difficult to construct a compromise regarding the land. Here was the trepidation that many Natives felt regarding the disrespectful treatment of animals by Western science and conservation. They did not see themselves as managing animals but, rather, as relating to them in a reciprocal manner: you killed to meet your need, not to control another's population. The latter was a dangerous idea to hunters who did not see the environment as a biotic machine in need of adjustment. Currie was satisfied, though he knew the hunters were dubious about his plan. "They'll do it just right," he assured the reporter, "those people are wise practicing conservationists." The romantic and the scientific worked neatly together for him, but the narrative of management could not be reconciled so easily out on the land.[49]

For another fifteen years in James Bay the preservation program continued to garner interest among reporters. Stories in *Weekend Picture Magazine, Saturday Night,* and the *Toronto Star* all recounted the state of affairs in James Bay during the 1920s and 1930s and the cooperative effort to restore the region. Clearly, whites in James Bay and elsewhere in the North were increasingly interpreting the Cree world from the outside and using that world as the foundation for a great many environmental and cultural purposes. Here is where Olaus Murie and J.W. Anderson found some of their audience for their reminiscences of the region. In a world increasingly concerned with the environment and with Native peoples, the Canadian North became a powerful symbolic resource – that lens through which whites could look at their own world as well as another.[50]

This was never truer than with regard to the great wealth of anthropological data that was collected in these decades regarding the Cree and their hunting. Numerous anthropological and ethnographic studies were carried out during the postwar period, and these have been invaluable in interpreting the historical record of the region. Some things strike me, though, as I read these studies as historical texts themselves. For the most part, these researchers were interested in hunting culture, and so they focused on the practices and beliefs that surrounded the Cree living on their land. In some respects they were looking for Conn's "ancient custom," but they were more sophisticated than that. They knew they were studying a twentieth-century people and so they noted and interpreted change, what they often referred to as acculturation. But quite often hunting was seen as the traditional aspect of Cree life and was separated from acculturative aspects. Here again is the cognitive dissonance between old and new, expected and unexpected, and this is not surprising. Seeing hunting as traditional is part of my argument as well, though I want to see it as part of the acculturative process too. Few anthropologists ever really tried to overcome that dissonance and to understand the whole of what they saw, and so when this information came to be used within the political and legal process after 1970, it was easy to lose the subtlety of those interpretations. Hunting was never interpreted as a modern activity, as the product of a Cree kind of progress, and quite often anthropological evidence was used to bolster the two-dimensional picture of an essential hunter and a natural moral economy.[51]

By the 1960s, a large body of knowledge concerning the Cree and the lands of James Bay had been constructed in various places within the culture to the south. All of it in some respect involved getting information and cooperation from Cree hunters to the north. Because the Cree still used their lands almost exclusively, and because all the various constructions of understanding had not been incorporated into one place, none of this had any particular effect on those living in the bay. Yet, the Cree environment had changed dramatically in the thirty years since the Depression, when the Cree had been an almost completely isolated people in an environment that was largely unknown to those outside of James Bay. Beaver reserves had changed the environment, and this had aided Cree hunters in their attempt to live on the lands; at the same time, however, Cree culture had adapted to the new system of regulation. Because whites had to rely on the Cree for the success of these programs, the Cree were able to influence the character of bureaucratic action for their own cultural ends and to continue the history of negotiated change with the outside world. They had also

FIGURE 6.2   *Mistassini Post, 1968.* This picture shows the wall-tents that most Cree lived in during the summer when they were gathered there. During this period there were some more permanent houses, but most of Mistassini's residents went to the land in late August or September to spend the season hunting and trapping. The Hudson's Bay Company post and Anglican Church are not shown in this view.

developed the ability – an ability that they would continue to need – to work with white bureaucrats within a Western legal structure.[52]

By the 1960s, events to the south were changing rapidly, particularly in the culture and environment of Quebec. Forces were at work, within Québécois society and the provincial government, that would forever change its relationship with the lands and people of James Bay. James Bay would become part of the Québécois consciousness as Quebec challenged its relationship with Ottawa, which, in turn, shaped the relationship between Ottawa and the Cree. The beaver reserves had resulted in the reorganization and reinvigoration of Cree hunting, but it relied on the exclusive use of the land by the Cree, and this was only possible if Quebec had no use for it. With the coming of the Quiet Revolution and the birth of Québécois technocratic nationalism, James Bay became part of the future of a reborn province: popular and political consciousness had caught up with political boundaries. The end of the reserve system marked both the end of a land-use plan and the moment when the outside narrative about the Cree and their land poured back north and flooded the entire region.

7

Flooding the Garden

*After two years we have been discussing the settlement of the
claims put forward by the James Bay Cree and the Inuit of Northern
Quebec. The media have talked about land and money. But what,
in fact, is the real meaning of this Agreement? This is not just an
Agreement dealing with territorial and financial issues that involve
a population of 10,000 souls. This is not just an Agreement between
a government and a group of persons forming a part of our society.
This is an Agreement that foresees the rational organization of a
territory of 410,000 square miles – with all that this objective implies.*

*– John Ciaccia, negotiator of JBNQA to the
National Assembly, November 5, 1975*[1]

There is a sign in Radisson, Quebec, along the road near the administration building. It is one of those multidirectional mileage signs that people put up as a joke in remote places: Ottawa, 1,100 kilometres; Amsterdam, 5,300 kilometres; Los Angeles, 5,990 kilometres, and so on. The sign marks this place as a frontier, and like all those kinds of signs, in addition to the humour there is also a more serious message about being on the periphery of the world. Radisson is indeed nowhere near the centre of anything. The town sits near the site of the Robert Bourassa dam, and it is the administrative headquarters for the La Grande complex, but beyond that it is surrounded by the bush. Its original purpose was to serve as the base for the construction crews who built the dams, but now only some of the town's three hundred or so residents work directly for Hydro-Québec. Most hydro workers commute from the south on ten-day shifts, and it takes surprisingly few people to run the complex on a day-to-day basis. The rest of the town seems to be involved in government or the service industry, either ancillary to the dams or aimed at tourists: sport hunters come here for the caribou, fishers to ply the lakes and rivers, and five or six thousand people a year come to tour the dam.

The people of Radisson – non-Natives here have recently been calling themselves Jameseans – are, I suppose, the modern equivalent of the western pioneers. They have left distant places and staked out territory to try to build new homes and raise families in this remote region, but this is a different kind of frontier than was found in the western United States or Canada. Though this feels like a nice little community, there will be no wave of immigrants following behind to fill up the land and reorganize it into a replica of the St. Lawrence Valley. This is the modern frontier, the resource frontier, and the landscape has been reorganized by workers who came and left. The dams are part of this reorganization, but there is a much larger occupation of this land than is represented by the few hundred Jameseans or even by the vast territory covered by the reservoirs. This region is now part of Quebec: it is not only within its political boundaries but also within its imaginative frontier. This place is on the fringes of the province; nevertheless, most of the people who come to tour the hydroelectric facility each year are from Quebec. They come here because this place is a source of pride as well as of power. It is an icon to Québécois culture's modernity, and it is at the heart of a cultural narrative.

Radisson is here because, during the same century that the Cree struggled with impoverishment and then helped to create the reserve system, Quebec underwent its own internal evolution, which culminated in what has been called the Quiet Revolution of the 1960s. After Confederation in 1867, for a number of reasons, Quebec focused largely on a vision of Franco-Canadian society that had little imaginative use for the northern lands that were incorporated into the province after Confederation: up to the Eastmain River in 1898 and Ungava in 1912. But even as the beaver reserves were being developed, a younger generation of Quebeckers began to question this isolation and to create a new francophone narrative that would change the province's political partnership with the rest of Canada and with its northern territory. These sentiments took political wing in 1959 with the death of Premier Maurice Duplessis and the election of Liberal Jean Lesage.

The changes that came in the next six or seven years affected all of Quebec society; as they relate to this story, however, they marked a radical shift in Quebec culture's relationship to its environment. Quebec, which for so long had looked to the land as its agrarian base, the cultural soil in which language and religion took root and bore fruit, quickly began to see an economic and cultural use for its non-agricultural regions. There were resources for a new society up here – material and imaginative resources – and Quebeckers began to resent anglophone usage of what they saw increasingly as their land. Chief among these resources were rivers that could be used to power a growing economy. The nationalization and politicization of rivers and electric power in Quebec is central to the reorganization of the North and to the creation of the frontier I talked about in Radisson.

The politics of the Quiet Revolution found their way to James Bay in 1970 in the dreams of Robert Bourassa and the Quebec Liberal Party. In that year, the province began the construction of the first of the four dams that would create the initial La Grande River hydroelectric complex. In that same year, the Cree began their legal battle with the province – a battle that has become both famous and infamous in the arena of Native land claims and Native rights. Both these developments changed the geography of James Bay. The dams were completed between 1978 and 1984 – more have been added since – but even before the first water began to rise, legal action and political negotiation had already led to shifts in environmental discourse that are as crucial to the history of the region as is the flooding of the land. The 1970s marked not only the flooding of Cree land but also a cultural watershed for the Cree – the moment in their history when all the other narratives that had been developing outside the region became central to their future as a people. It is tempting to look at the dams as the driving force of environmental change, a force to which the imaginative forces were only adjunct – they are so physically dominant, after all – but the dams could not have been built without conceptual changes in Quebec society or without the application of a new political and technical discourse about the land. With both wires and words, the La Grande project integrated a distant region into the technical geography of an international electrical grid and into a cultural narrative that understood the land in a way that was anathema to Cree tradition.[2]

We have seen that this was not the first time that new narratives had come to the bay, but it was the first time that outside political, scientific, and economic discourses had been so tightly tied to the changing material use of the land. The technical prowess of Hydro-Québec, a new technocratic Québécois government, and the economic needs of a burgeoning modern economy formed a unified force in James Bay that had no precedent. Cree narrative and Cree hunting ceased to have the weight that they had had in previous encounters, and, for the first time, the Cree were forced to define themselves in terms dictated by outsiders. These terms came first in the Quebec Court's attempt to understand the James Bay region in *Kanatewat v. The James Bay Development Corporation*, a lawsuit that the Cree brought to stop the development, and it has defined much of the last thirty-five years in the region. The Cree left their lands in order to protect them, but though they carried their narrative understanding with them, it had little meaning outside the region. During the hearing, the Court developed an interpretation of James Bay – one that was decidedly sympathetic to the Cree but one that conformed to its own cultural and environmental expectations. It was this understanding that later became codified in the negotiation of the James Bay and Northern Quebec Agreement (JBNQA), which was signed in 1975. Starting at that moment, and continuing into the twenty-first century, the Cree have been trying to reassert their cultural presence within this new technological and narrative environment.

It was in the Court's process of discovery – an ironic but meaningful term here – that, for the Cree, the narrative shift began, moving away from what they wanted to say about their land and towards what they were expected to say. They argued that they needed the land as it was, but the questions that were asked of them and the answers that they were allowed to give recorded only the material relationship that they had with it. In short, the legal process took the material facts of Cree life and placed them into the very different narrative framework of science and progress, and this change in language, this new "rational organization" of James Bay, as Minister John Ciaccia so rightly called it at the ratification of the JBNQA, was more important to the Cree than the actual legal interpretation that the Court put on its understanding. The Court's limited decision in favour of the Cree stood for only a few days before being overturned, but the understanding and information gathered during the hearing became firmly entrenched.

What this means is that the Cree have had to become a political and legal people within this new geography and have had to learn a new way of negotiating power in order to maintain themselves and their relationship to the land. It has been noted by many how rapidly and effectively the Cree reacted to the building of the dams, and they have pointed to the educated younger leaders who were able to further their cause when the time came. This is certainly true, but the fact that the Cree as a people had been negotiating with Europeans and North Americans for centuries in various ways should not be overlooked. The negotiation in the 1970s was novel in some respects, the context shifted dramatically away from James Bay, but in other ways it was directly related to all the negotiations since the 1670s. As the Cree struggle to adapt themselves to the post-JBNQA environment, we are reminded that they have been adapting to new circumstances for centuries, and, while these most recent circumstances are very challenging, the situation is not hopeless.

The JBNQA can and should be seen as a landmark treaty that gave a Native people a new kind of self-determination not seen before in North America. It also ought to be interpreted as a cultural watershed for the Cree and their place on the lands of James Bay because it changed radically the Cree's historical ability to define that land largely within their own language and assumptions about culture and nature. Since 1975, the Cree have continued to talk about the land as they understand it and their place in it, but they have also been forced to explain their cultural use of the land to outsiders within a legal and political framework that is not flexible enough to hold many of their cultural concepts. The land, instead of being solely the centre of a cultural cosmos, has become a source of political and environmental debate both inside and outside Cree culture. In a sense, they are still moving between narratives, but now the land has been changed and the context of those narratives has become increasingly complex.[3]

Even within this book, this chapter represents a narrative as well as a physical dislocation that I think is worth embracing as the dissonance is analogous to the shifting cultural contexts that mark this aspect of Cree history. They had to leave James Bay to try to protect it, and we have to leave it too. Whereas in previous chapters I noted the development of a non-Native narrative outside the bay but focused on the internal history of the region, in this chapter my focus shifts to events on the outside because they now begin to reshape both the land and the narrative of the Cree. Events in the bay are still important, and we will get back there, but what happened in Montreal between 1972 and 1975 must take precedence for a while. It is here where the Québécois story and the Cree story converged.

The convergence really began on the evening of April 30, 1971, when Premier Robert Bourassa stood before a crowd of a few thousand Liberal Party faithful in the Québec Coliseé and addressed them in the narrative of Nouveau Québec. The size of the crowd in the stadium was an accurate indication of Bourassa's political health that spring: things had not gone well in his first year of leading the province. He had been elected on the promise of one hundred thousand jobs and had produced almost none; the unfolding of the October Crisis the previous fall had made him appear weak and ineffective to many Quebeckers as Prime Minister Trudeau stole his thunder, invoking the War Measures Act when the Front de libération du Québec first kidnapped British trade commissioner James Cross and then killed Quebec labour minister Pierre Laporte. Bourassa's image as the new, young, competent technocrat, a new brand of Québécois politician, was shattered in those few days when he found himself caught between a powerful federal edifice and a violent push for liberation and separation.[4]

That evening, Bourassa moved his politics north, taking with him Quebec's premier Crown corporation known as Hydro-Québec. He announced the beginning of the huge hydroelectric project that Quebec would create in the watershed of James Bay, and, calling it the "Project of the Century," he told Quebec society to look north and to rethink this region and its uses to the province. With that speech he moved the cultural boundaries of the province: James Bay would be "the key to the economic and social progress of Québec, the key to the political stability of Québec, and to the future of Québec." It would put a hundred thousand people to work, produce power to fulfill the needs of the province, and leave a surplus to be exported to the New England states. James Bay had been under tentative study by Hydro-Québec for nearly fifteen years, but when Bourassa needed it most, Hydro-Québec would play its part by channelling the national pride that Quebeckers felt for the corporation into this massive project. Hydro-Québec's involvement in provincial politics and provincial nationalism was nothing new; Bourassa's project fit well within the historical patterns of Hydro-Québec's development. But with this expansion north, he did succeed in bringing James Bay within the province in a way that the political territorial transfers of 1898 and 1912 had never done.[5]

The La Grande project as proposed by Bourassa would cover an area of 166,500 square kilometres, and the size of the project spoke to the size of the political needs of the time. The planned project running at full power would be able to produce 8.5 million kilowatts of power. This was three times the electricity created by the Churchill Falls facility in Labrador, the biggest hydro plant in North America when it came online in 1971. The four original dams along the La Grande River would utilize the 380-metre drop in elevation over a distance of 500 kilometres to create the electricity, and, in addition to these four dams, the project would create eighteen spillways and control structures along with 130 kilometres of dykes – all of these designed to focus the waters of this and other watersheds on the four powerhouses. The La Grande complex, then, would comprise the whole of the La Grande basin, half of the Great Whale River basin (the latter was dropped later in negotiations), 28 percent of the Caniapiscau and Koksoak basins, and most of the Opinaca River basin. In the coming decades, it would take in 90 percent of the Eastmain River to the south, and the Rupert River diversion which began in the summer of 2007 will push most of that river north as well.[6]

Harnessing the potential of James Bay's hydro power – feeding it through turbines, into transformers, and down high-tension lines – has since then been the technical dream of a generation of Québécois engineers and politicians. Beginning that night, it became a dream closely tied to the other dream of that generation – the driving dream of a reshaped Québécois nationalism that grew out of the Quiet Revolution. This was a dream not only of cultural and linguistic distinction but also of technological and economic distinction. Now James Bay was a region of vast potential for a people who could muster the imagination and the technical skill to exploit it, and Hydro-Québec had grown to represent the best of what the Québécois could develop. In this way, it is really impossible to separate Hydro-Québec and La Grande either from the politics of cultural distinction in Quebec or from the politics of sovereignty.[7]

Not only was the James Bay Project a way of rebuilding Bourassa's power in general, but it was also a way of keeping that power away from René Lévesque and the newly formed separatist Parti Québécois (PQ). As minister of natural resources, Lévesque had argued for the nationalization of electricity in the province under Hydro-Québec. During "Electricity Week" in 1962, he told a crowd that it would be the first step towards the decolonization of Quebec. He had then convinced the Lesage government to move on nationalization by threatening to resign if it did not fight an election over the issue. The Liberals had retained control of the legislature, and, in 1963, Hydro-Québec had become a Crown corporation and controlled all of the electric utilities in the province. Throughout the 1960s, it had grown into a powerful interest in the international business market, and when Lévesque deserted the Liberal Party to create the Parti Québécois in 1968, he saw Hydro-Québec as both a tool for liberating the province and as a means for furthering the political power of his new party. Robert Bourassa's announcement that new economic strength would be drawn from the rivers of the James Bay region meant that his Liberals would also draw power away from the PQ. He went on to optimistically predict an energy usage rate that would continue to double every ten years, as it had since Second World War – a prediction reached not by engineers but by politicians. Big was the order of the day. Yet, in April of 1971, there is little doubt that Bourassa not only expected the project to be economically positive, to stimulate hope and collective pride, but also to create jobs and win votes.[8]

In July 1971, the Quebec legislature passed Bill 50, creating the James Bay Development Corporation (SDBJ) to control not only hydro but also forestry, mining, and tourism in the region. The bill changed the entire legal structure under which the Cree reserves had been constructed. The province had always maintained that it would have the right to develop its resources, when and if it decided to do so, and that the leases to the federal government would be voided in that event. Quebec had been willing to establish the reserves in James Bay because the resources were not needed, nor was it technically possible before the 1960s to harness the hydroelectrical potential and to deliver it from such a distance, but by 1970 the technical problems had been solved and the resources were needed. With Bill 50, the province unceremoniously, and without any hesitation about whether they had the legal right to do so, began the surveying and road construction. Though the federal government still had its obligation to Natives, given the federal Liberals' fear of the separatist PQ, they were disinclined to interfere with Bourassa's plans, and it was left to the Cree to meet the new challenge brought to their culture and the lands of James Bay.[9]

The first meeting of the Cree as a regional, political people took place at Mistassini Post on June 28, 1971. Connected by bonds of friendship and family among hunters, the Cree had never before considered themselves bound together governmentally. There had been no need for this, and neither of the governments to the south really thought of the Cree as a single people, except in the broadest of terms. The HBC had been the connecting link between the various bands as far as government was concerned, along with the small organization of fur reserve workers. This Mistassini meeting began to change that as two generations of Cree met to discuss their shared problems. Older chiefs brought younger men to translate for them, and the younger chiefs brought older trappers for advice and guidance.[10]

This meeting was also significant for the presence of the Indians of Quebec Association (IQA), which was quick to declare its solidarity with the Cree. It was in fact the IQA's money and organization that enabled the Cree to meet. Then a political organization controlled by members of southern tribes, the IQA had offered successful resistance to Trudeau's Native policy in Ottawa, and now it offered its assistance to the Cree in fighting the Quebec agenda. The IQA immediately saw the Cree as part of a pan-Native movement in Quebec and Canada, and, while in the end this was not a comfortable fit for the Cree, for the moment the assistance was welcome. They drafted a resolution to Jean Chrétien, then the federal minister of Indian Affairs, and this was the first step towards the longest interlocutory hearing in the history of the Canadian courts.[11]

During this entire process, Chrétien maintained what he called "alert neutrality" in an attempt to maintain the relationship between the Liberal governments of Quebec and Canada, but in many ways alert neutrality became a de facto abrogation of federal responsibility and an abandonment of forty years of cooperation with the Cree concerning the lands of James Bay. The Trudeau government did not act to address the Cree request for aid, and Chrétien's office claimed never to have received their resolution: the document has never been found. From the Native perspective, Trudeau's brand of liberal nationalism was every bit as culturally myopic as was Lévesque's Quebec nationalism, and the situation was only made more complicated as the Middle East embraced its own kind of nationalism in the form of the 1973 oil embargo, which put the La Grande project in a new international political light. Cree hunters continued to use their lands and hunt for their living but under a growing cloud of unease that came with the presence of work crews and surveyors as well as this new global context.[12]

On April 18, 1972, another gathering of Cree leaders took place, this time in Fort George, where the decision was made to go south to fight the project. It was at this meeting that the Inuit of Quebec first joined the Cree because, though the dams were not on their territory, they felt threatened by their presence. On May 3, 1972, the Cree and Inuit filed for an injunction on the work being done in James Bay, holding a press conference in Montreal to announce their intended actions against Bill 50. With this they entered both the legal and political arenas. Their claim was that the bill was unconstitutional and that the work done by Hydro-Québec should be stopped, at least until some settlement could be reached. Here too they entered into the Canadian consciousness. They met with Chrétien in early May to discuss the federal role in their dispute with Quebec, but the increasingly dire political reality meant the Cree problem would stay provincial business. PQ demands for independence continued to gather support with the electorate, threatening national stability. Shortly afterward, on May 16, 1972, the plan for the first phase of the La Grande project was delivered to the Natural Resources Committee of the Quebec legislature. Work began later that same month, and the infrastructure of roads, running up along the coast to Fort George and inland to the La Grande 2 dam site, was already in place by the summer of 1972. The working season would be over that year before the Cree were able to enter the Superior Court in Montreal.[13]

On October 25, 1972, the attorneys for the Cree – James O'Reilly, Robert Litvack, and Peter Hutchins – made their petition before Justice Albert Malouf, and on November 17 the hearing began in earnest. Their case, though it took seven months to present, was fairly simple. They argued that legal precedent, both before and after Confederation, gave the Cree rights on the lands of James Bay that had never been extinguished; the wording of the 1912 transfer of this territory to Quebec had specifically required a settlement of Native land claims in a treaty patterned on the numbered treaties elsewhere in Canada. This had not been done. The Cree claimed that they still depended on this land in its present state for their livelihood and that the hydro development was infringing upon these rights. For their part, Hydro-Québec's attorneys argued that Quebec had the right to exploit its natural resources as it saw fit, and even if there was a need to treat with the Natives in the area, the legal balance of convenience was on their side. They argued that the project should not be postponed because every non-working day would cost their client money. The general thrust of Jacques Le Bel, Romeo Boulanger, and Roger Thibodeau's presentation was aimed at showing that the Cree, after three centuries of contact with Europeans, lived and thought much like any Canadian citizen.[14]

Arguing the first aspect of the Cree case was simple enough; it involved citing precedent that began with the English Crown's first dealings with the Natives of North America, and it followed that legal, diplomatic relationship through Confederation to the present. The second part was far more complicated. It involved understanding the land, along with the Cree relationship to the land, and there was no text or list of texts that covered this subject. Local knowledge was extensive within the context of the hunt, but geographically, scientifically, and ethnographically the specifics of James Bay were still only superficially synthesized. There was a lot of information out there, as we have seen, but it was scattered and unorganized. Creating a rational picture of it would entail a long, sometimes ad hoc process of legal testimony by the Cree and their expert witnesses. And it was the nature of the questions asked that would come to define the limits of that picture.

For the first two-and-a-half days, Chief Billy Diamond of Rupert House stood to give evidence, and during this time the tone of the proceeding was established. He was first asked to locate Rupert House on the map, then to identify the area that his people used for hunting and trapping. He was asked to estimate that territory's area, which he put at 50,000 square kilometres, and to mark on the map the area that his father's family used as a trapline. This became the formulaic set of questions that, in an attempt to show how completely the Cree occupied the land, was asked of all the Native witnesses. As a child, Diamond had been sent to a provincial boarding school in Ontario and had received an education in English. As a result he was accustomed to this kind of information gathering, with its emphasis on quantity rather than quality, and he answered these questions easily and without hesitation.[15]

Other older hunters, those without this specific education, found these questions inappropriate. They understood the questions, but they did not understand the reasons why someone would ask them in the first place. Canadians put value on information that the Cree had never thought to collect. This was partly because they did not need it and partly because to collect this kind of data showed a kind of disrespect that jeopardized their relationship with the land. It is in this difference in values that the shift in language begins to appear. Diamond was asked to explain how the Cree hunted and trapped their lands, and he explained the yearly cycle of the hunt, giving a list of the kinds of animals that were used. He was also asked to estimate the percentage of their diet that the Cree got from the bush, which he put at 90 percent. He then gave a brief history of the recent events in James Bay and entered into evidence some pictures he had taken of the work sites he had visited.[16]

Le Bel's cross-examination of Diamond set the rhythm for his questioning of the other Native witnesses as well. He asked Diamond about the use of airplanes to go to and from traplines, which, by then, had become the practice among some Cree hunters. He also asked about the use of snowmobiles for travelling in the bush and showed incredulity when Diamond told him that the Cree at that time did not use them on their lands:

Well, Chief, if their trap line is, for example, 80, 90 miles inland, how is it possible for them to bring back the game?

They use a sleigh and dog-team ...

Dog-team?

... and the mother carries her children on her back and they walk on snowshoes and the husband may carry a packsack on his back and the heavier equipment is left on a sleigh and the dogs pull the sleigh and the man may help, the trapper may help the dogs by having a strap attached to the sleigh and pulling and carrying at the same time.

And each and every time, members are going to their trap line, they bring dogs and sleighs with them?

Yes.

If they go to their territory by plane?

Yes, the dogs are taken.[17]

In spite of the critical and mistrusting tone of Le Bel's examination – the job of a cross-examining attorney after all – his incredulity was genuine; it seemed impossible for him to think of surviving in this wilderness without relying on machines or, more important, that anyone might find it more convenient to live without machines. Le Bel was asking about survival in a wilderness wasteland, and Diamond was describing the simple facts of living in the bush. Le Bel was trying to show how dependent the Cree had become on technology, and Diamond was trying to explain that the Cree interpreted technology with a different set of values than that used by those in the South. The planes and snowmobiles, which Le Bel saw as part of the same useful technology, the Cree hunter saw, respectively, as a machine that dropped him off and eased his burden and as a machine that had to be gassed, maintained, and stored when not in use. This was the logic that the Cree had been applying to Western technology for centuries. "Most of the people are going to their trap line by plane though?" Le Bel asked again, coming back to his original point regarding how the Cree used Western technology. And so the proceedings moved on.[18]

Diamond was brought back a few days later to go beyond the statistical evidence and to elaborate on what he had been prevented from saying about the Cree understanding of their place in the world in his earlier testimony. Le Bel had objected to the hearsay nature of Diamond's statements about Cree identity, but Malouf had reversed his initial ruling, deciding later to hear the testimony. Diamond's elaborations were one of the few articulations of Native understanding in the long months of testimony. Diamond was asked what effects he saw for his people:

with the development of the James Bay area as outlined in the initial phase of the James Bay Project, we see the planification [sic] of roads into James Bay. We see the planification of transmission lines from La Grande to the Montreal area. There will no doubt, there'll be other development in James Bay, such as "Acnow" Development [a Quebec corporation] and my people are not prepared to [meet] the impact of this development. My people have gradually developed themselves, on their own time.

The Cree were not a primitive people, and they had taken much from Western technology and culture, but these projects were of a different order of magnitude and they threatened to bring in a new level of change. Change and continuity had existed side by side, but the projects would alter this dramatically. Diamond continued:

> and with the construction of transmission lines, roads in the area, there is the removal of trees and top soil and it will affect the traditional ways of life of my people. When it affects the traditional way of life of the Indian people, then their culture will be affected. If their culture is affected then their pride will be affected. We have lots of pride in being Indian, we have lots of pride in being able to live directly from the land and we want to continue this pride. The Indians of Rupert House and James Bay area wish to continue to live the traditional way of life.[19]

Diamond's testimony is a watershed in the understanding of James Bay. This was the clearest statement regarding the original objective of the Cree and their traditional way of life made in the entire hearing. His testimony only touched on the dual themes of gradual development and the traditional lifeways that were so important in the Cree past – the fact that the Cree were then a twentieth-century people, practising a twentieth-century way of life – but they were never highlighted. This was probably smart courtroom strategy, given that La Bel wanted to portray the Cree as just like everyone else, but it also hobbled the Cree case in some meaningful ways.

Whether he did so consciously or not, Diamond stressed the effects of roads and future development while neglecting to mention the dams and the flooding. The last thirty-five years have shown that roads and the access they have given have been at least as disruptive as has the flooding, if not more so. Certainly this is the case in the Waskaganish region, which is Diamond's home. He saw these future problems and spoke abstractly and hypothetically to try to make his point, but most of the other Cree were hesitant to speak of anything beyond their own personal experience and were more than a little puzzled at the kinds of information they were being asked to provide to the Court. Some of them did not have the language to go beyond the minimum rudiments of the questions, even with the help of the translator; others were simply viewing the world from a perspective that made those questions meaningless. Diamond's point was lost in the end, and the information gathered was almost exclusively statistical and scientific.

Over the next two months, two or three Cree witnesses were heard each day, and the questioning became almost a matter of form as both sides sought information and tried to come to an understanding of this territory and its people. In the end, this information became so rote that the two sides agreed on what would be allowed into the record without testimony. O'Reilly stipulated these facts for one hunter, and Le Bel agreed to let it be entered without testimony:

> One: that he has a trapline, number 33, within the Eastmain hunting ter-
> ritory that includes the area on the north side of the Eastmain River and
> both sides of the Opinaca, and that his trapline is presently being used;
> Two: that for several years, he has used his trapline every year, for periods
> from three to seven months; Three: that when he is not on his trapline, he
> also hunts and fishes around the settlement, throughout the year; Four: that
> he catches beaver, lynx, otter, bear, mink, rabbit, ptarmigan; Five: that he
> catches the following fish: pike, sturgeon, Whitefish, walleye, sucker and
> the big catfish species, the exact name of which is unknown; Six: that he
> catches the following birds: geese, blue geese, loon, ducks and white owl;
> Seven: that he and all of his family, one wife and six children, eat approxi-
> mately 80% of country food, when in and around the settlement; Eight:
> that he has gone up the Opinaca River a considerable length; Nine: that
> his children hunt and fish around the settlement when they are home from
> school. These are the facts which my Confreres have admitted that witness
> would testify to.[20]

Slowly, Cree life began to be a matter of accepted and predictable statistical fact and hunting an occupation rather than an active and changing relationship with a dynamic and unpredictable environment.[21]

Each witness was asked to mark out his trapline with coloured pencil, one or two thousand hectares on a provincial map. When the chiefs of the bands appeared, they were asked to sketch the whole community's trapping territory so that a visual picture of Cree use could be more fully developed. This was rough estimation, with each hunter using what landmarks he could find on the map, and there were occasional revisions. Matthew Neeposh had marked out the extent of the Mistassini territory for the Court, but when Chief Smally Petawabano took the stand he redrew the border farther north. Despite these discrepancies, estimates were entered into the record as fact. In one respect, these revisions were relatively unimportant in that the map was simply meant to give the Court a generalized view of the extent of the land the Cree used. But this generalized perception of

Cree use, this abstraction of the land, began slowly to erode the precise and intimate relationship that these hunters shared with this landscape. The underlying cultural and environmental facts were absent in the Court's picture. The extent of use was clear, but the meaning of that use never emerged.[22]

When witnesses were asked to estimate the size of their territory, or the band territory, there were a variety of responses. Petawabano, who seemed fairly comfortable with the questioning, hesitated only a little when asked the size of the Mistassini land: "well, I'm no expert on that, but according to my estimation, it was approximately 80,000 square miles." Chief William Gull, of Waswanipi, would not put a figure on the size of his territory, telling the Court that he did not think of the bush as an area of square miles and that in the bush there were no boundaries to measure. When asked about how they were measured in the record, he was clear in stressing the lack of boundaries in the bush: "no, people hunted all over and even traplines were just for beaver when they came." For him, at least, the structure of the reserves had been an accommodation. Both men spoke through interpreters, although Petawabano, who was thirty-four, spoke English fairly well, and this difference in language skills may have made it easier for him to understand the context of the questions. Both men were on shifting ground, though. Clear and measurable boundaries were recorded in Ottawa, but, before now, they had never been applied directly to the land without Cree cultural mediation. The Cree had defined these boundaries as they saw fit, but now the lines on the map were redefining them. It is worth mentioning here, because it seems strange, that there was almost no investigation of the reserve system in the whole of the proceedings, and it does not enter into Malouf's deliberations.[23]

This shift in perspective was true of other data as well, and there is a clear sense that some of these hunters saw that they were being boxed in by this process. The hunters showed a marked hesitancy to quantify their land or the animals on it. Steven Tapiatak, of Fort George, marked out his territory on the map but tried carefully to point out that his outline was really only a guess. When he was asked how many fish could be caught in a summer at the first rapids of the La Grande River, he would offer no guess. When asked how many miles it was from the village to the rapids, he answered that he could not tell the number of miles "because I do not measure the area I travel." He was then asked to estimate the number of beaver he caught during a year, to which he responded: "I cannot estimate. All I can tell you is that I trap beaver every year." This hesitancy, conscious or unconscious, was frustrating, almost comical at times. When Matthew

Neeposh was asked, in cross-examination, how high the trees were in a recently burned area of his trapline, he answered that he did not know how high the trees were because he had "never really gone and measured the trees." When Le Bel pushed him for a guess he held his hand above the floor and Le Bel read into the record: "six, eight inches, something like that. It has been reduced to four inches now!" Le Bel's irritation with Neeposh is telling.[24]

This hesitancy was not due to an inability to understand or to calculate; rather, it was due to a refusal to think about the land and the game in terms of numbers and statistics or to speak hypothetically. When Litvack tried to establish how the late break-up on the bay might affect the salmon season, he asked John Watt to hypothesize what would happen if the ice did not go out until the middle of August. Watt's response: "I can't answer that [because] I never see the ice in the middle of August." Georges Pachano, when asked to estimate the number of fish he caught, would not give a number. When asked if he had not kept track, he replied emphatically: "No, I didn't keep track of the number of fish I catch in a year. It wasn't intended by the Creator who created the fish that the Indian keep track of all the fish that he kills."[25] It would be disrespectful, and therefore dangerous, to tally fish as though they were possessions. Again, there is a sense that the Cree saw where this was headed.[26]

These kinds of exchanges between the Cree and the attorneys highlight the very different languages of understanding that were present in the courtroom. As Richard Preston has noted, an answer of "I don't know" does not necessarily mean a lack of information; rather, it often means something more like, "I don't know how to reply to your question in a way that will be satisfactory to both of us." In his work with the Cree, Preston found that, if his questions could be phrased in a culturally appropriate way – especially if his phrasing showed a grasp of the general topic in Cree terms – then information could be attained. But the Court never displayed this level of cultural sophistication; rather, it demanded knowledge on its own terms. It wanted to interpret the region in terms of commodity, and the Cree refused to think of things along those lines. Matthew Shanush, chief of Eastmain, was asked if he knew about an Eastmain trapping cache that had been destroyed by Hydro-Québec workers and the amount of monetary compensation that the corporation gave the Cree. He was aware of the compensation, "but not in the means of what was destroyed, but in means of money, and the money that was compensated to the trapper is nothing compared to what he had obtained from these traps and from what he would obtain in the future if he still had these traps." The Cree were used to money, but clearly it could not be equated with the potential of the cache. In a similar vein, when Steven Tapiatak was asked how much money he had made the previous year, he could only guess at one thousand dollars as he "did not keep track." François Mianiscum replied in the same way to Le Bel when asked to guess what he made from guiding each year. "Is that more than what he earns from trapping?" asked Le Bel. The translator replied, "he says, he doesn't know how much he gets from hunting because everything changes each year, it's different, he doesn't get the same amount from hunting, he doesn't make the same amount from hunting."[27]

It would be easy to pass this off as a lack of record keeping skills, but it was more than that. Mianiscum probably had a pretty clear idea of how much he had earned, but each year for the Cree involved a changing set of facts that was contingent upon things that were beyond the hunter's direct control. To become too confident in and reliant upon records was dangerous. This held true of compensation that might be received for the flooded lands. "When you talk about money, it means nothing," said Job Bearskin, "there will never be enough to pay for the damage that has been done. I'd rather think about the land and think about the children. What will they have; money means nothing." A little later in his testimony, he made reference to the garden that existed in the region and how that – not money – was the legacy of the Cree to their children.[28]

At moments like this in the testimony one can glimpse how the Cree understood their relationship to the land and their identification with the animals. O'Reilly asked John Weapiniccapo, of Eastmain, if he had seen a change in the animals on his land since Hydro-Québec had blasted on the river:

> There was a difference in the number of animals as compared to the number that were there before the blasting and also blasting makes a lot of noise and also when they're doing blasting on the river, well, there's a large amount of water that's being blown into the air.
>
> What effect does this large amount of water, going into the air, have?
>
> I cannot tell you the exact effect, but all I can say is that the smell after the blasting, is not, it wasn't pleasant to me, [and] I'm pretty sure that it wasn't any more pleasant to the animals than it was to me.[29]

This displays a level of sensitivity and identification that grows from living in the bush, and it relates to more than simply hunting: it relates to being a hunter. At another point, O'Reilly asked a question that went to the heart of the Cree identification with the land and their self-identity as hunters:

> Okay, now, how long have you been a trapper, Chief Shanush, or hunter?
>
> I don't think he quite understood the sentence. [Interpreter speaking]
>
> Has he been a hunter or a trapper since he was a child?
>
> He says, I've been hunting, trapping now ever since I was young because I was born on the trap land and I was raised there.[30]

Shanush didn't think of himself as a professional hunter – something that he could either be or not be. "Hunter" was an identity he had held since he was old enough to act upon it. This was also evident in John Watt's testimony, under Le Bel's cross-examination, when he told him that everybody in Fort Chimo was a hunter. Le Bel wanted him to enumerate how many were full-time hunters.

> That I couldn't answer because they are men and the women and grown kids, they [are] all hunters.
>
> Full-time?
>
> It's full-time. [interpreter in response to Watt's nod]
>
> Can you give me, Mr. Watt, an approximate figure of the full-time hunters, men and women?
>
> That question I could not answer because there everybody is involved in this and everybody has some work and a few works then finishes then go off for hunting. They would just sort of take turns.
>
> I want to be sure, Mr. Watt, that you make a distinction, the difference between full-time and part-time hunters. I'm talking about full-time hunters. You are talking also about part-time hunters.[31]

Watt finally and grudgingly accepted the parameters of the question and guessed at sixty full-time hunters, but in his mind they were all hunters: some of them worked at jobs, but that did not change who they were. All this speaks obliquely to a different relationship with the landscape of James Bay and gives clues regarding a Cree way of thinking that was never explored throughout the eight months of *Kanatewat*.

Cultural blind spots came out in other Court presumptions as well. The whole notion of progress was an issue that Le Bel wanted to stress, and, while he met some procedural objections from O'Reilly, he met no philosophical ones. O'Reilly objected to the leading nature of the questions when Le Bel seemed to be telling Sally Matthew, of Fort George, about the benefits of schools, hospitals, and other technology without letting her come to her own conclusions. Le Bel wanted her to agree that these things had improved life in the settlement and were now necessary; O'Reilly objected to the nature of the questions, but he did not address the basic assumption that all technological progress was inherently necessary. Billy Diamond's point that some technological change helped and some did not was lost and Malouf, too, wanted to admit progress as a given. He told the attorneys that he did not want "to anticipate any proof which either party wishes to make or intends to make, but it seems to me that these are matters which could readily be admitted by the parties. I'm speaking of progress."[32]

No matter how the Court decided, progress would come to James Bay, and this would form the context of Cree life. Twenty years later, in 1992, then grand chief Matthew Coon Come still struggled with this presumption when fighting new hydro development on Cree land. "I am not against development or all construction over economic activity and all the rest," he argued, "that is not the position of the Crees of northern Québec. We know that some development is necessary, and we understand that there is value in progress and advancement. We are not attempting to avoid high technology, machinery, electricity, and other signs of progress. But I must ask if every project, if every new structure, every new highway, if every dam is really 'development.'" This was at question in the courtroom, and the answer seemed a nearly foregone conclusion.[33]

Native testimony finished in January. Some witnesses were recalled at later points in the trial to clarify their testimony, but the majority of witnesses from January on were scientists and experts on the engineering of dam projects. Hydro-Québec called some white witnesses from the region to refute some of what the Cree had said, but, under cross-examination, most of them had to admit that their knowledge of the Cree was limited to contact in white towns like Chibougamau. It was the scientists who were asked to organize the territory for the Court in a way that the Cree had not. The Cree had helped create a map of the land and its various traplines, but they had not been asked how their land worked, only what they had harvested from it.

It was also left to the expert witnesses to establish the history and longevity of the Cree occupation of the James Bay area and to quantify that
use for the record. It was they who were able to put numbers on what
the Cree witnesses had only spoken of in general terms. Anthropologist
Harvey Feit provided an overview of the historical record pertaining to
the Cree that relates closely to the chronology of *Home Is the Hunter*. He
began with Father Albanel's visit in 1672 and continued through the fur
trade and missionary eras of the nineteenth century. Government records
of the present century completed the trail. Adrian Tanner established the
precontact usage of the area by citing the few archaeological studies that
had been conducted in the region. Edward Rogers corroborated these
archaeological opinions, but, for lack of hard evidence, neither he nor
Tanner could answer questions in any great detail: "We just don't know
where the sites are. There's, as I say, there's been no work done [there].
It's a fascinating blank in the map." Historical analysis of the region was
pretty thin at that time as most of the fur trade and economic history of
the Canadian North was focused on the western side of Hudson Bay and
James Bay. The Court was given no details regarding how the Cree had
dealt with the fur trade or the HBC.[34]

Expert witnesses were able to put quantities on the pattern of living that
the Cree had described. Through them the Court learned that one specific
Mistassini hunting group, in the winter of 1969-70, survived mostly on
moose, caribou, and beaver but that they also consumed otter, porcupine,
geese and ducks, mink, marten, squirrel, and ptarmigan; all of these added
up to 4,839.6 kilograms of meat for the winter. Of that, 904.9 kilograms
was caribou, 2,096.8 kilograms was moose, 697 kilograms was beaver, and
646.8 kilograms was various kinds of fish. The rest of the 4,839.6 kilograms
was made up of smaller game. These statistics were produced by full-time
hunters who comprised 61 percent of the Mistassini band. Part-time
hunters made up another 20 percent, and the remaining 19 percent did
no trapping at all.[35]

For the Waswanipi band the figures were similar, with 56.2 percent of
the men in this community following the pattern of full-time hunting,
and 26 percent practising part-time hunting. Only 8.7 percent, however,
practised no hunting or trapping at all. This was during the winter; during
the summer, the statistics were very different. In the summer, 66 percent
of the men worked at part-time jobs around the community, and only
25.3 percent were unemployed. The result of these various labours was
that 82.4 percent of the food for these Cree families came from the bush;

therefore, 17.6 percent came from the store. When translated in monetary terms and compared with other money earned, this meant that country food accounted for 52.1 percent of their annual income. Ten percent of their income came from the furs that they trapped during the winter, and 20.2 percent came from the wages they earned during the summer. The rest of their annual income came from federal allowances such as old age pensions and welfare. It was estimated that the yearly market value of meat gathered in the villages of Eastmain and Paint Hills was $280,000, while the value of that gathered from Fort George was $560,000. Moreover, by breaking down the statistics according to age, it was shown that there was no decrease in hunting activity in the younger generation, although the young did have more experience at wage labour than did older men.[36]

The weight of statistical evidence was daunting, but the imposition of inductive reasoning was important to the proceedings as these figures were arrived at in a number of ways. Researchers actually took some down in the bush when the hunters brought in the animals, and some were recorded when researchers interviewed the hunters shortly after their seasonal return to the village. Other hunters had been asked to keep a journal of their success during the winter and return it the researcher in the spring. The figures were cross-checked with other members of the group, and, in the words of Feit, "there was an attempt to establish scientific validity here and these figures have scientific validity in the sense that they are cross-checked and they're internally consistent." All of these statistics were consistent, but they represented only one or two years of data. Yet they came to represent the Cree standard of living, despite the Cree insistence that things change from year to year and that subsisting in the bush, for them, was not a matter of statistics.[37]

All this production of and reliance upon statistical understanding led to some confusion. O'Reilly asked Tanner to explain to the Court that the number of fur-bearing animals reported to the government of Quebec were, in fact, only those that had been sold in trade and did not include those used by the Cree themselves or those considered too damaged to trade. He was trying to establish that hunting numbers were higher than the statistics indicated. At this point there was an objection from the re-sponding attorneys. They did not believe that a witness could contradict the official record of the province; the number of fur-bearers trapped was a matter of public record. Interestingly, the Court upheld their objec-tion, and while Malouf was willing to admit that O'Reilly was trying to show a greater reliance on trapping by the Cree, he would not allow the question:

The only ruling I am making for purposes of the record and so that you will understand it, is that I will not allow an individual to give two statistics or to disclose that there are two statistics, one which he divulged to the Government Agency, for reasons which are still unknown to me, and "B," that he had a private, an additional bookkeeping arrangement to show the number of animals he really killed, which is not the same as the number that he gave to the Government official. That's my ruling.[38]

Malouf may have felt that he was protecting the Court from confusion, but, like the lines on the map, which had never been applied to the landscape from within, this statistical information had never been meaningful in James Bay. Hunters had given bureaucrats numbers within a certain context, and they had become official statistics. Now official statistics were not to be contradicted, and they were directly related to the use and conception of the region. The fact that the Cree had been setting their own quotas, using animals according to their own needs, and maintaining their cultural understanding of beaver and other food animals – all of which had created the apparent contradiction – was never admitted into the court record.

Other expert witnesses spoke to the Cree's reactions to the project, laying out the personal and cultural effects of development. John Berry, a professor of psychology, gave evidence on the damaging effects of acculturation upon people who came into contact with a more dominant culture – the dynamics of assimilation, integration, and rejection, as he enumerated them. This acculturation created stress among people who wanted to maintain their cultural identity, and, according to Berry, the Cree were beginning to show signs of this kind of stress. Because the Hydro-Québec lawyers were themselves trying to show how acculturated the Cree had become, experts for the Cree tended to ignore the long relationship that had existed between the Cree and whites. Paul Bertrand, an anthropologist for Hydro-Québec, argued that no culture could expect to maintain a distinct identity in an increasingly global and technological world. He argued that the Hydro-Québec projects in James Bay would act as a "salutary shock" to the Cree culture and would help the Cree bootstrap themselves into the modern world. He believed that the Cree would have to change in order to survive. This argument was also made, in less confrontational language, in a report written on the state of Cree society by Richard Salisbury in the early 1970s. This report would become the basis of his book, *A Homeland for the Cree*, published in 1986, in which he argues that the projects and the settlement had helped bring the Cree together as a regional people.[39]

None of these insights into the changes that the Cree were facing addressed the changes that, over the centuries, they had made in adapting to the presence of European culture in the region. This was because the latter did not fit the needs or the understanding of either side's argument. The Cree lawyers presented contact as a seemingly recent event, something new to the Cree, while the Hydro-Quebec lawyers maintained that assimilation had already occurred. These arguments are not surprising, but they skewed the Court's interpretation. More important, none of these experts saw that the change that was now occurring was one in which the Court proceedings were directly involved. The trial itself was changing the region and its people. Leaving aside the glaring irony of his assertion in a Montreal courtroom about the impossibility of maintaining distinct identity, Bertrand was, to a degree, correct about the need for change. The Cree had been facing the need to change for centuries, but the context of change was now shifting around them both in the bay and in the courts. From all sides there was a concerted effort to fight the notion that the Cree were a modern people, one with their own definition of what it meant to be modern.

The remainder of the expert witnesses testified concerning two areas: the engineering of the whole complex of dams and their effect upon the environment of the North. There was a monumental mustering of evidence, and forty professionals were called to testify to what these dams would mean to the ecosystems around eastern James Bay. Climatologists, geologists, and, especially, biologists were called upon to give opinions. Predictably, those called by O'Reilly were negative about the projects, while those called by Le Bel were positive. What was significant about all the testimony was that those who opposed the projects did so based on their perception that the dams were being built without a proper scientific understanding of the region. For all of them, the important issue was that there was not nearly enough information to form adequate opinions and that further study was needed. All of them brought the scant data that they were able to collect about the region and laid out a method of investigation that would improve the understanding of the bay to the point where decisions regarding hydro development could be made rationally. For them, this method was crucial to successful development.

The first of these witnesses, and the one with the most seniority, was Professor Kenneth Hare from McGill University. Hare brought with him a systematic understanding of the environment of northern Quebec and a set of ideals that guided the use of that understanding. He bounded the region of the hydro project within the forest-tundra and woodland zones between the 59th and 52nd parallels, the true tundra being to the north and the true forest to the south. He laid these zones out on a highly detailed map of the peninsula. Using these maps, and his understanding of the region, Hare was able to delineate for the Court the topology of land formations, starting with the coastal plains and rising inland through the band of muskeg swamps to the interior. In this way, a generalized geographical understanding developed that was detached and distinct from the individual subsistence geography as the hunters in the bay had known it. Gone were the watershed maps of the tallymen.[40]

Hare explained the various wetland habitats that existed within this geography and the negative effect that the flooding would have upon them. He told the Court about the caribou herds that range along the northern regions of James Bay and the traditional routes that they used. He admitted that scientific understanding of the caribou in Quebec was almost non-existent: "I do not believe that the habits of the interior caribou are known at all, sir. I know of no expert studies of this." The thrust of his testimony was that the northern environment was delicate and did not adapt easily or quickly to changes: "In the north, there is [sic] only a very limited number of species; the northern vegetation and the northern fauna are made up of a limited number of different kinds of plant and different kinds of animal. And most of them are highly specific. They have exact requirements and they are adapted to a specific environment." He concluded that the state of knowledge was so scant that it would be improvident to develop the territory at present.[41]

Significantly, it was this lack of knowledge about which Hare was most adamant. He emphasized that they were dealing with a region that was the size of Europe, that there were "only a handful of scientists" who ever worked in the interior, and that developers were basing their work "on the flimsiest of evidence. I would say that over the peninsula as a whole, we have got to the stage where we have done the reconnaissance. We have taken the first look, but in most areas of science we have done very little detailed work indeed." For Hare, study and measurement were synonymous with management and control. In his opinion, what was needed was the kind of study and management that the Scandinavians practised in their forests and tundra. He noted that "they try to see the development as a comprehensive development so that one part of the environment isn't benefited at the expense of another. They are, of course, very sophisticated in their development of hydroelectric power. And their land management practices are a joy to behold to somebody in my business; they control land use to an extraordinary extent even to the extent of the reindeer herding practices of the Lapps."[42]

Hare was a proponent of development, if it were to be done in what he considered to be a responsible manner, but the lack of understanding of the North worried him, and he knew enough to be very concerned about these changes:

> It will be different and I will confess that I would prefer it to be left alone. That's an emotional reaction of a person who spends his life studying. The emotional reaction arises from the fact that these are delicate systems. The southern environment, the ones of the tropics and the temperate latitudes adapt, rebuild, accommodate themselves. Those of us who work in the north are constantly faced with a nightmare that the northern regimes do not do this and they require nursing, they require a kind of sensitive treatment which we don't yet know how to administer. So my answer is the environment will be different and I will add that myself, I would prefer that the northern environments be not [sic] disturbed until we can do, we can understand how to do it.[43]

Clearly, Hare cared deeply for the region and understood it on a personal level that others in the Court could not. Unlike the Cree hunters, Hare discounted his own personal involvement with the region in order to rationalize it, to generalize about its rules, and to predict what would happen. These were powerful methodological assumptions and were as important for dam building as they were for environmental science. They were as important as the idea of progress, and the Court came to frame its understanding within them. The last witness testified on May 24, 1973, and lawyers for the two sides made their final arguments from June 13 through June 21.

On the morning of June 18, 1973, Peter Hutchins, a junior counsel for the Cree, stood to address the Court. He tried to focus on the cultural meaning that the land held for the Cree. In doing this he was fighting the current of language and evidence that had flowed through the courtroom over the previous months. The great wealth of knowledge that had been collected did not contain the specifics he needed, and he wrestled with his lack of evidence. The Cree to him were a "special race" with "special concepts," and, in order to make its decision, the Court had to understand the attitudes of the petitioners towards the land. Hutchins attempted to introduce the Cree cultural narrative into the equation, but the language of the hearing ensured that his vocabulary was limited and vague: English did not provide the words or concepts for which he grasped.[44]

Hutchins tried to encapsulate for the Court the meaning of these special cultural concepts: that the Cree were at home on every part of the land, that they knew it intimately, and that they gathered their existence from all of it. Hutchins argued that the land was the centre of Cree culture and that their tradition was the land, with its physical and spiritual resources, and that they were tied inextricably to it in its natural state. He told the Court that the Cree felt that they belonged to the land: "The land is the centre of [their] existence. It is peace, it is tranquility, it is harmony with nature." The Cree were a Native people, and they had a unique concept of the land "and this is a communal concept. The land for them is a home and it is also a garden and it is a garden in two senses." In the first sense, it was a place to gather resources for daily living; in the second, it was a place of cultural origin. "They are of the Garden," Hutchins concluded.[45]

He was absolutely right in what he was trying to communicate, but while the Court knew intimately the natural facts of this region and the quantifiable aspects of Cree hunting, it had only a surface understanding of the Cree garden. This metaphor is clearly one with which many Cree are comfortable, but, under the circumstances, what was the Court to do with it? How could the Court deal with an actual physical location that was a Garden of Eden, one that Hydro-Québec was about to flood? The Cree had not been asked to articulate any of their relationships to the land, and so any human engagement with the land on a symbolic level was outside the Court's ability to assess or, indeed, even comprehend. Hutchins could only sketch it out in broad terms: "This project is the clash of two ways of life, of two diametrically opposed cultures, but with only one possible outcome: the effective subjugation of the petitioners. Part of the last frontier, the last wilderness, the territory of the petitioners is being mechanized, My Lord, and indelibly stamped, and [the] petitioners, the inhabitants of that territory are bewildered." In his need for words he fell back on romanticism to make his point: the garden, in the end, became a wilderness filled with unchanged people who were unprepared for modernity.[46]

By what were the Cree bewildered? That becomes the real question here. Certainly they were not bewildered by the concept of a dam (their knowledge of the habits of beaver would preclude this) nor by the power of Western technology (with which they had had a long and often beneficial relationship). What they were bewildered by was a system of knowledge and a concept of nature that would use the power of technology to create this particular kind of dam. They were bewildered by a definition of progress that required that their land be used in this way, by a definition of progress that disregarded the totality of their land in order to reshape it for strictly human use. But the Court's knowledge was predicated on the acceptability of these definitions as, in many ways, they were the foundation upon which the Court itself was built. Malouf took the case under advisement for most of the rest of 1973, not giving his judgment until November 15. His 180-page judgment summarized the gathering of statistical and scientific information, and, in the end, this rationalized understanding would be the most important aspect of the hearing.

"This has been a long hearing." So Malouf began his judgment in favour of the Cree and Inuit plaintiffs. Despite the length of the document, and the detail with which Malouf recounted the various testimonies, the judgment served mostly to indicate the facts that he ruled to be outside the parameters of the injunction. As a legal document, it asserted little beyond the opinion that the Cree had some kind of rights in James Bay and that Quebec should stop construction until it could be determined what they were. He first declared that this was by no means a final hearing on the issue of Native rights in the region, that he was simply imposing a halt to construction so that the value of the land would remain unchanged for both parties until the issue of rights could be resolved. That was the legal mandate, and he would stay within its bounds. Malouf then went on to winnow out all those Natives involved in the case but not living in the territory covered by Bill 50. In his opinion, they had no legal interest in the case. This included the IQA as well as the Inuit who lived outside the region. Even the Northern Quebec Inuit Association, headquartered in Fort Chimo, which was within the affected area, was disqualified. The rest of the petitioners named in the suit were individuals who lived in the area and who had given their power of attorney to the legal team. Thus, there was no band or council before the Court, only individuals.[47]

Malouf made a detailed study of both the treaty history and the jurisprudence involving Aboriginal title and rights in Canada. In some respects, this was a review of the plaintiff's case, and, in others, it was his own understanding of the case. It was clear, however, that, history notwithstanding, he felt that Quebec had an obligation to treat with the Cree simply by virtue of the Quebec Boundaries Extension Act, 1912.[48] Having gone this far, he again made it clear that he would not define the nature and extent of "Indian Title" in this case, but he felt it was obvious that the material examined in this part clearly shows that at the very least the Cree Indians and Eskimo have been exercising personal and usufructuary rights over the territory and the lands adjacent thereto. They have been in possession and occupation of these lands and exercising fishing, hunting, and trapping rights therein since time immemorial. It has been shown that the Government of Canada entered into treaties with Indians whenever it desired to obtain lands for the purposes of settlement or otherwise. In view of the obligation assumed by the Province of Québec in the Legislation of 1912 it appears that the Province of Québec cannot develop or otherwise open up these lands for settlement without acting in the same manner that is, without the prior agreement of the Indians and Eskimo.[49]

He went on to support his view that the Cree had rights that should be examined further, but the only decision he set down was to deny Hydro-Québec's request that the balance of convenience be placed with them. He concluded by saying that he did not have "the slightest doubt that [the] petitioners have established a strong prima facie case. I am convinced that they have a clear right to an interlocutory order of injunction."[50]

This was the strongest statement that Malouf would make on the rights of the Cree, though he was clearly moved by his personal feelings for those Cree whom he had encountered. Just as Hare set aside his personal feelings for the land, so Malouf set aside his personal feelings for the Cree in order to apply the "objective" gaze of the law, and his decision was drawn within very tight parameters. Even if it had stood, it would have left the Cree with the responsibility of having to prove the larger argument of Native rights. As a legal statement, it asserted very little and was, in fact, overturned only five days later by the Superior Court of Quebec, which put the balance of convenience with Hydro-Québec.

More important to this history, the new understanding of James Bay developed in Malouf's courtroom was firmly in place when Quebec offered the Cree a negotiated settlement. Malouf's statement that Quebec had not fulfilled its obligation to treat with the Cree may have moved the province to approach them, but it did so from a strong position. For their part, the Cree moved their fight from the legal to the political arena because they rightly perceived that, while the reversal weakened their legal chances for further appeal, it gave them political leverage with Quebec – leverage that they might lose if they delayed. The fulcrum on which this political leverage was based, however, was the new rationalization of James Bay, which saw the Cree use of the land as functionally different from, but conceptually similar to, the other uses proposed. The Cree drove the hardest bargain that they could; but, legally, hunting became just another way of using the natural resources of James Bay.

Thus, as a political document, the judgment takes on far more importance than it had as a legal document. Malouf asserted the Cree's right to clarify their legal relationship to the land, and his judgment also provided an eighty-page summary of all the evidence given about the environment of James Bay. All the language of scientific and anthropological understanding, and the assumptions bound up in that language, were contained in this document, which the Cree took with them as they moved their case from the courts into the arena of political negotiation and public relations. It was here that they would have to make a new kind of argument not only to politicians in Quebec but also, eventually, to the people of Canada and the northeastern United States.

Two things must be considered with regard to the Cree decision to negotiate with Quebec. The first is simply that they did decide to negotiate, even though the initial offer from the government made them very unhappy. The Cree continue to cite the duress they were under to strike a quick deal, and they continue to question the validity of some of the clauses of the JBNQA. Second is the meeting of chiefs that took place on August 8, 1974, and at which they finally made the break with the IQA and formed the Grand Council of the Crees. The IQA, an increasingly radical pan-Indian organization, had criticized the Cree for trying to negotiate an agreement that did little for the other Natives of Quebec. For their part, the Cree questioned both the effectiveness of the IQA in fighting the Cree battle and its involvement with radical groups such as the American Indian Movement in the United States. The newly formed Grand Council was the Cree's first regional government and the first political body in the James Bay region. The Cree took back to James Bay not only the little money that they had in the IQA but also James O'Reilly, the IQA's chief legal council. Negotiations continued through the spring of 1974 with John Ciaccia, a former deputy of Jean Chrétien's and a newly elected member of Quebec's legislature. For weeks the negotiations went nowhere, until the idea of categorizing the land of James Bay was developed. This proved to be the point that allowed the other issues to be settled. The agreement was signed on November 11, 1975, after more than a year of negotiating and political manoeuvring to get the principle passed by both the provincial and federal governments.[51]

The terms of the agreement are many and complicated. In fact, the complete legal meaning of the agreement was still in question, with regard to the future development of hydro power in the area, when the Cree signed the most recent agreement with Quebec, the so-called Peace of the Brave, which was meant to clarify parts of the JBNQA. Things are still in flux, but the JBNQA gave Quebec the right to build the La Grande project, and, in exchange, the Cree received a large cash settlement – $130 million – and the right to a regional government. Practically speaking, this meant setting up a government to manage the monies received in the agreement and a bureaucracy to take over from the limited federal organization with which the Cree had been dealing before. The JBNQA cut in two very different directions in relation to the hunter's life in the bush and to his life in the villages. As it related to the community life of the Cree, the JBNQA created a great deal of self-determination and control for each village and for the Cree as a regional people. Sections 11A through 21 of the document deal with the development of the Cree Regional Authority and all the ancillary structures that come under its control. The Cree Regional Authority is the corporate vehicle through which the Grand Council of the Crees exercises its authority; all of the communities of James Bay are incorporated under it and all have equal representation. Under these sections, the structures of local and regional government were laid out, including political officers and how they are elected, their duties and services, and qualifications for both holding office and voting in elections. The formality of the agreement was new in terms of community operations as, though the Cree had been electing their chiefs in community meetings for much of the twentieth century, the political authority of these positions was now much more substantial.

In other respects, the Cree Regional Authority was placed in direct control of services that, until then, had been controlled by the federal government. The Authority took over the ownership of the hospital at Great Whale and the responsibility for health services in the region. All these services would be overseen by a Cree board of health and social services, which would also be responsible for the social well-being of Cree in the region. Part of this restructuring involved the creation of a single school municipality comprising all the Cree communities of James Bay. The Cree School Board would be responsible for the education of Cree children. Both primary and secondary education would be handled within James Bay, and Cree children would not have to leave their communities to attend boarding schools in the South. Significantly, it was agreed that the Cree could educate their children both in Cree and in English, despite the growing francophone tide in Quebec that led to the passage of the language law, Bill 101, shortly after the agreement was signed.[52]

The judicial district of Abitibi was modified to include all the Cree communities and to exclude the non-Native communities in the area. Justices of the peace – who, preferably, would be Cree – would handle minor justice issues, while circuit judges would take care of more serious issues. The latter would be federal judges, but the agreement stated that they "must be cognizant with the usages, customs, and psychology of the Cree." While the courts would be under federal control, their scheduling and rulings would have to be flexible with regard to the customs of the region. This would apply to the enforcement of the law as well. Both local Cree police forces (for the individual communities) and special Cree units of the Quebec provincial police force would be created for the region. These police forces would be under the authority of the province but would be based in Cree communities and staffed by qualified Cree, which meant that they should be in tune with the psychology of Cree communities. In sum, the JBNQA reshaped the Cree communities by inserting a new layer of Cree control between the Canadian governments and the Cree, focusing the latter on their own political structures within the region.[53]

But out in the bush the consequences of the agreement were very different from what they were in the communities. The JBNQA legitimized the physical changes wrought by the La Grande project, with a few minor concessions, and it extinguished Native claims regarding that and future development. Most significantly, it established a new language regarding the environment – a language that the Cree would have to use when speaking of their land to non-Natives. The structure roughed out in the courtroom in Montreal was now crystallized in the language of the agreement, and the land was divided. The 55th parallel was established as the dividing line between the Cree to the south and the Inuit to the north; this was the boundary between the Cree Regional Authority and the Northern Quebec Inuit Association. The whole of the territory was subdivided into three categories for the purposes of development and legal control. Category 1 lands, which surrounded the eight Cree communities and comprised 5,589 square kilometres each, were almost exclusively under Cree control. It was here that their legal authority was strongest, and, while these lands might be taken for development, there were strict guidelines and compensation regimes according to which this could be done. Category 2 lands comprised 65,086 square kilometres, were shared by all the communities, and were not under the same degree of Cree as were Category 1 lands. The Cree still held exclusive rights to hunting and fishing on these lands, but it was easier for Quebec to develop their resources without penalty. Category 3 lands could be used by all parties and were controlled

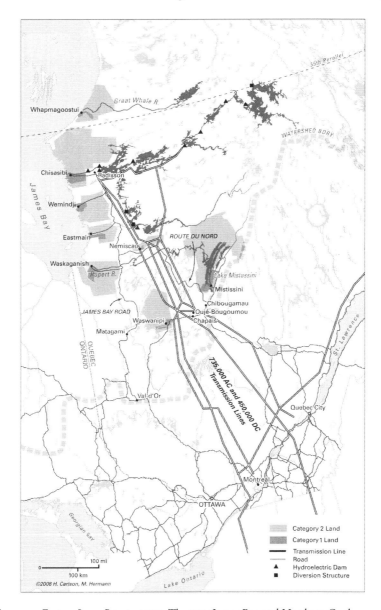

MAP 7.1   *Eastern James Bay, post-1975.* The 1975 James Bay and Northern Quebec
Agreement reorganized the region both physically and legally. The land was broken
into categories and land beyond the immediate area of the Cree villages was opened to
development. Over the past thirty years, the La Grande Complex has grown to dominate much of the land north of the Eastmain River, and numerous high-tension corridors
have been run south; clear-cutting has also affected a majority of the land south of the
Eastmain.

by the province. The Cree were not excluded from using these lands, but neither were non-Natives.

These lands, unlike the earlier territories and traplines, were clearly defined within the parameters of global terminology. Pages of the JBNQA are taken up in describing the exact location of each Cree village, and the agreement calls for an on-site survey of each of these within three years of its ratification. For the first time Cree lands were defined not by watersheds, traplines, and family agreements but, rather, by latitude, longitude, mean sea-level geodesic benchmarks, and resource harvesting management. La Société des travaux de correction du complexe La Grande (SOTRAC) was incorporated as a non-profit organization whose purpose was to deal with the effects of the La Grande hydro complex. Part of its mandate was to re-organize traplines that would be partially or completely flooded by the four dams on the La Grande River and to attempt to trap out or relocate animals whose territory would also be flooded. It was also to alter subsistence hunting to make it fit with the new regime on the river; SOTRAC would implement programs to "increase the efficiency of subsistence hunting and to maintain subsistence harvesting potential at the highest level practical." These programs would include aerial inventorying of beaver lodges and caribou herds and the use of enhanced communications. SOTRAC would study the operation of possible animal farms for fur-bearing animals and the "installation of food preservation facilities to enhance barter or trade opportunities within and between the Cree communities of fish, meat, game, and other subsistence harvest foods." SOTRAC would also study and develop plans for the environmental enhancement of fisheries.[54]

The JBNQA set up a schedule for the creation of environmental and social impact reports on all large-scale development within Category 1 and Category 2 lands. This process was designed to help ameliorate the effects of development on the Cree, but the language of the treaty fell clearly on the side of Western interpretation. In general, the impact assessment procedure was to "contribute to an understanding of the interactions between Native people, the harvesting of wild life resources and the economic development of the Territory, and also to promote understanding of ecological processes." The reports should categorize land, water, air, and people, and how they should be interrelated ecologically and economically. These interrelation-ships now held more meaning than did those between the hunter and the hunted, and hunting, fishing, and trapping were brought within the legal regime of the document. Each Native was given the "right to harvest," which was defined as the right to kill animals both for community use and for commercial use in the fur trade or in commercial fisheries. This harvest was to be subjected to the principle of conservation, which was defined as "the pursuit of the optimum natural productivity of all living resources and the protection of the ecological systems of the Territory so as to protect endangered species and to ensure primarily the continuance of the traditional pursuits of the Native people, and secondarily the satisfaction of the needs of non-Native people for sport hunting and fishing." These principles of conservation and management were to apply equally to all categories of land and to the hunter's relationship with the bush.[55]

This, then, was the reorganization of James Bay along a new set of ideas about the environment, and these changes hark back in an ironic way to the worst fears of the defendants in the *Kanatewat* case. At the time, the focus was on the physical changes that would come with the dams, and in his closing arguments, James O'Reilly summarized the effects that he foresaw:

> From a peaceful hunting and fishing territory, providing a home and livelihood to [the] petitioners, James Bay will become the center of the largest hydroelectric project in America, with all the changes and disruptions that the urbanization of land implies. The phenomenon of technological power will have burst suddenly onto the scene in Northern Québec, sweeping everything in its path.[56]

His attention was focused on the disruption of James Bay by Hydro-Québec's bulldozers, and he placed his witnesses and arguments in opposition to that development. He had spent seven months trying to prove that his clients had rights to the land upon which they lived, and he had succeeded. He had taken the Court from only the vaguest understanding of the territory and the projects and given it a clear picture of the interrelatedness of environment and technology. But the interconnection between culture and nature had been missed. The James Bay hydroelectric development and the agreement that made it possible became a great challenge to a set of values that had grown around the northern environment over thousands of years and persist into the twenty-first century. Manifest within the phenomenon of technological power was the phenomenon of Western knowledge, the narrative of politics and science, and, in that respect, many of O'Reilly's witnesses and arguments were of a piece with those of his opponents.

The full expression of that linkage was embodied within the JBNQA in a way that it never was in vague land transfers. Quebec moved ahead not only with hydro development and all the other aspects of development that were laid out in the JBNQA but also with the full reorganization of Cree lands within the political and cultural understandings of the West. This is the rationalization of the land in which the town of Radisson was built, and it is within this narrative geography that people live and work. But out on the land all around Radisson are Cree hunting camps, and people continue to live and work there as well, within another rationalization of the land. Hunting was protected legally within the JBNQA, and, in fact, money from the agreement was negotiated to subsidize this use of the land; but the agreement also opened up all this land to other possible uses, leaving the bush camps of the Cree on very unstable ground. This is a position in which many, if not most, Native people have found themselves during their histories, and, in the past, such moments were the beginning of very long troubles, many of which still exist. But the Cree entered this particular moment at the end of the twentieth century and not the end of the nineteenth century. And, even as many of history's lessons shed light on the post-JBNQA environment, nothing is certain.

8

Conclusion: Journeys of Wellness, Walks of the Heart

Culture is not a fixed condition but a process: the product of interaction between the past and the present. Its toughness and resiliency are determined not by a culture's ability to withstand change, which indeed may be a sign of stagnation of life, but its ability to react creatively and responsively to the realities of a new situation.

— *Lawrence W. Levine,* Black Culture
and Black Consciousness[1]

The sun is rising behind the spruce trees in bright red this morning, and the ice crystals on the dark green needles are tinged with a rose colour that makes them glow. I'm guessing that it was in the minus twenties last night, from the way the trees were popping and snapping before the sun started to rise, and my breath is a steady flow of steam as I walk out into the bush. Behind me our tents are all in a row, with smoke coming out of their chimneys now; everyone is awake and the mid-March light is growing fast. It's just shy of twenty-five years since I first came to this region, since that day on Coldwater Lake, and that deep quiet is still here in the trees and on this land, though not in as many places now. Today I am with the Oujé-Bougoumou Cree on their land at the southern edge of the James Bay region. Their ancestors traded at Mistassini, Rush Lake, and Pike Lake posts, though their history is a little cloudier than is that of others in the region. Many of them were not part of the reserve system because their land was in the Lake Dore region, around the mining town of Chibougamau, and so they were affected by resource extraction long before the other Cree. As I mentioned briefly before, by the time that the reserves were being started they had already been told to move once, and by the 1960s they had been moved four times in order for the mining to continue. Their community was so disrupted during that time that, when the JBNQA was negotiated and signed, they were largely forgotten and got nothing out of the settlement until the 1980s. Today I am walking on their lands, and the story of the re-establishment of their community is a hopeful aspect of the present here in James Bay. It's an important part of the way I want to end.

I've been invited to join this group for a couple of days of their sixteen-day journey this year. This particular group is made up predominantly of teens who have been encouraged to go to the bush in order to have time to think about some of the problems they're facing in their lives. These walks have become a part of many of the communities up here, and it was these same kind of walkers who were being welcomed back to Mistissini in the ceremony I mentioned earlier. This growing tradition of walks is an attempt to reconnect people with the land and with their cultural identity – a healing tool for all the cultural stress and disturbance that has gone on up here since the dams and the new resource management regime. This is literally and symbolically a new path for the people out onto the land, which is still at the centre of who they are as a people. They have not lost hope in their land – in any of its many dimensions – and this is the legacy that these kids will inherit, even with all of the changes here.

When I was in Mistissini it was a very emotional experience for many of those walkers – completing their journey, finding something within themselves that resonated with the bush and the traditions of their people. There was a lot of laughter and tears as they made their way up the hill towards the lodges. I don't want to romanticize this, but I think it was a profound connection with their memory of themselves that they were experiencing. It was not a re-enactment of something out of the past; rather, it was a new articulation of what it is to be Cree and to live in this region where they come from as a people. This is my interpretation of what I saw. I also believe it was a political act, though this too is only my interpretation. There is nothing overtly political about these walks; they are doing them for themselves. But those walkers had been crossing Category 2 and Category 3 lands for the weeks prior to their arrival in Mistissini. In my mind, they had, in a sense, been reoccupying these lands. Symbolically, they were taking back lands that had been taken under the James Bay agreement; they were continuing to tell themselves into the story of the land. In part, that is what is happening on this walk. Oujé-Bougoumou (see p. IX)was given its own Category 1 lands when it was created, but they, too, have a connection with the Category 2 and Category 3 lands in this area. They too are continuing the story now.[2]

FIGURE 8.1   *Tenting with the Oujé-Bougoumou Cree.* The tent that we used in March 2007 was made of lightweight Egyptian cotton, the stove inside was made of sheet metal. The floor of packed snow was covered with spruce bows in the traditional fashion and we used bearskins as sleeping mats. It made a bright, warm, and portable dwelling.

Our group eats breakfast together, and then we gather for a circle in the communal tent. There's not too much formal talking, but the walkers are reminded that it would be good if they used their time during the day to think about the trip and about what they would like to get out of it – how they would like it to change their lives when they get back to family and community. These are all good kids, but they've had some problems and they need to get in touch with something out here to heal themselves. My hosts have told me that there should not be much talking on the trail, they need some time to think, and anyone familiar with outdoor education will be familiar with this aspect of personal healing and development (though there is much more to this experience, given the history up here). I, too, am looking forward to the chance to do some thinking about this place. After we've joined in a prayer, we go outside for a group picture taken on somebody's cell phone – a useful piece of technology – and we begin the day's journey through the bush.

It's good to be walking after so many days on the road. I'm feeling stiff at first and have to concentrate on keeping my feet apart so the shoes don't trip me up. The snow is beautiful powder, and it's piled deep in the dark green spruce, though the trail is well packed. This is the boreal forest, spire-like spruce with a few birches here and there. The spruce are bearded with stringy moss, which gives them a slightly shaggy quality, but that moss is valuable stuff when it comes time to light a fire. It is dry, as are the twigs upon which it grows, and a ball of it is almost guaranteed to ignite in all but the wettest conditions. As we crest and then descend a small rise we head out over an open area that I think is probably pretty swampy in the warm weather. You only get to walk like this in the winter around here; in the summer this would probably be muskeg and walking would be nearly impossible. There isn't a sound of anything but the wind in the trees this morning, not a car or a plane – not anything. All of this is what I still find so compelling about James Bay. There is a barren beauty here that has to be experienced. When I talk to people about this forest I can tell that they think of it as bleak and foreboding, and maybe that's true if you're used to only the hardwoods of eastern North America. The beauty here is a little harsher, starker maybe, a little like the desert or the high mountains – though I find this forest much more liveable than those places.

The end of this story is the part that I am most worried about telling. I'm worried because it is likely the most important part to get right, given the ongoing process in James Bay. All of those issues that I raised about history and politics at the beginning of *Home Is the Hunter* are at the forefront now, and I am well aware that the political nature of historical writing only becomes more powerful as one approaches the present. I have made a great deal about outside narratives in this region, about how they have affected this land; yet, in many ways, the preceding pages have been a continuation of that process. I also know how poorly historians often do when dealing with current issues. The temptation is always to make predictions based on the past, and that at least I won't do – for the most part, anyway. So much has happened and so many things have changed over the last generation or two that it is difficult to know even where to start to talk about the events of those years. The luxury of historical perspective is gone, and the pace with which events have occurred has jumped exponentially. But, given a historical foundation, they may make some sense.

The danger in the previous chapter, with its focus on dramatic alterations to narrative and physical environment, is that it will leave the reader with the sense that the 1970s were a kind of denouement for the Cree and the lands of James Bay as they once had been. I once saw it this way myself, but this is not the conclusion that I wish to come to now. Though the sweeping nature of change during the last thirty-five years sometimes threatens to overcome hope, what I have been able to learn up here, and from the historical record, has taught me that the Cree and their land are strong and resilient and that there is every chance – if they are lucky – that they will find some way to adapt to these latest changes that will enable them to maintain control over their world. Change has and will come to James Bay, as it has always done. The Cree have dealt with it before, and there is every reason to hope that they will be able to do so again, especially given the resources that they have from both inside and outside.

The fact remains, though, that the negotiation between Cree culture and outsiders now occurs at a multitude of levels, from the strictly local encounters between Cree and sport hunters on Category 3 lands to the encounters between the Grand Council of the Crees and the Canadian government in conference rooms in Ottawa. It occurs within a political and economic geography that now sees James Bay as an important part of the future of southern Canada and the United States. The logs rolling south from James Bay are going to US markets, and last week, when I stood on that dam on the La Grande River – renamed for Robert Bourassa after his retirement in 1994 – there was no mistaking the connection between that place and my home in Vermont. The four sets of high-tension lines that bisect James Bay run to the St. Lawrence Valley and continue across the border. The electrical market, like all energy markets these days, is booming, and, though Quebec ships less than 10 percent of its power to the United States, the latter is a very important piece of its market. The connection is fascinating in its intricacy.

Because La Grande and other hydro facilities can be taken off and brought back on line within fifteen minutes, they provide Quebec with a powerful tool to use in the international market. The United States produces most of its power with fossil fuel or nuclear plants that take hours, even days, to get up to speed, and so it doesn't like to turn them off, even when that means the price of power falls when demand is low. At those times, Quebec turns off its facilities and buys cheap power from outside – for pennies a kilowatt hour – and it keeps its water for when the price is high, in the winter and summer, selling back to the United States for an exponential profit. It is an enviable business model, and Quebec watches the energy market the way that other brokers watch stocks. This integrated energy market is part of the geography of James Bay now, and Americans are among its residents in Vermont, New York, and even as far away as Pennsylvania.

As a result of the James Bay Agreement, this is the new situation in the region, and the preceding resource connection is part of what I want to focus on in these last few pages. Yet, as I think about the events of the last thirty-five years, it seems important that, while we have integrated Cree lands into our resource use, we have only partially integrated the Cree people into our narrative geography. We do not think of them when we use the electricity generated up here, or the timber that is cut on their lands, and there is something fundamentally problematic in that. The Cree have been forced to integrate us and our lands into their story and to engage with us as fully as possible to mitigate what we are doing to theirs. We, on the other hand, have relegated this engagement with their culture to the work of a few bureaucrats. Only occasionally do they break into the public consciousness, during particularly trying times, and even then we tend to fall back on some of those same romantic understandings of Natives that challenge their cultural process. This disengagement and romanticization is an ethical lapse on our part, and it is every bit as problematic as is our use of their land.

To try to comprehend the events of the last thirty-five years in relation to the history of James Bay is to struggle with all of the various ways that physical and narrative geographies have been rearranged and how this has affected the Cree. First, the Cree have had to enter fully into the political and legal narrative of the Canadian state. They are now citizens of a country whose politics are deeply affected by arguments about cultural distinction, and they live in the very province that has made those arguments its central political theme for nearly fifty years now. If the Cree are to survive within the Canadian state, they need to continue to make their own assertions about cultural distinction, Native rights, and some kind of Cree sovereignty over their land. As difficult as that is, they have no choice. The JBNQA became a founding political document for the Cree and, because of this and their complicated relationship with the governments of Quebec and Canada, they have become a political people.[3]

Billy Diamond, who became the first grand chief after helping to negotiate the original agreement, observed in 1991 that the index of the JBNQA "reads like the constitution of a new country. This is exactly what it was meant to be."[4] This may be coming to pass now, but the struggle to develop this interpretation has been difficult, and many times the Cree leadership has been disappointed by the treatment the Cree have received from Canadian governments over the decades. Very few in Ottawa or Quebec City have been willing to accept Diamond's interpretation, and they think of the JBNQA in very different terms. Matthew Coon Come, grand chief until 1999, has interpreted the agreement as being in many ways just a more legalistic and nuanced version of all the hegemonic Aboriginal treaties of the past, meant mostly to box Native peoples in and gain control of their land. Canadian bureaucrats would likely not appreciate the political implication of Coon Come's argument, but, in truth, they really have not seen the JBNQA as being fundamentally different from agreements of the past. This has been the great impasse that the Cree have had to try to overcome within the political arena by arguing that Eeyou Istchee is in some ways sovereign and distinct.[5]

This impasse and the need to create opportunity for their people has led some Cree to take a more conciliatory and cooperative stance towards development. This seems to have been the political philosophy of Ted Moses, grand chief until the summer of 2006, when he chose to negotiate a new agreement with Quebec in 2002. *La Paix des Braves* (the Peace of the Brave), as it is called, is a multi-billion-dollar treaty that allows the province to build the new diversion project on the Rupert River but that creates some vitally needed Cree control over logging in the region and that gives them an economic and developmental stake in its future. Moses argued that this was a "nation-to-nation" agreement, that it would alter the way that the Cree and the province would interact in the future. Under Moses' leadership, the Cree moved much closer to the province than they had in the past. In reaching for more sovereign status, *La Paix des Braves* ties the Cree more closely to the future of development on their land and is meant to ensure that they will benefit both financially and politically.[6]

More than any of the other agreements that the Cree have signed over the last thirty-five years, *La Paix* has been a source of debate within Cree society. The treaty negotiations were carried out largely in secret by both the Grand Council and Quebec, and the communities were only given a few weeks to decide whether or not to support the deal by referendum. All the villages except for Chisasibi voted for the agreement, though Waskaganish and Nemiska have recently held referenda voting against the Rupert River diversion, which is at the heart of *La Paix*. The situation is very complex when it comes to development in the region and whether or not the Cree should become more closely tied to the culture and the politics of the South. Many see the development and the promised jobs as the way forward, but a good many see the continued occupation and cultural definition of the land as still being vital to the future of the Cree. This walk I am on this morning is part of that process, I now believe, though it's taken me a while to see how this kind of trip is related to the political aspects of Cree life.

I said earlier that Cree politics and Cree culture should not be conflated, and this is worth repeating because it is so easy to do when speaking of recent events. Just as I used to see a denouement in the 1970s, so I used to think that the Cree political relationship with Canada was more important than what was happening in James Bay. I now think this was a serious error and that, in many ways, the mechanisms of politics are a lot like the internal combustion engines I talked about at the outset of this story. Politics creates a noisy narrative – too often full of sound and fury – that breaks the quiet of the bush and fills the world of James Bay with French and English. It, too, holds its own temptations towards hubris and towards changing the Cree relationship with the land. In order to see the meaning of politics for the Cree, the land must be seen not just as a political concept but as the place where political action finds meaning within powerful cultural activity. The people out walking this land and hunting on it are occupying Eeyou Istchee too, but this is far more than a simple matter of sovereignty.

It is at the level of cultural meaning that the second feature of narrative geography's effects on the Cree comes to bear. As I said, the Cree have only occasionally broken into the public consciousness of the larger societies to the south, though far more in Canada than in the United States. It is likely that a majority of Canadians know something of the Cree story as it is in the media periodically, though what they know might be restricted to politics and treaty negotiations. A great majority of Americans probably know nothing of the region and its people. If they live in the northeastern United Sates they might remember the campaign, in the early 1990s, to stop the Great Whale River project. But even northeasterners are more likely to know about Hydro-Québec, because of its corporate sponsorship of public radio and other cultural outlets, than they are the Cree. Even those who know something of the Cree may not have all the information they need to judge the situation or to understand their part in it.

Cree leaders are rightfully known for being sophisticated political advocates, but more often than not the Cree people are still presented as they were back at the time of the *Kanatewat* case – as a simple people unprepared for modernity, living in one of the world's last wildernesses. There is often a great deal of political expediency in this portrayal, especially if the point is to win a short-term victory over an immediate threat to a river or public health. But this poses a danger to the long-term relationship between peoples who are now part of each other's worlds, whether they want to be or not. If *Home Is the Hunter* has shown anything, I hope it is that the

Cree are a deeply sophisticated people, a people with an intellectual and philosophical heritage that has stood the test of time, and that their leaders did not learn to be as effective as they are out of thin air. The Cree are continuing to tell their story of the land, and they have made us a part of that story; not surprisingly, we don't come off very well much of the time. It is now time for us to include the Cree in our story – not the Cree as we imagine them to be but the Cree as we can best understand them. Part of this has to do with politics, but the more important part has to do with the Cree relationship to the land and its continuation through the last thirty or forty years.

The JBNQA was not ratified by Quebec until 1978, three years after the negotiators signed it. The defeat of Bourassa's Liberals by the PQ in 1976 changed the political picture both provincially and nationally, making the Cree position more difficult in several ways. Because René Lévesque had promised a referendum on separation and the Quebec legislature was kept busy with the cultural agenda of the PQ, northern issues got set aside. It was only by continuous lobbying that the Cree were able to get the legislature to act to sign the JBNQA into law. Even after its ratification, none of the money was released to implement it. The first phase of work on the hydro projects was completed in October 1979, but the Cree were in essentially the same position, financially and practically, as they had been seven years earlier. The agreement had granted them a great deal of power over their communities, but, without the funds needed to take action, that was of little value.

By the summer of 1980, the rapid but incomplete technological change that had come to the eight Cree communities began to show tangibly negative effects. Federal money had helped build houses by the dozens in the villages, but the indoor plumbing was connected to nothing but the trenches where the sewer pipe was supposed to be laid. The sewer projects were at a standstill because the federal government, which had started the projects in the 1970s, had stepped back in the hope that the Quebec would take over or that funds from the JBNQA would be used. Quebec failed to act. Meanwhile, the sewers in James Bay began to breed disease, and children began to fall sick with the same scourges that still kill children in the Third World: diarrhea and dehydration. At one point, 117 children were counted sick in the eight villages of James Bay, and three eventually died of gastroenteritis. But the province argued that this was now a Cree problem. The perception was that the JBNQA had made the Cree rich and that they should take care of themselves. Much of the last thirty-five years has been marked by this popular perception of vast Cree wealth and a struggle to get both governments to live up to their responsibilities under the JBNQA.

On paper, the JBNQA promised money, but the legislation never defined how, or when, or for what reasons that money would be released. No special office was set up in the provincial government to deal with the implementation of the JBNQA; rather, that task fell to the Secrétariat des activités gouvernementales en milieu amérindian et inuit, which handled Native affairs for the entire province. Quebec and the federal government argued over responsibility, and it took two more years of lobbying and lawsuits to get $62 million released to finish the sewers. It was here that the Cree learned the necessity of being their own best advocates. Governments had their own priorities, and these did not involve the Cree. Only lobbying and public opinion could move them. Lobbying in Ottawa had brought about the Tait Report, which severely criticized the government's inaction with regard to implementing the JBNQA. The Cree also took their case to the UN Conference on Indigenous Peoples in Geneva, and, in the end, they managed to make the whole issue simply too uncomfortable. Ottawa paid for the sake of political expediency, and this kind of action has continued to be an effective tool in the Cree struggle.[7]

The key to understanding the political logjam in this early period of the JBNQA is the 1980 Quebec referendum on Sovereignty Association. René Lévesque and the PQ, after four years in power, finally brought the separation issue to bear by asking the people of Quebec for permission to proceed with some kind of separation from Canada. At first Lévesque had been the uncomfortable heir to Bourassa's James Bay Project, but Hydro-Québec and the new economic power of Quebec were, by 1980, central to his argument for separation. The Cree's primary concern was getting the money out of the JBNQA, but the whole possibility of Quebec's forming a new political relationship with Canada was also terribly troubling. Politically, the Cree had come to rely on the ability to negotiate with both Quebec City and Ottawa and to balance one against the other. A Quebec outside of Canada would leave the Cree without any political counterweight, and there would be no telling what this would mean for them and the treaty for which they had fought. They found themselves involved in this quintessentially Canadian squabble simply to protect their new political position in Canada, and they fought for the "no" vote as a matter of their own preservation, even though being part of Canada had its problems too.

In response to the Quebec issue, Prime Minister Trudeau found new impetus for his long-standing desire to create a new Canadian constitution. The thrust of the PQ argument was that Quebec had suffered by agreeing to become part of Canada under the British North America Act, 1867, and Trudeau promised a new document that would recreate Canada along better lines. He agreed that Quebec had been ill served over time, but he thought the cause was a self-imposed distinction that kept the people of the province from fully participating in Canada as equal citizens. Trudeau's vision was not the PQ vision of an even more distinct and separate French society in North America but, rather, it was vision of a Canada in which there were no distinctions between citizens and all were equally protected under the Constitution. In other words, people should identify themselves as Canadians first. This presented the Cree with another serious problem. Because of Trudeau's insistence that no special status be given to Quebec, the language in the Constitution would also take away the special status of Natives in Canada. This would have been disastrous to all Native cultures, which survive on that fine line of special status created by their treaties – treaties that have given them precious little in material benefits but that have created a relationship with the government that at least acknowledges their cultural existence. In an interesting twist, the Cree leadership discovered that an uncle of one of its consultants was a bishop in the Vatican, and a meeting with the pope was arranged for late November 1982. John Paul II was sympathetic, and it was a coup for a delegation of Cree, representing the First Nations of Canada, to be received by the pope. Clearly, Trudeau was not taking his political cues from the Vatican, but the pontiff's statements were an embarrassment. What came of this battle was a very ambiguous clause in the Constitution that guaranteed the "treaty rights" of all Natives in Canada. Nobody knew what that meant, and it took another effort, before a first ministers conference, to get Section 35 of the Constitution changed to include all land claims agreements. With this, the JBNQA and other treaties were sanctioned within the new Constitution, though Quebec did not and has not signed it. So the matter is still in a state of uncertainty.

At the same time that all these events were unfolding within the governments and societies to the south, the La Grande facility had started generating power and sending huge amounts of water down the river into the bay. One of the things that opponents had worried about from the beginning was erosion caused by increased flow, but, given the minimal environmental impact regime in the province, these worries had received little attention. When the water started to flow things on the lower river began to change, including on the upstream side of Fort George Island. The increased flow began to wear away at the island so badly that, within a year, there were serious concerns for the community of Fort George. This is when the federal and provincial governments decided to move the people to the mainland on the south shore of the river, and the village of Chisasibi was built. As I noted, these people's lives have not stabilized even yet – nor has the river, according to local hunters in Chisasibi. Erosion continues to change the channels in unexpected ways as floods come not seasonally but according to the peak electrical needs of a distant people.

Even as the Fort George community was being moved, the trees left to rot under the new reservoirs started to leach methyl mercury into the waters. Methyl mercury is a naturally occurring compound, one that has been a part of the boreal environment from the end of the last ice age. But now a great quantity that had been locked up in trees and the soil was finding its way into the water and into the food chain. Fish in the reservoirs ingested the mercury and stored it in their fat and flesh, and those who ate these fish ingested it too. A casual eater might not notice any effect, but the Cree, who founded part of their subsistence on their fishing, were in greater danger. Mercury in high doses causes Minamata disease, a debilitating neurological syndrome first identified in Japan during the 1950s in victims of industrial poisoning. Some people began to show signs of this syndrome, but, most important, when the danger was discovered and the government warned people about eating too much fish, some Cree came to fear this once important food. The loss of faith in country food has been one of the serious unforeseen cultural side effects of this and other aspects of the James Bay projects. Nobody anticipated that the move away from country food – partly caused by a growing distrust of fish and other traditional foods – would cause such a dramatic rise in diabetes among the Cree. Within our own culture, over the last twenty-five years, an increasingly sedentary lifestyle and a diet full of sugars have caused the diabetes rate to rise dramatically. And, among the Cree, it has risen to the level of an epidemic. Many Cree now need dialysis, and mothers have to worry about the disease during pregnancy and childbirth. All these things became facts of life for people on the land in James Bay.[8]

While people in James Bay were dealing with sewers, relocation, and mercury, Robert Bourassa came back to power in 1985, bringing with him a plan for further expansion in James Bay. The next phase of development was to be focused on the Great Whale River to the north of the La Grande River, and when the announcement came that construction was slated to begin in 1991, the Cree organized to stop it. Because a large part of the justification for the new project involved selling power to the United States, the Cree actively engaged people in New York and New England to stand with them in their struggle. The fight took years, but activists on both sides of the border worked with the Cree and, together, they successfully lobbied legislatures in the South to cancel the contracts that comprised Hydro-Québec's profit margin on the project. The PQ came back to power in 1994, and, because it had other things on its agenda, it put Great Whale on the shelf. This was a victory for the Cree and their allies, but Hydro-Québec and the province learned valuable lessons from it, and they have put these to good use.[9]

Matthew Coon Come and other Cree had travelled south to New England and New York and created a network of relationships with politicians and citizens in order to convince them to stop participating in the James Bay projects. Coon Come put the case to Americans in no uncertain terms: "A project of this kind involves the destruction and rearrangement of a vast landscape, literally reshaping the geography of the land. This is what I want you to understand: it is not a dam. It is a terrible and vast reduction of our entire world. It is the assignment of vast territories to a permanent and final flood. The burial of trees, valleys, animals, and even the graves beneath tons of contaminated soil." This was really the moment when the Cree entered most forcefully into people's consciousness in the United States, and the projects were stopped when Americans did not participate in furthering the environmental and social disruption that had come with La Grande. I say the Great Whale project was stopped, though recently it has re-emerged as a possibility in the political rhetoric of Quebec. The world has changed since then, we need electricity in ever-increasing amounts now, and our memories of James Bay and the Cree have faded in those intervening years.[10]

The PQ called a halt to Great Whale because it wanted to spend its political capital on another referendum on separation, which was to be held in October 1995. Because of the failure of Trudeau's constitutional vision, along with many attempts to patch it back together, public opinion in Quebec was running in favour of some kind of sovereignty. The Cree were convinced that the PQ was determined to extinguish their right to their land, arguing that they had signed it away in the JBNQA, and so they were vocal in their opposition to Jacques Parizeau's independence program. But Coon Come wanted to make it clear that he was no federalist partisan either. "I'm not in the federalist camp," he said, "and neither am I in the separatist camp. I'm in the Cree camp. I'm here to protect the rights and interests of my people no matter what happens in Quebec." For him, the formula was quite clear: "Everything flows from the land. As long as we have it, the Cree will survive – no matter what happens in Quebec." The question remained, however, of how to protect the land given the rights that Quebec held to develop it. It was not only hydro development that was the problem during the 1990s.

In addition to the issues of rivers, the increased logging on Cree lands, beginning in the late 1980s, has become a dramatic problem for them. The building boom in the United States was fed on a great deal of Canadian lumber, and, during the 1990s, the lumbering operations that had been well to the south of Cree land expanded to the point where the whole southern part of their land was being cut. The logging has really been the mirror image of the vast landscape changes that the hydro diversions brought to the North. The roads have been steadily pushed north on a yearly basis, and many traplines have been devastated by clear-cutting. The Cree had Quebec in court over this issue for much of the late 1990s, and it was pressure from cutting that moved them towards negotiating and accepting *La Paix des Braves* six years ago. This agreement introduced a pattern of mosaic cutting, which was meant to alleviate those problems. It stipulates the percentage of an individual trapline that can be cut and lets the tallyman reserve those moose-yards and bear lands that are essential to the hunt. This has helped individual hunters, though at the expense of putting more traplines under the saw, and everybody seems to know that the cutting is happening too fast and that it will not be sustainable. They will run out of traplines before others have regenerated, and nobody can tell what will happen next, though the reintroduction of Great Whale as an idea, despite the apparent spirit of *La Paix*, may offer a clue.[11]

This is the broad historical outline, then, of the political and social issues that the Cree have faced since the signing of the JBNQA, and clearly what is said and done outside of James Bay is vitally important to people's lives there. The Cree reaction to the events of the last thirty-five years shows that their governments, both the Grand Council and the individual bands, have worked hard and have been very successful in engaging governments to the south. The latter have not always been enthusiastic partners, but they have often been pressured by the peculiar workings of the Canadian Constitution and sometimes by popular opinion on both sides of the border. This latter force has been too infrequently applied though, and, as I said a few pages back, our failure to include the Cree in our narrative has been an ethical lapse. I now want to investigate that idea a little more,

FIGURE 8.2   *Graffiti on the bridge at Oatmeal Falls.* This bridge is on the Rupert River, the focus of Hydro-Québec's latest damming project.

and I also want to bring this discussion back to James Bay and what is happening there today.

The James Bay road crosses the Rupert River at the bridge at Oatmeal Falls, and it flows from there another eighty or ninety kilometres to Waskaganish. The falls there are long and powerful, as they are in many places on that major waterway, and as I stood there on the bridge a few days ago I was once again left to wonder at the balance between their beauty and the electricity that is latent in them – judging by the graffiti on the bridge, others are troubled too. "Why Kill Me?" is painted prominently on one of the suspension towers – "I gave you life," "Love, from Rupert River." I spent time walking through the snow for the pleasure of hearing the falling water and watching the sunlight in the rime ice in the trees, but I had to fight to keep off despondency. I've been told by Hydro-Québec people that the river will only be reduced by 50 percent, but I have serious doubts about the truth of that. If it is true, then maybe it is meaningful, but nobody really knows what will happen to the fish and the fishing when the dams are closed; nobody can say what the loss or even the reduction of the first rapids near Waskaganish will mean to the people there.

The issues are so much more complex than they were fifteen years ago when Great Whale was stopped. We are now facing the end results of our two-hundred-year obsession with carbon-based fuels: we are caught between our love of power and our maturing understanding of what that power has cost us on a global scale. Hydro-Québec and others tell us that its power is an alternative to making power with fossil fuel, and though rotting vegetation in reservoirs does produce a great quantity of methane, one of the worst greenhouse offenders, it still seems a logical choice by some metrics. So Great Whale resurfaces along with the Rupert River project, and the trucks with earth-moving equipment begin to roll north out of the St. Lawrence. But do we have the right to ask the Cree to give up more land so that we can try to avoid the worst of what we have created? The Cree, like other northern people, will face some of the worst effects of global climate change whether we take their land or not. Should theirs be a double sacrifice?

Yet, it's too easy to simply decry Hydro-Québec for building dams or logging companies for cutting forests as we did in the past. It is too easy simply to call for the protection of untouched wilderness. I certainly do not disagree with wilderness protection, but it is too narrow to be the answer to this problem. And, as I hope I've made clear, James Bay is not a wilderness but, rather, a landscape occupied by people. It is even too easy to condemn Western culture for its gluttony and its overconsumption of the earth's resources. The scope of the criticism is better, but it generalizes it almost to the point of meaninglessness. We can blame governments or corporations like Hydro-Québec or the forces of globalization; but, in the end, if they are the problem, then it is because of us and the daily decisions we make as to where our resources originate. This is why we need to connect ourselves to the lands of James Bay and to write the Cree into our narrative.

James Bay has become something of a mirror for me, a way of looking outward towards another people and seeing myself and the meaning of my own people's actions in the past and in the future. In learning about the environment of James Bay, about Cree culture and the historical events that shaped this region, I have created an image in my mind; yet, as in the reflection caught in the glass of a framed picture, I have also seen myself as part of that scene, an image superimposed upon it. The image and the reflection bring home the hard answers to the questions I raised – that it is we who are ultimately responsible here, all of us – both individually and together. In a democracy, we as citizens can change energy policy and forest resource use; more important, in the marketplace, we as consumers can reshape the landscape of demand rather than the landscape of James Bay – if we choose to make changes to our own lives rather than to the lives of others, if we choose to let others follow their own path.

We are part of the geography of James Bay, we are on the land now as we sit at home in Vermont, New York, or southern Quebec. As I walk, I am thinking about how easy it is to forget that fact. I guess I am thinking too about how we are controlled by this geography of resource use. We have been told that we are addicted to oil – a bold statement of the obvious – but what is more correct is that we are addicted to resources in all their forms. Oil is just the most problematic one at this moment, at least from a geopolitical and climatological perspective. But many of our resources are problematic in a larger sense, and I would like us to think about the Rupert River project and clear-cutting in those terms. Whether or not these rivers are dammed, whether or not the new cutting regime works, if we do not change, then it will be another of the rivers up here or the trees in someone else's forest – another sacrifice for the Cree or some other people. This is happening, in part, because we do not know their stories and have not fit them into our own. So there are purely environmental issues here in James Bay, I suppose, but in the end they are all connected with cultural issues. And, the more I consider it, the harder it becomes for me to think of people and environments as separate. I walk through this forest listening to the wind, but I can't help but hear in my mind the crackling and buzzing of those high-tension wires back near Radisson – and, far away, the fan in my computer running when I sit to write about this place and its people. All these things are connected along the path I am walking.

If we are environmentally aware and we do not want to see the Rupert River stilled or Cree culture further threatened, then it is not just a matter of our "saving" the Rupert – or the forest or the Cree, for that matter – within our social, economic, and political process. It is that very process that is threatening them. The Cree are more than capable of taking care of themselves and their land; what they need is for others to do the same for themselves and their land. This was the failure of the Great Whale fight – that people thought they could save a river without really understanding themselves or the people they thought they were trying to save. This sounds unduly harsh, but I think it's accurate.

All right, that's all for the politics. I want to spend the rest of my time this morning taking in the beauty of this forest and thinking about all the years between now and my first visit here. I also want to spend time thinking about the people I am with – thinking about the strength it takes to put a people back together as a community and to keep them

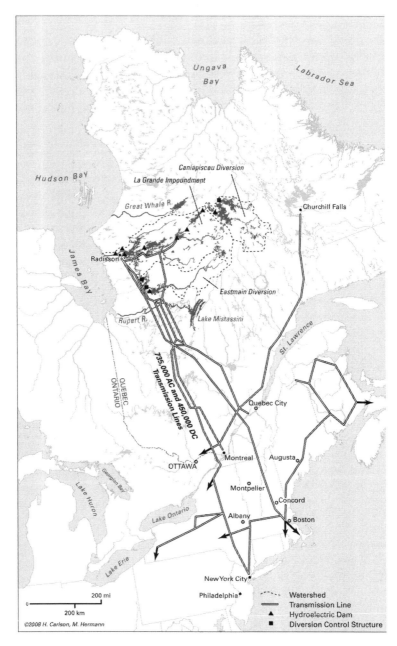

MAP 8.1 *James Bay hydroelectric project in a North American context.* The La Grande
River hydroelectric complex delivers power to the south via two 735,000-volt lines that
run to the St. Lawrence Valley (some of which cross the border) and a 450,000-volt
direct current line that runs directly to the Boston area (which is fed out from there).

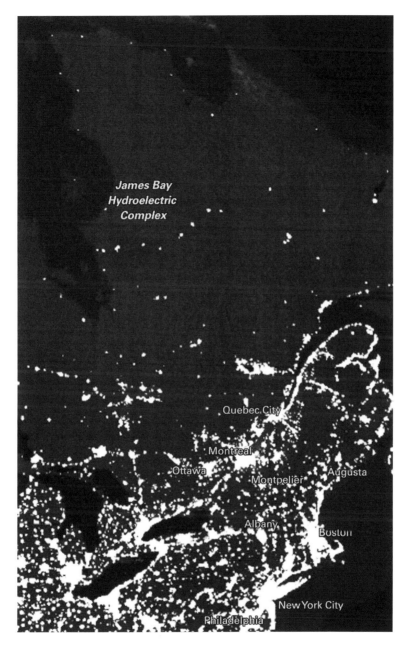

FIGURE 8.3 *Northeastern North America at night*. This satellite photo of northeastern North America highlights the cross-border power grid into which the La Grande feeds. The lights visible in the north are the various dams and substations associated with the project, as well as the Cree communities and Chibougamau. *NASA*

together and connected with the land. What the latest development on the Rupert River and the massive clear-cutting of land that I have seen along the road will mean, how it will affect the process that I see here and have seen in other villages, I really have no idea. But I know that this walk is an important part of the process. These walks are a response to the changes that have come with the JBNQA, and they are an aspect of the hunting relationship to the land, which is still being carried out here. Last night's dinner of moose and walleye came from this land, and as we sat by the stove on the spruce boughs and bearskins getting to know one another, we were reinventing something whose continuity stands in contrast to many more visible changes.

As I said, unlike most of the Cree territory, Oujé-Bougoumou land was further south, around what is now the town of Chibougamau, and when copper was discovered there prior to the Second World War these Cree people lost their land. Not until the early 1980s did they begin a renewed effort to gain recognition, and, with the help of the new Cree government, they were able to negotiate an agreement in 1992 that gave them recognition and a land base upon which to build a community. In this agreement they got some of their lands back and money to build the village that today sits by Lake Opemisca – a small place that radiates out from a central pavilion along streets that curve around to form a semicircle. Like many of the other villages today, it has the feeling of a nice little community in the woods, not too much different from many other places, though this one has been recognized by the United Nations as a model community. It is its people and its history that makes things different. This walk has happened on their hunting lands; in fact, this morning Anna, one of my hosts, pointed out to me where we crossed the boundary between two traplines. Part of the reason for these walks is to keep people in touch with that cultural landscape of the region and the memory of the people.[12]

These walks started in Mistissini, back in 1999, when Jimmy Gunner organized one to raise money for kidney dialysis equipment so that people wouldn't have to be away from their families while getting treatment. Since then, they have become an expression of Cree life, and the people who complete them find a source of pride and healing – the same kind of pride the Cree have always taken from being able to find nutritional and spiritual sustenance in the land. Many Cree still spend extended time on the land hunting and trapping and these walks are an extension of that. As noted, this group is made up of teens, but older people go out too and cover a great deal of territory. Part of the group I watched come in to Mistissini had come all the way from Chilton's old post on Lake Nichicun, covering the distance in about three weeks. As I have said, there are still tallymen for all the traplines, but these walks are a new part of the Cree story of the land. If the tallymen continue to steward the land and continue to shape the cultural geography of the region, then these walks are a way for more people to engage with all of that.

It is in their hunting, in these walks in the bush, in the connection with the land, that Cree culture continues to move like river water to find a path around the rocks: it adapts and yet remain whole. It is here, too, that the Cree tend the garden to bring forth both food and meaning from the land – to remember. I have heard these walks referred to by several names – journeys of recovery, journeys of wellness, walks of the heart – and I think all of them have several meanings. In some ways, they refer to the recovery of a person, but they also refer to the wellness of the land and the strengthening of the heart of the community that relies on the land. To make a landscape sacred is to sacrifice something to it rather than sacrificing it to some other perceived need. It means giving as much as you receive from the land in order to create a community with it. It also means placing words on the the land, naming it, and telling stories about it. In this I go back to Momaday, and this is what makes a garden in its fullest sense. It is a process that requires dealing with change while also maintaining a larger continuity. How the Cree will continue to tend to this work in their current situation I am not sure, but we would do well to think carefully about their tenacity. For myself, as I walk this morning and watch the ice crystals sparkle in the sunlight, I have hope; but I also know that I and my people have to tend to things ourselves.[13]

Postscript

As this book goes to press, grand chief Matthew Mukash and representatives from Ottawa met, on February 21, 2008, in Mistissini to sign a new agreement between the Cree and Canada that will fundamentally change the relationship between the two. This agreement does not change the James Bay and Northern Quebec Agreement (JBNQA) of 1975, but, for the next twenty years, the Cree Regional Authority (CRA) will assume control of much of Ottawa's responsibility under the 1975 treaty. The agreement calls for the parties to negotiate another agreement before this one expires, in 2028, so this is, to some extent, looked upon as a lasting pact. Other terms are as follows: The Cree will receive $1.35 billion and take control, under the CRA, of the administration of justice under their own Cree justice system; they will take over the administration and operation of much of the physical infrastructure in the region (roads, government offices, etc.); and, finally, they will take control of monies used for Cree trapping and for tourism in the region, along with the many other programs now run under the JBNQA. This new settlement is meant to bring to a close long-standing litigation over government non-compliance with aspects of the JBNQA, by giving the Cree more control over their own governance.

Even more important to my mind is the process of further negotiation stipulated in the agreement. The agreement creates a Cree–Canada Standing Committee that will deal exclusively with ongoing issues between the

two. It gives the CRA greater bylaw-making powers as a regional government, and it also calls for further negotiations that would alter the JBNQA
and create a "Cree Nation Government." In addition, the Cree–Canada
Standing Committee will continue negotiations on changing the environmental and social impact protocol under the JBNQA and on creating a
Cree regional police force (in addition to the community police that exists
now). All of this does not yet approach the kind of internal control and
Native governance that was created in Nunavut in 1999, but the tone of
the agreement leads one to think in these terms. It is perhaps premature
to argue, as Billy Diamond did about the JBNQA, that this is a kind of
founding constitution, but recent developments can't help but lead one
in that direction. While not wanting to make any predictions about the
future, one cannot help but be optimistic, given the past and the long
history of successful cultural and political negotiations that the Cree have
conducted both on and about their land.[1]

Notes

FOREWORD

1　James C. Scott, *Seeing Like a State: How Certain Schemes to Improve the Human Condition Have Failed* (New Haven/London: Yale University Press, 1998), 4.

2　"A History of Kitimat-Kemano Project," Institute of Electrical and Electronics Engineers (IEEE) website, http://www.ieee.ca/millennium/kitimat/kitimat_history.html; A. Ghate, "Building in Canada's Coast Mountains: The Challenging Kemano Hydro Project," *Hydro Review* 10, 7 (1991): 24-32. See also Ken Coates, "The Power to Transform: The Kemano Power Project and the Debate about the Future of Northern British Columbia," *Journal of Northern Studies* 1-2 (2007): 31-50.

3　Graeme Wynn, *Canada and Arctic North America: An Environmental History* (Santa Barbara, CA: ABC-Clio, 2007): 284-91, 309-10; Paul R. Josephson, *Industrialized Nature* (Washington, DC: Island Press, 2002), 15-41; Lionel Chevrier, *The St. Lawrence Seaway* (Toronto: Macmillan, 1959); Carleton Mabee, *The Seaway Story* (New York: Macmillan, 1961); Lowell J. Thomas, *The Story of the St. Lawrence Seaway* (Buffalo, NY: Stewart, 1957).

4　Wynn, *Canada and Arctic North America*, 310-11.

5　Peter Kulchyski, "Manitoba Hydro: How to Build a Legacy of Hatred," *Canadian Dimension* 38, 3 (May/June 2004): 24-27.

6　See "The Lost Villages Historical Society," at http://www.lostvillages.ca/.

7　*Report of the Royal Commission on Aboriginal Peoples* (1996), Vol. I, part II, section 11.3.4, "The Cheslatta T'en and the Kemano Hydro Project," available at http://www.ainc-inac.gc.ca/ch/rcap/sg/sg40_e.html#118. See also J.E. Windsor and J.A. McVey, "Annihilation of Both Place and Sense of Place: The Experience of the Cheslatta T'en Canadian First Nation within the Context of Large-Scale Environmental Projects," *Geographical Journal* 171, 2 (2005): 146-65.

8　Wynn, *Canada and Arctic North America*, 310; Thomas, *The Story of the St. Lawrence Seaway*.

9   See also "High Hopes for the James Bay Project," CBC Archives, May 2, 1971, at http://
    archives.cbc.ca/society/native_issues/topics/94-492/.
10 Bechtel Corporation, La Grande Project, at http://www.bechtel.com/spjames.htm.
11 J.I. Linton, "Guest Editorial: The James Bay Hydroelectric Project – Issue of the Century,"
    Arctic 44, 3 (1991): iii-iv.
12 US President Dwight D. Eisenhower's Farewell Address to the Nation, January 17, 1961: "In
    the councils of government, we must guard against the acquisition of unwarranted influence,
    whether sought or unsought, by the military industrial complex ... We should take nothing
    for granted. Only an alert and knowledgeable citizenry can compel the proper meshing
    of the huge industrial and military machinery of defense with our peaceful methods and
    goals, so that security and liberty may prosper together." Available in transcript at http://
    coursesa.matrix.msu.edu/~hst306/documents/indust.html and on video at http://www.
    youtube.com/watch?v=8yo6NSBBRtY; see also Frank Zelko, "Making Greenpeace: The
    Development of Direct Action Environmentalism in British Columbia," *BC Studies* 142,
    3 (Summer/Autumn 2004): 197-239.
13 Sean McCutcheon, *Electric Rivers: The Story of the James Bay Project* (Montreal: Black Rose,
    1991), 43.
14 Al Gedicks, *The New Resource Wars, Native and Environmental Struggles against Multinational
    Corporations* (Boston: South End Press, 1993), 19.
15 These developments can be traced in greater detail in Richard Salisbury, *A Homeland for
    the Cree: Regional Development in James Bay, 1971-1981* (Montreal/Kingston: McGill-Queen's
    University Press, 1986).
16 Boyce Richardson's career can be traced in his *Memoirs of a Media Maverick* (Toronto:
    Between the Lines, 2003). Richardson was a prescient commentator and early advocate of
    what we might now call "civil and sustainable society," as evidenced in his four pamphlets,
    published by the *Montreal Star* between 1969 and 1971 (*The Emergent Indian; Indians of
    the Northwest Territories; Chaos or Planning;* and *Pollution, Everybody's Business*). In 1972 he
    released *The Future of Canadian Cities* (Toronto: New Press), based on his many newspaper
    articles about Canadian urban problems and focused especially on citizens' involvement in
    their communities and attitudes towards urban land. I am grateful to Boyce Richardson
    for corresponding with me and for inviting me into his home in March 2007 for a wide-
    ranging and stimulating conversation about his career.
17 Michael Gnarowski, ed., *I Dream of Yesterday and Tomorrow: A Celebration of the James
    Bay Cree* (Kemptville, ON: Golden Dog Press, an imprint of Haymax Inc., 2003), 85.
18 I have written briefly of Richardson's films and their importance for environmental history
    in Graeme Wynn, "Northern Exposure," *Environmental History* 12, 2 (2007): 388-90; the
    quotes in this paragraph are drawn from this article.
19 The quotations in this paragraph come from Boyce Richardson, "Boyce'sPaper," available
    at http://www.magma.ca/~brich/, entry for 14 May 2008, My Log 233 (accessed May 19,
    2008). *Cree Hunters* won the Flaherty Award for 1974 from the British Society for Film
    and Television Arts for the best documentary in the tradition of Robert Flaherty, and a
    special award from the Melbourne Film Festival in 1975. Also relevant here are Boyce
    Richardson, *James Bay, the Plot to Drown the North Woods* (New York: Sierra Club and
    Toronto: Clarke, Irwin, 1972), and Boyce Richardson, *Strangers Devour the Land* (New
    York: Knopf, 1976/Toronto: Macmillan Canada, 1976; re-issued Post Mills, VT: Chelsea
    Green Publishing/Vancouver: Douglas and McIntyre, 1991). Some of a series of interviews

among the James Bay Cree undertaken by Boyce Richardson and his son Thom in 1999 are included in Michael Gnarowski, ed., *I Dream of Yesterday and Tomorrow.* More broadly of interest is another Richardson-Ianzelo film on Aboriginal rights, *Our Land Is Our Life* (National Film Board of Canada, 1975).

20   Richardson, *Flooding Job's Garden* (Tamarack Productions: 1991). See also James F. Hornig, ed., *Social and Environmental Impacts of the James Bay Hydroelectric Project* (Montreal: McGill-Queen's University Press, 1999), and Gaétan Hayeur, *Summary of Knowledge Acquired in Northern Environments from 1970-2000* (Montreal: Hydro-Québec, 2001).

21   Richardson, *Strangers Devour the Land*, 214, 284-86.

22   Bill Nichols, *Representing Reality: Issues and Concepts in Documentary* (Bloomington and Indianapolis: Indiana University Press, 1991), 145.

23   Clifford Geertz, "Thick Description: Toward an Interpretive Theory of Culture," in *The Interpretation of Cultures* (New York: Basic Books, 1973), 3-30.

24   E.P. Thompson, *The Making of the English Working Class* (London: Victor Gollancz, 1963). My reference is to the widely quoted statement in the preface: "I am seeking to rescue the poor stockinger, the Luddite cropper, the 'obsolete' hand-loom weaver, the 'utopian' artisan, and even the deluded follower of Joanna Southcott, from the enormous condescension of posterity," 12.

25   This is paraphrased from Carlson's response to reviewers of his manuscript, submitted to UBC Press, August 2, 2007.

26   Richardson, *Strangers Devour the Land*, 118-19.

27   Wynn, "Northern Exposure," 388-90.

28   Linton, "Guest Editorial," iv. See also "Remarks of Chief Violet Pachanos to the World Conference Against Racism (WCAR), Durban, South Africa, September 6, 2001" at http://groups.yahoo.com/group/protecting_knowledge/message/1785.

29   See J. Edward Chamberlin, *If This Is Your Land, Where Are Your Stories? Finding Common Ground* (Toronto: Alfred A. Knopf, 2003).

CHAPTER 1: INTRODUCTION

1   Frederick Turner, *Beyond Geography: The Western Spirit against the Wilderness* (New Brunswick: Rutgers University Press, 1980), 9.

2   For a good series of essays on this point, see James F. Hornig, ed., *Social and Environmental Impacts of the James Bay Hydroelectric Project* (Montreal: McGill-Queen's University Press, 1999).

3   N. Scott Momaday, "To Save a Great Vision," *The Man Made of Words: Essays, Stories, Passages* (New York: St. Martin's Press, 1997), 23. Momaday is speaking of the oral tradition, but many Native elders see writing as another powerful way of putting stories into social practice. See Julie Cruikshank, *The Social Life of Stories* (Vancouver: UBC Press, 1998), xiii. The idea that cultural and personal stories are integral to any history of Native peoples is also taken up in Julie Cruikshank, *Life Lived Like a Story* (Lincoln: University of Nebraska Press, 1990).

4   See also Donald L. Fixico, "Ethics and Responsibilities in Writing American Indian History," in *Natives and Academics: Researching and Writing about American Indians*, ed. Devon A. Mihesuah, 84-99 (Lincoln: University of Nebraska Press, 1998); Vine Deloria Jr., "Comfortable Fictions and the Struggle for Turf: An Essay Review of the *Invented Indian: Cultural Fictions and Government Policies*," in Mihesuah, *Natives and Academics*, 65-84.

5 Richard J. Preston, "How Cultures Remember: Traditions of the James Bay Cree and of Canadian Quakers," *Papers of the Thirty-first Algonquian Conference*, 302-3 (Winnipeg: University of Manitoba, 2000).

6 In this I am thinking of the kind of narrative structure that Northrop Frye explains as existing "on different rhythmical levels. In the foreground, every word, every image, even every sound made audibly or inaudibly by the words, is making its tiny contribution to the total movement. But it would take a portentous concentration to attend to such details in direct experience: they belong to the kind of critical study that is dealing with simultaneous unity." We can grasp the larger categories, "like the trees and houses that we focus our eyes on through a train window," but for him "the narrative is more like the weeds and stones that rush by in the foreground." See Northrop Frye, *Fables of Identity: Studies in Poetic Mythology* (New York: Harcourt, Brace, and World, 1963), 22. Despite this, however, I think that, in the blur of that simultaneous unity, we ought to be able to perceive some rhythm or pattern that would add to historical understanding, particularly when we have the actions of individuals to concentrate on as well.

7 See David Rich Lewis, *Neither Wolf Nor Dog: American Indians, Environment, and Agrarian Change* (New York: Oxford University Press, 1994); Roy Ellen, *Environment, Subsistence, and System: The Ecology of Small-Scale Social Formations* (Cambridge: Cambridge University Press, 1982); Benjamin Orlove, "Ecological Anthropology," *Annual Review of Anthropology* 9 (1980): 235-73; Marshall Sahlins, "Culture and Environment: The Study of Cultural Ecology," in *Horizons of Anthropology*, ed. Sol Tax, 132-47 (Chicago: Aldine Press, 1964).

8 N. Scott Momaday, *The Way to Rainy Mountain* (Albuquerque: University of New Mexico Press, 1969), 84. Momaday explains his notions of sacred in *The Man Made of Words* (New York: St. Martin's Press, 1997), 113-24.

9 This is also a challenge that comes from a diverse set of more general intellectual understandings of language, nature, and culture. Pierre Bourdieu, *Language and Symbolic Power* (Cambridge: Harvard University Press, 1991), 10, asks that we investigate words within the creation of social reality as that understanding is integral to our understanding of both politics and history. Paul Shepard, in *The Tender Carnivore and the Sacred Game* (Athens: University of Georgia Press, 1998), 202, argues that language is not so much a social act as an aspect of developmental cognition within *Homo Sapiens* – that individual cognition is the basis of social organization. And he also sees nature as the foundation of human culture for, as he says, "the mind has been nurtured and weaned" by its variety, and humans need to categorize in order to survive. Thus, for him, the individual in nature is vital to understanding culture.

10 What I'm getting at is that the collecting and categorizing of information and the creation of an official narrative described in Cruikshank, *The Social Life of Stories*, occurred in James Bay, but this official narrative did not replace local understanding or even affect much local activity until the 1970s. For a different perspective, see George E. Tinker, *Missionary Conquest: The Gospel and Native American Cultural Genocide* (Minneapolis: Fortress Press, 1993), 1-8. It was Thomas Kuhn, in *The Structure of Scientific Revolutions* (Chicago: University of Chicago Press, 1970), who first argued for the culture of scientific investigation and the rapid paradigmatic changes that occur within scientific explanations when they are faced with epistemological crises. These arguments about watershed shifts in human thought have been taken up by Foucault and others. This way of seeing the Native world has best been explored by Carolyn Merchant in *Ecological Revolutions: Nature, Gender, and Science*

in New England (Chapel Hill: University of North Carolina Press, 1989). Among Kuhn's critics, the most interesting for this study is Alasdair MacIntyre, whose "Epistemological Crises, Dramatic Narrative, and the Philosophy of Science," *The Monist* 60 (1977): 453-71, argues for enlarged human narrative schemata that hold both the outmoded understandings (which caused the crises in the first place) and the new explanations that resolve them. My argument is essentially a critical-rationalist one that relies heavily on an epistemology of negotiation and the creative praxis of culture as laid out by Karl Popper in *Conjectures and Refutations: The Growth of Scientific Knowledge* (London: Routledge and Kegan Paul, 1963), chap. 5; and Karl Popper, *The World of Parmenides: Essays on the Presocratic Enlightenment* (New York: Routledge, 1998).

11 In this I am using several different starting points. First, the many works of Edward Sapir in which he grapples with the relationship of individual humans to their linguistic and cultural surroundings (see note 19). I also start from David Carr's assertion, made in "Narrative and the Real World: An Argument for Continuity," *History and Theory* 25, 2 (1986): 117, that narrative inheres in reality and is not simply imposed. Also that language is not simply an ideal but is, instead, the stuff of the economic and political negotiation that Pierre Bourdieu argues for in *Language and Symbolic Power*. Finally, the avenue of thinking that I follow started with my reading William Cronon's "A Place for Stories: Nature, History, and Narrative," *Journal of American History* 78 (March 1992): 1347-76, and discovering the solutions he offers to the troubled relationship between narrative and history. Regarding Natives, narratives, and politics, Julie Cruikshank, in *Social Life*, xii-xiii, makes the provocative statement that, "if one has optimistic stories about the past, one can draw on internal resources to survive and make sense of arbitrary forces that might otherwise be overwhelming." Thus Native storytellers see an opportunity to subvert outside, dominant power orthodoxies and to mould the world around them. Along similar lines, Edward Sapir, in "Culture: Genuine and Specious," *American Journal of Sociology* 29 (1924): 417, argues that history defined as a science is destructive of culture because it does not allow a "creative use of the past."

12 Carr, "Narrative and the Real World," 126-28. Frank Kermode, in *The Sense of An Ending: Studies in the Theory of Fiction* (New York: Oxford University Press, 2000), uses apocalyptic traditions to give another insight into how inherent narrative structures, with their beginnings, middles, and ends, exist within our cultural understanding; James Clifford and George E. Marcus, eds., *Writing Culture: The Poetics and Politics of Ethnography* (Berkeley: University of California Press, 1986), 19.

13 Here I am trying to take both (1) the scientific approach to environment and (2) the cultural critique of science seriously within an "environmentalist paradigm." See David Arnold, *The Problem of Nature: Environment, Culture, and European Expansion* (Cambridge: Blackwell Publishing, 1996), 9-14. See also Michael M.J. Fischer, "Ethnicity and the Post-Modern Arts of Memory," in Clifford and Marcus, *Writing Culture*, where he points to this process in the creation of ethnic identity. To this I want to add environmental identity. For an interesting discussion of the reciprocal adaptation of culture and nature, see E.N. Anderson, *Ecologies of the Heart: Emotion, Belief, and the Environment* (New York: Oxford University Press, 1996), 123-34. In asserting the spatial aspect of language, I am not taking up the correlation that Saussure makes between polity and language but, rather, am trying to put into the environment the kinds of linguistic "fields" posited by Bourdieu. Gillian Beer, in *Arguing with the Past* (London: Routledge, 1989), suggests that, within us, there are narrative spaces of reading and writing that nest historically within

the spaces created by past readers and writers (and, again, I would add environment to this matrix). James Axtell's "The Power of Print in the Eastern Woodlands," *William and Mary Quarterly* 44, 2 (April 1987): 300-09, also takes up the power of words to affect consciousness and environment. Frye, in *Fables of Identity*, 14, notes that words exist between the tempo of music and the pattern of art; therefore, narrative has both a spatial and a temporal quality.

14 Calvin Martin, *The Way of the Human Being* (New Haven: Yale University Press, 1999). See also Turner, *Beyond Geography*, for an investigation of the need to see the spiritual side of Western culture's advent in North America.

15 See James Axtell, *Beyond 1492: Encounters in Colonial North America* (New York: Oxford University Press, 1992), 67-68; James Axtell, *After Columbus: Essays in the Ethnohistory of Colonial North America* (New York: Oxford University Press, 1988), 16; and Karen Ordahl Kupperman, *Indians and English: Facing Off in Early America* (Ithaca: Cornell University Press, 2000).

16 Joshua Piker, in *Okfuskee: A Creek Indian Town in Colonial America* (Cambridge: Harvard University Press, 2004), also argues for the need to understand the movement of individuals across community and cultural borders. See also the introduction to Richard White's, *Middle Ground: Indians, Empires, and Republics in the Great Lakes Region, 1650-1815* (New York: Cambridge University Press, 1991). James Clifford, *Writing Culture*, 10, points out that anthropologists can no longer distance other cultures from their connections with larger world forces – forces that frame research. And this, I think, holds true for Native histories as well. See also Henry Glassie's *Passing the Time in Ballymenone: Culture and History of an Ulster Community* (Philadelphia: University of Pennsylvania Press, 1982), in which he discusses the idea of history as a map of the past to be used in the present.

17 Leslie Marmon Silko, *Ceremony* (New York: Penguin, 1977), 126.

18 For an interesting history of the development and deployment of the idea of "primitive society" in the late nineteenth century, see Adam Kuper, *The Invention of Primitive Society: Transformations of an Illusion* (New York: Routledge, 1988); George W. Stocking, ed., *The Shaping of American Anthropology, 1883-1911: A Franz Boas Reader* (New York: Basic Books, 1974); Clifford Geertz, *The Interpretation of Cultures: Selected Essays* (New York: Basic Books, 1973), 35.

19 See Edward Sapir, *Selected Writings of Edward Sapir in Language, Culture, and Personality*. David G. Mandelbaum, ed. (Berkeley: University of California Press, 1949); "Language," *Encyclopedia of the Social Sciences* (New York: Macmillan, 1933), 9:155-69; "Language and Environment," *American Anthropologist* 14 (1912): 226-42; "Communication," *Encyclopedia of the Social Sciences* (New York: Macmillan, 1931), 4:78-81; "Culture, Genuine and Spurious," 401-29; "Cultural Anthropology and Psychiatry," *Journal of Abnormal and Social Psychology* 27 (1932): 229-42; "The Unconscious Patterning of Behavior in Society," *The Unconscious: A Symposium*, in E.S. Dummer, ed., 114-42 (New York: Knopf, 1927); "Why Cultural Anthropology Needs the Psychiatrist," *Psychiatry* 1 (1938): 7-12. I want to acknowledge, without losing sight of the meaning of individual historical actors, both (1) the power of Foucault's argument regarding the creation of categories such as "man" as aspects of our own culture's assertion of power and (2) the postmodern critique of historical tropes. See Joyce Appleby, Lynn Hunt, and Margaret Jacob, *Telling the Truth about History* (New York: W.W. Norton, 1994), 211-13. See also Christopher Norris, *What's Wrong with Postmodernism: Critical Theory and the Ends of Philosophy* (Baltimore: Johns Hopkins University Press, 1990).

20 For a discussion of the field of ethnohistory and its approaches see Alfred G. Bailey, "Retro-spective Thoughts of an Ethnohistorian," *Historical Papers* (Toronto: Canadian Historical Association, 1977); James Axtell, "Ethnohistory: An Historian's Viewpoint," *Ethnohistory* 26 (1979): 1-13; Bruce Trigger, "Ethnohistory: Problems and Prospects," *Ethnohistory* 29 (Fall 1982): 1-19; Francis Jennings, "A Growing Partnership: Historians, Anthropologists and American Indian History," *Ethnohistory* 29 (1982): 21-34; Calvin Martin, "Ethnohistory: A Better Way to Write Indian History," *Western Historical Quarterly* 9 (1978): 41-56.

21 For the critique of anthropology as ahistorical, see Herbert S. Lewis, "The Misrepresenta-tion of Anthropology and Its Consequences," *American Anthropologist* 100, 3 (1998). See also Gerald Sider's *Between History and Tomorrow: Making and Breaking Everyday Life in Rural Newfoundland* (Peterborough, ON: Broadview Press, 2003), where he attempts to look at the process of historical change by connecting the anthropological concept of culture with Marx's economic concept of class. In order to do this he redefines both concepts. By root-ing culture in the social relations of production (the Marxian concept of class), Sider goes beyond the definition of culture as values, ideologies/rituals, and symbols. In doing this, he comes to grips not only with the ahistorical concept of culture used in anthropology but also with the essence of the Marxian understanding of the concept of class, which is itself inherently unhistorical and acultural. It is the play between these two concepts, with culture entering the discussion of class and class entering the discussion of culture, that transforms both and makes them useful for looking at historical change. See also James Clifford, *Writing Culture*, 18-20; Richard White, *Middle Ground*, xiii-xv; James Axtell, *Beyond 1492*, 67-68; and William S. Simmons, "Culture Theory in Contemporary Ethnohistory," *Ethnohistory* 35 (1988): 1-14.

22 Again, Edward Sapir points the way in his "Culture, Genuine and Spurious," noting that culture is historical and not genetic and that, while "genuine" culture satisfies the spiritual needs of the individual, there is always the danger of culture becoming stagnant and un-satisfying. It is the unsatisfied individual who works perpetually to remodel culture. For Sapir, dissatisfaction is psychological and spiritual, but I think there is a material aspect that makes the argument for tension and change even more compelling. Unfortunately, much anthropology has suffered under the notion, most famously put forward by Ruth Benedict, that there is no tension between culture and its members. See her *Patterns of Culture* (Boston; Houghton Mifflin, 1934), 251-78. Also see Edward Sapir, "Why Cultural Anthropology Needs the Psychiatrist," in which he discusses the creation of new "traditions" by people negotiating their way through changing historical situations and how powerful certain individuals can be during times of turmoil.

23 René Dubos, *Man Adapting* (New Haven: Yale University Press, 1965), a study of the import-ance of human history and culture in understanding adaptation to disease, takes a similar view of human environmental relationships. As he writes in his introduction, "human life is thus the outcome of the interplay between three separate classes of determinants, namely: the lasting and universal characteristics of man's nature, which are inscribed in his flesh and bone; the ephemeral conditions which man encounters at a given moment; and last but not least, man's ability to choose between alternatives and to decide upon a course of action." For more on environmental history, see Donald Worster, *Dust Bowl: The Southern Plains in the 1930s* (New York: Oxford University Press, 1979); "Doing Environmental Hist-ory," in *The Ends of the Earth: Perspectives on Modern Environmental History* (New York: Cambridge University Press, 1988), 289-307; "History as Natural History: An Essay on Theory and Method," *Pacific Historical Review* 53 (1984): 1-19; William Cronon, "The Uses

of Environmental History," *Environmental History Review* 17 (1993): 1-22; David Demeritt and William Cronon, "Ecology, Objectivity, and Critique in Writings on Nature, *Journal of Historical Geography* 20 (1994): 22-37; William Cronon, "A Place for Stories: Nature, History, and Narrative," 1347-76; Richard White, "American Environmental History: The Development of a New Historical Field," *Pacific Historical Review* 54(1985): 297-335; J.R. McNeill, "Observations on the Nature and Culture of Environmental History," *History and Theory* 42 (2003): 5-43.

24 Mary Louis Pratt, in "Fieldwork in Common Place," in Clifford and Marcus, *Writing Culture*, 27-50, explores the ways in which narrative insinuates itself even into scientific writing, which has tried to deny narrative as being subjective and, thus, as counter-productive to understanding culture. Her argument is that narrative continues to find a place in anthropology because we need it in order to understand culture. Analysis is by its nature deconstructive, while narrative is constructive. Richard Preston, in *Cree Narrative* (Montreal: McGill-Queen's University Press, 2002), argues that narrative is the cognitive foundation of Cree culture, that it is the means by which the Cree locate themselves within a contingent and changing world. Julie Cruikshank, in *The Social Life of Stories*, deals with Native narrative in a different and larger context. David Carr, in "Narrative and the Real World," 130, posits a connection between his group narrative and the Hegelian idea of *Geist* – "an I that is We, a We that is I" – and points to how cognizant Hegel was of the fragile nature of the relationship between the individual and the group. This is a connection that Bourdieu raises in *Language and Symbolic Power*, 106, where he talks about the "alchemy" of how individual acts create the group, which, in turn, creates the individual. All of this is even clearer when we include environment in the discussion.

25 Library and Archives Canada (LAC), Olaus Johan Murie Fonds, MG 30, B102, "Diary," June 22, 1914, November 25, 1914.

26 Here, I believe, is what Foucault means when he discusses the individual in *The Order of Things: An Archeology of the Human Sciences* (New York: Pantheon Books, 1970), 351, 379-80, where he argues for seeing individuals and groups of individuals rather than the category "Man." He sees these individuals moving within a cultural structure, and he famously predicts the end of the category "Man," seeing it as the untenable "double articulation of the history of individuals upon the unconscious of cultures and of the historicity of those cultures upon the unconscious of individuals."

27 I have argued that this power is not by necessity disruptive and destructive, as some would characterize it, but that human narration should be seen as a "natural" part of the environment, just as change should be seen as a natural part of human culture. David Carr's *Time, Narrative, and History: An Essay in the Philosophy of Time* (Bloomington: Indiana University Press, 1986) deals at greater length with the notion of creating community in narrative. In "Narrative and the Real World," 123-24, Carr positions the narrative experience not only within the cognitive existence of past, present, and future but also within the cultural roles that we all play (storyteller, audience, and narrative character). This is a theme taken up by a number of critics of the narrative form, foremost among them being Hayden White, Michel Foucault, and Louis O. Mink, all of whom see narrative as a kind of distortion of reality. Paul Ricoeur, in *Time and Narrative* (Chicago: University of Chicago Press, 1984), 1:52-94, is more ambivalent about narrative, seeing it as redescription of reality and as a kind of "creative imitation" of reality, which he labels "mimesis." Paul Nadasdy's *Hunters and Bureaucrats: Power, Knowledge, and Aboriginal-State Relations in the Southwest Yukon* (Vancouver: UBC Press, 2004) is an insightful study of the effects of official language and

knowledge on the hunting culture of Yukon Natives that uses Foucauldian critique as one of its theoretical foundations. See also Christopher Norris, *What's Wrong with Postmodernism: Critical Theory and the Ends of Philosophy* (Baltimore: Johns Hopkins University Press, 1990), 1-7.

28 Carolyn Merchant, in *Ecological Revolutions*, sees a similar mechanism for radical historical change in moments when cultures face crises in both economic production and cultural reproduction at the same time. Hers is a Marxian interpretation that is related, in a way, to Gerald Sider's arguments (cited in note 21). For me, these moments are important, but I also see that major historical change occurred in much more subtle ways in James Bay long before the revolutionary moment. See also Bourdieu, *Language and Symbolic Power*, 169.

CHAPTER 2: IMAGINING THE LAND

1 As translated by Gilbert Herodier and quoted in Boyce Richardson, *Strangers Devour the Land: A Chronicle of the Assault upon the Last Coherent Hunting Culture in North America, the Cree Indians of Northern Quebec, and Their Vast Primeval Homelands* (New York: Alfred A. Knopf, 1976), 151.

2 Certainly, the metaphor might have come out of Native horticultural tradition, but, as will become clear in following chapters, it was likely borrowed from non-Native newcomers.

3 Robert Bourassa, *Power from the North* (Scarborough, ON: Prentice-Hall, 1985), 8.

4 John McPhee, *Annals of the Former World* (New York: Farrar, Straus, and Giroux, 1998), 636; LAC, Robert Bell Fonds, MG 29, B15, vol. 2, file 14, Robert Bell, "The Commercial Importance of Hudson's Bay," 1; Bourassa, *Power from the North*, 2.

5 LAC, Hudson's Bay Company Records, MG 20, B133/a/13, Mistassini Post Journals, 10; LAC, Olaus Johan Murie Fonds, MG 30, B102, "Hudson's Bay Diary," June 22, 1914; Harvey A. Feit, "James Bay Crees' Life Projects and Politics: Histories of Place, Animal Partners and Enduring Relationships," in *In the Way of Development: Indigenous People, Life Projects, and Globalization,* eds. Mario Blaser, Harvey A. Feit, and Glenn McRae (New York: Zed Books, 2004), 93-94; Matthew Coon Come, "Survival in the Context of Mega-Resource Development: Experiences of the James Bay Cree and the First Nations of Canada," in *In the Way of Development,* ed. Mario Blaser, Harvey A. Feit, and Glenn McRae (New York: Zed Books, 2004), 155; James Axtell, *Beyond 1492: Encounters in Colonial North America* (New York: Oxford University Press, 1992), 59-60. Coon Come quote in Barry Came, "Fighting for the Land: Matthew Coon Come Challenges the Separatists," *Maclean's,* February 27, 1995, 16-20.

6 Frank G. Speck and George G. Heye, *Hunting Charms of the Montagnais and the Mistassini* (New York: Museum of the American Indian, 1921), 19; Kerry M. Abel, *Drum Songs: Glimpses of Dene History* (Montreal: McGill-Queen's University Press, 1993), 40-42; Richard Preston, *Cree Narrative: Expressing the Personal Meanings of Events,* National Museum of Man, Mercury Series (Ottawa: Canadian Ethnological Service, 1975), 21. See also Richard Preston, *Cree Narrative,* 2nd ed. (Montreal: McGill-Queen's University Press, 2002), 64, 237.

7 LAC, Hudson's Bay Company Records, Waswanipi Journals, B227/a/14, 7; Preston, *Cree Narrative,* 2nd ed., 72-73.

8 See Margaret Pearce, "Encroachment by Word, Axis, and Tree: Mapping Techniques from the Colonization of New England," *Cartographic Perspectives* 48 (2004): 24-38.

9   McPhee, *Annals,* 394-95, 657.

10   Ibid., 388-402; F. Kenneth Hare, "Climate and Zonal Divisions of the Boreal Forest Formation in Eastern Canada," *Geographical Review* 40 (January 1950): 615.

11   Keith Crowe, *History of the Aboriginal Peoples of Northern Canada* (Montreal: McGill-Queen's University Press, 1974), 1; LAC, Robert Bell Fonds, MG 29, B15, vol. 61, file 45, J. Macintosh Bell, "Between Lake Superior and the East Coast of James Bay, 1901," 14; Geological Survey of Canada, RG 45, vol. 196, notebook 739, 1.

12   Sean McCutchen, *Electric Rivers: The Story of the James Bay Project* (Montreal: Black Rose Books, 1991), 7; Lewis Robinson, *Resources of the Canadian Shield* (Toronto: Methuen, 1969), 66.

13   LAC, Robert Bell Fonds, MG 29, B15, vol. 61, file 45, J. Macintosh Bell, "Between Lake Superior and the East Coast of James Bay," 16; MG 29, B15, vol. 61, file 49, R.W. Brock, "A Report on the Country between Waswanipi and Mistassini Lakes, 1896," 4; Hudson's Bay Company Records, MG 20, Waswanipi Post Journals, B227/a/13, 13.

14   LAC, James Bay Collection, cabinet 39, AA-20, *Kanatewat v. James Bay Development Corporation,* Kenneth Hare, AA-20, vol. 10, 94; Peter G. Sly, *Human Impacts on the Hudson Bay Bioregion: Its Present State and Future Environmental Concerns* (Ottawa: Hudson Bay Programme, 1994), 21-22; I. Hustrich, "On the Forest Geography of the Labrador Peninsula," *Acta Geographica* 10 (1949): 6-35.

15   Hare, "Climate and Zonal Divisions," 620.

16   LAC, *Kanatewat,* Don Gill, AA-20, vol. 15, 8.

17   Robert J. Naiman, "Ecosystem Alteration of Boreal Forest Streams by Beaver (*Castor Canadensis*)," *Ecology* 67 (1986): 1254; Jim O'Brien, "The History of North America from the Standpoint of the Beaver," in *Free Spirits: Annals of the Insurgent Imagination*, Paul Buhle, 45-54 (San Francisco: City Lights Books, 1982).

18   Naiman, "Ecosystem Alteration," 1266-67.

19   LAC, Olaus Johan Murie Fonds, MG 30, B 102, "On the Shores of Hudson's Bay," 4.

20   A.R.E Sinclair, Dennis Chitty, Carol I. Stefan, Charles J. Krebs, "Mammal Population Cycles: Evidence for Intrinsic Differences during Snowshoe Hare Cycles," *Canadian Journal of Zoology* 81 (February 2003): 216-20; Cole Burton, Charles J. Krebs, Eric B. Taylor, "Population Genetic Structure of the Cyclic Snowshoe Hare (*Lepus americanus*) in South-western Yukon, Canada," *Molecular Ecology* 11 (September 2002): 1689-701.

21   Sly, *Human Impacts on the Hudson Bay Bioregion*, 35-36; LAC, *Kanatewat,* AA-20, vol. 15; LAC, MG 30, B102, 10; LAC, Albert Peter Low Fonds, MG 30, B33, vol. 1, Albert Peter Low, "1902 Journal on Hudson's Bay," 29.

22   LAC, *Kanatewat,* AA-20, Don Gill, AA-20, vol. 15, 6-8, 17-22.

23   Edward A. Johnson, *Fire and Vegetation Dynamics: Studies from the North American Boreal Forest* (Cambridge, UK: Cambridge University Press, 1992), 1-3; LAC, Geological Survey of Canada Records, RG 45, vol. 220, notebook 2492, 35-40; Stephen J. Pyne, *Fire in America: A Cultural History of Wildland and Rural Fire* (Princeton: Princeton University Press, 1982), 1-66; Julian Harris Salomon, "Indians that Set the Woods on Fire," *Conservationist* 38 (March-April 1984): 35-39; Luc Sirois and Serge Payette, "Reduced Postfire Tree Regeneration along a Boreal Forest–Forest-Tundra Transect in Northern Québec," *Ecology* 72 (1991): 619-27.

24   LAC, Hudson's Bay Company Records, MG 20, Nitchequon Post Journals, B147/a/15, 8; Abitibi District Reports, B1/e/2, 2; B1/e/4, 3; South River District Reports, B206/e/1, 1; Waswanipi Post Journals, B227/a/25, 7.

25 LAC, Hudson's Bay Company Records, MG 20, Andrew Graham, "Observations on Hudson's Bay," E2/4, 1; Axtell, *Beyond 1492*, 154; A. Cooke, "The Exploration of New Quebec," in *Le Nouveau Quebec: Contribution à l'étude de l'occupation humaine*, ed. J. Malaurie and J. Rousseau (Paris: Mouton and Co., 1964); M. Laliberté, "La forêt boréale," in *Images de la préhistoire du Québec: Recherches amérindiennes au Québec*, ed. Claude Chapdelaine (Montréal: Recherches amérindiennes au Québec, 1973).

26 LAC, Hudson's Bay Company Records, MG 20, Andrew Graham, "Observations on Hudson's Bay," E2/9, 213; Preston, *Cree Narrative*, 2nd ed., 24; LAC, Ecclesiastical Records, MG 17, Church Missionary Society (CMS), reel A-87, "Roy Fleming Journal," April 12, 1859; Hudson's Bay Company Records, MG 20, Nitchequon Post Journals, B147/a/15, 19.

27 LAC, *Kanatewat*, Harvey Feit, AA-20, vol. 9A, 92; Calvin Martin, *Keepers of the Game: Indian-Animal Relationships and the Fur Trade* (Berkeley: University of California Press, 1978), 5; John H. Dowling, "Individual Ownership and the Sharing of Game in Hunting Societies," *American Anthropologist* 70 (1968): 502-7.

28 Don W. Dragoo, "Some Aspects of Eastern North American Prehistory: A Review 1975," *American Antiquity* 41 (January 1976): 3-28; LAC, CMS, reel A-88, John Horden, "Diary," April 22, 1856; Roy F. Fleming Fonds, MG 30, D55, vol. 4, file 30, "The Geese of James Bay," newspaper clipping saved by Fleming, October 1949; Colin Scott, "Science for the West, Myth or the Rest: The Case of James Bay Cree Knowledge Construction," in *Naked Science: Anthropological Inquiry into Boundaries, Power and Knowledge*, ed. Laura Nader (New York: Routledge, 1996), 78-81.

29 There is still debate over whether these lands associated with particular hunters were an Aboriginal creation or something that was brought over by Europeans. See Shepard Krech III, *The Ecological Indian: Myth and History* (New York: W.W. Norton, 1999); LAC, CMS, reel A-103, J.H. Keen, "Journal," September 3, 1878.

30 LAC, George Barnley Journal, MG 20, J40, September 22, 1840; LAC, Hudson's Bay Company Records, MG 20, Pike Lake Post Journals, B163/a/10, 13.

31 LAC, *Kanatewat*, Billy Diamond, AA-20, vol. 3, 20-21. Preston, *Cree Narrative*, 2nd ed., 206; LAC, Olaus Johan Murie Fonds, MG 30, B102, "Hudson's Bay Journal," July 15, 1914.

32 LAC, *Kanatewat*, Edward Rogers, AA-20, vol. 13, 85.

33 Several detailed descriptions of the Cree yearly cycle can be found. The best include Edward S. Rogers, *Quest for Food and Furs: The Mistassini Cree, 1953-1954* (Ottawa: National Museum of Canada, 1973); and Adrian Tanner, *Bringing Home Animals: Religious Ideology and Modes of Production of the Mistassini Cree Hunters* (New York: St. Martin's Press, 1979).

34 For other descriptions of the depth of subsistence cycles, see William Cronon, *Changes in the Land: Indians, Colonists, and the Ecology of New England* (New York: Hill and Wang, 1983); and Richard White, *The Roots of Dependency: Subsistence, Environment, and Social Change Among the Choctows, Pawnees, and Navajos* (Lincoln: University of Nebraska Press, 1983).

35 Edward S. Rogers, *The Hunting Group-Hunting Territory Complex among the Mistassini Indians* (Ottawa: National Museum of Canada, Bulletin 195, 1963); "The Individual in Mistassini Society from Birth to Death," *Contributions to Anthropology 1960* (Ottawa: National Museum of Canada, Bulletin 190, 1963); *The Material Culture of the Mistassini* (Ottawa: National Museum of Canada, Bulletin 218, 1967); "The Mistassini Cree," In *Hunters and Gatherers Today*, ed. M.G. Bicchieri (Toronto: Holt Rinehart and Winston, 1972).

36 LAC, Hudson's Bay Company Records, MG 20, Kaniapiskau Post Journals, B98/a/4, 1; Neoskweskau Post Journals, B143/a/5, 21; Mistassini Post Journals, B133/a/6, 2; B133/a/48,

1; Eleanor Leacock, "The Montagnais-Neskapi Band," in *Contributions to Anthropology: Band Societies* ed. D. Damas (Ottawa: National Museum of Canada, 1969); LAC, Olaus Johan Murie Fonds, MG 30, B102, "Hudson's Bay Journal," September 8, 1914; Preston, *Cree Narrative*, 2nd ed., 28.

37 Adrian Tanner argues that modern negotiations were an inversion of the usual Cree stance regarding exclusion of outsiders, but I think the Cree have always expanded their negotiations with outsiders if they deemed them powerful and necessary. See Tanner, "Culture, Social Change, and Cree Opposition to the James Bay Hydroelectric Development," in *Social and Environmental Impacts of the James Bay Hydroelectric Project*, ed. James F. Hornig (Montreal: McGill-Queen's University Press, 1999), 133; Daniel B. Fusfeld, "Economic Theory Misplaced: Livelihood in Primitive Society," in *Trade and Market in the Early Empires*, ed. Karl Polanyi, Conrad M. Arensberg, and Harry W. Pearson, 342-56 (Glencoe, IL: The Free Press, 1957). See also Calvin Martin, *Keepers of the Game: Indian-Animal Relationships and the Fur Trade* (Berkeley: University of California Press, 1978); Richard Preston, "A Survey of Ethnographic Approaches to the Eastern Cree-Montagnais-Neskapi," *Canadian Review of Sociology and Anthropology* 12, 3 (1975): 268-77.

38 Richard J. Preston, *Cree Narrative*, 2nd ed., 200-6; *Cree Narrative: Expressing the Personal Meanings of Events*, 182; Frank Speck, *Naskapi: The Savage Hunters of the Labrador Peninsula* (Norman: University of Oklahoma Press, 1935).

39 Scott, "Science for the West," 72; See Calvin Martin, *The Way of the Human Being* (New Haven: Yale University Press, 1999), 77-103, for an alternative understanding of this issue.

40 LAC, George Barnley Journal, MG 20, J40, October 8, 1840; James Olaus Murie Fonds, MG 30, B102, "Hudson's Bay Journal," February 18, 1915.

41 Adrian Tanner, *Bringing Home Animals: Religious Ideology and Modes of Production of the Mistassini Cree Hunters* (New York: St. Martins Press, 1979), 73.

42 Tanner, *Bringing Home Animals*, 90-91; LAC, Hudson's Bay Company Records, MG 20, Kaniapiskau Post Journals, B98/a/3, 7.

43 Preston, *Cree Narrative*, 2nd ed., 30-33; Tanner, *Bringing Home Animals*, 90-93.

44 LAC, Hudson's Bay Company Records, MG 20, B186/e/5, 9.

45 LAC, George Barnley Journal, MG 20, J40, January 15, 1841; Adrian Tanner, "Notes on the Ceremonial Hide," in *Papers of the Fifteenth Algonquian Conference*, ed. William Cowan, 91-105 (Ottawa: Carleton University Press, 1984).

46 LAC, Olaus Johan Murie Fonds, MG 30, B102, "Hudson's Bay Journal," September 28, 1915; Hudson's Bay Company Records, MG 20, Waswanipi Post Journal B227/a/66, 45.

47 Preston, *Cree Narrative: Expressing the Personal Meanings of Events*, 140-41; Claude Levi-Strauss, *The Savage Mind* (Chicago: University of Chicago Press, 1966), 1-16; Scott, "Science for the West," 73; Harvey A. Feit, "Hunting and the Quest for Power: The James Bay Cree and Whitemen in the Twentieth Century," in *Native Peoples: The Canadian Experience*, ed. R. Bruce Morrison and C. Roderick Wilson, 171-207 (Toronto: McClelland and Stewart, 1986).

48 LAC, William Walton Letterbook, MG 30, D133, "Annual Letter," January 6, 1904; Preston, *Cree Narrative*, 2nd ed., 201.

49 LAC, Hudson's Bay Company Records, MG 20, Eastmain Post Journals, B59/a/1,1814, 5; LAC, Olaus Johan Murie Fonds, MG 30, B102, "On the Shores of Hudson's Bay," 25.

50 James McKenzie, "The King's Posts and Journal of a Canoe Jaunt Through the King's Domains, 1808, The Saguenay and the Labrador Coast ...," *Les bourgeois de la Compagnie du Nord-Ouest: Récits de voyages, lettres, et rapports inédits relatifs au Nord-Ouest canadien,*

ed. L.R. Mason (Québec City: De l'Imprimerie Générale A. Coté et cie, 1889-90 [reprint, New York: Antiquarian Press, 1960]), 2:415; Preston, *Cree Narrative,* 2nd ed., 200.

51 LAC, Robert Bell Fonds, MG 29, B15, vol. 62, file 17, "Indian Mythology," 1889; Harvey A. Feit, "Hunting and the Quest for Power," 177-78.

52 Preston, *Cree Narrative,* 2nd ed., 252; Lyle Dick, "Pibloktoq (Arctic Hysteria): A Construction of European-Inuit Relations?" *Arctic Anthropology* 32, 2 (1995): 1-42.

53 Lou Marano, "Windigo Psychosis: The Anatomy of an Emic-Etic Confusion," *Current Anthropology* 23, 4 (1982): 385-412; J.M. Cooper, "The Cree Witiko Psychosis," *Primitive Man* 6 (1936): 20-21; Robert A. Brightman, "The Windigo in the Material World," *Ethnohistory* 35, 4 (1988): 337-79; Kristen Borré, "The Healing Power of the Seal: The Meaning of Inuit Health Practice and Belief," *Arctic Anthropology* 31, 1 (1994): 1-15; A. Irving Hallowell, "Psychic Stress and Culture Patterns," *American Journal of Psychiatry* 42 (1936): 1291-310; Ruth Landes, "The Abnormal among the Ojibwa Indians," *Journal of Abnormal and Social Psychology* 33 (1938): 14-33; Richard Preston, "Ethnographic Reconstruction of Witigo," in *Papers of the Ninth Algonquian Conference,* ed. William Cowan, 61-67 (Ottawa: Carleton University Press, 1978); Regina Flannery, Mary E. Chambers, and Patricia A. Jehle, "Witiko Accounts from the James Bay Cree," *Arctic Anthropology* 18 (1982): 57-77; Jennifer S.H. Brown, "Cure and Feeding of Windigos: A Critique," *American Anthropologist* 73 (1971): 2-22.

54 Preston, *Cree Narrative,* 2nd ed., 267n15; LAC, CMS, reel A-89, Horden Journal, June 16, 1860; Hudson's Bay Company, MG 20, Nitchequon Post Journals, B147/a/23, 31.

55 LAC, Hudson's Bay Company Records, MG 20, Mistassini Post Journals, B133/a/29,24-25.

56 Richard J. Preston, "The Witiko: Algonkian Knowledge and Whiteman Knowledge," in *Manlike Monsters on Trial: Early Records and Modern Evidence,* ed. M. Halpin and M. Ames, 111-31 (Vancouver: UBC Press, 1980).

57 Literally, *Kwashaptam* means "he conjures it," or "he who enters a conjuring tent" (Preston, *Cree Narrative,* 2nd ed., 257). Because the term "conjuror" (or *jongleur* in French) has pejorative meanings (fraudulent creation, or the creation of a spectacle for the sake of entertainment), I use the Cree term. My hope is that this imparts a more accurate idea of how the concept functioned in the Cree environment.

58 Literally, "big man." *Mistabeo* is interpreted as a helping spirit and the term is related to *powakum* (to dream).

59 Preston, *Cree Narrative,* 2nd ed., 78-80; see also Alice Ahenakew, *Ah-ayitaw isi e-ki-kiskeyihtahkik maskihkiy / They Knew Both Sides of Medicine: Cree Tales of Curing and Cursing Told by Alice Ahenakew,* ed. H.C. Wolfart and Freda Ahenakew (Winnipeg: University of Manitoba, 2000).

60 The actual tent into which the hunter goes to perform.

61 LAC, CMS, reel A-82, Letter of the Bishop of Montreal, December 16, 1844; Preston, *Cree Narrative* 2nd ed., 78-114; Canadian Museum of Civilization, Harvey Feit Papers, B 359, file 6, "The Power to 'See' and the Power to Hunt: The Shaking Tent Ceremony in Relation to Experience, Explanation, Action, and Interpretation in the Waswanipi Hunter's World," 1983, 10.

62 J.W. Anderson, *Fur Trader's Story* (Toronto: Ryerson Press, 1961), 101.

63 LAC, Records of the Hudson's Bay Company, MG 20, Rupert's House District Reports, B186/e/1, 4.

64 Ibid.

65 Canadian Museum of Civilization, Colin Scott Papers, B377, folder 7, "Encountering the White Man," 14.

CHAPTER 3: INLAND ENGAGEMENT

1 LAC, Hudson's Bay Company Records, MG 20, Nitchequon Post Journals, B147/a/26, 2.

2 In the 1990s, the village was renamed Mistissini to differentiate it from the lake and the old HBC post. This was done when the other villages took their modern Cree names. I refer to the HBC post as "Mistassini Post" and to the present community as "Mistissini."

3 E.E. Rich, *The History of the Hudson's Bay Company, 1670-1870* (London: Hudson's Bay Record Society, 1958-59), 1:21-36.

4 W.A. Kenyon, *The History of James Bay 1610-1686: A Study in Historical Archaeology* (Toronto: Royal Ontario Museum, 1986), 76-85; David Denton, *A Visit in Time: Ancient Places, Archaeology, and Stories from the Elders of Wemindji* (Nemiska, QC: Cree Regional Authority Administration Regionale Crie, 2001), 16.

5 Rich, *History of the Hudson's Bay Company*, 1:304-12; Daniel Francis and Toby Morantz, *Partners in Furs: A History of the Fur Trade in Eastern James Bay, 1600-1870* (Montreal and Kingston: McGill-Queen's University Press, 1983), 62-63. For a description of the west, see Kerry M. Abel, *Drum Songs: Glimpses of Dene History* (Montreal: McGill-Queen's University Press, 1993), 45-57.

6 Francis and Morantz, *Partners in Furs*, 37-38, 101-2.

7 Canadian Museum of Civilization, B377, folder 7, Colin Scott, "Encountering the Whiteman: Myth, History, and the Ideology of Reciprocity," McMaster University, June, 1985, 3-8.

8 Toby Morantz, "Northern Algonquian Concepts of Status and Leadership Reviewed: A Case Study of the Eighteenth Century Trading Captain System," *Canadian Review of Sociology and Anthropology* 19 (1982): 482-502; Francis and Morantz, *Partners in Furs*, 41-43; Karen Ordahl Kupperman, *Indians and English: Facing Off in Early America* (Ithaca: Cornell University Press, 2000), 71-72, 185-93.

9 Arthur Ray, *The Canadian Fur Trade in the Industrial Age* (Toronto: University of Toronto Press, 1990), 28-29, 51-55.

10 LAC, Hudson's Bay Company Records, MG 20, Temiskamay Post Journals, B215/a/22, 2; Nitchequon Post Journals, B147/a/3, 18, 20; MG 30, George Barnley Journal, September 11, 1840, January 15, 1841, June 13, 1841, Rupert's House Journals, B186/a/66, 61, Peter C. Mancall, *Deadly Medicine: Indians and Alcohol in Early America* (Ithaca: Cornell University Press, 1995).

11 Toby Morantz, "The Fur Trade and the Cree of James Bay," in *Old Trails and New Directions. Papers of the Third North American Fur Trade Conference*, ed. C. Judd and A. Ray (Toronto: University of Toronto Press, 1980), 55; Ernest Voorhis, ed., *Historic Forts and Trading Posts of the French Regime and the English Fur Trade Companies* (Ottawa: Department of Interior, 1930).

12 K.G. Davies, ed., *Northern Quebec and Labrador Correspondence, 1819-1835* (London: Hudson's Bay Record Society, 1963), 6n1. See also Jennifer S.H. Brown, *Strangers in Blood: Fur Trade Company Families in Indian Country* (Vancouver: UBC Press, 1980), 153-77.

13 LAC, Hudson's Bay Company Records, MG 20, Nitchequon Post Journals, B147/a/27, 2; Alfred G. Bailey, *The Conflict of European and Eastern Algonkian Cultures* (Toronto: University of Toronto Press, 1930), 117-19; Harold Innis, *The Fur Trade In Canada* (Toronto: University of Toronto Press, 1930), 386; Mary Black-Rogers, "Varieties of 'Starving': Semantics and Survival in the Subarctic Fur Trade, 1750-1850," *Ethnohistory* 33, 4 (1986): 353-83; George Colpitts, *Game in the Garden: A Human History of Wildlife in Western Canada to 1940* (Vancouver: UBC Press, 2002), 14-38; Charles A. Bishop, *The Northern Ojibwa and the Fur Trade: An Historical and Ecological Study* (Toronto: Holt, Rinehart, and Winston, 1974), 111-14; D.W. Moodie, "Agriculture and the Fur Trade," in *Old Trails and New Directions. Papers of the Third North American Fur Trade Conference*, ed. C. Judd and A. Ray, 272-90 (Toronto: University of Toronto Press, 1980).

14 LAC, Hudson's Bay Company Records, MG 20, Temiskamie Post Journals, B215/a/1, 1-2.

15 Ibid., 3-6.

16 Ibid., 6-8.

17 Ibid., 8-9.

18 Ibid., B215/a/3, 11.

19 Ibid., B215/a/2; B215/a/3, 11-13; Morantz, "Fur Trade and the Cree of James Bay," 48-49. See also Cornelius J. Jaenen, *The Meeting of the French and Amerindians in the Seventeenth Century* (London: University of Western Ontario Press, 1970); LAC, George Barnley Journal, MG 20, J40, June 30, 1841; LAC, Ecclesiastical Records, MG 17, CMS, reel A-102, J. H. Keen to Wright, July 11, 1877; Canadian Museum of Civilization, Rolf Knight Fonds, box 40, file 6, 7.

20 LAC, Hudson's Bay Company Records, MG 20, Abitibi Post Journals, B1/a/1, 1; Nemiscau Post Journals, B142/a/1, 1; Temiskamie Post Journals, B215/a/24, 13; Waswanipi Post Journals, B227/a/2, 6; Kaniapiskau Post Journals, B98/a/1, 4; Mistassini Post Journals, B133/a/3, 23, B133/a/19, 8, B133/a/26, 16, B133/a/32, 4, B133/a/34, 24, B133/a/35, 9; Nitchequon Post Journals, B147/a/18, 6, B147/a/19, 9; Pike Lake Journals, B163/a/10, 4; CMS, MG 17, reel A-114, Letter of August 31, 1886.

21 LAC, Hudson's Bay Company Records, MG 20, Mistassini Post Journals, B133/a/53, 35; Nitchequon Post Journals, B147/a/15, 6, B147/a/32, 2; Temiskamay Post Journals, B215/a/12, 6; Waswanipi Post Journals, B227/a/7, 21.

22 LAC, Hudson's Bay Company Records, MG 20, Mistassini Post Journals, B133/a 16, 26.

23 Francis and Morantz, *Partners in Fur,* 41; LAC, Hudson's Bay Company Records, MG 20, Rupert's House Journals, B186/a/3.

24 LAC, Hudson's Bay Company Records, MG 20, Mistassini Post Journals, B133/a/8, 8; Temiskamay Post Journals, B215/a/4, 12; South River House Journals, B206/a/1, 16.

25 LAC, Hudson's Bay Company Records, MG 20, Nitchequon Post Journals, B147/a/11, 12, B147/a/12, 6, B147/a/19, 11, B147/a/32, 3.

26 LAC, Hudson's Bay Company Records, MG 20, Mistassini Post Journals, B133/e/8, 3, B133/e/9, 3; Pike Lake Journals, B163/a/14, 10; Temiskamay Post Journals, B215/a/24, 16; Pike Lake Journals B163/a/26, 7.

27 LAC, Hudson's Bay Company Records, MG 20, Mistassini Post Journals, B133/a/1, 5; B133/a/14, 15-18; Neoskweskau Post Journals, B143/a/4, 14-21; Neoskweskau Post Journals, B143/a/18, 4; Temiskamay Post Journals, B215/a/8, 10; Mistassini Post Journals, B133/a/4, 17, B133/a/6, 3, 17; Nitchequon Post Journals, B147/a/1, 10-11, B147/a/21, 25.

28 LAC, Hudson's Bay Company Records, MG 20, Nitchequon Post Journals, B147/a/1, 27; Temiskamay Post Journals, B215/a/9, 11; Pike Lake Journals B163/a/7, 10.

29 LAC, Hudson's Bay Company Records, MG 20, Neoskweskau Post Journals, B143/a/1, 1, 10; Mistassini Post Journals, B133/a/17, 29; Pike Lake Journals, B163/a/7, 11; Nitchequon Post Journals, B147/a/21, 16.

30 LAC, Hudson's Bay Company Records, MG 20, Neoskweskau Post Journals B143/a/1, 1, 10; Mistassini Post Journals, B133/a/17, 29; Pike Lake Post Journals, B163/a/7, 11; Nitchequon Post Journals, B147/a/21, 16; Fort Nescopie Post Journals, B139/a/14,13; Temiskamay Post Journals, B215/a/17, 21; Nitchequon Post Records B147/a/23,26.

31 Harvey A. Feit, "James Bay Crees' Life Projects and Politics: Histories of Place, Animal Partners and Enduring Relationships," in *In the Way of Development*, ed. Mario Blaser, Harvey A. Feit, and Glenn McRae, 105-8 (New York: Zed Books, 2004).

32 LAC, Hudson's Bay Company Records, MG 20, Neoskweskau Post Journals, B143/a/1, 1; Nitchequon Post Journals, B147/a/3, 16-17; Fort Nescopie Post Journals, B139/a/14, 14; MG 30, B102, "Olaus Johan Murie Hudson's Bay Diary, 1914-1915," April 2, 1915; Hudson's Bay Company Records, MG 20, Nitchequon Post Journals, B147/a/23, 26, B147/a/1, 21; Temiskamay Post Journals, B215/a/21, 17; Nitchequon Post Journals, B147/a/12, 10; B147/a/14, 9; Waswanipi Post Journals, B227/a/14, 6; Kaniapiskau Post Journals, B98/a/4, 12; Nitchequon Post Journals, B147/a/11, 17. See also Katherine A. Spielmann, *Farmers, Hunters, and Colonists: Interaction between the Southwest and the Southern Plains* (Tucson: University of Arizona Press, 1991), 1-18, 155-71; Wilcomb E. Washburn, "Symbols, Utility, and Aesthetic in the Indian Fur Trade," in *Aspects of the Fur Trade*, ed. Russell W. Findley, 50-55 (St. Paul: Minnesota Historical Society, 1967).

33 LAC, Hudson's Bay Company Records, MG 20, Temiskamay Post Journals, B215/a/4, 3; Mistassini Post Journals, B133/a/26, 20.

34 LAC, Hudson's Bay Company Records, Mistassini Post Journals B133/a/44, 18; B133/a/28, 15; MG 20, CMS, MG 17, reel A-88, Journal of Bishop John Horden, June 14, 1856; Waswanipi Post Journals B227/a/63, 48.

35 LAC, Hudson's Bay Company Records, MG 20, Temiskamay Post Journals, B215/a/27, 11; Nitchequon Post Journals, B147/a/2, 15; Kaniapiskau Post Journals, B98/a/1, 14.

36 LAC, Hudson's Bay Company Records, MG 20, Mistassini Post Journals, B133/a/17, 17, 25. Family relationships between Natives and HBC traders and their effects on the fur trade are the subject of Jennifer S.H. Brown's *Strangers in Blood*. See also Gary Anderson, *Kinsmen of Another Kind: Dakota-White Relations in the Upper Mississippi Valley, 1650-1862* (Lincoln: University of Nebraska Press, 1984).

37 Sylvia Van Kirk, *Many Tender Ties: Women in Fur-Trade Society in Western Canada, 1670-1870* (Norman: University of Oklahoma Press, 1980), follows the development of marriages between fur traders and Native women. James Bay fits within her early analysis of these relationships as being mutually beneficial. But whereas in western Canada these relationships became complicated with the coming of white women and the consequent social dynamic that led to the marginalization of the Métis population, on the Eastmain they remained much more closely tied to local definitions. See also Abel, *Drum Songs*, 80-87.

38 LAC, Hudson's Bay Company Records, MG 20, Neoskweskau Post Journals, B143/a/1, 9; B143/a/6, 5. B143/a/15, 2; Temiskamay Post Journals, B215/a/24, 22; Pike Lake Post Journals, B163/a/21, 6. See also Brown, *Strangers in Blood*; Jennifer S.H. Brown, "Linguistic Solitudes and Changing Social Categories," in *Old Trails and New Directions. Papers of the Third North American Fur Trade Conference*, ed. C. Judd and A. Ray, 145-59 (Toronto: University of Toronto Press, 1980).

39 LAC, Hudson's Bay Company Records, MG 20, Neoskweskau Post Journals, B143/a/10, 15.
40 Ibid., Rupert's House District Reports, B186/e/5, 9.
41 Ibid., Pike Lake Post Journals, B163/a/12, 11.
42 Ibid., Mistassini Post Journals, B133/a/8, 16; B133/a/9, 4-5; B133/a/3, 4; Waswanipi Post Journals, B227/a/15, 27; Rupert's House District Reports, B186/e/4, 7; Waswanipi Post Journals, B227/a/1, 24; Pike Lake Journals, B163/a/2, 24; Waswanipi Post Journals B227/a/14; B227/a/1, 27, 34; Mistassini Post Journals, B133/a/2, 13, 17.
43 LAC, Hudson's Bay Company Records, MG 20, Mistassini District Reports, B133/e/4, 1; Neoskweskau Post Journals, B143/a/5, 9; Toby Morantz, "'Gift-Offerings to Their Own Importance and Superiority': Fur Trade Relations, 1700-1940," in *Papers of the Nineteenth Algonquian Conference*, ed. William Cowan (Ottawa: Carleton University Press, 1988), 141.
44 A Made Beaver was the unit of exchange used by the HBC. One prime beaver pelt was equal to a Made Beaver and other furs and trade goods were reckoned on that basis.
45 LAC, Hudson's Bay Company Records, MG 20, Mistassini Post Journals, B133/a/15, 35; Kaniapiskau Post Journals, B98/a/2, 7; Bishop, *Northern Ojibwa*, 148-49; Nitchequon Post Journals, B147/a/11, 9.
46 LAC, Hudson's Bay Company Records, MG 20, Mistassini Post Journals, B133/a/43, 23; B133/a/45, 19, 30; B133/a/46, 3, 7.
47 LAC, Hudson's Bay Company Records, MG 20, Rupert's House Post Journals, B186/a/42, 9; B186/a/27, 43-48; Temiskamay Post Journals, B215/a/23, 5.
48 LAC, Hudson's Bay Company Records, MG 20, Temiskamay Post Journals B215/a/2, 11; B215/a/4, 4, 10; B215/a/7, 4; Neoskweskau Post Journals, B143/a/15, 5; Nitchequon Post Journals, B147/a/26, 3, 12; B147/e/1, 2; CMS, reel A-79, E.A. Watkins to secretaries, January 7, 1853.
49 LAC, Geological Survey of Canada, RG 45, vol. 182, notebook 1169.
50 Provincial Archives of Ontario, Gladman Family Papers, MU 1385, Select Committee Minutes, May 26, 1857; LAC, Geological Survey of Canada, RG 45, vol. 182, notebook NS 1168, 5; LAC, Robert Bell Fonds, MG 29, B15, vol. 2, file 11, "Report on the East Coast of Hudson's Bay, 1877"; Hudson's Bay Company Records, MG 20, Rupert's House Journals, B186/a/15; B186/a/26, 21; B186/a/30, 9; B186/a/42, 12; B186/a/66, 9, 11; B186/e/6, 4; B186/e/15, 7; Rupert's House District Reports, B186/e/18; LAC, Mary Jackman Fonds, MG 30, C210.
51 LAC, Hudson's Bay Company Records, MG 20, Waswanipi Post Journals, B227/a/39, 5, 9.
52 Ibid., Mistassini Post Journals, B133/a/8, 3; B133/a/19, 23; Mistassini District Reports, B133/e/3, 2; B133/e/2, 1.
53 LAC, Hudson's Bay Company Records, MG 20, Mistassini Post Journals, B133/a/25, 23; Mistassini District Reports, B133/e/3, 2; B133/e/7, 2; Mistassini Post Journals, B133/a/23, 5; Pike Lake Post Journals, B163/a/26, 11, 16; Mistassini Post Journals, B133/a/34, 3; B133/a/39, 4, 6.
54 LAC, Hudson's Bay Company Records, MG 20, Waswanipi District Reports, B227/e/7, 2; Waswanipi Post Journals, B227/a/11, 2; B227/a/27, 10.
55 LAC, Hudson's Bay Company Records, MG 20, Waswanipi Post Journals, B227/a/3, 15; B227/a/6, 10; B227/a/12, 7; B227/a/14, 12; Waswanipi District Reports, B227/e/13, 6-7.
56 LAC, Hudson's Bay Company Records, MG 20, Rupert's House Post Journals, B186/a/58, 24; Temiskamay Post Journals, B215/a/30, 4; Mistassini District Reports, B133/e/5, 3;

Nitchequon Post Journals, B147/a/23, 22; Mistassini Post Journals, B133/a/8,5; Nemiscau Post Journals, B142/a/8,2; Morantz, "Fur Trade and the Cree of James Bay," 41-43.

57 CMS, MG 17, reel A-79, Horden to Venn, June 26, 1852; reel A-79, E.A. Watkins to secretaries, July 10, 1853. For details of the European conceptual and material relationship predicated on the expectations of agriculture, see Brian Donahue, *The Great Meadow: Farmers and the Land in Colonial Concord* (New Haven: Yale University Press, 2004); Katherine A. Spielmann, *Farmers, Hunters, and Colonists: Interaction between the Southwest and the Southern Plains* (Tucson: University of Arizona Press, 1991); Carolyn Merchant, *Ecological Revolutions: Nature, Gender, and Science in New England* (Chapel Hill: University of North Carolina Press, 1989).

58 LAC, Hudson's Bay Company Records, MG 20, Great Whale Post Journals, B372/a/16, 20; George Barnley Journal, MG 20, J40, September 30, 1841.

59 LAC, Hudson's Bay Company Records, MG 20, Nitchequon Post Journals, B147/a/18, 9-10; LAC, Robert Bell Fonds, MG 29, B15, vol. 45, file 10, "Bell Diary Book, 1877."

CHAPTER 4: CHRISTIANS AND CREE

1 LAC, Ecclesiastical Records, MG 17, CMS, reel A-88, Horden Journal, February 2, 1853.

2 James Axtell, "Some Thoughts on the Ethnohistory of Missions," *Ethnohistory* 29, 1 (1982): 35-41

3 Stan MacKay, "An Aboriginal Christian Perspective on the Integrity of Creation," in *Native and Christian: Indigenous Voices on Religious Identity in the United States and Canada*, ed. James Treat (New York: Routledge, 1996), 52.

4 See John Webster Grant, *Moon of Wintertime: Missionaries and the Indians of Canada in Encounter since 1534* (Toronto: University of Toronto Press, 1984), 96-118.

5 See Carol L. Higham, *Noble, Wretched, and Redeemable: Protestant Missionaries to the Indians in Canada and the United States, 1820-1900* (Albuquerque: University of New Mexico Press, 2000); George E. Tinker, *Missionary Conquest: The Gospel and Native American Cultural Genocide* (Minneapolis: Fortress Press, 1993); Jennifer S.H. Brown, "Reading Beyond the Missionaries, Dissecting Responses," *Ethnohistory* 43, 4 (1996): 716; James P. Ronda, "Generations of Faith: The Christian Indians of Martha's Vineyard," in *American Encounters: Natives and Newcomers from European Contact to Indian Removal, 1500-1850*, ed. Peter C. Mancall and James H. Merrell (New York: Routledge, 2000), 139; David J. Silverman, "Indians, Missionaries, and Religious Translation: Creating Wampanoag Christianity in Seventeenth Century Martha's Vineyard," *William and Mary Quarterly* 62, 2 (2005): 141-74; Richard Preston, "James Bay Syncretism: Persistence and Replacement," in *Papers of the Nineteenth Algonquian Conference*, ed. William Cowan (Ottawa: Carleton University Press, 1988), 153; James Treat, ed., *Native and Christian: Indigenous Voices on Religious Identity in the United States and Canada* (New York: Routledge, 1996), 8-9, 10.

6 LAC, George Barnley Journal, MG 24, J40, reel A-20, April 26, 1841; Kerry M. Abel, *Drum Songs: Glimpses of Dene History* (Montreal: McGill-Queen's University Press, 1993), 113.

7 William Walton, "Those Who Would Lead the Indian to Christ Must First Learn to Stand in Their Moccasins!" *The Canadian Churchman* 70, 42 (November 25, 1943), 669; Preston, "James Bay Syncretism," 149.

8 LAC, CMS, MG 17, reel A-87, F. Hamilton Fleming, Sept 16, 1859, Letter to Venn.

9   Jennifer S.H. Brown, "'I Wish to Be as I See You': An Ojibwa-Methodist Encounter in Fur Trade Country, Rainy Lake, 1854-1855," *Arctic Anthropology* 24, 1 (1987): 25-26; Canadian Museum of Civilization, Rolf Knight Fonds, box 40, file 5, "Bush Post Community: The Anthropologist Observed."

10 LAC, Ecclesiastical Records, MG 17, CMS, reel A-79, David Rupert's Land to Venn, August 10, 1852; J.R. Miller, *Skyscrapers Hide the Heavens: A History of Indian-White Relations in Canada* (Toronto: University of Toronto Press, 1991), 189-211.

11 LAC, Ecclesiastical Records, MG 17, CMS, reel A-88, Horden Journal, April 4, 1853; CMS, reel A-125, Memorandum, March 18, 1873. See also Ramsey Cook, *1492 and All That: Making a Garden Out of a Wilderness* (Toronto: Robarts Centre for Canadian Studies, 1992).

12 Reuben Gold Thwaite, ed., *Jesuit Relations and Allied Documents* (Cleveland: Burrows Press, 1896-1901), 68:55; Alfred G. Bailey, *The Conflict of European and Eastern Algonkian Cultures, 1504-1700* (Toronto: University of Toronto Press, 1969), 128.

13 Thwaite, *Jesuit Relations and Allied Documents*, 68:43; LAC, Robert Bell Fonds, MG 29, B15, vol. 54, file 12; vol. 64, file 17.

14 Toby Morantz, *The White Man's Gonna Getcha: The Colonial Challenge to the Crees in Quebec* (Montreal: McGill-Queen's University Press, 2002), 75; G. Carrière, *Les Missions catholiques dans l'est du Canada et l'honorable Compagnie de la Baie d'Hudson, 1844-1900* (Ottawa: Université d'Ottawa, 1957).

15 LAC, Ecclesiastical Records, MG 17, CMS, reel A-79, E.A. Watkins to secretaries, January 7, 1853; John Horden to Reverend Venn, September 8, 1853; CMS, reel A-111, Bishop of Moosonee to Fenn, June 26, 1883; Provincial Archives of Ontario, Cotter Fonds, Letterbook 1883-89, James Cotter to Vincent, June 22, 1887; Cotter to E.J. Peck, July 8, 1887; Abel, *Drum Songs*, 114; LAC, Ecclesiastical Records, MG 17, CMS, reel A-77, Letter from Benjamin Harrison, January 28, 1822.

16 Joyce M. Banks, "The Church Missionary Society Press at Moose Factory: 1853-1859," *Journal of Canadian Church Historical Society* 26, 2 (1984): 71; LAC, Ecclesiastical Records, MG 17, CMS, reel A-79, David Rupert's Land to Venn, August 10, 1852.

17 Higham, *Noble, Wretched, and Redeemable*, 103, 106-16; LAC, Ecclesiastical Records, MG 17, CMS, reel A-120, Bishop of Moosonee to Baring Gould, September 14, 1898; J.A. Lackey Annual Letter. For a description of the CMS mission in the west, see Abel, *Drum Songs*, chap. 6.

18 LAC, Ecclesiastical Records, MG 17, CMS, reel A-79, Horden to W. Knight, January 26, 1852; CMS, reel A-88, Horden Journal, September 2, 1851; LAC, George Barnley Journal, MG 20, J40, Letter from Alder, March 11, 1840; June 30, 1840; November 4, 1840; November 12, 1840; January 30, 1841; John S. Long, "The Reverend George Barnley and the James Bay Cree," *Canadian Journal of Native Studies* 6, 2 (1986): 313-31; Banks, "The Church Missionary Society Press at Moose Factory: 1853-1859," 70.

19 Charles Leith and Arthur Leith, *A Summer and Winter on Hudson's Bay* (Madison, WI: Self-published by Leith, 1912), 52-53; Hudson's Bay Company Records, MG 20, Mistassini Post Journals, B133/a/46, 21; James Axtell, "The Power of Print in the Eastern Woodlands," *William and Mary Quarterly* 44, 2 (1987): 300-09.

20 LAC, George Barnley Journal, MG 20, J40, November 13, 1841.

21 Ronda, "Generations of Faith," 155-56.

22 Shamanic belief in general involves the individual's journeying through spiritual geography, which is intimately connected with physical geography. These journeys to heaven and hell

were an adaptation of Christian spiritual space to a Native world. Significant in James Bay is the connection of those spiritual travels to the hunt. The poles that make up the tent of the *kwashapshikan* represent the trees in which the bones of the hunted were hung, and the journey made during the performance is, in many cases, tied to the quest for food. Conceptual places like heaven and hell fit easily within this spiritual geography of the hunt without shattering Native belief. In fact, aspects of Christianity may help the hunter in his relationship with his environment and the other-than-human beings. See Harvey Feit, "The Power to 'See' and the Power to Hunt: The Shaking Tent Ceremony in Relation to Experience, Explanation, Action, and Interpretation in the Waswanipi Hunter's World," Canadian Museum of Civilization, B359, f6.

23 Jennifer S.H. Brown, "The Track to Heaven: The Hudson Bay Cree Religious Movement of 1843," *Proceedings of the Thirteenth Algonquin Conference* (Winnipeg: University of Manitoba, 1983); Robert R. James and J.H. Kelley, "Observations on Crisis Cult Activities in the Mackenzie Basin," in *Problems in the Prehistory of the North American Sub-Arctic*, ed. J. Helmer, S. Van Dyke, and F.J. Kense, 153-64 (Calgary: University of Calgary Archaeology Association, 1977); A.F.C. Wallace, "Revitalization Movements: Some Theoretical Considerations," *American Anthropologist* 58 (1956): 264-81; Walton, "Those Who Would Lead," 670; Karen Ordahl Kupperman, *Indians and English: Facing Off in Early America* (Ithaca: Cornell University Press, 2000), 139-41; Daniel Francis and Toby Morantz, *Partners in Fur: A History of the Fur Trade in Eastern James Bay, 1600-1870* (Montreal: McGill-Queen's University Press, 1983), 165-66; LAC, Ecclesiastical Records, MG 17, CMS, reel A-88, Horden to secretaries, July 3, 1854.

24 Fannie Hardy Eckstorm, *Old John Neptune and Other Maine Indian Shamans* (Orono: University of Maine Press, 1980), 9-10.

25 LAC, Hudson's Bay Company Records, MG 20, Pike Lake Post Journals, B163/a/5, 12; Waswanipi Post Journals, B227/a/11, 8; Mistassini Post Journals, B133/a/19, 28, B133/a/22, 21, B133/a/25, 24; Waswanipi Post Journals, B227/a/25,24; Mistassini Post Journals, B133/a/22, 35; Mistassini Post Journals, B133/a/23, 7.

26 LAC, Hudson's Bay Company Records, MG 20, Waswanipi District Reports, B227/e/13, 2.

27 LAC, Ecclesiastical Records, MG 17, CMS, reel A-79, E.A. Watkins to secretaries, January 7, 1853; Watkins to secretaries, July 10, 1853.

28 LAC, Ecclesiastical Records, MG 17, CMS, reel A-79, Watkins to secretaries, July 10, 1853; Morantz, *White Man's Gonna Getcha*, 76, 83.

29 LAC, Ecclesiastical Records, MG 17, CMS, reel A-80, Horden to C.C. Finn, September 9, 1872; CMS, reel A-125, Memorandum, March 18, 1873.

30 Morantz takes the translation of Wapatchee's name from the priest who translated it as "The King of Prayer," but "prayer boss" or "prayer chief" would relate more to local hunting culture.

31 LAC, Ecclesiastical Records, MG 17, CMS, reel A-102, J.H. Keen to Wright, July 11, 1877.

32 LAC, Ecclesiastical Records, MG 17, CMS, reel A-112, Bishop of Moosonee to Fenn, February 19, 1884; reel A-102, July 11, 1877, Keen to Wright; reel A-113, Bishop of Moosonee to Fenn, September 16, 1885; reel A-80, Horden to J. Chapman, September 1, 1857; reel A-80, Vincent to secretary, September 15, 1873; September 14, 1874; Horden to J. Chapman, September 1, 1857; Canon Bertal Heeney, ed., "Thomas Vincent," *Leaders of the Canadian Church* (Toronto: Musson, 1920), 2:240.

33 Heeney, "Thomas Vincent," 241.

34 LAC, Ecclesiastical Records, MG 17, CMS, reel A-95, Vincent to committee, September 4, 1862; Heeney, "Thomas Vincent," 241.

35 LAC, MG 30, D133, Walton Letterbook, Walton to My Dear Reverend, January 4, 1905.

36 See Kupperman, *Indians and English*, 204-11; LAC, Ecclesiastical Records, MG 17, CMS, reel A-80, Horden to Venn, August 9, 1858; MG 30, D133, Walton to unnamed reverend, January 4, 1905; Annual Letter, January 6, 1904.

37 Ronald Niezen, "Healing and Conversion: Medical Evangelicalism in James Bay Cree Society," *Ethnohistory* 44, 3 (1997): 466.

38 LAC, MG 30, D133, William Walton Letterbook, 2; James Axtell, *Beyond 1492: Encounters in Colonial North America* (New York: Oxford University Press, 1992), 105, 115-17.

39 LAC, Ecclesiastical Records, MG 17, CMS, reel A-80, Watkins to Reverend J. Chapman, August 15, 1856; Horden to unknown, September 7, 1868; Brown, "I Wish To Be as I See You," 21.

40 LAC, George Barnley Journal, MG 20, J40, June 1, 1841; CMS reel A-112, Horden Journal, June 25, 1884; reel A-80, June 24, 1868, Horden to Reverend J.; CMS, reel A-114, Nevitt Journal, August 31, 1886; LAC, Ecclesiastical Records, MG 17, CMS, reel A-114, Nevitt Journal, August 18, 1886.

41 LAC, Ecclesiastical Records, MG 17, CMS, reel A-79, E.A. Watkins to secretaries, January 18, 1854; CMS, reel A-80, March 17, 1854; E.A. Watkins to J. Chapman, August 15, 1856; CMS, reel A-79, Watkins to secretaries, January 18, 1854.

42 LAC, MG 17, CMS, reel A-80, May 10, 1858, Horden to Venn; reel A103, July 6, 1878, Keen to Wright.

43 J.W. Anderson, *Fur Trader's Story* (Toronto: Ryerson Press, 1961), 58, 100.

44 LAC, Hudson's Bay Company Records, MG 20, Mistassini Post Journals, B133/a/25, 21; B133/a/38, 24; B133/a/39, 2.

45 LAC, Hudson's Bay Company Records, MG 20, Nitchequon Post Journals, B147/a/13, 27; B147/a/14, 8; B147/a/15, 8; Mistassini Post Journals, B133/a/53, 9; B133/a/59, 40; Waswanipi Post Journals, B227/a/61, 10.

46 LAC, Hudson's Bay Company Records, MG 20, Temiskamay Post Journals, B215/a/26, 19; Waswanipi Post Journals, B227/a/32, 19; Nitchequon Post Journals, B147/a/21, 27-28; B147/a/13, 27.

47 LAC, Ecclesiastical Records, MG 17, CMS, reel A-104, E.J. Peck Diary, August 8, 1879; LAC, George Barnley Journal, MG 20, J40, January 15, 1841; December 7, 1841; LAC, Ecclesiastical Records, MG 17, CMS, reel A-88, Horden Journal, March 13, 1853; LAC, William G. Walton Papers, MG 30, D133, Walton Letterbook, 3.

48 LAC, Hudson's Bay Company Records, MG 20, Nitchequon Post Journals, B147/a/16, 8; B147/a/14, 23; Waswanipi Post Journals, B215/a/29, 1; B215/a/33, 2; LAC, Ecclesiastical Records, MG 17, CMS, reel A-87, F. Hamilton Fleming, "Journey to the Log Tent," April 10, 1859; CMS, reel A-88, Horden Journal, April 20, 1856; Waswanipi Post Journals, B227/a/30, 4; CMS, reel A-120, Bishop of Moosonee to Committee of CMS, July 27, 1897; LAC, George Barnley Journal, MG 20, J40, September 18, 1841; CMS, reel A-87, Fleming Journal, May 1, 1859. For other hide ceremonies, see Adrian Tanner, "Notes on the Ceremonial Hide," in *Papers of the Fifteenth Algonquian Conference*, ed. B. Cox, 91-105 (Ottawa: Carleton University Press, 1984).

49 LAC, Ecclesiastical Records, MG 17, CMS, reel A-88, Horden Journal, April 10, 1853; CMS, reel A-89, Horden Journal, May 21, 1860; CMS, reel A-80, Horden to secretary, September 10, 1871.

50 Anthony Wallace, *Death and Rebirth of the Seneca* (New York: Vintage, 1972); James Axtell, *After Columbus: Essays in the Ethnohistory of Colonial North America* (New York: Oxford University Press, 1988), 98.

51 LAC, George Barnley Journal, MG 20, J40, June 17, 1840; March 22, 1841; LAC, Ecclesiastical Records, MG 17, CMS, reel A-79, Horden to Venn, June 26, 1852.

52 LAC, George Barnley Journal, MG 20, J40, August 10, 1842; October 6, 1842; October 28, 1842. LAC, Ecclesiastical Records, MG 17, CMS, reel A-79, Horden to Venn, September 8, 1851; LAC, Robert Bell Fonds, MG 29, B15, vol. 54, file 13.

53 LAC, Ecclesiastical Records, MG 17, CMS, reel A-79, Horden to Reverend W. Knight, February 2, 1854; LAC, William G. Walton Papers, MG 30, D133, Walton Letterbook, 10-14; LAC, Ecclesiastical Records, MG 17, CMS, reel A-80, Horden to Venn, May 10, 1858; MG 30, D133, William G. Walton Papers, Annual Letter, January 6, 1902; LAC, Walton Letterbook, 8; LAC, CMS, reel A-103, Keen Journal, June 27, 1878; LAC, Roy F. Fleming Fonds, MG 30, D55, vol. 4, file 28, *Globe and Mail* clipping, December 13, 1950, Don Delaplante; LAC, William G. Walton Papers, MG 30, D133, Walton to reverend, January 4, 1905; Axtell, *After Columbus*, 90.

54 Jeremiah, 16:16.

55 LAC, George Barnley Journal, MG 20, J40, June 7, 1840; Ecclesiastical Records, MG 17, CMS, reel A-79, Horden to Knight, January 26, 1852; LAC, George Barnley Journal, August 27, 1841; Ecclesiastical Records, MG 17, CMS, reel A-80, Fleming to Venn, August 24, 1857; LAC, William G. Walton Papers, MG 30, D133, Walton Letterbook, Annual Letter, January 6, 1904.

56 LAC, CMS, MG 17, reel A-89, Moose Factory, September 3, 1861, Horden to Venn.

57 LAC, Ecclesiastical Records, MG 17, CMS, reel A-119, Walton to unknown, March 19, 1896; CMS, reel A-89, Horden to Venn, August 8, 1865.

58 Morantz, *White Man's Gonna Getcha*, 87-89.

59 Canadian Museum of Civilization, Frank Sun Manuscript, "Aspects of Syncretism between Traditional Cree and Christian Religious Beliefs," 48, 64, 77.

60 Richard Preston, "James Bay Syncretism," 147-55; John S. Long, "Manitu, Power, Books, and Wiihtikow: Some Factors in the Adoption of Christianity by Nineteenth-Century Western James Bay Cree," *Native Studies Review* 3, 1: 1 (1987): 1-30.

61 LAC, CMS, MG 17, reel A-88, Horden Journal, February 2, 1853; Ridington, "From Hunt Chief to Prophet," 9-10; Preston, "Cree Narrative: Expressing the Personal Meaning of Events," 21; Preston, *Cree Narrative,* 2nd ed. (Montreal: McGill-Queen's University Press, 2002), 237.

62 Louis Charbonneau-Lassay, "Christ the Hunter and the Hunted," *Parabola* 16, 2 (1991): 23-24.

CHAPTER 5: MARGINAL EXISTENCES

1 LAC, Hudson's Bay Company Records, MG 20, Mistassini Post Journals, B133/a/67, 32.

2 LAC, Indian Affairs Records, RG 10, vol. 6754, file 420-20-1-2, "Proceedings of the North American Wildlife Conference," February 3-7, 1936. See also Charles A. Bishop, *The Northern Ojibwa and the Fur Trade: An Historical and Ecological Study* (Toronto: Holt, Rinehart and Winston, 1974), 77-100.

3 LAC, CMS, reel A-79, September 1, 1854, Horden to Lay Secretary.

4 John Patrick Gillese, *Weekend Picture Magazine*, November 10, 1951.
5 LAC, Hudson's Bay Company Records, MG 20, Mistassini Post Journals, B133/a/48, 4-8
6 Ibid., 8-12.
7 LAC, Hudson's Bay Company Records, MG 20, Mistassini Post Journals, B133/a/50, 27; B133/a/52, 40; B133/a/54, 32; B133/a/53, 8.
8 LAC, Hudson's Bay Company Records, MG 20, Mistassini Post Journals, B133/a/56, 36; B133/a/56, 18-19.
9 LAC, Hudson's Bay Company Records, MG 20, Mistassini Post Journals, B133/a/59, 14-16.
10 Paul Hacket, *"A Very Remarkable Sickness": Epidemics in the Petit Nord, 1670-1846* (Winnipeg: University of Manitoba Press, 2002), 8-15; LAC, Hudson's Bay Company Records, MG 20, District Manager's Reports, A74/12; LAC, William G. Walton Papers, MG 30, D133, Walton Letterbook; LAC, A.P. Low Fonds, MG 30, B33, Journal, September 30, 1902; Toby Morantz, *The White Man's Gonna Getcha: The Colonial Challenge to the Crees in Quebec* (Montreal: McGill-Queen's University Press, 2002), 45.
11 LAC, Hudson's Bay Company Records, MG 20, Mistassini Post Journals, B133/a/13, 8-10; B133/a/29, 8; B133/a/44, 6.
12 LAC, Hudson's Bay Company Records, MG 20, Mistassini Post Journals, B133/a/31, 14-20.
13 LAC, Ecclesiastical Records, MG 17, CMS, reel A-113, December 4, 1885, Bishop of Moosonee to Wigram; reel A-115, January 18, 1887, Bishop of Moosonee to "My Christian Friend"; reel A-80, September 7, 1858, F.H. Fleming to Venn; LAC, Hudson's Bay Company Records, MG 20, Nitchequon Post Journals, B147/a/29, 1; Waswanipi Post Journals, B227/a/39, 13; LAC, Ecclesiastical Records, MG 17, CMS, reel A-98, Vincent Journal, August 8, 1860; LAC, Robert Bell Fonds, MG 29, B15, vol. 2, file 25, "Diseases among the Indians," 4-5; Morantz, *White Man's Gonna Getcha*, 43-44.
14 LAC, Ecclesiastical Records, MG 17, CMS, reel A-80, October 11, 1858, Horden to Venn; LAC, Robert Bell Fonds, MG 29, B15, vol. 2, file 25, "Diseases among the Indians," 1885, 6; LAC, Hudson's Bay Company Records, MG 20, Mistassini Post Journals, B133/a/42, 19; B133/a/44, 6; Waswanipi Post Journals, B227/a/49, 26-27, B227/a/63, 61-64.
15 LAC, Robert Bell Fonds, MG 29, B15, Volume 62, File 22, "Diseases Among the Indians Frequenting York Factory," 1885; Morantz, *White Man's Gonna Getcha*, 43-45; LAC, Hudson's Bay Company Records, MG 20, Mistassini District Reports, B133/e/17, 1; Waswanipi Correspondence, B227/b/3, 3; Rupert's House Journals, B186/a/111, 8-9; LAC, Robert Bell Fonds, MG 29, B15, vol. 2, file 25, "Diseases among the Indians," 4-5; A.P. Low, *Report of Explorations in the Labrador Peninsula in 1892-93-94-95* (Ottawa: Geological Survey of Canada, 1896), 70-71; Frank G. Speck, "Mistassini Hunting Territories in the Labrador Peninsula," *American Anthropologist* 25, 4 (1923): 454.
16 LAC, Hudson's Bay Company Records, MG 20, Waswanipi Journals, B227/a/63, 61-64; Hacket, *"A Very Remarkable Sickness,"* 12.
17 Harvey A. Feit, "Hunting and the Quest for Power: The James Bay Cree and Whitemen in the Twentieth Century," in *Native Peoples: The Canadian Experience*, ed. R. Bruce Morrison and C. Roderick Wilson (Toronto: McClelland and Stewart, 1986), 172-73; see Alfred Crosby, *The Columbian Exchange: Biological and Cultural Consequences of 1492* (Westport, CT: Praeger, 2003); Calvin Martin, *Keepers of the Game: Indian-Animal Relationships and the Fur Trade* (Berkeley: University of California Press, 1978).
18 Dominion of Canada Annual Reports of the Department of Indian Affairs 1864-1990, http://www.collectionscanada.gc.ca/indianaffairs/; LAC, Ecclesiastical Records, MG 17,

CMS, reel A-98, Vincent Journal, May 22, 1860; reel A-82, Bishop of Montreal to Venn, December 16, 1844; Hudson's Bay Company Records, MG 20, Mistassini Post Journals, B133/a/20, 24; Nitchequon Post Journals, B147/a/3, 10; Rupert's House Journals, B186/a/66, 53.

19 Arthur Ray, *The Canadian Fur Trade in the Industrial Age* (Toronto: University of Toronto Press, 1990), 28-29, 51-55; Morantz, *White Man's Gonna Getcha*, 32.

20 LAC, Ecclesiastical Records, CMS, reel A-117, Bishop of Moosonee to Wigram, May 21, 1892; LAC, Hudson's Bay Company Records, MG 20, Rupert District Reports, B186/e/26; Rupert's House Post Journals, B186/a/28; Mistassini Post Journals, B133/a/50, 4-6.

21 Eleanor Leacock and N. Rothschild, eds., *Labrador Winter: The Ethnographic Journals of William Duncan Strong, 1927-1928* (Washington, DC: Smithsonian Institute, 1994), 116. See also Richard Preston, *Cree Narrative,* 2nd ed. (Montreal: McGill-Queen's University Press, 2002).

22 LAC, Hudson's Bay Company Records, MG 20, Rupert River District Report 1891-1904, A74/1, 377-382.

23 LAC, Hudson's Bay Company Records, MG 20, District Manager's Reports A74/3, 37; A74/4, 37; A74/5-9.

24 LAC, Ecclesiastical Records, MG 17, CMS, reel A-89, Horden Journal, June 28, 1861.

25 LAC, Hudson's Bay Company Records, MG 20, Mistassini Post Journals, B133/a/23, 30; Nitchequon Post Journals, B147/a/22, 6; Pike Lake Journals, B163/a/3, 13; Rupert's House Journals, B186/a/66, 29; Rupert's House District Reports, B186/e/6, 6; Waswanipi Post Journals, B227/a/13, 26.

26 LAC, Hudson's Bay Company Records, MG 20, Waswanipi Post Journals, B227/a/16, 5; Mistassini Post Journals, B133/a/38, 18.

27 LAC, MG 20, J40, George Barnley Journal, June 5, 1840; LAC, Hudson's Bay Company Records, MG 20, Rupert's House Journals, B186/a/21, 20; B186/a/24, 12; Mistassini Post Journals, B133/a/17, 6; Temiskamay Post Journals, B215/a/20, 16; Pike Lake Journals, B163/a/21, 22; B163/a/27, 9; B163/a/28, 8-9; Waswanipi Post Journals, B227/a/26, 5; B227/a/47, 4; B227/a/49, 32; Rupert's House Journals, B186/a/111, 27.

28 LAC, Hudson's Bay Company Records, MG 20, Nitchequon Post Journals, B147/a/21, 25.

29 Ibid., Mistassini Post Journals, B133/a/64, 40; LAC, Geological Survey of Canada, RG 45, vol. 220, notebook 2492, 3, 11; LAC, Hudson's Bay Company Records, MG 20, Mistassini Post Journals, B/133/a/63, 3, 32.

30 LAC, Hudson's Bay Company Records, MG 20, District Manager's Reports, A74/10, 24; Mistassini Post Journals, B133/a/70, 45, 69; Waswanipi Post Journals, B227/b/3, 27.

31 Morantz, *White Man's Gonna Getcha*, 99, 100-4; Feit, "Hunting and the Quest for Power," 186-87; J.W. Anderson, *Fur Trader's Story* (Toronto: Ryerson Press, 1961), 53; LAC, MG 30, B33, Albert Peter Low Fonds, Journal of 1902, 30; LAC, William Walton Papers, MG 30, D133, Walton Letterbook, 26-27; LAC, MG 20, J40, "Reverend George Barnley Annual Letter, January 6, 1904," 26-27.

32 LAC, Hudson's Bay Company Records, MG 20, District Manager's Reports, A74/14; Canadian Museum of Civilization, Harvey Feit Papers, B 359, file 6, "The Power to 'See' and the Power to Hunt: The Shaking Tent Ceremony in Relation to Experience, Explanation, Action, and Interpretation in the Waswanipi Hunter's World," 1983, 22; Canadian Museum of Civilization, Rolf Knight Papers, box 40, file 6, "Rupert House Summary Report," 1961, 3.

33 LAC, Hudson's Bay Company Records, MG 20, Waswanipi Post Journals, B227/a/ 57, 24.

34 LAC, Hudson's Bay Company Records, MG 20, Mistassini Post Journals, B133/a/68, 17. W.A. Anderson, *Angel of Hudson's Bay: The True Story of Maud Watt* (Toronto: Clarke Irwin, 1961), 119-20; LAC, Hudson's Bay Company Records, MG 20, Mistassini Post Journals, B133/a/76, 14; Waswanipi Post Journals, B227/a/58, 41; B227/a/58, 3; B227/a/63, 48; Waswanipi Post Journals, B227/a/58, 1, 10, 39; B227/a/59, 76.

35 LAC, Hudson's Bay Company Records, MG 20, Waswanipi Post Journals, B227/a/60, 4-11.

36 Ibid., Mistassini Post Journals, B133/a/70, 45, 69; B133/a/72, 4; B133/a/73, 2; Waswanipi Post Journals, B227/a/63, 2.

37 Feit, "Hunting and the Quest for Power," 189-90; LAC, Hudson's Bay Company Records, MG 20, Nitchequon Post Journals, B147/a/41, 2; Matthew Coon Come, "Survival in the Context of Mega-Resource Development: Experiences of the James Bay Cree and the First Nations of Canada," in *In the Way of Development*, ed. Mario Blaser, Harvey A. Feit, and Glenn McRae (New York: Zed Books, 2004), 153-65.

38 LAC, Hudson's Bay Company Records, MG 20, Nitchequon Post Journals, B147/a/11, 38, 61-64.

39 Alexander Clúny, *The American Traveller: Containing Observations on the Present State, Culture, and Commerce of the British Colonies in America* (London: Dily, 1769), 8-27; Richard I. Ruggles, *A Country So Interesting: The Hudson's Bay Company and Two Centuries of Mapping, 1670-1870* (Montreal: McGill-Queen's University Press, 1991); G. Malcolm Lewis, *Cartographic Encounters: Perspectives on Native American Mapmaking and Map Use* (Chicago: University of Chicago Press, 1998), 1-55; Debra Lindsay, *Science in the Subarctic: Trappers, Traders, and the Smithsonian Institution* (Washington, DC: Smithsonian Institution Press, 1993), 7-9, 42-43.

40 LAC, Hudson's Bay Company Records, MG 20, Mistassini Post Journals, B133/a/13, 12; "Sidney Coolidge," *Appleton's Cyclopedia of American Biography*, vol. 1 (New York: D. Appleton and Company, 1887-89), 723.

41 Morris Zaslow, *The Opening of the Canadian North, 1870-1914* (Toronto: McClelland and Stewart, 1971), 81-85; LAC, Robert Bell Fonds, MG 29, B15, vol. 2, file 14, "The Commercial Importance of Hudson's Bay," 1.

42 LAC, Geological Survey of Canada, RG 45, vol. 220, notebooks 1171-73; vol. 239, notebook 372, 2; Zaslow, *Opening of the Canadian North*, 154; Morris Zaslow, *Reading the Rocks: The Story of the Geological Survey of Canada, 1842-1972* (Toronto: Macmillan, 1975), 119-68; *The Northward Expansion of Canada* (Toronto: McClelland and Stewart, 1988).

43 LAC, Albert Peter Low Fonds, MG 30, B33, vol. 1, "1902 Journal on Hudson's Bay," 13. See H.V. Nelles, *The Politics of Development: Forests, Mines, and Hydro-electric Power in Ontario, 1849-1941* (Toronto: Macmillan, 1974); David Massell, *Amassing Power: J.B. Duke and the Saguenay River, 1897-1927* (Montreal: McGill-Queen's University Press, 2000).

44 LAC, Geological Survey of Canada, RG 45, vol. 220, notebook 2485, 11; notebook 2486, 1902, 3.

45 LAC, Albert Peter Low Fonds, MG 30, B33, vol. 1, "1902 Journal on Hudson's Bay," 1-4; Anderson, *Fur Trader's Story*, 185; LAC, J.M. Bell Fonds, MG 29, B15, vol. 61, file 49, 1.

46 Morantz, *White Man's Gonna Getcha*, 39-40; Zaslow, *The Opening of the Canadian North*, 156; Anderson, *Fur Trader's Story*, 58, 99; LAC, Geological Survey of Canada, RG 45, vol. 217, notebook NS 3948, March 10, 1923; Jack Bradford, *Canadian Northern Railway and the*

Men Who Made It Work (Markham, ON: Initiative Publishing House, 1980); H.V. Nelles, *The Politics of Development: Forests, Mines, and Hydro-electric Power in Ontario, 1849-1941* (Toronto: Macmillan, 1974).

47 LAC, Hudson's Bay Company Records, MG 20, Mistassini Post Journals, B133/a/73, 8; B133/a/76, 13; Bruce W. Hodgins, *Canoeing North into the Unknown: A Record of River Travel, 1874-1974* (Toronto: Natural Heritage/Natural History, 1994), 63-80; Brian Back, *The Keewaydin Way, 1893-1983* (Temagami, ON: Keewaydin Camps, 1983); James West Davidson, *Great Heart: The History of a Labrador Adventure* (New York: Kodansha International, 1997).

48 LAC, Hudson's Bay Company Records, MG 20, Mistassini Post Journals, B133/a/70, 56.

49 Olaus Johan Murie, *Journeys to the Far North* (Palo Alto, CA: Wilderness Society and American West Publishing Company, 1973).

50 Murie, *Journeys to the Far North*, 28; See Boyce Richardson, *Strangers Devour the Land: A Chronicle of the Assault upon the Last Coherent Hunting Culture in North America, the Cree Indians of Northern Quebec, and Their Vast Primeval Homelands* (New York: Alfred A. Knopf, 1976), 4-6.

51 LAC, Olaus Johan Murie Fonds, MG 30, B102, "Hudson's Bay Diary, 1914-1915," September 18, 1914.

52 Paul Lawrence Farber, *Finding Order in Nature: The Naturalist Tradition from Linneaus to E.O. Wilson* (Baltimore: Johns Hopkins University Press, 2000); Trevor Harvey Levere, *A Curious Field-Book: Science and Technology in Canadian History* (Toronto: Oxford University Press, 1974).

53 Murie, "Hudson's Bay Diary, 1914-1915," September 18, 1914; Lindsay, *Science in the Subarctic*, 63-70.

54 LAC, Olaus Johan Murie Fonds, MG 30, B102, "On The Shores of Hudson's Bay," 15.

55 Ibid., "Hudson Bay Diary, 1914-1915," December 27, 1914.

56 "Waives" is a common nickname for a goose.

57 LAC, Olaus Johan Murie Fonds, MG 30, B102, "On the Shores of Hudson's Bay," 17; "Hudson's Bay Diary, 1914-1915," November 1, 1914

58 Ibid., "On The Shores of Hudson's Bay," 1-2.

59 Ibid., "Hudson's Bay Diary," July 15, 1914.

60 Ibid., "On the Shores of Hudson's Bay," 17.

61 Ibid., "Hudson's Bay Diary," February 19, 1915. "On The Shores of Hudson's Bay," 16-17.

62 Murie, *Journeys to the Far North*, 37.

CHAPTER 6: MANAGEMENT AND MORAL ECONOMY

1 LAC, Indian Affairs, RG 10, vol. 6752, file 420-10-1-3, Hugh Conn, 1943 Fur Conservation Report.

2 In this period after 1930, the village became increasingly identified as Rupert House and not Rupert's House. Before the village was renamed Waskaganish this was the way that it appeared on maps and in government documents for the most part. This was never universal, but I will use Rupert House from this point on.

3 Provincial Archives of Ontario (PAO), James Watt Papers, MU 1385, Letter to G.R. Ray, January 20, 1923; Frank G. Speck, "Mistassini Hunting Territories in the Labrador Peninsula," *American Anthropologist* 25, 4 (1923): 459.

4 Farley Mowat, *The People of the Deer* (Boston: Little, Brown, 1952).

5 LAC, Indian Affairs, RG 10, vol. 6532, file 1A-1256-19; vol. 6518, file IND-15-1-203; vol. 6955, file 371/20-2; vol. 7553, file 41, 074-2.

6 J.R. Miller, *Skyscrapers Hide the Heavens: A History of Indian-White Relations in Canada* (Toronto: University of Toronto Press, 1991), 99-116; J.R. Miller, *Shingwauk's Vision: A History of Native Residential Schools* (Toronto: University of Toronto Press, 1996); K. Tsianina Lomawaima, *They Called It Prairie Light: The Story of Chilocco Indian School* (Lincoln: University of Nebraska Press, 1994); Elizabeth Graham, *The Mush Hole: Life at Two Indian Residential Schools* (Waterloo, ON: Heffle Publishing, 1997).

7 LAC, Indian Affairs, RG 10, vol. 6112, file 350-1, W.L. Tyrer to Secretary of Indian Affairs, March 8, 1932; Russell Fernier to Tyrer, March 26, 1932; vol. 6112, file 350-1, Tyrer to Secretary of Indian Affairs, March 8, 1932; Telegram from Tyrer to Indian Affairs, August 10, 1940; Telegram from Tyrer to Hoey at Indian Affairs, August 15, 1940; vol. 8798, file 371/25-13-019; LAC, Indian Affairs and Northern Development, RG 22, vol. 1201, file 371/1-1, 1950 Report on Schools by Superintendent of Education, 4-18; RG 10, vol. 7187, file 371/25-1-011, Report of Neville F. Pearce, September 30, 1955; vol. 6843, file 486/29-2, V.N. Gran, "Report on Great Whale River."

8 PAO, Watt Papers, MU 1385, July 12, 1929, Letter to Parsons; August 16, 1929, Letter to V.W. West (District Manager of Charlton Island).

9 PAO, Watt Papers, MU 1385, August 16, 1929, Letter to V.W. West (District Manager of Charlton Island); August 17, 1929, Watt to West.

10 PAO, Watt Papers, MU 1385, August 17, 1929, Watt to West.

11 Ibid.; Harvey A. Feit, "James Bay Crees' Life Projects and Politics: Histories of Place, Animal Partners and Enduring Relationships," in *In the Way of Development*, ed. Mario Blaser, Harvey A. Feit, and Glenn McRae (New York: Zed Books, 2004), 100-1.

12 LAC, Hudson's Bay Company Records, MG 20, Rupert's House Journals, B186/a/58; B186/b/36, 12; Richard I. Ruggles, *A Country So Interesting: The Hudson's Bay Company and Two Centuries of Mapping* (Montreal: McGill-Queen's University Press, 1991), 126.

13 LAC, Hudson's Bay Company Records, MG 20, Rupert's House Journals, B186/a/58; Mistassini Journals, B133/a/27; James W. Anderson, *Fur Trader's Story* (Toronto: Ryerson Press, 1961), 184; Arthur J. Ray, "Some Conservation Schemes of the Hudson's Bay Company, 1821-1850: An Examination of the Problems of Resource Management in the Fur Trade," *Journal of Historical Geography* 1 (1975): 49-68.

14 PAO, Watt Papers, MU 1385, letter to unnamed banker, July 5, 1932; letter to Parsons, April 23, 1932; George Colpitts, "Conservation, Science, and Canada's Fur Farming Industry, 1913-1945," *Social History/Histoire sociale* 30, 59 (1997): 77-108.

15 PAO, Watt Papers, MU 1385, Richard to Maud Watt, August 2, 1944.

16 LAC, Indian Affairs, RG 10, vol. 6755, file 420-10-4-1-4, 1942, Nottaway Beaver Preserve Annual Report.

17 David Massell, "Power and the Peribonka, A Prehistory: 1900-1930," *Quebec Studies* 38 (2004): 87-103.

18 PAO, Watt Papers, MU 1385, August 2, 1944, Richard to Maud Watt; undated letter from 1932.

19 LAC, MG 30, A96, Kanaupascou Post, vol. 1, file 2, "Hudson [sic] Bay Company Canada's Fur Trade."

20 Speck, "Mistassini Hunting Territories in the Labrador Peninsula," 461.

21   PAO, Watt Papers, MU 1385, "Rough Draft of Speech to Indians," n.d.
22   LAC, Indian Affairs, RG 10, vol. 6754, file 420-10-4-1, April 26, 1932; file 420-10-4-1, Mackenzie to Tyrer, March 16, 1933; file 420-10-4-1, Tyrer to Mackenzie, March 1, 1933.
23   LAC, Indian Affairs, RG 10, vol. 6754, file 420-10-4-1, Alec Cooper, July 4, 1933.
24   Ibid., Report from Rupert's House, 1936.
25   Ibid., Watt to Parsons, December 7, 1937.
26   Ibid., Parsons to MacInnes, March 5, 1937; Parson to MacInnes, July 8, 1937.
27   LAC, Indian Affairs, RG 10, vol. 6754, file 420-10-4-1, Tyrer to Secretary of Indian Affairs, January 18, 1937; T.R.L. MacInnes, Deputy Secretary of Indian Affairs, to L.A. Richard, February 23, 1937.
28   LAC, Indian Affairs, RG 10, vol. 6754, file 420-10-4-1, Orders in Council, April 25, 1938; Harold McGill Memorandum, June 22, 1938; file 420-10-4-1-2, November 10, 1938.
29   LAC, Indian Affairs, RG 10, vol. 6755, file 420-10-4-1-3, First Annual Report for Old Factory Preserve, 1942; Conn Memorandum, August 7, 1941; vol. 6752, file 420-10-1-3, 1943 Report for Indian Affairs Branch; vol. 6755, file 420-10-4-1-3, Allen to Richard, August 9, 1941; file 420-10-4-1-3, Telegram from Allen to Watt, August 30, 1941; Quebec Orders in Council, October 30, 1941; vol. 6755, file 420-10-4-1-3, Richard to Camsell, September 2, 1942.
30   LAC, Indian Affairs, RG 10, vol. 6755, file 420-10-4-1-3, Fur Supervisors Report, August 18, 1942; vol. 6752, file 420-10-1-3, 1943 Report for Indian Affairs Branch.
31   LAC, Indian Affairs, RG 10, vol. 6755, file 420-10-4-1-3, C.W. Jackson to Richard, December 15, 1942.
32   Ibid., Conn to Allen, August 15, 1942.
33   LAC, Indian Affairs, RG 10, vol. 6754, file 420-10-4-1-2, Lariviere to D.J. Allen, Superintendent of Mines and Resources, February 26, 1941.
34   LAC, Indian Affairs, RG 10, vol. 6755, file 420-10-4-1-4, 1943 Annual Report; 1942, Nottaway Beaver Preserve Annual Report; R.H. Cheshire (HBC) to D.J. Allen, May 5, 1943; L.A. Richard to D.J. Allen, May 7, 1943; Quebec Orders in Council 6261, August 6, 1943; vol. 6754, file 420-10-4MI-1, Macleod to Conn, December 13, 1948. For history of Quebec colonization, see Joseph D. Conwill, "Return to the Land: Quebec's Colonisation Movement," *History Today* (April 1984): 16-21; Christian Morissonneau, *La Terre Promise: Le Mythe du Nord Québécois* (Montréal: Hurtubise HMH, 1978); Gerard Ouellet, *Aux Marches du Royaume de Matagami: Rochebaucourt* (Québec: Department of Colonization, 1947).
35   LAC, Indian Affairs, RG 10, vol. 6755, file 420-10-4-4, D.J. Allen to Charles Fremont, April 4, 1944; Abitibi Report, vol. 6755, 1944; Sheva Thomas, Rupert's House (Chief of Abitibi) to Department of Indian Affairs, October 25, 1944; vol. 6753, file 420-10-2-1, RCMP reports, June 23 and July 16, 1948; Conn to RCMP, July 14, 1948.
36   J.M. Cooper, "Is the Algonquian Family Hunting Ground System Pre-Columbian?" *American Anthropologist* 41 (1939): 66-90; Harvey Feit, "The Construction of Algonquian Hunting Territories," in *Colonial Situations: Essays on the Contextualization of Ethnographic Knowledge,* ed. G. Stocking, 109-34 (Madison: University of Wisconsin Press, 1991); LAC, Indian Affairs, RG 10, vol. 6752, file 420-10-1-3, 1943 Report for Indian Affairs Branch.
37   LAC, Indian Affairs, RG 10, vol. 6752, file 420-10-1-3, 1943 Report for Indian Affairs Branch.
38   Ibid.
39   Ibid.; vol. 6755, file 420-10-4-1-3, Conn to Allen, August 8, 1941.

40 LAC, Indian Affairs, RG 10, vol. 6752, file 420-10-1-3, 1943 Report for Indian Affairs Branch.

41 Ibid.; 1948 Old Factory Annual Report.

42 LAC, Indian Affairs, RG 10, vol. 6752, file 420-10-1-1, To the Indian Agent at Mistassini, Quebec, July 5, 1947.

43 Ibid., H. Lariviere to Indian Affairs in Ottawa, July 11, 1947.

44 LAC, Indian Affairs, RG 10, vol. 6754, file 420-10-4M1-4-NO-1, Memorandum from D.J. Allen, August 16, 1948; P.H. Watt to Conn, May 24, 1949; vol. 6752, file 420-10-1-3, 1943 Report for Indian Affairs Branch; vol. 6754, file 420-10-4M1-1, Conn to Demark, September 9, 1949; file 420-10-4M1-4-NO-1, Conn to Demark, March 7, 1950.

45 LAC, Indian Affairs, RG 10, vol. 6754, file 420-10-4-OL-1, Henry Cooke and Bishop Renison to Indian Affairs, June 27, 1947; file 420-10-4M1-4-NO-1, Conn to Dr. D.P. Moore, Director of Indian Health Service, November 27, 1947.

46 LAC, Indian Affairs, RG 10, vol. 6754, file 420-10-4M1-4-NO-1, Richard to Mrs. J.C.S. Watt, January 20, 1948.

47 Ibid., vol. 6755, file 420-10-4-4, H. Lariviere, November 19, 1944; Conn to Lariviere, November 13, 1944; LAC, Indian Affairs and Northern Development, RG 22, series A-1-a, vol. 177, file 32-2-19, Charles Fremont to Jean Lesage, September 22, 1953 (with original spelling).

48 LAC, Indian Affairs and Northern Development, RG 22, series A-1-a, vol. 177, file 32-2-19, "Report on Federal-Provincial Beaver Disease Meeting," November 26, 1953; Indian Affairs, RG 10, vol. 8409, file 301/20-14-3-3, J.H. Gordon, Superintendent of Welfare, to R.L. Boulanger, Superintendent of Indian Agency, February 25, 1957; see Paul Nadasdy, *Hunters and Bureaucrats: Power, Knowledge, and Aboriginal-State Relations in the Southwest Yukon* (Vancouver: UBC Press, 2004), 1-27.

49 Calvin Martin, *The Way of the Human Being* (New Haven: Yale University Press, 1999), 106-13; Robert Trumbull, "Indians Kill Only for Food," *Globe and Mail*, June 22, 1955, 17.

50 John Patrick Gillese, "The Beaver Has Come Back," *Weekend Picture Magazine*, November 10, 1951; *Saturday Night*, April 17, 1948 (*Toronto Star*).

51 Bernard Bernier, "The Social Organization of the Waswanipi Cree Indians," in *Anthropology of Development*, ed. Norman A. Chance (Montreal: McGill University Press, 1967); Norman A. Chance, *Developmental Change among the Cree Indians of Quebec* (Montreal: McGill University Cree Project, 1970); Norman A. Chance, ed., *Conflict in Culture: Problems of Developmental Change among the Cree* (Ottawa: Canadian Research Centre for Anthropology, 1968); N. Elberg, J. Hyman, and R. Salisbury, *Not by Bread Alone: The Use of Subsistence Resources among James Bay Cree* (Montreal: McGill-Queen's University Press, 1972); A. Kerr, *Subsistence and Social Organization in a Fur Trade Community: Anthropological Report on the Rupert House Indians* (Ottawa: National Committee for Community Health Studies, 1950); Rolf Knight, *Ecological Factors in the Changing Economy and Social Organization among the Rupert's House Cree*, Anthropological Papers of the National Museum of Canada, no. 15 (Ottawa: Department of the Secretary of State, 1968); Leonard Mason, *The Swampy Cree: A Study in Acculturation*, Anthropological Papers of the National Museum of Canada, no. 13 (Ottawa: Department of the Secretary of State, 1967).

52 Canadian Museum of Civilization, Rolf Knight, box 40, file 6, "Rupert's House Summary Report, 1961," 7; Toby Morantz, *The White Man's Gonna Getcha: The Colonial Challenge to the Crees in Quebec* (Montreal: McGill-Queen's University Press, 2002), 60.

CHAPTER 7: FLOODING THE GARDEN

1 John Ciaccia, negotiator of the James Bay and Northern Quebec Agreement (JBNQA) and head of Secrétariat des Activitiés Governmentales Milieu Amerindian et Inuit, to the National Assembly, November 5, 1975, *James Bay and Northern Quebec Agreement* (Montreal: Quebec National Library, 1976), xiii.

2 Hans M. Carlson, "A Watershed of Words: Litigating and Negotiating Nature in Eastern James Bay, 1971-1975," *Canadian Historical Review* 85, 1 (2004): 63-84.

3 Ibid.

4 Roy MacGregor, *Chief: The Fearless Vision of Billy Diamond* (Middlesex, UK: Penguin Books, 1990), 54; Graham Fraser, *PQ: René Lévesque and the Parti Québécois in Power* (Toronto: Macmillan, 1984), 56.

5 MacGregor, *Chief*, 53; Sean McCutchen, *Electric Rivers* (Montreal: Black Rose Books, 1991), 31.

6 LAC, *Kanatewat v. JBDC*, James Bay Collection, Cabinet 39, AA-20, vol. 19, Einar Skinnarland; Judgement, 53-54.

7 Louis Balthazar, *Bilan du nationalisme au Québec* (Montréal: Éditions de l'Hexagone, 1986); Dale C. Thomson, *Jean Lesage and the Quiet Revolution* (Toronto: Macmillan, 1984).

8 Thomson, *Jean Lesage*, 240-44; Edmour Germain, "Hydro-Québec: A French-Canadian Goal," *Public Utilities Fortnightly*, April 23, 1964, 33; Lawrence James Boyle, *The Development of the Hydroelectric Industry* (Ann Arbor, Michigan: University Microforms International, 1974), 2, 15, 33-36; McCutchen, *Electric Rivers*, 33-36.

9 LAC, *Kanatewat*, Judgment, 5; McCutchen, *Electric Rivers*, 34-35; David Massell, *Amassing Power: J.B. Duke and the Saguenay River, 1897-1927* (Montreal: McGill-Queen's University Press, 2000).

10 Harvey A. Feit, "James Bay Crees' Life Projects and Politics: Histories of Place, Animal Partners and Enduring Relationships," in *In the Way of Development*, ed. Mario Blaser, Harvey A. Feit, and Glenn McRae (New York: Zed Books, 2004), 102, 105-6.

11 MacGregor, *Chief*, 38; LAC, Billy Diamond, *Kanatewat*, AA-20, vol. 1, 20.

12 LAC, *Kanatewat*, AA-20, vol. 1, 17-20.

13 MacGregor, *Chief*, 38.

14 See Curtis Cook and Juan Lendau, eds., *Aboriginal Rights and Self-Government* (Montreal: McGill-Queen's University Press, 2000), 168-85.

15 See MacGregor, *Chief*, chap. 2.

16 LAC, *Kanatewat*, Billy Diamond, AA-20, vol. 1, 1-43.

17 LAC, *Kanatewat*, AA-20, vol. 3, 33-34.

18 Toby Morantz, "The Fur Trade and the Cree of James Bay," in *Old Trails and New Directions: Papers of the Third North American Fur Trade Conference*, ed. C. Judd and A. Ray (Toronto: University of Toronto Press, 1980), 45.

19 LAC, *Kanatewat*, Billy Diamond, AA-20, vol. 4, 38-39.

20 LAC, *Kanatewat*, AA-20, vol. 13, 102.

21 Boyce Richardson, *Strangers Devour the Land: A Chronicle of the Assault upon the Last Coherent Hunting Culture in North American, the Cree Indians of Northern Quebec, and Their Vast Primeval Homelands* (New York: Alfred A. Knopf, 1976), 38-40.

22 LAC, *Kanatewat*, AA-20, vol. 9A, 113.

23 LAC, *Kanatewat*, Smally Petawabano, AA-20, Volume 9A, 115; William Gull, AA-20, vol. 6, 25, 33.

24 LAC, *Kanatewat,* Steven Tapiatik, AA-20, vol. 6, 73-92; Matthew Neeposh, AA-20, vol. 5, 25-26

25 LAC, *Kanatewat,* Georges Pachano, AA-20, vol. 15, 17.

26 LAC, *Kanatewat,* John Watt, AA-20, vol. 4, 60.

27 Richard Preston, *Cree Narrative,* 2nd ed. (Montreal: McGill-Queen's University Press, 2002), 70; LAC, *Kanatewat,* Matthew Shanush, AA-20, vol. 4, 17; François Mianiscum, AA-20, vol. 5, 49.

28 LAC, *Kanatewat,* Joe [Job] Bearskin, AA-20, vol. 65, 30.

29 LAC, *Kanatewat,* John Weapiniccapo, AA-20, vol. 13, 106.

30 LAC, *Kanatewat,* AA-20, vol. 3, 95.

31 Ibid., vol. 4, 54.

32 Ibid., vol. 12, 57.

33 Matthew Coon Come, quoted in Donald A. Grinde and Bruce E. Johansen, *Ecocide of Native America: Environmental Destruction of Indian Lands and Peoples* (Santa Fe: Clear Light Publishing, 1995), 231; Harvey A. Feit, "James Bay Crees' Life Projects and Politics," 92.

34 LAC, *Kanatewat,* Harvey Feit, AA-20, vol. 9A, 96-98; Edward S. Rogers, AA-20, vol. 13, 77-78.

35 LAC, *Kanatewat,* AA-20, vol. 12, 79, 104.

36 Ibid., J.A. Spence, vol. 29; vol. 9A, 84-90, 102.

37 LAC, *Kanatewat,* AA-20, vol. 9A, 88.

38 Ibid., Albert Malouf, AA-20, vol. 12, 91.

39 Ibid., John W. Berry, AA-20, vol. 17; Paul Bertrand, AA-20, vol. 53; Richard F. Salisbury, *A Homeland for the Cree: Regional Development in James Bay, 1971-1981* (Montreal: McGill-Queen's University Press, 1986).

40 LAC, *Kanatewat,* Hare, AA-20, vol. 10, 64.

41 Ibid., 42, 55.

42 Ibid., 43-44, 74.

43 Ibid., Hare, 77.

44 LAC, *Kanatewat,* Peter Hutchins, AA-20, vol. 75, 6

45 Ibid., 11.

46 Ibid., 10.

47 LAC, *Kanatewat,* Malouf, "Judgement," 6, 11. For more detail of the judgment, see Carlson, "A Watershed of Words."

48 LAC, *Kanatewat,* Malouf, "Judgement," 30.

49 Ibid., 37.

50 Ibid., 149-50.

51 MacGregor, *Chief,* 123, 125.

52 Rebecca Anne Auten-Grenier, "Bill 101: Controversies in the Law," Independent Writing Project, University of Maine, 2001.

53 Government of Quebec, *James Bay and Northern Quebec Agreement* (Quebec City: Editeur officiel du Québec, 1976), 291.

54 *James Bay and Northern Quebec Agreement,* 25, 169.

55 Ibid., 332, 359.

56 LAC, *Kanatewat,* James O'Reilly, "Judgement," AA-20, vol. 72, 10.

CHAPTER 8: CONCLUSION

1 Lawrence W. Levine, *Black Culture and Black Consciousness: Afro-American Folk Thought from Slavery to Freedom* (New York: Oxford University Press, 1977), 5.
2 Harvey A. Feit, "James Bay Crees' Life Projects and Politics: Histories of Place, Animal Partners and Enduring Relationships," in *In the Way of Development*, ed. Mario Blaser, Harvey A. Feit, and Glenn McRae (New York: Zed Books, 2004), 93.
3 See Harvey A. Feit, "Political Articulations of Hunters to the State: Means of Resisting Threats to Subsistence Production in the James Bay and Northern Quebec Agreement," *Etudes/Inuit/Studies* 3 (1979): 69-85; J.S. Frideres, "The James Bay Cree (Eeyouch) and Inuit of Quebec: New Dimensions in Aboriginal Politics and Law," *Native Studies Review* 12 (1999): 5-12; Jane Jenson and Martin Papillon, "Challenging the Citizenship Regime: The James Bay Cree and Transnational Action," *Politics and Society* 28 (2000): 245-64; Colin Scott, ed., *Aboriginal Autonomy and Development in Northern Quebec and Labrador* (Vancouver: UBC Press, 2001).
4 Billy Diamond, "Renewed Struggle of the Cree for Control of Their Northland," *Canada Speeches* 5, 4 (1991): 28. For more of Billy Diamond's views, see Billy Diamond, "Villages of the Damned," *Arctic Circle* (fall 1990) 24-30; "Aboriginal Rights: The James Bay Experience," in *The Quest for Justice: Aboriginal People and Aboriginal Rights*, ed. J. Anthony Long (Toronto: University of Toronto Press, 1985), 265-85; "A Debate on the Positive and Negative Aspects of the Implementation of the Agreement," in *Baie James et Nord Quebecois: Dix ans après*, ed. S. Vincent and G. Bowers (Montréal: Recherches, amérindiennes au Québec, 1988).
5 Matthew Coon Come, "Survival in the Context of Mega-Resource Development: Experiences of the James Bay Cree and the First Nations of Canada," in *In the Way of Development*, ed. Mario Blaser, Harvey A. Feit, and Glenn McRae (New York: Zed Books, 2004), 160. For more on Coon Come's views, see "Charlottetown and Aboriginal Rights: Delayed But Never Relinquished," *Policy Options politiques* 6 (2002-3): 72; "Where Can You Buy a River," *Northeast Indian Quarterly* 8 (1991): 6-11. For an overview of the history of Native rights and land claims in Canada, see J.R. Miller, *Skyscrapers Hide the Heavens: A History of Indian-White Relations in Canada* (Toronto: University of Toronto Press, 1991), 211-67; J.R. Miller, "Aboriginal Rights, Land Claims, and the Struggle to Survive," in *Sweet Promises: A Reader on Indian-White Relations in Canada*, ed. J.R. Miller, 405-21 (Toronto: University of Toronto Press, 1991).
6 Ted Moses, "Eeyou Governance beyond the Indian Act and the JBNQA," April 18, 2002, Article 1, available at http://www.gcc.ca.
7 Naila Clerici, "The Cree of James Bay and the Construction of Their Identity for the Media," *Canadian Issues/Themes Canadiens* 21 (1999): 143-65.
8 For more detail on the environmental and social costs of the James Bay projects, see Philip Awashish, "The Stakes for the Cree of Quebec," in Vincent Bowers, *Baie James et Nord Québécois*; Peter G. Sly, *Human Impacts on the Hudson Bay Bioregion: Its Present State and Future Environmental Concern* (Ottawa: Hudson Bay Programme, 1994); Peter Gorrie, "The James Bay Power Project: The Environmental Cost of Reshaping the Geography of Northern Quebec," *Canadian Geographic*, February/March 1990, 21-31; James F. Hornig, ed., *Social and Environmental Impacts of the James Bay Hydroelectric Project* (Montreal: McGill-Queen's University Press, 1999).

9   Glenn McRae, "Grassroots Transnationalism and Life Projects of Vermonters in the Great Whale Campaign," in *In the Way of Development*, ed. Mario Blaser, Harvey A. Feit, and Glenn McRae, 111-29 (New York: Zed Books, 2004).

10 Matthew Coon Come, "A Reduction of Our World," in *Our People, Our Land: Perspectives on the Columbus Quincentenary*, ed. Kurt Russo (Bellingham, WA: Lummi Tribe and Kluckholn Center, 1992), 82; Donald A. Grinde and Bruce E. Johansen, *Ecocide of Native America: Environmental Destruction of Indian Lands and Peoples* (Santa Fe: Clear Light Publishing, 1995), 231.

11 Naomi C. Heindel, "Land Use Change in Northern Québec: A Remote Sensing Analysis in James Bay" (Honours thesis, Dartmouth College, 2007), 32-38.

12 Andre Picard, "A Dispossessed People Come Home," *Globe and Mail*, December 4, 1993: A1, A6; J. Frenette, *The History of the Chibougamau Crees: An Amerindian Band Reveals Its Identity* (Chibougamau, QC: Cree Indian Centre of Chibougamau, 1985).

13 N. Scott Momaday, *The Man Made of Words: Essays, Stories, Passages* (New York: St. Martin's Press, 1997), 113-17.

POSTSCRIPT

1   The full text of the new agreement can be found on the Grand Council website at www.gcc.ca.

Bibliography

ARCHIVAL SOURCES

Provincial Archives of Ontario

James Watt Papers (MU 1385)
Gladman Family Fonds (MU 1385)
McTavish Fonds (MU 1385)

Library and Archives Canada

Albert Peter Low Fonds (MG 30, B33)
Ecclesiastical Records (MG 17):
    United Society for the Propagation of the Gospel (FA-285, FA-181)
    Church Missionary Society (FA-23, reels A-77, A-79 to A-82, A-87 to A-90, A-95, A-97,
        A-98, A-99, A-102, A-103, A-104, A-111 to A-121, A-125)
    Methodist Records (FA-164)
    Miscellaneous Fur Trade Records (MG 19)
    George Barnley Journal (MG 20, J40)
Edward Alexander McGregor Fonds (MG 30, A125)
Geological Survey of Canada (RG 45):
    Vols. 295, 296, 239, 182, 220, 182, 226, 196, 197, 199, 213, 214, 217
Hudson's Bay Company Records (MG 20):
    District Managers' Reports (A74)
    Abitibi Post Journals (B1/a, vol. 1-22)
    Abitibi District Reports (B1/e, vol. 1-8)
    Ashuampmuchuan Journals (B7/a)
    Ashuampmuchuan Correspondence (B7/b)
    Big Lake Journals (B19/a, vol. 1-3)
    Big Lake District Reports (B19/e)
    Chicoutimi Journals (B36/a)

Chicoutimi Correspondence (B36/b)
Eastmain Journals (B59/a, vol. 1-127)
Eastmain Correspondence (B59/b, vol. 1-33)
Eastmain District Reports (B59/e, vol. 1-18)
Kaniapiskau Journals (B98/a, vol. 1-4)
Lac St. Jean Journals (B111/a, vol. 1-6)
Mistassini Journals (B133/a, vol. 1-61)
Mistassini Correspondence (B133/c)
Mistassini District Reports (B133/e, vol. 1-18)
Nescopie Journals (B139/a, vol. 1-17)
Nescopie District Reports (B139/e)
Nemiskau Journal (B142/a, vol. 1-9)
Neoskweskau Journals (B143/a, vol. 1-21)
Neoskweskau Reports (B143/e, vol. 1-5)
Nichikun Journals (B147/a, vol. 1-38)
Correspondence (B147/c)
Nichikun District Reports (B147/e)
Pike Lake Journals (B163/a, vol. 1-28)
Pike Lake Correspondence (B163/c)
Rupert's House Journals (B186/a, vol. 1-110)
Correspondence (B186/b, vol. 1-72)
Rupert's House Reports (B186/e, vol. 1-33)
Rush Lake Journals (B187/a)
South River House Journals (B206/a)
South River House District Reports (B206/e)
Temiskamay Journals (B215/a, vol. 1-34)
Temiskamay Reports (B215/e, vol. 1-4)
Waswanapi Journals (B227/a, vol. 1-53)
Waswanapi Letters (B227/b, vol. 1-15)
Waswanapi Reports (B227/e, vol. 1-13)
Winokapau Post Journals (B237/a, vol. 1-6)
Pointe Bleu Journals (B329/a, vol. 1-4)
Observations on Hudson's Bay (E2/, vol. 1-12)
Samuel Iserhoff, "Research of an Hundred Years Ago" (E93/, vol. 31)
King's Post Reports (E20)
Indian Affairs Records (RG 10):
Agency Records, Pointe Bleu Agency, 1881-1960
Annual Reports of Indian Affairs, 1864-1990
James Bay District Office, 1927-73
Quebec Fur Conservation, 1932-50
Fur Conservation, Wolves (vol. 6731, file 420-1-5)
James Bay and Abitibi Agencies, 1938-44 (vol. 6732, file 420-1-5-1-1)
Quebec Fur Conservation, 1946-50 (vol. 6752, file 420-10-1-1)
Correspondence, 1942 (vol. 6752, file 420-10-2-1)
Correspondence, 1943-45 (vol. 6752, file 420-10-2-2)
Beaver Preserves (vol. 6753, file 420-10-4)
Abitibi Preserves (vol. 6753, file 420-10-4AB-1-1)

Live Trapping (vol. 6753, file 420-10-4LT-1)
Mistassini Correspondence (vol. 6754, file 420-10-4M1-1)
Nottaway Correspondence, 1938-41 (vol. 6754, file 420-10-4-1-2)
Nottaway Reports, 1947-50 (vol. 6754, file 420-10-4M1-4)
Old Factory Correspondence, 1947-48 (vol. 6754, file 420-10-4)
Rupert River Preserve, 1932-38 (vol. 6754, file 420-10-4-1)
Nottaway Correspondence, 1942-46 (vol. 6755, file 420-10-4-1-4)
Nottaway Correspondence, 1941-42 (vol. 6755, file 420-10-4-1-3)
Fur Conservation, 1944-46 (vol. 6755, file 420-10-4-4)
Quebec fur Conservation, 1960-61 (vol. 8408, file 301/20-133)
Quebec fur Conservation, 1960-63 (vol. 8408 file 301/20-13-4)
James Bay Agency General Correspondence on fur Conservation, 1960 (vol. 8409, file 301/20-14-11-2)
General Correspondence fur, Quebec (vol. 8409, file 301/20-14-3-3)
Restigouche Agency, 1901-70
Superintendency Records, Sept Isle District Office, 1923-70
Indian Affairs and Northern Development (RG 22, Series A-1-a):
Beavers (vol. 177, file 32-2-19)
Schools, 1950 (vol. 1203, file 371/1-1)
James Bay Collection, *Kanatewat v. James Bay Development Corporation* (Cabinet 39, AA-20, vols. 1-78)
John Coldwell Fonds (MG 30, C82)
Mary Jackman Fonds (MG 30, C216)
Olaus Johan Murie Fonds (MG 30, B102)
Révillon Frères (MG 28)
Robert Bell Fonds (MG 29, B15)
Roy F. Fleming Fonds (MG 30, D55)
William G. Walton Papers (MG 30, D133)

Museum of Civilization

Colin Scott. 1977-81. Wemindji. 1982. Interviews/Life Histories MCC/CMC ARCHIVES DOCS ETHNO, box 403, file 3; box 377, file 7; box 348, file 8; box 339, file 9.
Frank Sun. 1979. Wemindji. Life Histories MCC/CMC ARCHIVES DOCS ETHNO, box 316, file 8; box 371, file 1; box 288, file 11.
Harvey Feit. 1968-70. Waswanapi Interviews/Life Histories MCC/CMC ARCHIVES DOCS ETHNO, box 359, file 6; box 25, file 21; box 389, file 4; box 419, file 6; box 382, files 5 and 6; box 392, file 5.
MCC/CMC ARCHIVES DOCS ETHNO, box 40, file 5 and 6; box 161, file 2.
Rolf Knight. 1961. Rupert House. Fieldnotes.

SECONDARY SOURCES

Abel, Kerry M. *Drum Songs: Glimpses of Dene History*. Montreal: McGill-Queen's University Press, 1993.
Ahenakew, Alice. *Ah-ayitaw isi e-ki-kiskeyihtahkik maskihkiy/They Knew Both Sides of Medicine: Cree Tales of Curing and Cursing Told by Alice Ahenakew*. Ed. H.C. Wolfart and Freda Ahenakew. Winnipeg: University of Manitoba Press, 2000.

Anderson, E.N. *Ecologies of the Heart: Emotion, Belief, and the Environment.* New York: Oxford University Press, 1996.

Anderson, Gary Clayton. *Kinsmen of Another Kind: Dakota-White Relations in the Upper Mississippi Valley, 1650-1862.* Lincoln: University of Nebraska Press, 1984.

Anderson, James W. *Fur Traders Story.* Toronto: Ryerson Press, 1961.

Anderson, W.A. *Angel of Hudson Bay: The True Story of Maud Watt.* Toronto: Clarke, Irwin, 1961.

Appleby, Joyce, Lynn Hunt, and Margaret Jacob. *Telling the Truth about History.* New York: W.W. Norton, 1994.

Arnold, David. *The Problem of Nature: Environment, Culture, and European Expansion.* Cambridge: Blackwell Publishing, 1996.

Averyt, William. "Canada-US Electrical Trade and Environmental Politics." *Canadian-American Public Policy* 12 (1992): 1-56.

Awashish, Philip. "The Stakes for the Cree of Quebec." In *Baie James et Nord Québécois: Dix ans après,* ed. S. Vincent, and G. Bowers. Montréal: Recherches amérindiennes au Québec, 1988.

Axtell, James. *Beyond 1492: Encounters in Colonial North America.* New York: Oxford University Press, 1992.

–. "Ethnohistory: An Historian's Viewpoint." *Ethnohistory* 26 (1979): 1-13.

–. *The Invasion Within: The Contest of Cultures in Colonial North America.* New York: Oxford University Press, 1985.

–. "The Power of Print in the Eastern Woodlands." *William and Mary Quarterly* 44 (1987): 300-09.

–. "Some Thoughts on the Ethnohistory of Missions." *Ethnohistory* 29, 1 (1982): 35-41.

Bailey, Alfred G. *The Conflict of European and Eastern Algonkian Cultures, 1504-1700.* Toronto: University of Toronto Press, 1969.

–. "Retrospective Thoughts of an Ethnohistorian." *Historical Papers.* Toronto: Canadian Historical Association, 1977.

Banks, Joyce M. "The Church Missionary Society Press At Moose Factory: 1853-1859." *Journal of Canadian Church Historical Society* 26, 2 (1984): 69-80.

Bauer, George W. "Cree Tales and Beliefs." *Northeast Folklore* 12 (1971): 6-70.

Beer, Gillian. *Arguing with the Past.* London: Routledge, 1989.

Berkes, Fikret. "Some Environmental and Social Impacts of the James Bay Hydroelectric Project, Canada." *Journal of Environmental Management* 12 (1981): 157-72.

Bernier, Bernard. "The Social Organization of the Waswanipi Cree Indians." In *Anthropology of Development,* ed. Norman A. Chance. Toronto: McGill University Press, 1967.

Bishop, Charles, A. *The Northern Ojibwa and the Fur Trade: An Historical and Ecological Study.* Toronto: Holt, Rinehart and Winston, 1974.

Black-Rogers, Mary. "Varieties of 'Starving': Semantics and Survival in the Subarctic Fur Trade, 1750-1850." *Ethnohistory* 33 (1986): 353-83.

Borre, Kristen. "The Healing Power of Seals: The Meaning of the Inuit Health Practice and Belief." *Arctic Anthropology* 31/1 (1994): 1-15.

Bourassa, R. *James Bay.* Montreal: Harvest House, 1972.

–. *Power from the North.* Scarborough, ON: Prentice-Hall, 1985.

Bourdieu, Pierre. *Language and Symbolic Power.* Cambridge: Harvard University Press, 1991.

Boyle, Lawrence James. "The Development of the Hydro-electrical Industry in Quebec." Ann Arbor, MI: University Microforms International, 1974.

Breton, Albert. "The Economics of Nationalism." *Journal of Political Economy* 72 (1964): 376-86.

Brightman, R. "The Windigo in the Material World." *Ethnohistory* 35 (1988): 337-80.

Brown, Jennifer S.H. "Cure and Feeding of Windigos: A Critique." *American Anthropologist* 73 (1971): 2-22.

–. "'I wish to be as I see you': An Ojibwa-Methodist Encounter in Fur Trade Country, Rainy Lake, 1854-1855." *Arctic Anthropology* 24 (1987): 23-29.

–. "Reading beyond the Missionaries, Dissecting Responses." *Ethnohistory* 43 (1996): 713-19.

–. *Strangers in Blood: Fur Trade Company Families in Indian Country.* Vancouver: UBC Press, 1980.

–. "The Track to Heaven: The Hudson Bay Cree Religious Movement of 1843." In *Proceedings of the Thirteenth Algonquin Conference*, ed. William Cowan. Winnipeg: University of Manitoba Press, 1983.

Brown, Jennifer S.H., and Robert Brightman. *The Orders of the Dreamed: George Nelson on Cree and Northern Ojibwa Religion and Myth, 1823.* Winnipeg: University of Manitoba Press, 1988.

Burch, Earnest S., Jr. "The Inupiat and the Christianization of Arctic Alaska." *Etudes/Inuit/Studies* 18 (1994): 81-108.

Burton, Cole, Charles J. Krebs, and Eric B. Taylor. "Population Genetic Structure of the Cyclic Snowshoe Hare (*Lepus americanus*) in Southwestern Yukon, Canada." *Molecular Ecology* 11 (2002): 1689-703.

Came, Barry. "Fighting for the Land: Matthew Coon Come Challenges the Separatists." *Maclean's*, February 27, 1995, 16-20.

Carr, David. "Narrative and the Real World: An Argument for Continuity." *History and Theory* 25, 2 (1986): 117-31.

–. *Time, Narrative, and History: An Essay in the Philosophy of History.* Bloomington: Indiana University Press, 1986.

Carrière, G. *Les Missions catholiques dans l'est du Canada et l'honorable Compagnie de la Baie d'Hudson, 1844-1900.* Ottawa: Université d'Ottawa, 1957.

Chance, Norman A., ed. *Conflict in Culture: Problems of Developmental Change among the Cree.* Ottawa: Canadian Research Centre for Anthropology, 1968.

Chance, Norman A. *Developmental Change among the Cree Indians of Quebec.* Montreal: McGill University Cree Project, 1970.

Charbonneau-Lassay, Louis. "Christ the Hunter and the Hunted." *Parabola* 16 (1991): 23-25.

Clerici, Naila. "The Cree of James Bay and the Construction of Their Identity for the Media." *Canadian Issues/Themes Canadiens* 21 (1999): 143-65.

Clifford, James, and George E. Marcus, eds. *Writing Culture: The Poetics and Politics of Ethnography.* Berkeley: University of California Press, 1986.

Colpitts, George. *Game in the Garden: A Human History of Wildlife in Western Canada to 1940.* Vancouver: UBC Press, 2002.

Conference on the History of Canadian Science, Technology, and Medicine. *Science, Technology, and Canadian History.* Kingston, ON: Second Conference on the History of Canadian Science, Technology, and Medicine, 1981.

Conference on the Study of the History of Canadian Science, Technology, and Medicine. *Critical Issues in the Canadian Science, Technology, and Medicine.* Kingston, ON: First Conference on the History of Canadian Science, Technology, and Medicine, 1979.

Conwill, Joseph D. "Return to the Land: Quebec's Colonisation Movement." *History Today*, April 1984, 16-21.

Cooke, A. "The Exploration of New Quebec." In *Le Nouveau Québec: Contribution à l'étude de l'occupation humaine*, ed. J. Malaurie and J. Rousseau. Paris: Mouton and Co., 1964.

Cook, Curtis, and Juan Lendau, eds. *Aboriginal Rights and Self-government.* Montreal: McGill-Queen's University Press, 2000.

Cook, Ramsay. *1492 and All That: Making A Garden Out of a Wilderness.* Toronto: Robarts Centre for Canadian Studies, 1993.

Coon Come, Matthew. "A Reduction of Our World." In *Our People, Our Land: Perspectives on the Columbus Quincentenary*, ed. Kurt Russo. Bellingham, WA: Lummi Tribe and Kluckholn Center, 1992.

–. "This Is a Terrible and Vast Reduction of Our Entire World." In *Ecocide of Native America*, ed. Donald Grinde and Bruce Johansen. Santa Fe: Clear Light Publishers, 1995.

Cooper, J.M. "The Cree Witiko Psychosis." *Primitive Man* 6 (1933): 20-21.

–. "Is the Algonquian Family Hunting Ground System Pre-Columbian?" *American Anthropology* 41 (1939): 66-90.

Craik, Brian, and Byers Casgrain. "Making a Living in the Bush: Land Tenure at Waskaganish." *Anthropologica* 28 (1986): 175-86.

Cronon, William. *Changes in the Land: Indians, Colonists, and the Ecology of New England.* New York: Hill and Wang, 1983.

–. "A Place for Stories: Nature, History, and Narrative." *Journal of American History* 78 (1992): 1347-76.

Crosby, A.W. *Ecological Imperialism. The Biological Expansion of Europe, 900-1900.* Cambridge: Cambridge University Press, 2004.

Crosby, Alfred. *The Columbian Exchange: Biological and Cultural Consequences of 1492.* Westport, CT: Greenwood Publishing, 1972.

Crowe, Keith. *History of the Aboriginal Peoples of Northern Canada.* Montreal: McGill-Queen's University Press, 1974.

Cruikshank, Julie, in collaboration with Angela Sidne, Kitty Smith, and Annie Ned. *Life Lived Like a Story: Life Stories of Three Yukon Elders.* Lincoln: University of Nebraska Press, 1990.

Cruikshank, Julie. *The Social Life of Stories: Narrative and Knowledge in the Yukon Territory.* Lincoln: University of Nebraska Press, 1998.

Culler, Jonathan. *On Deconstruction: Theory and Criticism after Structuralism.* Ithaca, NY: Cornell University Press, 1982.

D'Anglure, Bernard Saladin. "A New Look at Shamanism, Possession and Christianization." *Etudes/Inuit/Studies* 21 (1997): 21-36.

Danto, Arthur C. *Narration and Knowledge Including the Integral Text of Analytical Philosophy of History.* New York: Columbia University Press, 1985.

Davidson, James West. *Great Heart: The History of a Labrador Adventure.* New York: Kodansha International, 1997.

Davies, K.G., ed. *Northern Quebec and Labrador Journals and Correspondence, 1818-1835.* London: Hudson's Bay Record Society, 1963.

–. *Letters from Hudson Bay, 1703-40.* London: Hudson's Bay Record Society, 1965.

Day, Gordon M. "Western Abenaki." In *Handbook of North American Indians*. Vol. 15: *Northeast*. General ed. William C. Sturtevant. Vol. ed. Bruce G. Trigger. Washington, DC: Smithsonian Institution, 1978.

Delâge, Denys. *Le pays renversé: Amérindiens et Européens en Amérique du Nord-est, 1600-1664*. Montréal: Boréal Express, 1985.

Denton, David. "From the Source to the Margins and Back: Notes on Mistassini Quartzite and Archaeology in the Area of the Colline Blanche." In *L'eveilleur et l'ambassadeur: Essais archéologiques et ethnohistoriques en hommage à Charles A. Martijn, Paleo-Québec 27*, ed. R. Tremblay. Montréal: Recherches Amérindiennes au Québec, 1998.

–. "La période préhistorique récente dans la région de Caniapiscau." *Recherches archéologiques au Québec* 19 (1989): 2-3.

–. *A Visit in Time: Ancient Places, Archaeology, and Stories from the Elders of Wemindji*. Nemiska, QC: Cree Regional Authority Administration Regionale Crie, 2001.

Diamond, Billy. "Aboriginal Rights: The James Bay Experience." In *The Quest for Justice: Aboriginal People and Aboriginal Rights*, ed. J. Anthony Long. Toronto: University of Toronto Press, 1985.

–. "A Debate on the Positive and Negative Aspects of the Implementation of the Agreement." In *Baie James et Nord Québécois: Dix ans après*, ed. S. Vincent and G. Bowers. Montréal: Recherches amérindiennes au Québec, 1988.

–. "Renewed Struggle of the Cree for Control of Their Northland." *Canada Speeches* 5, 4 (1991): 27-34.

–. "Villages of the Damned." *Arctic Circle*, fall 1990, 24-30.

Dick, Lyle. "Pibloktoq (Arctic Hysteria): A Construction of European-Inuit Relations?" *Arctic Anthropology* 32/92 (1995): 1-42.

Dowling, J.H. "Individual Ownership and the Sharing of Game in Hunting Societies." *American Anthropologist* 70 (1968): 502-07.

Dragoo, Don W. "Some Aspects of Eastern North American Prehistory: A Review 1975." *American Antiquity* 41 (1976): 3-27.

Dubos, René. *Man Adapting*. New Haven: Yale University Press, 1980.

Eagleton, Terry. *Literary Theory: An Introduction*. Minneapolis: University of Minnesota Press, 1996.

Eckstorm, Fannie Hardy. *Old John Neptune and Other Maine Indian Shamans*. Orono, ME: University of Maine Press, 1980.

Elberg, N., J. Hyman, and R. Salisbury. *Not by Bread Alone: The Use of Subsistence Resources among James Bay Cree*. Montreal: McGill-Queen's University Press, 1972.

Evans, Richard J. "From Historicism to Postmodernism: Historiography in the Twentieth Century." *History and Theory* 41 (2002): 79-87.

Farber, Paul Lawrence. *Finding Order in Nature: The Naturalist Tradition from Linneaus to E.O. Wilson*. Baltimore: Johns Hopkins University Press, 2000.

Feit, Harvey A. "The Construction of Algonquian Hunting Territories." In *Colonial Situations: Essays on the Contextualization of Ethnographic Knowledge*, ed. G. Stocking. Madison: University of Wisconsin Press, 1991.

–. "The Ethno-Ecology of the Waswanipi Cree." In *Cultural Ecology Readings on Canadian Indians,* ed. B. Cox. Toronto: McClelland and Stewart, 1973.

–. "The Future of Hunters in Nation-States: Anthropology and the James Bay Cree." In *Politics and History in Band Societies*, ed. E. Leacock and R. Lee. New York: Cambridge University Press, 1982.

–. "Hunting and the Quest for Power: The James Bay Cree and Whitemen in the Twentieth Century." In *Native Peoples: The Canadian Experience*, ed. R. Bruce Morrison and C. Roderick Wilson. Toronto: McClelland and Stewart, 1986.

–. "James Bay Crees' Life Projects and Politics: Histories of Place, Animal Partners and Enduring Relationships." In *In the Way of Development*, ed. Mario Blaser, Harvey A. Feit, and Glenn McRae. New York: Zed Books, 2004.

–. "Mistassini Hunters of the Boreal Forest." MA thesis, McGill University, 1969.

–. "Negotiating Recognition of Aboriginal Rights: History, Strategies, and Reactions to the James Bay and Northern Quebec Agreement." *Canadian Journal of Anthropology* 1 (1980): 159-72.

–. "Political Articulations of Hunters to the State: Means of Resisting Threats to Subsistence Production in the James Bay and Northern Quebec Agreement." *Etudes/Inuit/Studies* 3 (1979): 69-85.

–. "Waswanipi Realities and Adaptations: Resource Management and Cognitive Structure." PhD diss., McGill University, 1978.

Fisher, A.D. "The Cree of Canada: Some Ecological and Evolutionary Considerations." *Western Canadian Journal of Anthropology* 11 (1969): 126-39.

Flannery, Regina. "Some Aspects of James Bay Recreative Culture." *Primitive Man* 9, 4 (1936): 49-56.

Flannery, Regina., M.E. Chambers, and P. Jehle. "Witiko Accounts from the James Bay Cree." *Arctic Anthropology* 18 (1982): 57-77.

Fletcher, Christopher, and Laurence J. Kirmayer. "Spirit Work: Nunavimmiut Experiences of Affliction and Healing." *Etudes/Inuit/Studies* 21 (1997): 205.

Flores, Dan. "Place: An Argument for Bioregional History." *Environmental History Review* 18 (1994): 1-18.

Foucault, Michel. *The Order of Things: An Archaeology of the Human Sciences*. New York: Vintage Books, 1970.

–. *Power/Knowledge: Selected Interviews and Other Writings, 1972-1977*. New York: Pantheon, 1980.

Francis, Daniel, and Toby Morantz. *Partners in Furs: A History of the Fur Trade in Eastern James Bay, 1600-1870*. Montreal and Kingston: McGill-Queen's University Press, 1983.

Fraser, Graham. *PQ: René Lévesque and the Parti Québécois in Power*. Toronto: Macmillan, 1984.

Frenette, J. *The History of the Chibougamau Crees: An Amerindian Band Reveals Its Identity*. Chibougamau, QC: Cree Indian Centre of Chibougamau, 1985.

Frideres, J.S. "The James Bay Cree (Eeyouch) and Inuit of Quebec: New Dimensions in Aboriginal Politics and Law." *Native Studies Review* 12 (1999): 5-12.

Frye, Northrop. *Fables of Identity: Studies in Poetic Mythology*. New York: Harcourt, Brace, and World, 1963.

Fusfeld, Daniel B. "Economic Theory Misplaced: Livelihood in Primitive Society." In *Trade and Market in Early Empires: Economics in History and Theory*, ed. Carl Polanyi. New York: Macmillan, 1957.

Germain, Edmour. "Hydro-Quebec: A French Canadian Goal." *Public Utilities Fortnightly*, April 23, 1964, 33-39.

Geertz, Clifford. *The Interpretation of Cultures: Selected Essays*. New York: Basic Books, 1973.

Goldman, Laurence R., ed. *The Anthropology of Cannibalism*. Westport, CT: Greenwood Press, 1999.

Gorrie, Peter. "The James Bay Power Project: The Environmental Cost of Reshaping the Geography of Northern Quebec." *Canadian Geographic*, February/March, 1990, 21-35.

Graham, Elizabeth. *The Mush Hole: Life at Two Indian Residential Schools*. Waterloo, ON: Heffle Publishing, 1997.

Grant, J.W. *Moon of Wintertime: Missionaries and the Indians of Canada in Encounter since 1534*. Toronto: University of Toronto Press, 1984.

Hacket, Paul. *"A Very Remarkable Sickness": Epidemics in the Petit Nord, 1670-1846*. Winnipeg: University of Manitoba Press, 2002.

Hallowell, Irving A. "Bear Ceremonialism in the Northern Hemisphere." *American Anthropologist* 28 (1926): 1-175.

–. "Psychic Stress and Culture Patterns." *American Journal of Psychiatry* 42 (1936): 1291-310.

Hare, F. Kenneth. "Climate and Zonal Divisions of Boreal Forest Formation in Eastern Canada." *Geographical Review* 40 (1959): 615-35.

Hayden, Brian. "Population Control among Hunter/Gatherers." *World Archaeology* 4 (1972): 205-21.

Hayeur, Gaétan. *Summary of Knowledge Acquired in Northern Environments from 1970 to 2000*. Montreal: Hydro-Québec, 2001.

Heeney, Bertal, ed. *Leaders of the Canadian Church*, 2 vols. Toronto: Musson, 1920.

Heindel, Naomi C. "Land Use Change in Northern Quebec: A Remote Sensing Analysis of Logging in James Bay." Honours thesis, Dartmouth College, 2007.

Higham, Carol L. *Noble, Wretched, and Redeemable: Protestant Missionaries to the Indians in Canada and the United States, 1820-1900*. Albuquerque: University of New Mexico Press, 2000.

Hind, Henry Yule. *Explorations in the Interior of the Labrador Peninsula: The Country of the Montagnais and Nesquapee Indians*. London: Longman, Green, Longman, Roberts and Green, 1863.

Hodgins, Bruce W. *Canoeing North into the Unknown: A Record of River Travel, 1874-1974*. Toronto: Natural Heritage/Natural History, 1994.

Hornig, James F., ed. *Social and Environmental Impacts of the James Bay Hydroelectric Project*. Montreal: McGill-Queen's University Press, 1999.

Hustich, I. "On the Forest Geography of the Labrador Peninsula." *Acta Geographica* 10 (1949): 6-35.

Jaenen, Cornelius J. *The Meeting of the French and Amerindians in the Seventeenth Century*. London, ON: University of Western Ontario Press, 1970.

Jameson, Frederic. *The Political Unconscious: Narrative as a Socially Symbolic Act*. Ithaca, NY: Cornell University Press, 1981.

Jennings, Francis. "A Growing Partnership: Historians, Anthropologists and American Indian History." *Ethnohistory* 29 (1982): 21-34.

Jenson, Jane, and Martin Papillon. "Challenging the Citizenship Regime: The James Bay Cree and Transnational Action." *Politics and Society* 28 (2000): 245-64.

Johnson, Edward A. *Fire and Vegetation Dynamics: Studies from the North American Boreal Forest*. Cambridge, UK: Cambridge University Press, 1992.

Kenyon, Walter Andrew. *The History of James Bay, 1610-1686: A Study in Historical Archaeology*. Toronto: Royal Ontario Museum, 1986.

Kermode, Frank. *The Sense of an Ending: Studies in the Theory of Fiction*. New York: Oxford University Press, 1968.

Kerr, A. *Subsistence and Social Organization in a Fur Trade Community: Anthropological Report on the Rupert's House Indians*. Ottawa: National Committee for Community Health Studies, 1950.

Knight, Rolf. *Ecological Factors in the Changing Economy and Social Organization among the Rupert's House Cree*. Anthropological Papers of the National Museum of Canada, no. 15. Ottawa: Department of the Secretary of State, 1968.

Krech, Shepard, ed. *Indians, Animals, and the Fur Trade: A Critique of Keepers of the Game*. Athens, GA: University of Georgia Press, 1981.

Krech, Shepard. *The Ecological Indian: Myth and History.* New York: W.W. Norton, 1999.

Kuper, Adam. *The Invention of Primitive Society: Transformations of an Illusion*. New York: Routledge, 1988.

Kupferrer, Harriet. "Impotency and Power." In *Political Anthropology*, ed. M. Swartz, A. Tanner, and A. Tuden. Chicago: Aldine Publishing, 1966.

Kupperman, Karen Ordahl. *Indians and English: Facing Off in Early America*. Ithaca, NY: Cornell University Press, 2000.

Laliberté, M. "La forêt boréale." In *Images de la préhistoire du Québec: Recherches amérindiennes au Québec*, ed. Claude Chapdelaine. Montréal: Recherches amérindiennes au Québec, 1973.

Landes, Ruth. "The Abnormal among the Ojibwa Indians." *Journal of Abnormal and Social Psychology* 33 (1938): 14-33.

Leacock, Eleanor. "The Montagnais-Naskapi Band." In *Contributions to Anthropology: Band Societies*, ed. D. Damas. Ottawa: National Museum of Canada, 1969.

–. "The Montagnais Hunting Territory and the Fur Trade." *American Anthropological Association Memoir 78*, 56, 5, pt 2 (1954).

–. "Status among the Montagnais-Naskapi of Labrador." *Ethnohistory* 5 (1958): 200-9.

Leacock, Eleanor., and N. Rothschild, eds. *Labrador Winter: The Ethnographic Journals of William Duncan Strong, 1927-1928*. Washington, DC: Smithsonian Institution, 1994.

Lee, Richard B., and Irven de Vore, eds. *Man the Hunter*. Chicago: Aldine Publishing Company, 1968.

Leith, Charles, and Arthur Leith. *A Summer and Winter On Hudson Bay.* Madison, WI: Self-published by Leith, 1912.

Levere, Trevor Harvey. *A Curious Field-Book: Science and Technology in Canadian History*. Toronto: Oxford University Press, 1974.

Levi-Strauss, Claude. *The Savage Mind*. Chicago: University of Chicago Press, 1966.

Lewis, David Rich. *Neither Wolf nor Dog: American Indians, Environment, and Agrarian Change*. New York: Oxford University Press, 1994.

Lewis, Herbert S. "The Misrepresentation of Anthropology and Its Consequences." *American Anthropologist* 100 (1998): 716-31.

Lewis, G. Malcolm. *Cartographic Encounters: Perspectives on Native American Mapmaking and Map Use*. Chicago: University of Chicago Press, 1998.

Long, John S. "The Reverend George Barnley and the James Bay Cree." *Canadian Journal of Native Studies* 6, 2 (1986): 313-31.

Lindsay, Debra. *Science in the Subarctic: Trappers, Traders, and the Smithsonian Institution*. Washington, DC: Smithsonian Institution Press, 1993.

Lomawaima, K. Tsianina. *They Called It Prairie Light: The Story of Chilocco Indian School.* Lincoln: University of Nebraska Press, 1994.

Low, Albert P. *Report of Explorations in the Labrador Peninsula in 1892-93-94-95.* Ottawa: Geological Survey of Canada, 1896.

MacDonald, L. Ian. *From Bourassa to Bourassa: A Pivotal Decade in Canadian History.* Montreal: McGill-Queen's University Press, 1984.

MacGregor, Roy. *Chief: The Fearless Vision of Billy Diamond.* Middlesex, UK: Penguin Books, 1990.

Mancall, Peter C. *Deadly Medicine: Indians and Alcohol in Early America.* Ithaca, NY: Cornell University Press, 1995.

Mancall, Peter C., and James H. Merrell. *American Encounters: Natives and Newcomers from European Contact to Indian Removal, 1500-1850.* New York: Routledge, 2000.

Marano, Lou. "Windigo Psychosis: The Anatomy of an Emic-Etic Confusion." *Current Anthropology* 3 (1982): 385-412.

Marshall, Susan. *Light on the Water: A Pictorial History of the People of Waswanipi.* Waswanipi: Waswanipi Band, 1987.

Martin, Calvin. "Ethnohistory: A Better Way to Write Indian History." *Western Historical Quarterly* 9 (1978): 41-56.

–. "The European Impact on the Culture of a Northeastern Algonkian Tribe: An Ecological Interpretation." *William and Mary Quarterly* 31 (1974): 3-26.

–. *In the Spirit of the Earth: Rethinking History and Time.* Baltimore: Johns Hopkins Press, 1993.

–. *Keepers of the Game: Indian-Animal Relationships and the Fur Trade.* Berkeley: University of California Press, 1978.

–. *The Way of the Human Being.* New Haven: Yale University Press, 1999.

Martin, Paul-Louis. *La chasse au Québec.* Québec City: Boréal, 1990.

Martin, Wallace. *The Recent Theories of Narrative.* Ithaca, NY: Cornell University Press, 1986.

Mason, L.R., ed. *Les bourgeois de la Compagnie du Nord-Ouest: Récits de voyages, lettres, et rapports inédits relatifs au Nord-Ouest canadien.* Québec City: De l'Imprimerie Générale A. Coté et cie, 1889-90 (reprint, New York: Antiquarian Press, 1960).

Mason, Leonard. *The Swampy Cree: A Study in Acculturation.* Anthropological Papers of the National Museum of Canada, no. 13. Ottawa: Department of the Secretary of State, 1967.

Massell, David. *Amassing Power: J.B. Duke and the Saguenay River, 1897-1927.* Montreal: McGill-Queen's University Press, 2000.

–. "Power and the Peribonka, A Prehistory: 1900-1930." *Quebec Studies* 38 (2004): 87-103.

McCutchen, Sean. *Electric Rivers.* Toronto: Black Rose Books, 1991.

McKenzie, James. "The King's Posts and Journal of a Canoe Jaunt Through the King's Domains, 1808, The Saguenay and the Labrador Coast ...." In *Les bourgeois de la Compagnie du Nord-Ouest: Récits de voyages, lettres, et rapports inedits relatifs au Nord-Ouest canadien,* ed. L.R. Mason. Québec City: De l'Imprimerie Generale A. Coté et cie, 1889 90 (reprint, New York: Antiquarian Press, 1960).

McNeill, J.R. "Observations on the Nature and Culture of Environmental History." *History and Theory* 42 (2003): 5-43.

McPhee, John. *Annals of the Former World.* New York: Farrar, Straus, and Giroux, 1998.

Merchant, Carolyn. *Ecological Revolutions: Nature, Gender, and Science in New England.* Chapel Hill: University of North Carolina Press, 1989.

Mihesuah, Devon A., ed. *Natives and Academics: Researching and Writing about American Indians.* Lincoln: University of Nebraska Press, 1998.

Miller, J.R. *Skyscrapers Hide the Heavens: A History of Indian-White Relations in Canada.* Toronto: University of Toronto Press, 1989.

Miller, J.R., ed. *Sweet Promises: A Reader on Indian-White Relations in Canada.* Toronto: University of Toronto Press, 1991.

Mills, Antonia, and Richard Slobodin, eds. *Amerindian Rebirth: Reincarnation Belief among North American Indians and Inuit.* Toronto: University of Toronto Press, 1994.

Mitchell, W.J.T., ed. *On Narrative.* Chicago: University of Chicago, 1981.

Momaday, N. Scott. *The Man Made of Words.* New York: St. Martin's Press, 1997.

–. *The Way to Rainy Mountain.* Albuquerque: University of New Mexico Press, 1969.

Morantz, Toby. "Aboriginal Land Claims in Quebec." In *Aboriginal Land Claims in Canada: A Regional Perspective*, ed. Ken Coates. Toronto: Copp Clark Pitman, 1992.

–. "Dwindling Animals and Diminished Lands: Early Twentieth Century Developments in Eastern James Bay." In *Papers of the Eighteenth Algonquian Conference*, ed. W. Cowan. Ottawa: Carleton University, 1987.

–. "The Fur Trade and the Cree of James Bay." In *Old Trails and New Directions: Papers of the Third North American Fur Trade Conference*, ed. C. Judd and A. Ray. Toronto: University of Toronto Press, 1980.

–. "'Gift Offerings to Their Own Importance and Superiority.' Fur Trade Relations, 1700-1940." In *Papers of the Nineteenth Algonquian Conference*, ed. W. Cowan. Ottawa: Carleton University Press, 1988.

–. "Northern Algonquian Concepts of Status and Leadership Reviewed: A Case Study of the Eighteenth-Century Trading Captain System." *Canadian Review of Sociology and Anthropology* 19 (1982): 482-502.

–. "'Not Annual Visitors.' The Drawing in to Trade of Northern Algonquian Caribou Hunters." In *Actes du Quatorzième Congrès des Algonquinistes*, ed. W. Cowan. Ottawa: Carleton University Press, 1983.

–. "Old Texts, Old Questions: Another Look at the Issue of Continuity and the Early Fur-Trade Period." *Canadian Historical Review* 73 (1992): 167-93.

–. "Oral and Recorded History in James Bay." In *Papers of the Fifteenth Algonquian Conference*, ed. W. Cowan. Ottawa: Carleton University, 1984.

–. "'So Evil a Practice': A Look at the Debt System in the James Bay Fur Trade." In *Merchant Credit and Labour Strategies in Historical Perspective*, ed. Rosemary Ommer. Fredericton, NB: Acadiensis Press, 1990.

–. "Provincial Game Laws at the Turn of the Century: Protective or Punitive Measures for the Native Peoples of Quebec?" In *Papers of the Twenty-Sixth Algonquian Conference*, ed. D. Pentland. Winnipeg: University of Manitoba Press, 1995.

–. *The White Man's Gonna Getcha: The Colonial Challenge to the Crees in Quebec.* Montreal: McGill-Queen's University Press, 2002.

Morin, Michel. *L'usurpation de la souveraineté autochtone: Le cas des peuples de la Nouvelle-France et des colonies anglaises de l'Amérique du Nord.* Montréal: Les Editions du Boréal, 1997.

Morrison, Kenneth M. *The Embattled Northeast: The Elusive Ideal of Alliance in Abenaki-Euroamerican Relations.* Berkeley: University of California Press, 1984.

–. *The Solidarity of Kin: Ethnohistory, Religious Studies, and the Algonkean-French Religious Encounter.* Albany, NY: State University of New York Press, 2002.

Morissonneau, Christian. *La terre promise: Le mythe du Nord Québécois.* Montréal: Hurtubise HMH, 1978.

Murie, Olaus Johan. *Journeys to the Far North.* Palo Alto, CA: American West Publishing Company, 1973.

Nadasdy, Paul. *Hunters and Bureaucrats: Power, Knowledge, and Aboriginal-State Relations in the Southwest Yukon.* Vancouver: UBC Press, 2004.

Naiman, Robert J. "Ecosystem Alteration of Boreal Forest Streams by Beaver." *Ecology* 67 (1986): 1254-69.

Nelles, H.V. *The Politics of Development: Forests, Mines, and Hydro-Electric Power in Ontario, 1849-1941.* Toronto: Macmillan, 1974.

Niezen, R. "Healing and Conversion: Medical Evangelism in James Bay Cree Society." *Ethnohistory* 44 (1997): 463-91.

Norris, Christopher. *What's Wrong With Postmodernism: Critical Theory and the Ends of Philosophy.* Baltimore: Johns Hopkins University Press, 1990.

O'Brien, Jim. "The History of North America from the Standpoint of the Beaver." In *Free Spirits: Annals of the Insurgent Imagination*, ed. Paul Buhle. San Francisco: City Lights Books, 1982.

Ouellet, Gerard. *Aux marches du Royaume de Matagami: Rochebaucourt.* Québec City: Department of Colonization, 1947.

Pearce, Margaret, W. "Encroachment by Word, Axis, and Tree: Mapping Techniques from the Colonization of New England." *Cartographic Perspectives* 48 (2004): 24-38.

Picard, Andre. "A Dispossessed People Come Home." *Globe and Mail*, December 4, 1993, A1, A6.

Piker, Joshua. *Okfuskee: A Creek Indian Town in Colonial America.* Cambridge: Harvard University Press, 2004.

Pratt, Mary Louis. "Fieldwork in Common Place." In *Writing Culture: The Poetics and Politics of Ethnography*, ed. James Clifford and George E. Marcus. Berkeley: University of California Press, 1986.

Preston, Richard J. "Catholicism at Attawapiskat: A Case of Culture Change." In *Papers of the Eighteenth Algonquian Conference*, ed. William Cowan. Ottawa: Carleton University Press, 1987.

–. *Cree Narrative.* 2nd ed. Montreal: McGill-Queen's University Press, 2002.

–. *Cree Narrative: Expressing the Personal Meanings of Events.* Ottawa: Canadian Ethnological Service, Museum of Man, Mercury Series, 1975.

–. "Eastern Cree Notions of Social Grouping." In *Papers of the Eleventh Algonquian Conference*, ed. W. Cowan. Ottawa: Carleton University Press, 1980.

–. "Ethnographic Reconstruction of Witigo." In *Papers of the Ninth Algonquian Conference*, ed. William Cowan. Ottawa: Carleton University Press, 1978.

–. "James Bay Cree Culture, Malnutrition, Infectious and Degenerative Diseases." In *Papers of the Algonquin Conference,* ed. William Cowan. Ottawa: Carleton University Press, 2001.

–. "James Bay Cree Syncretism." In *Papers of the Nineteenth Algonquian Conference*, ed. William Cowan. Ottawa: Carleton University Press, 1988

–. "Ritual Hangings: An Aboriginal 'Survival' in a Northern North American Trapping Community." *Man* 64 (1964): 142-44.

–. "A Survey of Ethnographic Approaches to the Eastern Cree-Montagnais-Naskapi." *Canadian Review of Sociology and Anthropology* 12 (1975): 267-78.

–. "The Witiko: Algonkian Knowledge and Whiteman Knowledge." In *Manlike Monsters on Trial: Early Records and Modern Evidence*, ed. M. Halpin and M. Ames. Vancouver: UBC Press, 1980.

Preston, Susan. "Exploring the Eastern Cree Landscape: Oral Tradition As Cognitive Map." In *Papers of the Algonkian Conference*. Ottawa: Carleton University Press, 2000.

–. "Is Your Cree Uniform the Same as Mine? Cultural and Ethnographic Variations on a Theme." In *Papers of the Eighteenth Algonquian Conference*, ed. William Cowan. Ottawa: Carleton University Press, 1987

–. *Let the Past Go: A Life History Narrated by Alice Jacob*. Ottawa: National Museums of Canada, 1986.

Price, Richard. "Practices of Historical Narrative." *Rethinking History* 5 (2001): 357-65.

Pyne, Stephen J. *Fire in America: A Cultural History of Wildland and Rural Fire*. Princeton: Princeton University Press, 1982.

Ray, Arthur. *The Canadian Fur Trade in the Industrial Age*. Toronto: University of Toronto Press, 1990.

–. "Some Conservation Schemes of the Hudson's Bay Company, 1821-1850: An Examination of the Problems of Resource Management in the Fur Trade." *Journal of Historical Geography* 1 (1975): 49-68.

Rich, E.E. *The History of the Hudson's Bay Company, 1670-1870*. London: Hudson's Bay Record Society, 1958-59.

Richardson, Boyce. *Strangers Devour the Land: A Chronicle of the Assault upon the Last Coherent Hunting Culture in North America, the Cree Indians of Northern Quebec, and Their Vast Primeval Homelands*. New York: Alfred A. Knopf, 1976.

Ricoeur, Paul. *Time and Narrative*. 3 vols. Chicago: University of Chicago Press, 1983-85.

Ridington, Robin. "From Chief to Prophet: Beaver Indian Dreamers and Christianity." *Arctic Anthropology* 24 (1987): 8-18.

Robinson, Lewis. *Resources of the Canadian Shield*. Toronto: Methuen, 1969.

Rogers, Edward S. *The Hunting Group-Hunting Territory Complex among the Mistassini Indians*. Ottawa: National Museum of Canada, Bulletin 195, 1963.

–. "The Individual in Mistassini Society from Birth to Death." In *Contributions to Anthropology 1960*. Ottawa: National Museum of Canada, Bulletin 190, 1963.

–. *The Material Culture of the Mistassini*. Ottawa: National Museum of Canada, Bulletin 218, 1967.

–. "The Mistassini Cree." In *Hunters and Gatherers Today*, ed. M.G. Bicchieri. Toronto: Holt, Rinehart and Winston, 1972.

–. *The Quest for Food and Furs: The Mistassini Cree*. Ottawa: National Museum of Canada, Publications in Ethnology no. 5, 1973.

–. "The Yearly Cycle of the Mistassini Indians." *Arctic* 12 (1959): 131-39.

Ronda, James P. "Generations of Faith: The Christian Indians of Martha's Vineyard." In *American Encounters: Natives and Newcomers from European Contact to Indian Removal, 1500-1850*, ed. Peter C. Mancall and James H. Merrell. New York: Routledge, 2000.

Ruggles, Richard I. *A Country So Interesting: The Hudson's Bay Company and Two Centuries of Mapping, 1670-1870*. Montreal: McGill-Queen's University Press, 1991.

Sahlins, Marshall. "The Intensity of Domestic Production in Primitive Societies." In *Studies in Economic Anthropology*, ed. G. Dalton. Washington, DC: American Anthropological Association, 1971.

–. *Stone Age Economics*. Chicago: Aldine-Atherton, 1972.

Salisbury, Richard F. *A Homeland for the Cree: Regional Development in James Bay, 1971-1981*. Kingston and Montreal: McGill-Queen's University Press, 1986.

Salomon, Julian Harris, "Indians that Set the Woods on Fire." *Conservationist* 38 (1984): 34-40.

Sapir, Edward. *Language: An Introduction to the Study of Speech*. New York: Harcourt, Brace, and Company, 1921.

–. *Selected Writings of Edward Sapir in Language, Culture, and Personality*. Ed. David G. Mandelbaum. Berkeley: University of California Press, 1949.

Scholes, Robert, and Robert Kellog. *The Nature of Narrative*. New York: Oxford University Press, 1966.

Scott, Colin, ed. *Aboriginal Autonomy and Development in Northern Quebec and Labrador*. Vancouver: UBC Press, 2001.

–. "Between 'Original Affluence' and Consumer Affluence: Domestic Production and Guaranteed Income for James Bay Hunters." In *Affluence and Cultural Survival: 1981 Proceedings of the American Ethnological Society*, ed. Richard Salisbury and Elizabeth Tooker. Washington, DC: American Ethnological Society, 1984.

–. "Encountering the Whiteman in James Bay Cree Narrative History and Mythology." *Aboriginal History* 19 (1995): 21-40.

–. "Hunting Territories, Hunting Bosses, and Communal Production Among Coastal James Bay Cree." *Anthropologica* 28 (1986): 163-73.

–. "Science for the West, Myth for the Rest? The Case of James Bay Cree Knowledge Production." In *Naked Science: Anthropological Inquiry into Boundaries, Power and Knowledge*, ed. Laura Nader. New York: Routledge, 1996.

Shkilnyk, Anastasia M. "The Destruction of an Ojibwa Community: Relations with the Outside Society." In *Out of the Background: Readings on Canadian Native History*, ed. Ken Coates and Robin Fisher. Scarborough, ON: Thomson and Nelson, 1998.

–. *A Poison Stronger Than Love: The Destruction of an Ojibwa Community*. New Haven: Yale University Press, 1985.

Sider, Gerald. *Between History and Tomorrow: Making and Breaking Everyday Life in Rural Newfoundland*. Peterborough, ON: Broadview Press, 2003.

Silverman, David J. "Indians, Missionaries, and Religious Translation: Creating Wampanoag Christianity in Seventeenth-Century Martha's Vineyard." *William and Mary Quarterly* 62 (2005): 141-74.

Simmons, William S. "Culture Theory in Contemporary Ethnohistory." *Ethnohistory* 35 (1988): 1-14.

Sinclair, A.R.E., Dennis Chitty, Carol I. Stefan, and Charles J. Krebs. "Mammal Population Cycles: Evidence for Intrinsic Differences During Snowshoe Hare Cycles." *Canadian Journal of Zoology* 81 (2003): 216-20.

Sirois, Luc, and Serge Payette. "Reduced Postfire Tree Regeneration along a Boreal Forest–Forest-Tundra Transect in Northern Quebec." *Ecology* 72 (1991): 619-27.

Skinner, Alanson Buck. "Notes on the Eastern Cree." *Anthropological Papers of the American Museum of Natural History Papers*. Vol. 9, part 1. New York: American Museum of Natural History, 1911.

Slotkin, Richard. *Regeneration through Violence: The Mythology of the American Frontier, 1600-1860.* Middletown, CT: Wesleyan University Press, 1973.

Sly, Peter G. *Human Impacts on the Hudson Bay Bioregion: Its Present State and Future Environmental Concerns.* Hudson Bay Programme, 1994.

Speck, Frank G. "Ethical Attributes of the Labrador Indians." *American Anthropologist* 35 (1933): 559-94.

–. "Mistassini Hunting Territories in the Labrador Peninsula." *American Anthropologist* 25 (1923): 452-71.

–. *Naskapi: The Savage Hunters of the Labrador Peninsula.* Norman: University of Oklahoma Press, 1935.

Speck, Frank G., and George G. Heye. *Hunting Charms of the Montagnais and the Mistassini.* New York: Museum of the American Indian, 1921.

Speck, Frank G., and Loren Eiseley. "Montagnais-Naskapi Bands and Family Hunting Districts of the Central and Southern Labrador Peninsula." *Proceedings of the American Philosophical Society* 85 (1937): 215-42.

Spielmann, Katherine A. *Farmers, Hunters, and Colonists: Interaction between the Southwest and the Southern Plains.* Tucson: University of Arizona Press, 1991.

Stockman, George W., ed. *The Shaping of American Anthropology, 1883-1911: A Franz Boaz Reader.* New York: Basic Books, 1974.

Tanner, Adrian. *Bringing Home Animals: Religious Ideology and Modes of Production of the Mistassini Cree Hunters.* New York: St. Martin's Press, 1979.

–. "The New Hunting Territory Debate: An Introduction to Some Unresolved Issues." *Anthropologica* 28 (1986): 19-37.

–. "The Significance of Hunting Territories Today." In *Native People, Native Lands*, ed. B. Cox. Ottawa: Carleton University Press, 1987.

Thomson, Dale C. *Jean Lesage and the Quiet Revolution.* Toronto: Macmillan, 1984.

Thwaite, Reuben Gold, ed. *Jesuit Relations and Allied Documents.* Cleveland: Burrows Brothers, 1896-1901.

Tinker, George E. *Missionary Conquest: The Gospel and Native American Cultural Genocide.* Minneapolis: Fortress Press, 1993.

Treat, James, ed. *Native and Christian: Indigenous Voices on Religious Identity in the United States and Canada.* New York: Routledge, 1996.

Trigger, Bruce. "Ethnohistory: Problems and Prospects." *Ethnohistory.* 29 (1982): 1-19.

Turner, Frederick. *Beyond Geography: The Western Spirit against the Wilderness.* New Brunswick: Rutgers University Press, 1980.

Upton, L.F.S. "The Origins of Canadian Indian Policy." *Journal of Canadian Studies* 8 (1973): 51-61.

Van Kirk, Sylvia. *"Many Tender Ties." Women in Fur Trade Society, 1670-1870.* Winnipeg: Watson and Dwyer, 1980.

Voorhis, Ernest, ed. *Historic Forts and Trading Posts of the French Regime and the English Fur Trade Companies.* Ottawa: Department of Interior, 1930.

Wallace, A.F.C. "Revitalization Movements: Some Theoretical Considerations." *American Anthropologist* 58 (1956): 264-81.

Walton, William. "Those Who Would Lead the Indian to Christ Must First Learn to Stand in Their Moccasins!" *Canadian Churchman*, 70, November 25, 1943, 669-70.

Washburn, Wilcomb E. "Symbol, Utility, and Aesthetic in the Indian Fur Trade." In *Aspects of the Fur Trade*, ed. Russell W. Findley. St. Paul: Minnesota Historical Society, 1967.

White, Richard. *The Middle Ground: Indians, Empires, and Republics in the Great Lakes Region, 1650-1815*. Cambridge/New York: Cambridge University Press, 1991.

–. *The Roots of Dependency: Subsistence, Environment, and Social Change among the Choctaws, Pawnees, and Navajos*. Lincoln: University of Nebraska Press, 1983.

Wright, J.V. "The Prehistory of the Shield." In *Subarctic*, ed. June Helm. Washington, DC: Smithsonian Institution, 1976.

Zaslow, Morris. *The Northward Expansion of Canada*. Toronto: McClelland and Stewart, 1988.

–. *The Opening of the Canadian North, 1870-1914*. Toronto: McClelland and Stewart, 1971.

–. *Reading the Rocks: The Story of the Geological Survey of Canada, 1842-1972*. Toronto: Macmillan, 1975.

Index